THE NORTHERN SOUL SCENE

Studies in Popular Music

Series Editors: Alyn Shipton, lecturer in jazz history at the Royal Academy of Music, London, and at City University, London; and Christopher Partridge, Professor of Religious Studies, Lancaster University

From jazz to reggae, bhangra to heavy metal, electronica to qawwali, and from production to consumption, *Studies in Popular Music* is a multi-disciplinary series which aims to contribute to a comprehensive understanding of popular music. It will provide analyses of theoretical perspectives, a broad range of case studies, and discussion of key issues.

Published

Do You Want to Know a Secret?: The Autobiography of Billly J. Kramer
Billy J. Kramer with Alyn Shipton

Dub in Babylon: Understanding the Evolution and Significance of Dub Reggae in Jamaica and Britain from King Tubby to Post-Punk
Christopher Partridge

Falco and Beyond: Neo Nothing Post of All
Ewa Mazierska

Global Tribe: Technology, Spirituality and Psytrance
Graham St John

Heavy Metal: Controversies and Countercultures
Edited by Titus Hjelm, Keith Kahn-Harris and Mark LeVine

Nick Cave: A Study of Love, Death and Apocalypse
Roland Boer

Open up the Doors: Music in the Modern Church
Mark Evans

Send in the Clones: A Cultural Study of Tribute Bands
Georgina Gregory

Technomad: Global Raving Countercultures
Graham St John

*The Lost Women of Rock Music:
Female Musicians of the Punk Era* (second edition)
Helen Reddington

THE NORTHERN SOUL SCENE

EDITED BY
SARAH RAINE, TIM WALL AND NICOLA WATCHMAN SMITH

SHEFFIELD UK   BRISTOL CT

Published by Equinox Publishing Ltd.

UK: Office 415, The Workstation, 15 Paternoster Row, Sheffield, South Yorkshire S1 2BX
USA: ISD, 70 Enterprise Drive, Bristol, CT 06010

www.equinoxpub.com

First published 2019

© Sarah Raine, Tim Wall, Nicola Watchman Smith and contributors 2019.
Reprinted material copyright as indicated in the Acknowledgements.

All rights reserved. No part of this publication may be reproduced or transmitted in any form or by any means, electronic or mechanical, including photocopying, recording or any information storage or retrieval system, without prior permission in writing from the publishers.

British Library Cataloguing-in-Publication Data
A catalogue record for this book is available from the British Library.

Library of Congress Cataloging-in-Publication Data
Names: Raine, Sarah, 1985- | Wall, Tim. | Smith, Nicola Watchman.
Title: The northern soul scene / edited by Sarah Raine, Tim Wall and Nicola
   Watchman Smith.
Description: Sheffield, UK ; Bristol, CT : Equinox Publishing, 2019. |
   Series: Studies in popular music | Includes bibliographical references and index.
Identifiers: LCCN 2018025853 (print) | LCCN 2018027675 (ebook) | ISBN
   9781781795590 (ePDF) | ISBN 9781781795576 (hb) | ISBN 9781781795583 (pb)
Subjects: LCSH: Soul (Music)--England, Northern--History and criticism. |
   Soul (Music)--Social aspects--England, Northern--History.
Classification: LCC ML3537 (ebook) | LCC ML3537 .N66 2019 (print) | DDC
   781.64409427--dc23
LC record available at https://lccn.loc.gov/2018025853

ISBN: 978 1 78179 557 6 (hardback)
       978 1 78179 558 3 (paperback)
       978 1 78179 559 0 (ePDF)

Typeset by CA Typesetting Ltd.

We dedicate this book to the memory of David Sanjek, who first imagined the project and stimulated the discussions which carried it through to publication.

Before his death in 2011, David was a Professor of Popular Music and Director of the University of Salford Music Research Centre in Greater Manchester, UK. David is best known for updating his father's history of the US music industry, published as *American Popular Music and Its Business: The First Four Hundred Years*. His contribution to the study of popular music was extensive and his influence on those with whom he worked was profound; he became a close friend to several of the contributors to this book. He was particularly interested in the engagement of African American music and the music industry and popular culture, researching widely on the subject over the latter decades of his life. Before taking up his academic position at Salford, he spent over 15 years as Director of the Archives at Broadcast Music, Inc. (BMI) in the US, and advised organizations which safe-guarded American popular music's past and made it available to the public. He was an active member of the International Association for the Study of Popular Music (IASPM), the subject association for work in this area. *The Northern Soul Scene* project could have had no better mentor, and this book would not have been the same without his leadership.

Thank you, David.

Contents

	Acknowledgements	xi
	Introduction *Tim Wall, Sarah Raine and Nicola Watchman Smith*	1
	Musical Bookmark 1 *Portrait of Tom Page by William Ellis*	10
1	Long After Tonight is All Over *Stuart Cosgrove*	11
2	Welcome to Dreamsville: A History and Geography of Northern Soul *Joanne Hollows and Katie Milestone*	20
3	"Out on the Floor": The Politics of Dancing on the Northern Soul Scene *Tim Wall*	41
4	Beyond the Master Narrative of Youth: Researching Ageing Popular Music Scenes *Nicola Smith*	60
	Musical Bookmark 2 *Portrait of Sean Chapman by William Ellis*	81
5	Acquiring Rights and Righting Wrongs? *Ady Croasdell*	82
6	(Re)Marking Old Records, Making New Meaning: Debating the Questionable Home of Northern Soul *Nicola Watchman Smith*	99
	Musical Bookmark 3 *Portrait of Emily Jane by William Ellis*	119

7	Dave Godin and the Politics of the British Soul Community *Joe Street*	120
8	Myths on/of the Northern Soul Scene *Sarah Raine and Tim Wall*	142
	Musical Bookmark 4 *Portrait of John Manship by William Ellis*	164
9	Soul Survivors *John Barrett*	165
	Photographic Dossier *John Barrett*	174
10	Searching for the Subcultural Heart of Northern Soul: From Pillheads to Shredded Wheat *Andrew Wilson*	179
11	Soul Boy, Soul Girl: Reflections on Gender and Northern Soul *Katie Milestone*	197
	Musical Bookmark 5 *Portrait of Sammy Dee by William Ellis*	215
12	Northern Soul: Life with Soul is Better, Much Better *Dani Herranz*	216
	Photographic Dossier *Bethany Kane*	222
13	Interviews with Tony Palmer, Elaine Constantine, and Liam Quinn *Interviews conducted and edited by Tim Wall*	227
	Musical Bookmark 6 *Portrait of Harriet Dakin by William Ellis*	247

14 Nostalgia, Symbolic Knowledge and Generational Conflict   248
Lucy Gibson

15 The Voice of Participants on the Scene   268
With commentary from Mark Duffett, Sarah Raine and Tim Wall, and the voices of "Dean", "Esther", "Rob" and "Nancy"

    Photographic Dossier   287
    Richard Oughton

16 I'm Still Looking for Unknowns All the Time:
    The Forward (E)motion of Northern Soul Dancing   292
    Paul Sadot

    Musical Bookmark 7   311
    Portrait of Kev Roberts by William Ellis

17 "Groove Me":
    Dancing to the Discs of Northern Soul   312
    David Sanjek

    Musical Bookmark 8   330
    Portrait of Jenny Wilkes by William Ellis

Critical Reflection   331
    Tim Wall

Index   344

Acknowledgements

As a book with co-creation at its heart, we wish to thank all the writers, photographers, and participant voices that have contributed to this book. Without any one of these, an aspect of the rich diversity we bring together here would have been lost. This book is a credit to your hard work and enthusiasm. We also thank those in the northern soul scene who added their voices and portraits, and who hosted us at their events: "Nancy", "Rob", "Esther", and "Dean", "John", "Bobby", and "Michael", Sean Chapman, Harriet Dakin, Sammy Dee, John Manship, Emily Jane, Tom Page, Kev Roberts, and Jenny Wilkes. We hope that this book in some way speaks to your experiences and demonstrates the true diversity and richness of the northern soul scene.

We wish to thank Ashgate, Guildford Press, Popular Music (OUP), Ruta 66, and the University Press of Mississippi for their permissions to reprint seminal pieces on northern soul as part of this edited collection, in particular Cynthia Foster at the University Press of Mississippi whose flexibility and understanding made it possible for us to include David Sanjek's (2012) chapter, in whose memory this book is dedicated.

We thank Sara Cohen, Mark Duffett, and Nathan Wiseman-Trowse for their insightful and constructive comments at the very beginning of this process, alongside Alyn Shipton, Valerie Hall, Janet Joyce, Sarah Lee, and the rest of the editorial team at Equinox Publishing, who supported the book from its conception, graciously answered our queries, and showed no end of patience with our busy and conflicting academic schedules.

We also wish to acknowledge all those people behind the scenes who helped pull this book together, from indexing to finance, in particular Christina Aldridge, Dulcie Barnes, Yvette Burn, Nicola King, Geraldine Marshall, Marco Santucci, and Dan Whitehouse.

Our thanks are extended to the Higher Education team at Newcastle College for their flexibility and support during the latter stages of this process, and to Derek B. Scott, the late Sheila Whiteley, and Patrick Williams for their highly valued guidance and time.

Finally, we would like to thank the staff and students at Birmingham City University, and the Birmingham Centre for Media and Cultural Studies, for their unwavering support for this project and others like it, through which we hope to advance popular music research.

Introduction

Tim Wall, Sarah Raine and Nicola Watchman Smith

This book has the ambitious aim of trying to capture some of the diversity of activity and perspective of a music culture which has sustained itself for nearly fifty years. With its origins in the early 1970s, and roots further back in a half-century-long British engagement with African American music, the northern soul scene today is a multi-generational music participatory culture with strong dancefloor traditions and stories that articulate the past high points and struggles of the scene.

This is primarily an academic book and the editors and many of the contributors are published researchers. Part of our academic purpose is to find a new way to investigate a music culture in book form. We achieve this through a model of co-production between the editors, the contributors, and the wider scene we seek to capture. In doing so, we have produced a far more diverse insight into the northern soul scene than is usually the case with academic studies, and we therefore offer a model for future editorial teams who seek to do the same for other music cultures. In producing the book with members of the scene we study, we aim to ensure that the northern soul culture that matters so much to them will simultaneously be studied in a manner that is both respectful and critically engaged.

The vast majority of the editors and contributors have personal experience of the scene and its culture. They also characterize something of the diversity of the scene's participants in age, role on the scene, and viewpoints. They have, though, primarily been chosen because they each offer something distinctive in dissecting what really matters in northern soul. There will be much to take issue with; as editors, we have self-consciously chosen contributions that do not always align with our own views, and while there is much in common over the issues that are addressed, there is far less consistency amongst the contributions about what exactly northern soul is, and how it should be understood. We purposely aim to avoid a coherent story of what northern soul is today, or any simple history of how the scene got here.

We have selected a range of perspectives, to both represent the emerging sense of the scene that developed through an unfolding literature and the diversity of perspective which exists in earlier studies and those specially commissioned for the book. In doing so, we are aware that we are confronting some very strong but simplistic narratives about what northern soul is. A clear sense of the existing narratives about the scene are to be found on the Wikipedia entry for northern soul, which brings together common themes of its twentieth-century north of England origins, its 60s black American soundtrack, and its distinctive dance style. In this account northern soul is:

> a music and dance movement that emerged from the British mod scene, initially in northern England in the late 1960s ... mainly consists of a particular style of black American soul music based on the heavy beat and fast tempo of the mid-1960s sound ... by lesser-known artists, released only in limited numbers, often by small regional American labels ... dancing became more athletic, somewhat resembling the later dance styles of disco and break dancing. Featuring spins, flips, and backdrops, club dancing styles were often inspired by the stage performances of visiting American soul acts (https://en.wikipedia.org/wiki/Northern_soul, accessed 1 August 2017).

As a collectively-authored account, the Wikipedia entry represents a public understanding of northern soul, accessible to (and editable by) scene members and interested individuals but, unlike the one offered in this book, it is narrative driven by the desire to construct coherence and singular definition. It is this dominant narrative, reproduced in many other publications, which most often defines the scene for those outside, but it has also become common-sense amongst active members of the scene themselves. It is not that we wish to dispute any of this thumbnail portrait, but rather to explore the more complex and contradictorily cultural practices which underlie the definitional certainties that are commonly utilized in studying popular music cultures. As editors, we have consciously sought out a diverse range of viewpoints and positions in selecting the contributions to make the point that there is no single explanatory narrative. We have taken a stance against any singular or linear history of the scene and favoured a pluralism about what the scene means to its participants. This means bringing forth strongly-held views from the very different perspectives in the often-fractious debates which characterize the scene's present-day discourse. While many of the contributions assume that there is an authentic scene to be discovered, and some that they can speak more authoritatively on this than others, we have sought to explore not simply *what* people say happened and happens, but *what it produces* when they say it.

As an academic project, this edited book has been constructed as a research activity in itself.

Individual chapters provide significant insights into different aspects of the scene in themselves, and all the authors provide an authoritative contribution. However, by reading across the chapters the differences and some of the contradictions in account become apparent. Many of the authors of the chapters presented here explicitly address these differences and, by connecting the accounts, the dynamic of scene ideology begins to emerge, and a nuanced understanding of its culture should be achieved. Accordingly, we have not followed the usual line of simply bringing a number of different essays together, but see this as an active, co-produced piece of research in which all contributors, academic and non-academic alike, have been involved.

The project itself emerged from a day-long symposium on northern soul, organized by Dave Sanjek, at which many of the contributors first came together. That symposium took contributions from academics and key scene figures alike, and welcomed a wide audience of academics and scene participants to the University of Salford, Greater Manchester. From the beginning, the editors imagined a book that drew on existing material in print alongside newly commissioned articles and other forms of capture beyond typical written chapters. The book contains prominent contributions from photographers and the spoken insights of some in interview form. The book's content developed through a process of dialogue between editors and contributors, culminating in a further symposium at Birmingham City University, where we shared our insights with each other. This dialogue was not always easy, as one would expect in a scene that matters greatly to its participants. The book was launched through a series of events on the topic of northern soul, held at Birmingham City University in 2019. This points, of course, to the fact that this book is just the start of a wider discussion which develops because of your engagement as a reader and critic.

Insiders and outsiders to the northern soul scene

The editorial line has been constructed by three very different academics, with three very different relationships to the scene.

Sarah Raine. The daughter of a mod-era father, Sarah was familiar with the sound and lyrics of 1960s African American R&B, sufficiently expanded to include some key northern soul anthems. In February 2012, she was first introduced to the northern soul scene by her partner, attending an allnighter at the Blackpool Winter Garden. From this point, she learnt to dance to the records that she knew already, discovered new sounds that went beyond her childhood soundscape, and found within the scene a complexity and deep meaning worthy of a detailed and immersive research project. Several years later, Sarah is a postdoctoral researcher in popular music at Birmingham City University focusing on the experiences of the younger generation of the scene, a regular attendee at allnighters, and the co-editor of this publication which brings together a range of contributors for whom northern soul is a passion that transcends the boundaries between the working week and the weekend.

Tim Wall. With the crew cut of the skinhead and a yearning for the Crombie coat his mum wouldn't buy, Tim grew up listening and dancing to early sixties soul and ska. DJing in local youth clubs, a record-collecting obsession and a fanatical commitment to dancing made it easy for what became known as northern soul to seep into his teenage years. Favouring Blackpool eclecticism and soul purism over Wigan's high octane stomp, Tim continued his northern soul odyssey at Morecombe Pier while presenting a weekly soul radio show and studying at university, and then moved to Manchester, where soul nights continued unabated. Soul has taken its place alongside vast amounts of other music in both his listening, dancing and academic studies, but northern soul remains part of his sense of self. Middle age and fatherhood made nights out a bigger challenge, and relocation to the English Midlands meant a less active participation until the twentieth century brought a club at every junction of the M6, and the independence of his children, resulted in a more regular return to dancing. Now a media and cultural studies academic approaching retirement, he first started publishing on northern soul because he felt existing research just didn't capture the scene from the inside.

Nicola Watchman Smith. Growing up in a house filled with music and musicians, Nicola learned of rock music from her dad and of soul music from her mam. This musical induction instilled in her a deep passion for popular music and a personal preference for sixties sounds. After many failed teenage attempts to play an instrument she translated her love of pop music into research. Nicola gained an MA in popular music studies and a PhD based on a study of northern soul, which in her eyes was the only popular music culture that still had a story to tell. The scene felt, paradoxically, simultaneously familiar and unknown; a world of emotive, infectious vinyl records there to be explored. Nicola came to northern soul as a young researcher, possessing only a brief insight into the scene gleaned from her mam (her mother was an amazing dancer, who Nicola had not known had attended the Casino until she practised questions for a research interview with her). Now Nicola finds herself a northern soul devotee and in the very privileged position of being an academic who gets to spend her days writing about a music culture that means so much to so many (herself, and her late mam, included).

It is telling that we, the editors, have spent time here establishing our own insider credentials, a practice that we find ourselves, as popular music researchers and as fans, engaging in at conferences, in articles, and in conversation with those active on the scene and with those who are not. Just like the editors, most of the people who contributed to this book found different "ways in" to the scene. Through partners or friends, by curiosity or by accident, an interest in northern soul became central to both what each of these different people do and the ways in which they define themselves, to themselves and to others. And as many different definitions of the "true soulie" exist within the ways in which people talk about and do northern soul, some of the claims to be of the inside provided within this book will be viewed by different readers as more or less authentic, more or less valuable, and the speakers more or less allowed to speak about the scene on behalf of its members. Like all other books written on northern soul, this book too will be discussed and tested on- and off-line, the articles dissected, the authors researched, and the experiences detailed here will be tested alongside those of the reader. Equally, they will be placed alongside research on other music scenes, correlations and differences highlighted. The members of the northern soul scene, like many music-focused communities, police their boundaries; developing, sharing, and applying a hierarchy of membership based upon what a "true" northern "soulie" should know and do, extended crucially to their first encounters of the scene and the engagement that followed.

We do not claim to have captured the "authentic" voice of northern soul, but rather to have brought together its multiplicity in the knowledge that these discourses of insider and outsider exist and are powerful, both within the scene and academic analysis. As the scene has developed and expanded along generational and geographical lines, its boundaries have been tested and remade by individuals who wish to forge their own space on the dancefloor, behind the decks, online, or in the visual or written consideration of the scene. But they do this within these shared boundaries, expectations, and histories that draw the lines of the scene. This book, like social media platforms or the busy bar at an allnighter, is a forum for contestation, and we hope that this collection of chapters and photographs both speak to your own experiences (of northern soul, of popular music, of edited collections) and also force you to reconsider them.

Organizing our understanding of northern soul

The seventeen chapters of the book start with four of the key pieces of writing which established serious studies of northern soul culture over a thirty-year period, followed by original essays produced specifically for this book covering topics as diverse as northern soul as recorded music, dance, lived culture, ideology, and media form. Interspersed between this writing are a series of portraits of scene members celebrating the records they love, and three photo dossiers that capture the scene at different stages of its development.

The earliest writing reproduced is Stuart Cosgrove's 1982 intelligent piece of journalism on one of the scene's defining clubs, Wigan Casino. Originally in a niche, eclectic music magazine, and written at the point when the Casino had just closed, his account is remarkably prescient about the role of the club in the scene's future. We imagined this article twinned with Dave Godin's 1970s *Blues & Soul* columns, but we were not able to secure republishing rights. Nevertheless, the role of the magazine and Godin's journalism is well-represented in later chapters. Joanne Hollows' and Katie Milestone's 1998 chapter explicitly builds upon Cosgrove's analysis to open up a discussion of the "northern-ness" of northern soul. Their work takes in the exclusiveness of the scene and the division between production and consumption that characterizes northern soul, wrapped up in a reconsideration of community and subcultural theory.

In the chapter from 2006 that follows, Tim Wall critically engages directly with Hollows' and Milestone's propositions, but focuses on the micro-cultural aspects of how exactly people dance at a soul night and what this might mean. He sets this within the politics of gender, ethnicity, and class which characterize the scene. By contrast, Nicola Watchman Smith's contribution is more sociological, placing the scene within earlier attempts to understand youth music subcultures; critiquing those approaches and asking what it is to be an aging "soulie" on a scene that emerged from a then thirty-five-year-old youth culture, embracing new generations of participants. All four articles establish themes of place, cultural activity, and identity that run through the newly commissioned essays, interviews, and photo dossiers which follow, and so provided a base for the northern soul scholarship we explore here.

William Ellis's eight musical bookmarks (specially-commissioned portraits) link a range of participants on the scene with core records in their collections. Ellis, well known for his *One LP* portraits of musicians and music industry notables, transformed this idea into the *One 45* project specifically for this book to reveal the diversity of people involved in the scene and their choices of records, many of which may well be controversial. The photographs signal the central place recorded music and record collecting has within the scene and the lives of those who are involved. Ellis also took the photograph which adorns the front cover, created in response to our commission to capture the vitality of a northern soul night. Ellis's photographs are matched by three portfolios interlaced within the written word chapters, produced by photographers from "the inside", and which deal very differently with the scene and its participants.

Ady Croasdell, a well-known promoter on the scene and CD compiler and researcher for the Kent label, kicks-off the new pieces. Here he shares his expert knowledge on the sometimes dubious ways in which records have entered and been distributed within the scene, and sets out the implications for the artists who originally made the music on which the scene thrives. It pairs nicely with Nicola Watchman Smith's second contribution to the book, which builds on these notions of musical authenticity, cultural ownership, and socio-cultural identity that pervade the role of records in the scene. Specifically, she explores the significance of the distinctly British consumption of music which was recorded in a geographically and culturally distant place.

Joe Street's rigorously-researched chapter on *Blues & Soul* columnist and soul activist, Dave Godin, reveals the complexity of the man, his politics, and his relationship with the soul scene he championed. While Godin is rightly celebrated within the scene, as Street reveals, his critical position within British music culture made things uncomfortable for those with less idealistic intentions. Sarah Raine and Tim Wall also tackle Godin's legacy in their chapter on myths on/of the scene. Looking at a range of self-documenting media texts produced within the scene, Raine and Wall explore the way these texts construct and work with histories of the scene to produce a one-dimensional story of northern soul's past.

John Barrett's unique contribution ties the photographs he produced of the scene at the end of the twentieth century to his account of why and how they came to be taken and exhibited. John's own passion and commitment comes through both, and we are delighted to make some of these images available in print again. Although, as John points out, he believed he was working at the time to preserve what he feared was a music culture in decline, the following chapters display something of the dynamics and cultural politics of a scene with a long history and vibrant present. Andrew Wilson's contribution is worthy of note as a return to the issues he dealt with in his more traditional 2007 sociological study, *Northern Soul: Music, Drugs and Subcultural Identity*, but now engaged with from an explicitly personal perspective. The way different academic approaches reveal different truths about music culture is particularly striking. Here, he re-examines the emergence of a rare soul scene from the late 1960s and early 1970s through an autobiographical lens, produces a revisionist history of the Casino years as a period that destroyed the community of the early scene, and reappraises how we view drug-related criminality on the scene. It is a striking and thought-provoking contribution which marks out a distinctive role for the book as a whole. Katie Milestone's reflections on gender and northern soul are equally challenging to many of the certainties of the scene's histories, which usually proceed with an unchallenged, overwhelmingly male narrative. Rich with original primary material and thoroughly theorized, Milestone's account highlights women's relationships to northern soul and explores the scene's gender structures which are notably absent from most media produced within and about the scene.

While many of the contributors look at the northern soul scene as a distinctly British music culture, it has become international in scope, and Dani Herranz's 'La Vida con Soul es Mejor, Mucho Mejor' captures something of the debt the Spanish scene owes to the history of its UK origins. Translated from the Español first publication (*Ruta 66*), and reprinted here, Herranz reveals the same sort of passion and commitment that British "soulies" mobilized to sustain a music scene well over forty years old. This freshness of engagement is also evident in Bethany Kane's photographs of the new generation on the scene. While older members may sometimes read the way this generation present their membership credentials as ersatz, Kane reveals another dimension of the commitment and reimagining northern soul's past that is likely to sustain the scene way beyond what could have been imagined in the 1970s. It also reminds us that the European and generational reinterpretation of the 2000s is actually no different in substance than the recoding of 1960s African-American music carried out by the initiators of the scene decades before.

These questions of mediation are uppermost in the interviews with two very different directors of films of northern soul life of the 1970s, Tony Palmer and Elaine Constantine. The first a 1977 documentary on Wigan Casino; the second a fictional recreation of the scene from a few years earlier from the vantage point of the twenty-first century. These interviews reveal significant new insights into how these important celebrations of northern soul came about, and how they fit within the personal lives and political commitments of their directors. Matched by a third interview with Liam Quinn who was centrally involved in the creation of dance scenes in Duffy's 'Mercy' video and the *Soul Boy* (Shimmy Marcus, 2010) feature film, reading the perspectives of all three helps us understand how hard it is to represent a lived culture in a media text, and how hard it is to keep to one's vision in the commercial environment that media texts are produced.

Both Lucy Gibson, and the voices of the scene participants captured by Sarah Raine, and then interpreted by Mark Duffett, Raine and Wall, play further on the multi-generational nature of the scene. Gibson directly addresses issues touched on in the proceeding chapters, with the role of nostalgia, memory, and familiarity as a form of symbolic knowledge fore-fronted in the way scene participants position themselves as genuine "soulies". In setting out at some length the ways different generations of northern soul participants narrate their involvement, the "voices" chapter attempts quite a sophisticated form of academic dialogue. The mediation of personal experience by participants themselves is presented unadorned, followed by framed interpretations by three academics, each with different experiences of the scene, and each using different academic traditions, to reveal how academia seeks to make sense of the lived experience of northern soul.

Richard Oughton's photographs are starkly different from those of Barrett and Kane, although they share Barrett's interest in the vitality of the dancefloor and Kane's attention to a new generation of soul participant. They also capture British, Brazilian, and European northern events, and reveal something of the differences in dance style from the observational eye of a younger generation of still image documentarians. The overlap with Paul Sadot's ambitious chapter is also telling. Sadot follows Wilson in offering a new history of northern soul, this time one that focuses on the post-Wigan rare soul scene-within-a-scene, linked to an attempt to develop an understanding of dance styles and their relationship to the dynamics of scene history. Built around a set of key records that, for Sadot, say something important about northern soul as a developing participatory aesthetic, the article reads somewhat like Paul's dancing: energetic, engaged, and deeply rooted in the scene and its complex history.

The seventeenth chapter takes us back to where this project began, with an essay from David Sanjek. Based upon the paper Sanjek presented at the original Salford northern soul symposium, it is our posthumous recognition of Dave's important role in kicking off this whole experiment in co-produced music culture studies. To an American popular music academic like Dave, based in Salford, England, and an outsider to the scene who nevertheless shared the same infatuation with black American music, northern soul seemed to be at the same time both familiar and strange. And from the beginning this duality drove his interest. It is fitting that we cap the edited contributions with this essay as it covers most of the ground of the book, and captures much of Dave's eloquence and warmth as a human being, and a popular music academic. In the end, it says as much about this project as it does the northern soul scene. And for that, Dave, we are all very grateful.

Musical Bookmark 1

Tom Page photographed at Hull City Hall, February 2017
Betty Lloyd, 'I'm Catching On'. US BSC Records – 401 1965

> "It's a very special record to me, I think it was the first record I sort of fell in love with; first record I paid a lot of money for. I play it all the time; love it. It's just the first couple of drum beats then horns come in. It's proper sixties Detroit femme-driven soul. Fantastic!"

Tom Page is a DJ and record collector. Tom has spoken live as a guest on BBC Radio 4 and appeared in the film *Northern Soul* (dir. Constantine, 2014). He has been DJing since 2012, gaining a following within the soul scene and DJed everywhere from the 100 Club in London to Corfu. He has a regular set at the Rugby Soul Club All-Niters.

1   Long After Tonight is All Over*

Stuart Cosgrove

> *With last September's closure of the Wigan Casino an era in the northern soul phenomenon ended. Stuart Cosgrove describes the importance of the Casino to northern dancers and rare soul collectors, gives an outline of the movement and looks at the songs and singers.*

Jimmy Radcliffe's 'Long After Tonight Is All Over' is both an anthem and a requiem. It first established itself as a cult record by being the sound that signalled the end of all-night sessions at The Twisted Wheel club in Manchester which has long since had a legendary reputation as one of the havens of rare soul. A mid-tempo sound which is simultaneously about leaving and meeting again, it is the perfect end to allnighters where the dancers identify with the club and return to it regularly over the years. Soon after 9.00am on Sunday 20th September 1981 the opening bars of 'Long After Tonight Is All Over' signified not only the end of the night but proverbially "the end of an era": the closure of Wigan Casino, one of the greatest and most cherished venues of northern soul music. In talking about the Casino, words of praise of a club's formidable contribution to Britain's rare soul scene, it is also an obituary and a critique. Wigan Casino's eight-year history was marked by the seemingly endless sagas of achievement and controversy. The records it "discovered" and persevered with will live on at future venues and the dancers it gave space to will reappear elsewhere. But the venue itself is finished only to be remembered in legends and stories, some real and some imaginary, told in other places long after tonight is all over.

Northern Soul: Time Will Pass You By

When Tobi Legend recorded 'Time Will Pass You By' for Bell's subsidiary record label Mala in 1968, the company could not possibly have predicted that over twelve years later one of their least successful records would be known word for word by thousands of people in another continent. But put quite simply,

---

*   Originally published in *Collusion* 2 (1982).

'Time Will Pass You By' is not only a northern soul record: it is also a record about northern soul. Its lyrics hint at the scene's history and make reference to its defining style.

The chorus refers to a life of the streets and northern soul is primarily a sub-culture of the cities. From Edwin Starr's 'Backstreets' to Frankie Valli's 'The Night', it is a scene that thrives on images of darkness, street life, night-time and the slightly seedy environments of old dancehalls and railway stations. The most remembered all-night venues have been decaying clubs in the backstreets of old industrial cities. Wigan Casino was notoriously seedy, its toilets permanently ankle deep in piss, and rusty condensation dripped regularly from the high ceilings. It was no place for the faint of heart or the uncommitted sightseers attracted by northern soul's tempting atmosphere.

The Casino was a place for quickly moving feet. The soul enthusiasts who nimbly evaded puddles of piss to change into new clothes in toilet cubicles were the fancy dancers on whom the northern scene's reputation hinges. One of the consistent features of the rare soul scene has been its ability to reproduce superb dancers who can predict almost every beat and soulclap in a thousand unknown sounds. But northern soul dancing is not only the backdrops, swallow dives and spins that catch the eye of the onlooker; it is more importantly the ritual elegance of a dance style that glides from side to side but refuses to adopt a name. The *Daily Express* thought that they would christen it the "wheelie" but no one paid any attention because for northern soul the mass media is something to be ridiculed, a cross they have to bear every few years when white rock fails to produce good copy. The media attention, like the disjointed words of 'Time Will Pass You By', moves on to new images and new themes. Implicit in Tobi Legend's line "Life is just a precious minute", is a reminder that northern soul like other sub-cultures is transient and shifting. The people move from city to city. When a venue closes they move on to another and when records have had their time they disappear to reappear at a later time as memories and legends. The northern soul scene is a drug scene. It is a scene permanently living on the fringes of the law. Its clubs lose their licences; the trains that carry dancers from Manchester, Leeds and Crewe are invariably met by uniformed police and plain-clothed drugs squad members, and much of the activity of the scene is covered in friendly secrecy. Over the years Black America has had a catalogue of tragedies involving singers and songwriters. Charlie Parker became entrapped in an endless cycle of heroin addiction, Frankie Lyman and Billie Holliday both died through drugs, whilst Esther Phillips and Etta James, who have both recorded songs which had exposure in the northern clubs, reached the perimeters of addiction before rebuilding their careers.

At times, it seems as if the northern soul scene tries to re-live and imitate the imagery of Black America. The music, the black berets and gloves that were once fashionable on the scene, and the catalogue of deaths that have befallen the scene over the years means the two cultures have much in common. But the northern soul scene is predominantly a soft drugs scene. Although it has had its tragedies in the form of broken needles in the toilets and early deaths remembered in dedicated records over the sound systems of the allnighters, the northern scene is in fact more about amphetamines than hard drug taking. There has always been a current within the scene that has criticized its reputation as a drug culture arguing that the minority tarnish the image of the majority and their music. But for a number of reasons amphetamines and rare soul have a history together which is evident in the earliest days of the original mods and in the emergence of all-night clubs in the mid-sixties. The vast majority of northern soul aficionados take amphetamines not only because they act as a stimulant to keep dancers and record collectors awake, not only because they induce people to talk (and overtalk) and thus forge friendships with people from other towns, but also because amphetamines are part of a whole bundle of different factors that gather together to make up the *style* of northern soul. Since the early arrival of imported American soul music in Britain in the sixties, the rare records, the energetic dancing and the forbidden fruits of the local chemist shop have gone hand in hand. Whether it is right or wrong to take amphetamines is open to debate but to deny their complex co-existence with northern soul is to deny the truth. However, the motto on the badge commemorating the last night of Wigan Casino was not about drugs but about the music. In a final gesture of humour the motto read, "Time passed you by". The single most important feature of northern soul is its respect for the music of Black America.

Let the Music Play

The Blue Cat label is one of hundreds of small labels committed to releasing soul music that has a collectors' reputation on the rare soul scene. Its general reputation is founded on the Ad-Libs' classic 'Boy From New York City' but on the northern scene it is particularly associated with uptempo dance records by Sidney Barnes and Didi Noel. The latter's version of the catchy 'Let The Music Play' is both a classic and a testament ... Let the music play, let it play forever. There is a strong belief that northern soul is, by its very nature, special music. Music that transcends trends and fads to become music that will last forever. This belief in the supremacy of the music explains a very strong current of dedication within the scene which encourages regulars to adopt pseudonyms from rare record labels (Ric-Tic from Wolverhampton), to tattoo the names of legendary labels such as Okeh on arms and wrists and to set about collecting the entire catalogue of obscure and long forgotten labels.

The emphasis on rare soul and the relative uniqueness of the northern scene can be traced back to the first wave of imported soul music in the sixties. Originally the attraction of imported Black music was both its roots in dance beats and the manner in which it marked the owner out from those content with the formulaic records on the BBC playlist. The period of the mid-sixties saw the emergence of the mod sub-culture in Britain and the establishment of Black owned independent record companies in the USA. Although the mods disappeared (only to reappear in a different form in the late seventies), many of the companies like Berry Gordy's Motown group grew and diversified. The northern scene began to establish its own venues and they became increasingly distinctive as the policy of unique style became a more conscious policy in favour of rare, unknown soul. The collectors and the DJs turned their attentions away from the Motown labels when they became too well known and too readily available. This shift can be pinpointed from 1965 onwards. After years of distribution through other labels including London-American, Fontana, Oriole, and Stateside, in March 1965 Motown released the Supremes' 'Stop in the Name of Love' on their own Tamla Motown label. The search for music which maintained the distinctive features of the Detroit sound (uptempo beat, exchanging vocals and saxophone breaks) led the collectors of the North to explore other lesser known labels: Mirwood, Ric-Tic, Wingate, and Revilot. This shift towards lesser known American labels also coincided with a more general awareness of the R'n'B catalogue of companies like Cameo Parkway and Chess who were already established in the pop and blues markets respectively. It was during this period that the northern scene first discovered the recordings of people like Edwin Starr and Laura Lee (who later joined Motown when their recording company Ric-Tic was bought over by Berry Gordy). It also saw the appearance on the British soul scene of people like Jimmy Conwell, Earl Harrison and Leon Haywood who had no previous reputations.

The consolidation of rare soul as a defining feature of the northern scene also firmly established the central importance of Detroit as the mythical capital of the scene. Even today, years after Motown had moved their commercial base to the West Coast, Detroit labels have a special significance in the North. Ric-Tic, Wingate and Revilot remain strong favourites and have now been joined by a host of other Detroit labels including Premium Stuff, Magic City, Deto, Big Hit and Kool Kat. Similarly, Detroit has given birth to a formidable list of northern celebrities of whom Rose Batiste, Ronnie McNeir and Black Nasty are only a few. The Terra Shirma studio in Detroit has probably been the birthplace of more rare northern records than any other studio and the production work of the Detroit-based pair Richard "Popcorn" Wylie and Tony Hester is equally established. In fact, after many years, Popcorn Wylie's 'Rosemary What Happened' (an atmospheric dancer based on the story of *Rosemary's Baby*) remains a highly sought-after collectors' record.

The rare soul policy has at least three related factors. Firstly, rare music invariably means specialist venues offering the most complete collection of sounds and this in turn encourages northern fans to travel very long distances to clubs. Secondly, the laws of supply and demand invariably mean that high prices are asked and paid for rare records. This has tended to confuse and annoy outsiders who become indignant at the prices that records change hands for. The sale of James Fountain's 'Seven Day Lover' on William Bell's Atlanta-based Peachtree label generated hostility when around £200 changed hands. But there is always a semblance of sanity on the scene brought about by collectors who carry an encyclopaedic knowledge of the music, and often advise others including the DJs on their purchases. Perhaps the most immediate problem of rare soul, which far outstretches the importance of big prices, is the existence of bootlegging. The threat that a bootlegger may identify a rare record, press up illegal copies, and make them available at just over £1, is a pressing problem (and a problem of pressings). The northern scene has sought to combat the immediate problems of bootlegging by inventing a system of cover-ups whereby rare records are given a new title and are credited to artists who are either entirely fictional or who are established singers with an already proven reputation on the scene. Thus a record like the Coasters' recording of 'Crazy Baby' was referred to as 'My Heart's Wide Open' and was credited to a non-existent soul singer Freddie Jones. This white lie about Black music allows the record to establish itself with the dancers before it is prematurely released or bootlegged. The persistent problem with cover-ups is that it makes genuine collection more difficult and it tends to generate a cult of imitation. Disc jockeys have recently tried to cover a Wilson Pickett record which is neither particularly rare nor in any need of the kind of protection that the cover-up is designed to give.

Despite the northern scene's undeserved reputation as a sub-culture which sticks rigidly to old and inferior versions of the Detroit sound, there is in fact a massive range of northern records which defy this reputation. It is quite possible for a DJ to programme three records one after the other. The first might be a cover version of the Motown classic 'Love is Like an Itching in My Heart' by Jenny and the Jewels on Hit Records; the second might be a much slower ballad number like Keanya Colins's 'Love Bandit' which at times threatens to be a ballad; and the third might be the raucously progressive 'Psychedelic Soul' featuring the screeching sax and gruff vocals of Chicago session musician Saxie Russell. The range of northern soul is wide enough to encompass the sophisticated sixties R'n'B record 'Looking For You' by Garnett Mimms, the uptempo beat of Jackie Wilson's 'The Who Who Song', the Philly-influenced elegance of Oscar Perry's 'I Got What You Need' and the left field Miami funk of the Delreys Incorporated's 'Destination Unknown'. Although the relationship between a record and its rarity is always likely to be complex, it is difficult to make any sweeping generalizations about the quality of northern soul. Many records are not in fact prized for any intrinsic qualities but for their ability to generate atmosphere in the middle of an all-night session. Very few people would argue that Sam and Kitty's 'I've Got Something Good' was a good record but it is undeniably a record that builds up atmosphere and attracts the dancers. But there is quality in northern soul and there is a very high level of respect for some records. The name of the late Linda Jones has been trendily sprinkled on the pages of the *NME* and *The Face* but none of the clubs that those magazines give space to actually get round to playing any of Linda Jones's uniquely soulful records. The cult status that Linda Jones and Lorraine Ellison enjoy in conversation is rarely backed up in practice. The northern scene's dedicated exposure of 'My Heart Needs a Break' and 'I Just Can't Live My Life' remain Linda Jones's only consistent public exposure in Britain. If a catalogue of names is any guide to quality then the last night at Wigan Casino had much to commend it. Nancy Wilson, Jodi Mathis, Anne Sexton, Jean Carn, Alice Clark and Esther Phillips were only a small proportion of the female vocalists played through the night. The search for rare soul dancers continues and the easier access to the USA has given collectors more possibilities. A small army of soul experts regularly scan the surface of American cities driven on by the unshakeable belief that in the next rack will be a promotion copy of an uptempo sound which the company lost faith in. It should preferably be one of only a few in the world featuring the lead vocals of a guy recently convicted of murder, and the demanding saxophone of a bank robber. The northern rarity is a strange and irresistible breed: Darrell Banks, the singer who popularized many northern classics including 'Open the Door to Your Heart' and 'Angel Baby', murdered in a gunfight; Johnny Braggs, the singer of 'They're Talking About Me', convicted to three life sentences; and Frankie 'Love Man' Crocker, the talk-over DJ on 'Ton of Dynamite', jailed as a payola racketeer. The northern soul singer, like the scene itself, strays down the backstreets of a twilight world.

Come On Train

Don Thomas's excellent recording of 'Come On Train' on the independent San Francisco label NUVJ emerged at a critical period in the development of northern soul. The scene had two particularly thriving clubs in Wigan Casino and Blackpool's Mecca Highland Room. The scene was put under considerable adverse pressure by the media who turned to it in a brief search for something different. The appearance of several particularly crass and offensive articles in the *Daily Express* and the *Daily Mirror* together with the kiss of death from the unimaginative lips of Tony Blackburn (who actually recorded a "northern" record under the pseudonym of Lenny Gamble) threatened to devastate the scene. This problem was made worse by the attitude of two powerful DJs – Ian Levine who was then a regular at the Mecca and Russ Winstanley the managing DJ at Wigan. On the one hand the Mecca followed a policy of exclusive new rarities programmed alongside the more soulful kind of contemporary disco. The Casino meanwhile remained loyal to rare soul but also increased its output of old northern standards and at times was guilty of playing records which had no real place on a soul scene. This split became generally known as "oldies versus funk" even though both clubs still played many records in common. The situation was made worse by the other interests of the major DJs who, during the period of media attention, became involved with various different record companies. Ian Levine certainly used his position to advance his own productions with Chicago soul singers such as L.J. Johnson, Barbara Pennington and Evelyn Thomas. Some of the Wigan DJs were less than honest about their dealings with record companies and with the bootlegger Simon Soussan, one of the *enfant terribles* of northern soul. Almost simultaneously with some of these problems was the entry into the pop charts of a notoriously awful cover version of a record called "Ski-ing In The Snow" by the Invitations. The cover was made by a dire pop group calling themselves Wigan's Ovation (the name being a mixture of the north's top venue and a highly respected harmony group The Ovations who record on Goldwax). Needless to say, they had nothing whatsoever to do with northern soul. The enthusiasts knew they didn't but the media and many other music followers thought they did. Out of this debacle two tendencies emerged. Firstly, a significant number of people, many of whom had been long devotees, became more attracted to the emerging attractions of quality disco and later jazz/funk. Many of them left the scene to move to other soul clubs in Manchester, Leeds and London. Some of them like Steve Strange, Chris Sullivan and David Ball drifted elsewhere to indulge in a cocktail of Bowie, punk and futurism to re-emerge as Visage, Blue Rondo à la Turk, and Soft Cell. Many others drifted back towards the north when nothing else could satisfy the attraction of rare soul. The other current within the scene remained loyal to Wigan as a venue and to its mixed playlist. But the oldies and newies schism has remained a problem until the present day.

The closure of Wigan Casino was immediately followed by several competing attempts to establish a new replacement venue. The management of the Casino acting in their own best interests announced another allnighter for the week after the one that supposedly marked the end of an era. This announcement was almost certainly done to destabilize a new venture in the north jointly organized by one of the scene's most respected DJs, Richard Searling, and a collector of long standing, Bernie Golding. This new venture is undoubtedly the best future for the scene but it is open to doubt whether it can survive against the mammoth institution of the Wigan Casino management. Whatever the outcome the scene will rebuild its future because Jackie Wilson, Etta James, Jerry Williams, The High Keys, The Carstairs and Little Ritchie are undoubtedly more central to rare soul than the people who act as DJs for their records. In cities all over Britain they'll be waiting for the train to come on. Don Thomas's lyrics sum up the feeling of many northern soul fans faced with a future without the Casino: "Travelling from country and city to city, trying to find somewhere to belong ... So come on train."

About the author

Stuart Cosgrove is a journalist, broadcaster, and media executive, formerly working at *NME* and *The Face*, and Channel 4 where he was Controller of Arts and Entertainment and Head of Programmes (Nations and Regions). He presented BBC Radio Scotland's northern soul show *Floorfillers* in the 2000s. His personal involvement in the scene is captured in the autobiographical *Young Soul Rebels*, published by Polygon in 2017.

Long After Tonight is All Over — Northern Soul

Stuart Cosgrove

With last September's closure of the Wigan Casino an era in the Northern Soul phenomenon ended. Stuart Cosgrove describes the importance of the Casino to Northern dancers and rare soul collectors, gives an outline of the movement and looks at the songs and singers.

Junior Walker and the All Stars

Jimmy Radcliffe's "Long After Tonight Is All Over" is both an anthem and a requiem. It first established itself as a cult record by being the sound that signalled the end of all-night sessions at the Twisted Wheel club in Manchester which has long since had a legendary reputation as one of the havens of rare soul. A mid-tempo sound which is simultaneously about leaving and meeting again, it is the perfect end to all-nighters where the dancers identify with the club and return to it regularly over the years. Soon after 9.00am on Sunday 20th September 1981 the opening bars of "Long After Tonight Is All Over" signified not only the end of the night but proverbially 'the end of an era': the closure of Wigan Casino, one of the greatest and most cherished venues of Northern Soul music. In talking about the Casino, words of praise of a club's formidable contribution to Britain's rare soul scene, it is also an obituary and a critique. Wigan Casino's eight year history was marked by the seemingly endless sagas of achievement and controversy. The records it 'discovered' and persevered with will live on at future venues and the dancers it gave space to will reappear elsewhere. But the venue itself is finished only to be remembered in legends and stories, some real and some imaginary, told in other places long after tonight is all over.

Northern Soul: Time Will Pass You By

When Tobi Legend recorded 'Time Will Pass You By" for Bell's subsidiary record label Mala in 1968, the company could not possibly have predicted that over twelve years later one of their least successful records would be known word for word by thousands of people in another continent. But put quite simply "Time Will Pass You By" is not only a Northern Soul record it is also a record about Northern Soul. Its lyrics hint at the scene's history and make reference to its defining style . . .

As I sit here looking at the street,
Little figures, quickly moving feet,
Life is just a precious minute,
Open up your eyes and see,
Give yourself a better chance,
Because Time will pass you by.

The chorus refers to a life of the streets and Northern Soul is primarily a sub-culture of the cities. From Edwin Starr's "Backstreets" to Frankie Valli's "The Night" it is a scene that thrives on images of darkness, street life, night-time and the slightly seedy environments of old dancehalls and railway stations. The most remembered all-night venues have been decaying clubs in the backstreets of old industrial cities. Wigan Casino was notoriously seedy, its toilets permanently ankle deep in piss and rusty condensation dripped regularly from the high ceilings. It was no place for the faint of heart or the uncommitted sightseers attracted by Northern Soul's tempting atmosphere.

The Casino was a place for quickly moving feet. The soul enthusiasts who nimbly evaded puddles of piss to change into new clothes in toilet cubicles were the fancy dancers on whom the Northern scene's reputation hinges. One of the consistent features of the rare soul scene has been its ability to reproduce superb dancers who can predict almost every beat and soulclap in a thousand unknown sounds. But Northern soul dancing is not only the backdrops, swallow dives and spins that catch the eye of the onlooker, it is more importantly the ritual elegance of a dance style that glides from side to side but refuses to adopt a name. The Daily Express thought that they would christen it the "wheelie" but no one paid any attention because for Northern Soul the mass media is something to be ridiculed, a cross they have to bear every few years when white rock fails to produce good copy. The media attention like the disjointed words of "Time Will Pass You By" moves on to new images and new themes. Implicit in Tobi Legend's line "Life is just a precious minute," is a reminder that Northern Soul like other sub-cultures is transient and shifting. The people move from city to city. When a venue closes they move on to another and when records have had their time they disappear to reappear at a later time as memories and legends. The Northern Soul scene is a drug scene. It is a scene permanently living on the fringes

2 Welcome to Dreamsville:[1]
A History and Geography of Northern Soul*

Joanne Hollows and Katie Milestone

The northern soul scene in Britain is a regionally based dance and club network that centres around "rare" soul records from the 1960s and 1970s. With its roots in the soul clubs of the mid-1960s, northern soul is still alive today. Northern soul events are primarily held in the north and Midlands of England, although they exist on a lesser scale in different parts of Britain. Despite the distinctiveness and longevity of this largely "underground" scene, northern soul has attracted little attention in cultural analysis. With the notable exception of Stuart Cosgrove's 'Long After Tonight is All Over',[2] northern soul has tended to remain hidden in the footnotes of academic accounts of musical cultures and subcultures. In this chapter, we aim to open up a space for talking about northern soul rather than offering any definitive account of it.[3]

In this chapter, we hope not only to raise the profile of this marginalized scene within popular music criticism, but also to show how the case of northern soul raises more general questions about the cultural study of music. In particular, the chapter addresses debates about place and identity and the relationship between local musical scenes and global musical cultures. The analysis is organized around four main concerns: the "northern-ness" of northern soul; rarity, exclusivity and commodity exchange; the relationships between contexts of production and consumption; and the importance of place and pilgrimage within the northern soul scene. In negotiating these issues, we hope to highlight how the northern soul scene produces a sense of identity and belonging. In doing so, we hope to offer a different way of conceptualizing identity and the production of "community" in musical cultures from that offered by subcultural theory. In the process, questions about conception of musical value and commodity exchange within musical cultures will be highlighted.

---

* Originally published in A. Leyshon, D. Matless and G. Revill (eds.), *The Place of Music*, 1st ed. (London: Guilford Press, 1998).

The marginalization of northern soul in the cultural study of music is, at least in part, a product of both the predominance of subcultural theory[4] in analysing musical culture and the preoccupations of subcultural theorists. While Cosgrove's subcultural analysis of northern soul is informative, and we draw on his insights, the northern soul scene highlights the limitations of subcultural theory. Richard Middleton has noted that subcultural theorists were ill equipped to deal with cases such as northern soul where "subcultural identity is centrally focused on music" because they were more concerned with "music as symbol" than "music as music".[5] Furthermore, the romance and radicalism attributed to youth subculture was compounded by the way in which subcultural theorists privileged notions of progress, change, and the new, never quite freeing themselves from the association between "youth" and "the future". It is partly for these reasons that, as Gary Clarke has noted, subcultural theory focused on the "innovatory moment" of subcultures, so they seem to exist in a "synthetic moment of frozen historical time".[6] The longevity of musical cultures such as northern soul and the scene's fascination with music from a bygone era (the US soul music of the 1960s and early 1970s) meant that it failed to meet the theoretical requirements of subcultural theory.

The lack of attention paid to northern soul was also compounded by the fact that, until recently, scenes centring around discos and clubs have been marginalized from pop history.[7] The "authentic" subcultures of subcultural theory were usually located on the street. The street operated as a sign of "authenticity" because not only has it traditionally been a site that is difficult to regulate but also because unlike the club, the street is supposedly distanced from the world of commerce which, for subcultural theorists, is identified with ideological incorporation. By positioning the radicalism of subculture against the ideological pull of capitalist commerce, subcultural theorists not only ignored more commercial scenes but also overlooked the intersections between the subcultures they studied and commercial activity.[8] If, in considering northern soul, we hope to open up one part of a hidden history of club culture, then we also wish to argue that a consideration of commercial activities within the musical scene should be central to cultural analysis. The case of northern soul highlights the way in which the value of commodities such as records are not simply a product of processes of production or consumption but also a product of processes of exchange that need to be understood as meaningful cultural activities.

If northern soul has remained hidden from academic histories of pop, it is also a scene in which history and tradition are central values. This "soul underground" privileges a knowledge of musical histories and traditions that also inform the value of "rarity" within the scene. It is in relation to the values of history, tradition, and rarity that distinctions between the "authentic" and the "inauthentic" are constructed within northern soul. This is not to argue that northern soul is an "authentic" culture because it values "authenticity" but to consider how notions of "authenticity" are produced in different ways in different musical cultures. On one level, notions of "authenticity" and northern soul seem incompatible: as we have already noted, northern soul did not fit the criteria of authenticity fixed by subcultural theorists. Furthermore, musical cultures that are primarily organized around recorded music[9] are often seen as "inauthentic" in a folk discourse that privileges "live" music that is produced and consumed by "active" members of a "community".[10] Folk discourse, like subcultural theory, is suspicious of the commercial intervention of the cultural industries between producers in privileging the "authentic" as a sign of cultural value. For example, northern soul is based on a rejection of commercially successful records and as we go on to argue, privileges a sense of "roots" by stressing the importance of the sociological and musical origins of northern soul records within local musical cultures.[11]

If subcultural frameworks can provide only a limited understanding of northern soul, Schmalenbach's concept of the *Bund* makes it possible to think of the relationships between place and identity and to conceive of the northern soul scene as an "elective, unstable, effectual form of sociation".[12] Unlike conceptions of "community" in which a sense of belonging is based on ascriptive social relations, geographical proximity, and tradition, social relations in *Bund* are elective and based on sentiment, although, as we shall argue in the case of northern soul, they may aspire to produce their own traditions. In order to be sustained, the *Bund* must produce "a code of practices and symbols which serve as the basis for identification" and also produce a sense of belonging.[13] In the following discussion, we consider the practices and symbols that form the basis for identification in northern soul and highlight the ways in which these are bound up with the centrality of place within the scene.

A brief history of northern soul

The rare or northern scene has its roots in the early 1960s. As Stuart Cosgrove has argued, the first wave of soul import was favored by people who sought to distinguish themselves from "popular taste", "those content with the formulaic records on the BBC playlist".[14] A "rare" or "underground" soul scene emerged in the mid-1960s out of both the Mod scene and the rhythm and blues clubs of the north. This scene tended to reject "popular" Motown sounds in favour of undiscovered, and hence "rare" or "underground" Detroit labels.[15] At this point in the scene's history, there was still an emphasis on new or relatively new tracks. The tracks were less specifically dance-orientated tracks but instead, as DJ Richard Searling puts it, records that people liked so much that they made them want to dance.[16] At this time, the scene was associated with clubs such as the Mojo in Sheffield, the Wheel in Manchester, and the Catacombs in Wolverhampton.

In the early to mid-1970s the rare or northern soul scene underwent some changes. Also at this time the northern soul scene received some media attention, and as a consequence discussions of northern soul have often been "fixed" around this era. At this point the scene shifted to become a distinctive "rare" soul scene based around obscure old records by maintaining an emphasis on 1960s soul. There was also some shift of pace to fast up-tempo stompers and a corresponding shift in the speed and frenzy of dance, aided by the consumption of "speed".[17] Richard Searling has noted that black participants tended to drift away from the scene as the pace of the music accelerated.[18] After the Torch in Tunstall (Stoke on Trent) closed, Wigan Casino allnighters acted as a focal point for the scene from 1973, distinguished by high-speed soul that was suited to its cavernous interior. Wigan Casino, like the Torch before it, was also, crucially, well placed for motorway links.[19] Because Wigan became the focus for media attention, "northern soul" became equated with Wigan Casino, although it was only one of many clubs that held northern soul nights.

The 1970s not only saw a shift from slower to faster soul, but also the emergence of a schism within the scene between those who wanted to retain an emphasis on old soul and those who wanted to include new tracks. Furthermore, the increased publicity and popularity that the scene was receiving was seen as a danger to what was perceived as an underground movement that had made a cult out of obscurity. The media attention, along with the new/old split, threw the scene into crisis in the mid-1970s. Furthermore, although the scene valued "authentic" old soul, it demanded a constant supply of unheard, "rare" records. But the stocks of undiscovered up-tempo US soul records were diminishing. The scene had to evolve and was faced with two options: either it could stick with tradition, play "authentic" oldies, and end up with a stagnant playlist, or it could maintain the rarity and obscurity of the scene by shifting to new "rare" soul.[20] This second option could be achieved in two ways: first, through the production of custom-made northern soul tracks geared to the dancefloor which tried to keep some fidelity to the production values of 1960s soul; and second, by feeding into a living Afro-American dance music tradition by absorbing new black musics. Both options were taken up by Ian Levine, a DJ from the Blackpool Mecca. Levine went to the United States to try and produce new northern soul sounds and raise the quality of custom-made new tracks.[21] He also began to introduce new dance music which would eventually lead some people away from northern soul into nights organized around 1970s Philadelphia dance music (the basis for the 1980s "rare groove" scene) and others into an emergent jazz-funk scene.[22]

After the closing of Wigan Casino in 1981, the northern soul scene shifted pace again, often moving into smaller venues and centring around slower tracks from the 1960s and early 1970s. Obscure up-tempo tracks might have been used up, but there was still a ready supply of slower tracks, and, although rarities are once more getting hard to come by, new disks still occasionally emerge. The scene is also sustained through small-scale media such as DJ Richard Searling's show on the northern radio station *JFM* and music papers such as *Black Echoes*, *Soul Underground*, and *Blues & Soul*. Despite the occasional "discovery" of northern soul by the southern taste-making, "style" magazines such as *The Face* and *I-d*, contemporary northern soul is no youth culture, with the average age of participants at today's events pushing forty. Indeed, increasingly, the northern soul scene revolves around memory and familiarity, rather than rarity. As Cosgrove argues, legends and memories have always played an important part in the scene as well as being an important theme within the lyrics of many northern soul tracks.[23] Northern soul not only places value on a musical tradition but also on the scene's own traditions.

The "northern-ness" of northern soul

The term "northern soul" was coined by Dave Godin of *Blues & Soul* magazine after a visit to an allnighter at the Twisted Wheel in 1970 to describe a distinctive soul scene that existed north of Watford, and mainly in the north and the Midlands. However, in order to understand the "northern-ness" of the scene, it is also necessary to place it in relation to the "regionally-based 'supremacy'" of the southeast.[24] In the late 1960s and early to mid-1970s – the time of the scene's heyday – soul was generally unfashionable among white audiences. The northern soul scene, which valued unfashionable musical traditions, was seen as backward and risible. Despite a few notable exceptions to the rule (Mersey-beat, for example), until the 1980s the provinces in Britain were seen as places where people indulged in watered-down versions of what London was doing years ago, a form of geographical "trickle-down" thesis, although more appropriately in this case a "trickle-up" thesis.

As Bourdieu argues, forms of cultural capital are not only unequally distributed between classes, but are also unequally distributed in a "socially ranked geographical space".[25] The literal "cultural capital" of Britain, London, has the power to make distinctions between the legitimate and the illegitimate, in both traditional and newer cultural forms, and thus to distinguish between what is "in" and what is "out" or unfashionable. If forms of cultural capital are not simply distributed in social space but also in geographical space, it is important to note that distinction between the legitimate and the illegitimate aren't simply distinctions between "high" and "popular" culture but are even made within popular culture, including youth culture.[26]

If the distribution of cultural capital in geographical space, cross-cut by the unequal distribution of cultural capital in social space, leads to London's superiority as a national centre of economic, social, and cultural capital, then this is also based on a refusal of, and distinctiveness from, the regions as "culturally deprived" and "backward". Northern soul might best be thought of as a refusal of this refusal – that is, as a refusal of the South's claims to legitimacy and distinction.[27] The northern soul scene was not simply a watered-down version of a southern scene but was instead "produced" within the north. Because the scene was organized around old American records it didn't need London's economic and cultural power in order to survive. In this way, both a provincial and basically a workingclass form of northern soul rejects the legitimacy of more powerful taste formation within the United Kingdom (while also being unable to displace them).[28]

Rarity, exclusivity, and commodity exchange

If music is central to the northern soul scene for dancing, it is also crucial as a rare commodity. Northern soul nights are the site not only for dance but also for the exchange of records. The club is also a marketplace.[29] While the emphasis on rarity and obscurity has led some people to dismiss northern soul as elitist, this misses the point that strategies of distinction operate in all aspects of popular music.[30] Furthermore, the investment in particular forms of cultural capital that are recognized within the field of northern soul cannot only be used to create a profit in cultural distinction but can also be converted into economic capital. Northern soul records can exchange hands for hundreds, and sometime thousands, of pounds.[31] This not only highlights the centrality of commercial activity in many youth cultures – a fact ignored when authenticity is defined against the commercial – but also points to the importance of the processes of exchange and consumption as a source of both the cultural and the economic value of music. This challenges two dominant arguments to be found in music criticism, both of which privilege production as the source of value. The first argument, heavily reliant on folk discourse, claims that musical values are homologous with the values of the community in which the music is produced. The second, not unrelated, argument, draws on Marxist economics to argue that the cultural and economic value of music is fixed in the production process. Instead, the case of northern soul illustrates that value is not only determined by the logic of production but that economic, cultural and symbolic value are produced through exchange and consumption practices in different cultural contexts.[32]

Records are not only bearers of musical meaning but are also material objects and commodities. Appadurai's work on the "social lives of things" is useful in thinking about the "conditions in which economic objects circulate in different 'regimes of value' in time and space".[33] For Appadurai, "Demand, desire, reciprocal sacrifice and power interact to create social value in specific social situations".[34] It is in this context that records can be seen to have value both as commodities and as bearers of musical meaning, and why these factors need to be thought through together. As Will Straw argues, different musical cultures have their own logic which is a product of how value is constructed: "Cultural commodities may themselves pass through a number of distinct market and populations in the course of their lifecycle. Throughout this passage, the markers of their distinctiveness and their bases of value may undergo significant shifts."[35] Furthermore, the practice and processes of exchange need to be understood as social activities that help to create and sustain northern soul.

Northern soul can be used to challenge the production-dominated Marxist view of the music industry and folk notions of musical communities because it highlights the "commodity candidacy" of records that had moved out of the commodity state.[36] The "socially regulated paths"[37] that these 1960s soul records on minor labels were doomed to follow was, if they were lucky, a six-month shelf life. Many didn't even make it to the commodity state in the first place and remained unreleased. However, as they moved into a different "regime of value" – the northern soul scene that valued obscurity – the commodity candidacy of these records was highlighted. In this way, the northern soul scene worked with an opposite set of values to the record industry (and very similar values to music critics): it was the unpopularity and lack of commercial success of these records that made them so highly prized and gave them the mark of authenticity.

Appadurai argues that diversions from the socially regulated paths of commodities are always competitively inspired.[38] In the northern soul scene, it is DJs and dealers who make these diversions and who stand to make both a profit in cultural distinction and an economic profit from rare records. As Will Straw argues, DJs act as "intellectuals within a given musical terrain" and are "engaged in struggles for prestige and status".[39] The ability of DJs to act as intellectuals comes from the high amounts of cultural capital they possess within this particular musical terrain or cultural field. In the northern soul scene, as in contemporary dance-music cultures in the United Kingdom, it is the DJs who are as much stars of the scene as recording artists, and it is their names that are used to sell events. However, although DJs define the value of records, they also need records to define their own value.[40]

Northern soul events can be thought of as "tournaments of value", "complex periodic events which are removed in a culturally well-defined way from the routines of economic life".[41] For Appadurai, tournaments of value are status competitions between people in power, in this case DJs. Success in these competitions, argues Appadurai, is partly measured by the skill through which commodity paths are diverted or subverted.[42] One of the main ways in which DJs in the northern soul scene hype up the records' rarity value and their own prestige is through the use of white labels. By sticking white labels over the original labels and retitling them, DJs increase the exclusivity of records. The previous history of the commodity is temporarily eradicated in the process.[43] As DJ Richard Searling points out, this is also a source of entertainment within the scene.[44] Furthermore, as he also acknowledges, it is a means of transforming cultural capital into economic profit. The other function of white labels is to discourage bootlegging, the illegal copying of are records which often occurred, especially in the scene's heyday.[45] Bootlegging undermined the values of authenticity and rarity that were central to the northern soul scene. Whereas bootlegs in some musical cultures are valued because of their rarity, within northern soul bootlegs lack the life history necessary to be valued. As with religious relics, verifying the object's history is central to its value.[46] By temporarily disguising the origins of records through the use of white labels, DJs prevented bootleggers from identifying the heritage of the music and thus from authenticating the fabricated.[47]

Urban north United Kingdom to urban north United States

Thus the value of records that originally were the product of black America in the 1960s changed as they moved from one regime of value to another. However, this does not mean that continuities between the original context of production and the northern soul scene should be ignored. If northern soul refuses the authority of "the south" of England, it allies itself with the American north, in particular with cities such as Detroit. Iain Chambers has commented on the appeal of what he calls "the sweet promise of the neon-streaked streets of American nights and pleasures".[48] On one level, then, northern soul is yet another example of the ways in which British working-class culture has produced an "imaginary" identification with America as an "escape" from native cultural traditions, an identification which offered a more "extensive ... sense of the possible".[49] The identification with "America" is, however, contradictory. On the one hand, both the authentication of old disks as US products and the association of these disks as the product of particular places in the United

States is important within northern soul. On the other hand, the "America" that is consumed is the "pop cultural myth" of America rather than the "USA as a real place".[50]

If the northern soul scene attempts to build a regionally based culture by bypassing and rejecting the limitations of the national, it does so by positioning itself in relation to global relations. However, to claim that northern soul represents a local appropriation of global cultural flows is insufficient because the music used to "produce" the northern soul scene is not drawn from a "globalized" international culture. This is not to argue that northern soul exists "outside" of global capitalism nor to argue that the independent labels on which northern soul was originally released were somehow "independent" of the agendas of the global music industry in general and thus were more "authentic", although this attitude may well exist within the scene. Rather, we wish to stress that northern soul's privileging of a regional identity, based on the rejection of the national, needs to be understood as based on interregional affiliations at a global level. The sense of regionality in northern soul is produced out of material circumstances – the clubs, the fans, and so on – but also depends on other regional "reference groups", and "on ideas and fantasies that are themselves mediated globally" through international flows of images.[51]

The regional base of northern soul – England's north and Midlands – is not of course a region in which northern soul is the only musical scene. Indeed, as Will Straw argues, what is more interesting is the diversity of musical practices within localities.[52] Instead, northern soul's interregional association with Detroit, and other Rust Belt cities to a lesser extent, directs us to the "ways in which the making and remaking of alliances between communities are the crucial political processes within popular music".[53] Northern soul also highlights the ways in which the politics of identity associated with processes of globalization and localization, which are taken as products of post-Fordism and postmodernization and are often associated with the impact of new communication technologies, are not in fact novel but have a long history within diasporic musical cultures.

The value of the records used within northern soul is not only their "Americanness" but more specifically an identification with black urban America (a point that has been made about a range of postwar British youth subcultures).[54] As Cosgrove has argued, not only is "the single most important feature of Northern Soul its respect for the music of Black America", but the scene also "tries to relive and imitate the imagery" of African-American culture.[55] As has already been noted, the northern soul scene respects history rather than novelty, and this attitude corresponds with the wider claims about the importance of history in black music. For example, Gilroy has argued that "black music has ... only partially obeyed the rules of reification and planned obsolescence. Its users have sometimes managed to combine the strongest possible sense of fashion with a respectful, even reverent, approach to the historical status of their musical culture which values its longevity and its capacity to connect them to their historical roots".[56] Of course for white northern soul fans, the relationship to black America is "imagined". On the one hand, musically and lyrically the tracks offer a sense of history, but on the other, they make connections with, and fetishize, the history of the "Other". Thus, while attempting to draw connections between the urban American north and the urban English north, we are not seeking to equate the experience of white British and black American. Indeed, the fetishization of black musical cultures by white Britain needs to be understood in relation to "an exotic fantasy, not the reality of living under [specific forms of] oppression".[57]

However, just because the relationship to black urban America is "imagined", this does not diminish its power and significance within the northern soul scene. To ignore different engagements with musical form by distinguishing "true" soul fans from "fake" soul fans reproduces the politics of exclusion and inclusion inherent in subcultural theory and accentuated in the case of white fans of music identified as "black".[58] Gilroy suggests that thinking of musical cultures in term of Edward Said's concept of an "interpretive community" might be more profitable.[59] In this way, it is possible to think of an interpretive community of soul fans that extends from the streets of Detroit through the northern soul scene and into the bedrooms of young women lip synching to Diana Ross records. These fans are linked by certain possibilities within soul music and the discourses within which the meaning of soul is produced. As Shepherd has argued, while musical meaning is neither immanent in the sound nor in the lyrics, "the sounds of music restrict significantly the range of affective states and meaning that can be invested in them. For that reason, the sounds of a particular musical event will always be likely to encourage the investment of certain traces and resonances".[60]

As we have already argued, the respect for history and tradition within black music is present in northern soul's sounds and words. The ways in which soul privileges "ecstasy" and "solidarity"[61] is built on in the dance-floor culture of northern soul. Furthermore, the way in which vocals tend to follow the beat in many northern soul tracks produces a sense of urgency and movement, creating a music for socializing and dancing.[62] There are also lyrical possibilities in the music of the northern soul scene that become meaningful in the context of the urban British north. For Cosgrove, the appeal of soul in the British north lies in its attempts to deal with the pain of city living.[63] Although these songs deal with images of poverty, suffering, and "life in the backstreets", they also at both lyrical and musical levels offer some attempt to temporarily transcend problems. This is partly a result of the gospel heritage of soul. The imagery of a desolate northern landscape is central to many northern soul tracks.[64] For British soul fans, it is this identification with an imaginary American urban landscape that allows the daytime's urban decay to be produced as the night-time's glamour. In a global culture, "mediascapes", "images of the world created by the media", blur the lines between "realistic" and "fictional" landscapes.[65] Therefore, although there are various possibilities already in the sounds and imagery of northern soul, this doesn't determine consumption. As Shepherd argues, "Affect and meaning have to be created anew in the specific social and historical circumstances of each instance of music's creation and use".[66]

The importance of the sounds of the Rust Belt in the northern soul scene also needs to be understood in relation to Fordist production methods. Soul not only emphasizes suffering and redemption, it also celebrates leisure time as the time free from industrial processes and reclaims the body from the world of work as an instrument of pleasure.[67] Although many northern soul songs are love songs, this format can be used to explore emotional exploitation and male rationality which can also offer a critique of industrial exploitation. For example, Eloise Laws's 'Love Factory' uses industrial metaphors to demonstrate how the rationality of Fordist production methods has invaded the "private" sphere of the emotions.[68]

To conclude this section, in understanding the ways in which records, and as we shall see, places, are used within the northern soul scene, it is therefore necessary to combine the analysis of meanings located in the musical text with meanings that become attached and embedded in the music through use. As we have seen, in northern soul, the meaning of the music and the meaning of records as material objects are both important and interrelated because they help to sustain a sense of identity and belonging within the scene. Furthermore, as we have argued, northern soul values music that is not only unpopular in the present but was often condemned to oblivion at the time it was produced. It is the significance that accrues to northern soul music through use that adds to its value. It is through becoming integrated into the northern soul scene that these records acquire a new "reality". One of the clearest illustrations of this point is to be found in Henry Jenkins's work on fan cultures, in which he quotes a children's story that tells the tale of how toys are made "real": "Real isn't how you are made. It's a thing that happens to you. When a child loves you for a long, long time, not just to play with, but REALLY loves you, then you become real".[69]

Place, pilgrimage, and identity

The relationship between place and identity in northern soul is, as we have already seen, based on a regional rejection of the south of England and an affiliation with the black north of America. However, this far from exhausts the significance of place in northern soul. The sense of "community" within northern soul is not one based on locality or neighbourhood but instead is "produced" through travel and an attachment to the spaces that are usually considered mundane but that acquire an "aura" as sacred places because they are central to the scene. In this last section, we explore the ways in which travel, place, and identity are interrelated in the production of the northern soul scene.

Members of the northern soul scene would, and still do, travel hundreds of miles to attend a particular event.[70] Travel within the scene both reproduces and subverts aspects of traditional daytripping. Northern soul events are associated with the weekend and with special bank-holiday events. In some ways, this draws on the older notion of the "dance train" of the early 1930s that carried single, working-class youths from Manchester and Salford to Saturday night dances at Blackpool's Tower Ballroom.[71] With some of the key sites in the northern soul geography located in seaside resorts – for example, Blackpool, Morecambe, and Cleethorpes – the scene reproduces traditional working-class leisure patterns. This integration of older working-class cultural practices into the scene again reinforces the value of tradition within northern soul. As Rob Shields has argued, the "liminal 'time-out'" offered by daytrips and holidays is "partly accomplished by a movement out of the neighbourhoods of 'everyday life' to specific resort towns".[72] Travel to these sites then reproduces older working-class leisure patterns in which trips are tied to a move from "production spaces" to "consumption spaces",[73] drawing on the place-image of seaside resorts as sites of "liminality".

However, the northern soul scene both uses and subverts aspects of traditional daytripping. Although it subverts the idea of daytripping by "nighttripping", it is also based on organized bus trips and train travel that integrate the act of travel into the collective practices of the scene. Members can also collect embroidery patches from these sites which can be sewn on to the hold-alls[74] associated with the scene.[75] If the practice of clubbing and travelling "produced" this scene out of dispersed members, then columns in magazines also worked to produce a sense of "community" by giving details of such events as northern soul marriages and meetings between characters on the scene.[76] This sense of a dispersed community and the scene as a migrant scene also connects with the importance of displacement and migration in many northern soul songs.

If travel to seaside resorts can be explained in terms of traditional working-class leisure practices, what is less easy to explain is why fans travelled to places like Wigan and Tunstall which are mundane "production places" rather than "consumption spaces". On one level, it is the very act of travel that is crucial to the scene, building on the ritualistic pleasure of "going out" which can be seen in more recent club cultures. Furthermore, as Hetherington argues in his work on New Age travellers, an act of pilgrimage allows both for identity renewal and a symbolic escape from everyday life.[77] The specific sites that motivated travel, and that changed over time (often due to attempts to regulate nightclubs), were not specific towns so much as specific clubs. As Shields has argued, certain sites when appropriated "become socially important not only for their empirical facilities but for their qualities as what William Whyte called 'schmoozing' spaces which support personal and group identification".[78] The centrality of particular clubs to the scene, enshrined in treasured embroidered patches, operates in a similar way to the centrality of the music. Through acts of consumption, these sites become "re-enchanted", acquiring "an aura of symbolic values".[79]

The collective practice through which mundane urban sites become "re-enchanted" are integrated with identity formation within the northern soul scene. As we have already noted, Hetherington has drawn on Schmalenbach's concept of the *Bund* as "an intense form of affectual solidarity, that is inherently unstable and liable to break down very rapidly unless it is consciously maintained through the symbolically mediated interactions of its members".[80] Furthermore, the *Bund* requires "self-conscious, ritualised and symbolic practices of group maintenance".[81] The activity of travel and the use of "sacred places" such as the Torch and Wigan Casino as sites of "social centrality" need to be understood, alongside other ritualized practices within the scene discussed earlier, as practices that help to maintain the dispersed community of northern soul fans. The emphasis on tradition and legend within the scene, which we have noted throughout, is a mechanism through which the scene both produces and reproduces a collective history in which place-images are central.[82] Stories, legends and traditions are important mechanisms for maintaining a club scene through the times it is suspended and relatively inactive, nurtured only through infrequent fanzines, radio shows, and listening to the music at home.[83]

By thinking about identity formation in the northern soul scene with reference to the concept of the *Bund*, it is possible to solve some of the problems in thinking about identity in relation to musical cultures. One of the major problems with subcultural theory was its emphasis on a "subcultural identity" which, while arising out of structural positions also seemed to transcend all other identities that members of subcultures could inhabit. As Angela McRobbie puts it, "[f]ew writers seemed interested in what happened when a mod went home after a weekend on speed".[84] Members of musical scenes are not simply "teds", "mods", "punks", or "northern soulies" but also mothers, sons, husbands, and workers. Furthermore, they may also, for example, be fans of *Coronation Street* or the Stoke City football club. As Rob Shields argues, we often claim that "'we wear many hats' … Each momentary identification corresponds to a role in a given social 'scene' – a scene dominated by a group and the group ethos".[85] It is through specific consumption practices attached to travel and to particular sites that a sense of collectively and "affectual solidarity"[86] is produced and reproduced within northern soul. It is through these practices that the *Bund* can be maintained despite being unstable and despite the fact that members have a diverse range of identification.

Writing this piece, it became clear that religious associations continually reoccur in our discussions of the northern soul scene. On the one hand, this association is clearly evident in the nature of soul with the strong relationships between many soul performers and the church, its gospel roots, and the sense of ecstasy and transcendence that most soul offers, however secularized. On the other hand, the sense of a religious fervour also comes out of our discussion of the practices associated with the scene, whether in phrases like "Keep the faith" or in the sense of "possession" in northern soul dancing or even in the status of records as relics, clubs as sacred places or shrines, and travel as pilgrimage. The emotional attachments that are central to affective "communities" or *Bund* have been downplayed in subcultural accounts of musical cultures, quite possibly because of the "feminine" association of these qualities. Yet the desire for a sense of attachment, of belonging and of having "a place", are central to the northern soul scene, in both the music and the practices associated with it. This sense of tradition and faith in the production of the northern soul "community" offers a different way of understanding musical cultures to the portraits of innovatory subcultural moments. Although northern soul puts far more emphasis on place than most musical cultures, it also provides a signpost toward other popular music cultures that are increasingly spread across generations and divorced from a simple association with youth.

If, as we have noted throughout, the attachment to place in the northern soul scene is complex, the scene also begins to challenge some of the assumptions embedded in the current theoretical popularity of notions of "liminal spaces". Both Shields's and Foucault's concepts have useful applications, but neither can, nor should, be applied too liberally. While northern soul draws on the liminal status of seaside resorts in some of its central sites, it is rather difficult to conceive of Wigan and Tunstall as "liminal spaces". Certainly, both towns are "places on the margins" of the centres of economic and cultural power. Their landscapes share many aspects of industrial and deindustrial urban centres but lack the cultural infrastructure of the city. In this sense, they are "liminal". However, they lack the place-image of pleasure that Shields attributes to seaside resorts.

While the clubs involved may operate as consumption spaces, many of these are far from "glamorous" in any normal sense of the word. Yet within the northern soul scene, they are sites that motivate pilgrimage and memorabilia. If northern soul draws on a preconstructed "placemyth"[87] of Detroit, then the myths attached to places such as the Torch are a product of the scene alone. The value of these sites is not just a product of the DJs associated with them, the sound quality, and so on – although these are important – but their importance as sites of social centrality within the scene and the histories constructed by the scene. It is through these processes that a weekend in Wigan or Stoke becomes a meaningful experience, just as value is added to the music through processes of consumption. To return to this story of how toys become real, "[o]nce you are Real, you can't be ugly, except to people who don't understand".[88]

By using the work of Schmalenbach and Hetherington to think about how the production of a sense of belonging and identity in northern soul is also bound up with the production of sites of social centrality and a sense of place, we hope to offer an alternative way of thinking about the relationships between musical cultures, identity, and place. Furthermore, the case of northern soul highlights the complexity of the relations between space, power, and musical cultures. Northern soul also highlights the importance of understanding how musical cultures are not only conscious productions but must be consciously reproduced, reworked, and maintained in order to sustain a scene.

Acknowledgements

Thanks to Kevin Hetherington, Mark Jancovich, and Martin Parker for their help and comments.

About the authors

Joanne Hollows is an independent researcher and writer. She was formerly Reader in Media and Cultural Studies at Nottingham Trent University. Her research spans a range of areas including popular music, feminism and popular culture, food and domestic cultures. Her books include *Feminism, Femininity and Popular Culture* (Manchester University Press, 2000), and *Media Studies: A Complete Introduction* (Hodder, 2016). Joanne's current research interests in music focus on the strange relationships between cycling and music cultures.

Katie Milestone is Senior Lecturer in Cultural Studies and Sociology at the Manchester Metropolitan University. Her research interests focus on gender and popular culture, creative industries, place and identity and popular music. Her doctoral studies at the Manchester Institute for Popular Culture on music and place, and her long-standing personal and academic interest in northern soul, led to published work and research events about the scene. The second edition of her jointly authored book *Gender and Popular Culture* will be published by Polity Press, and she is writing a Major Works Collection on the same subject for Routledge. She is currently working on research into dance music culture and gender, place and identity in the creative industries.

Notes

1. S. Ambrose, *Welcome to the Dreamville* (1965). Originally released on Musicor in the United States and on Stateside in the United Kingdom. Reissued on *Up All Night*. Vol. 2: *Thirty Hits from the Original Soul Underground* (Charly, 1993).

2. S. Cosgrove, "Long After Tonight is All Over", *Collusion* 2 (1982): 38–41. Since this chapter was written, there have been some publications that extend some of the debates we touch on. On northern soul, see K. Milestone, "Love Factory: The Sites, Practices, and Media Relationships of Northern Soul", in S. Redhead *et al.* (eds.), *The Club Cultures Reader: Readings in Popular Cultural Studies* (Oxford: Blackwell, 1997), pp. 152–67. Also of interest is S. Frith and C. Gillett (eds.), *The Beat Goes On: The Rock File Reader* (London: Pluto, 1996). It is also important to note that many of the debates we engage with in this article have also been developed in more depth in S. Thornton, *Club Cultures: Music, Media, and Subcultural Capital* (Cambridge: Polity Press, 1995).

3. In particular, although we provide a "reading" of northern soul, there is obviously a need for some ethnographic work on the scene.

4. See, e.g., S. Hall and T. Jefferson (eds.), *Resistance Through Rituals* (London: Hutchinson, 1976); and D. Hebdige, *Subculture: The Meaning of Style* (London: Methuen, 1979).

5. R. Middleton, *Studying Popular Music* (Milton Keynes, UK: Open University Press, 1990), p. 166.

6. G. Clark, "Defending Ski-jumper: A Critique of Theories of Youth Subculture", in S. Frith and A. Goodwin (eds.), *On Record: Rock, Pop, and the Written Word* (London: Routledge, 1990), p. 83.

7. S. Thornton, "Strategies for Reconstructing the Popular Past", *Popular Music* 9/1 (1990): 87–95.

8. See, e.g., A. McRobbie, "Second-hand Dresses and the Role of Ragmarket", in A. McRobbie (ed.), *Zoot Suits and Second-hand Dresses* (Basingstoke, UK: Macmillan, 1989); R. Middleton, *Studying Popular Music* (Milton Keynes, UK: Open University Press, 1990); J. Shepherd, "Value and Power in Music: An English-Canadian Perspective", in V. Blundell *et al.* (eds.), *Relocating Cultural Studies: Developments in Theory and Research* (London: Routledge, 1993), pp. 171–206.

9. However, this is not to neglect the importance of "live" acts during the late 1960s and the 1970s; see, e.g., "The Torch Story", *Blues & Soul* 103 (1973): 12–14.

10. S. Frith, "Art versus Technology: The Strange Case of Popular Music", *Media, Culture, and Society* 8 (1986): 26–79.

11. S. Redhead and J. Street, "Have I the Right?: Legitimacy, Authenticity, and Community in Folk's Politic", *Popular Music* 8/2 (1989): 177–83.

12. K. Hetherington, "The Contemporary Significance of Schmalenbach's Concept of the Bund", *Sociological Review* 42/1 (1994): 16. As Hetherington points out, Schmalenbach's concept has been used as a way out of Tonnies's opposition between *Gemeinschaft* and *Gesellschaft*. *Bunde* are neither inspired by the unconscious sense of belonging in traditional ascriptive "communities" nor by rationality, but instead are an "intentional" and "conscious phenomenon derived from mutual sentiment and feeling" (p. 9). As Freund puts it, the *Bund* "would be a place for the expression of enthusiasms, of ferment, and of unusual doings" (cited, p. 6).

13. Ibid. As Hetherington points out, similar ideas have emerged more recently in Maffesoli's conception of the "neotribe" in which forms of solidarity are "elective and affectual" rather than ascriptive as they are in older notions of the tribe ("Contemporary Significance", p. 14).

14. Cosgrove, "Long After Tonight", p. 39.

15. Although as Cosgrove has argued, Detroit is "the mythical capital of the scene" ("Long After Tonight", p. 40), rare soul would also be taken from other minor labels operating out of cities such as Chicago and Philadelphia. Some slower tracks would also be taken from "deeper" soul sounds of the South.

16. Taken from authors' interview with Richard Searling, December 1992.

17. As Cosgrove argues, "amphetamines and rare soul have a history together" dating back to the Mod scene in the 1960s and institutionalized in the first allnighters in the mid-1960s ("Long After Tonight", p. 39). Although not everyone at an allnighter would take drugs, speed did play an important part in producing the scene, in a similar way to the centrality of ecstasy in rave cultures. In dance cultures, speed is not only valued for its energizing effects but the rituals of acquiring and taking speed have a symbolic role in producing the event of clubbing.

18. From interview material, see n. 16.

19. "The Torch Story".

20. See Cosgrove, "Long After Tonight", p. 41.

21. For a fuller discussion of the problem of custom-made northern soul and the production of a new-release scene, see T. Cummings, "Northern Soul: After the Goldrush", *Black Music* (1975): 8–14.

22. Cosgrove, "Long After Tonight", p. 41.

23. Ibid., p. 38.

24. D. Massey, *Space, Place and Gender* (Cambridge: Polity Press, 1994), p. 109.

25. P. Bourdieu, *Distinction* (London: Routledge, 1984), p. 124.

26. S. Thornton, "Moral Panic, the Media, and British Rave Culture", in A. Ross and T. Rose (eds.), *Microphone Fiends: Youth Music and Youth Culture* (New York: Routledge, 1994), p. 188.

27. Even in more sympathetic accounts of the South, it is claimed that the southern soul scene lacked the institutional framework (clubs and record shops) that enabled the appreciation of rare soul and thus is seen as "deprived". See, e.g., F. Elson, "Check out the North", *Blues & Soul* 120 (1973): 2.

28. E.g., in an interview with Dave Godin, soul journalist Neil Rushton claimed that "when the current disco bubble bursts, it will be of the upmost [sic] importance that somewhere there is a continuing audience for good music, and it happened before when the south, and London in particular, abandoned soul in favour of more fickle idols, no doubt the north will continue to carry the torch and the banner regardless. I think it's safe to say that the north is the only part of Britain where soul has ever approached anything like being an 'in' trend and it will always continue to draw a certain amount of strength and force from that region" (*Blues & Soul* 200 [July 6, 1976]: 11).

29. This also draws on older working-class leisure traditions in the north. This argument is expanded in J. Hollows and K. Milestone, "Inter-city Soul", paper presented at the British Sociological Association annual conference "Contested Cities", April 1995, University of Leicester.

30. Thornton, "Moral Panic"; G. Vulliamy, "Music and Mass Culture Debate", in J. Shepherd *et al.* (eds.), *Whose Music?: A Sociology of Musical Languages* (London: Latimer Press, 1977), pp. 179–200.

31. E.g. Frank Wilson's 'Do I Love You', which was released on a Motown subsidiary label on Christmas Day 1966 and immediately withdrawn. Only one copy of this record is known to exist and the record is valued at £5,000 ("Antique Records Road Show", BBC Radio 1, September 1992).

32. See, e.g., M. Poster (ed.), *Jean Baudrillard: Selected Writings* (Cambridge: Polity Press, 1988).

33. A. Appadurai, "Introduction: Commodities and the Politics of Value", in A. Appadurai (ed.), *The Social Life of Things: Commodities in Cultural Perspective* (Cambridge: Cambridge University Press, 1986), p. 4.

34. Ibid.

35. W. Straw, "Systems of Articulation: Logics of Change: Communities and Scenes in Popular Music", *Cultural Studies* 5/3 (1991): 374.

36. Appadurai, "Introduction", p. 13.

37. Ibid., p. 17.

38. Ibid.

39. Straw, "Systems of Articulation", p. 375.

40. This draws on Appadurai's analysis of the kula system of the Western Pacific. Appadurai cites Munn's observation on kula exchange in Gawa that "[a]lthough men appear to be agents in defining shell value, in fact, without shells, men cannot define their own value; in this respect, shells and men are reciprocally agents of each other's value definition" (Appadurai, "Introduction", p. 20).

41. Ibid., p. 21.

42. Ibid.

43. Paul Gilroy has argued that in the sound systems of the 1960s and 1970s, the reliance on imported music and the removal of labels should be understood as a critique of commercialization and as subverting "the emphasis on acquisition and individual ownership which the markers of black music cultures identified as an unacceptable feature of black culture" (P. Gilroy, *There ain't No Black in the Union Jack* [London: Hutchinson, 1987], p. 167). While not wishing to generalize to other musical cultures from northern soul, Gilroy's argument depends on searching out anti-capitalist elements as signs of resistance in

black music cultures, a romantic view that may ignore the calculative and profit-motivated dimensions in these cultures.

44. From an interview with authors.
45. Cosgrove, "Long After Tonight", p. 40.
46. Appadurai, "Introduction", p. 23.
47. When northern soul gained increased popularity in the mid-1970s, authenticity and rarity were not only threatened by bootleggers but by rereleases. As Idris Walters observed in 1975, northern soul fans "would prefer to have to pay £2.50 for a single as long as it's going to stay rare, but, more and more, they are in danger of shelling out £5.00 for something that they aren't told will be on general release at 60p in the time it takes to get changed. The vigilance of the bootleggers and the legitimate record companies have combined to produce a new regime – overprovision, Northern soul for idiots, trans-Atlantic high finance" (I. Walters, "Is Northern Soul Dying on its Feet?" Republished in H. Kureishi and J. Savage (eds.), *The Faber Book of Pop* [London: Faber and Faber, 1995], p. 454).
48. I. Chambers, *Urban Rhythms* (London: Macmillan, 1985).
49. I. Chambers, *Border Dialogues: Journeys in Postmodernity* (London: Routledge, 1990). There are numerous accounts of the appeal of "America" to the British working classes. See, e.g., I. Chambers, *Popular Culture: The Metropolitan Experience* (London: Methuen, 1966); P. Miles and M. Smith, *Cinema, Literature and Society* (London: Croom Helm, 1987).
50. S. Frith, "Anglo-America and its Discontents", *Cultural Studies* 5/3 (1991): 266.
51. Ibid.
52. Straw, "Systems of Articulation", p. 368.
53. Ibid., p. 370.
54. See, e.g., Hebdige, *Subculture*.
55. Cosgrove, "Long After Tonight", p. 39.
56. P. Gilroy, *Small Acts: Thoughts on the Politics of Black Cultures* (London: Serpents Tail, 1993), pp. 238–39.
57. V. Walkerdine, *Schoolgirl Fictions* (London: Verso, 1990), p. 209. On the difficulty of talking about "black cultures", see S. Hall, "What is This 'Black': in Black Popular Culture?" in G. Dent (ed.), *Black Popular Culture* (Seattle: Bay Press, 1992), pp. 21–37.
58. This can also result in some essentialist tendencies. For a review of this debate, see, e.g., P. Gilroy, "Sounds Authentic: Black Music, Ethnicity, and the Challenge of a Changing Same", *Black Music Research Journal* 11/2 (1991): 110–31.
59. Gilroy, *There ain't No Black*, p. 187.
60. Shepherd, "Value and Power in Music", p. 198.
61. R. Middleton, *Pop Music and the Blues* (London: Victor Goltancz, 1972), p. 218.
62. Ibid., p. 220.
63. S. Cosgrove, "Living in the City: A Soul Essay", paper delivered at the Unit for Law and Popular Culture, January 1991, Manchester Polytechnic.
64. Cosgrove, "Long After Tonight".
65. A. Appadurai, "Disjuncture and Difference in the Global Cultural Economy", *Theory, Culture and Society* 7 (1990): 299.
66. Shepherd, "Value and Power in Music", p. 188.

67. Gilroy, *There ain't No Black*, p. 202. While it is understood that the critique of productivism and reclaiming the body has additional meanings associated with slavery in African-American culture, this doesn't mean that the critique of productivism and celebration of leisure is in any way meaningless to the white British working class.

68. E. Laws, 'Love Factory' (1970). Sequel. Of course, Fordist production methods have also been closely associated with the production of Detroit soul, most notably in the case of Berry Gordy's Motown. Gordy, it is often claimed, drew on his experiences of working in the car industry at Motown, introducing rigorous quality control, a workshop of songwriters, and the repeated use of the same formula. More recently, a more sympathetic account of Motown production has been developed that challenges some previous assumptions. See J. Fitzgerald, "Motown Crossover Hits 1963–1966 and the Creative Process", *Popular Music* 14/1 (1995): 1–11.

69. M. W. Blanco, *The Velveteen Rabbit or how Toys Become Real*, cited in H. Jenkins, *Textual Poachers: Television Fans and Participatory Culture* (New York: Routledge, 1992), p. 50.

70. Despite the scene being associated with the north and Midlands of England, there were in fact many Scottish northern soul fans who would make regular trips across the border. There were also a few northern soul venues scattered around the south.

71. A. Davies, *Leisure, Gender, and Poverty: Working-class Culture in Salford and Manchester, 1930–39* (Milton Keynes, UK: Open University Press, 1992), p. 90.

72. R. Shields, *Places on the Margin: Alternative Geographies of Modernity* (London: Routledge, 1991), p. 85.

73. Ibid., p. 111.

74. As well as becoming part of the northern soul style, the hold-alls had a practical function. Sweaty from dancing, people would often change clothes during the course of a night.

75. One outlet for these badges was the International Soul Club which distributed sew-on patches and car stickers which included "Forever the Torch" and "Keep the Faith The Catacombs". Operating out of Newcastle-under-Lyme (Stoke on Trent), the International Soul Club boasted 30,000 members in 1973. For 10 pence a year membership, the club offered details of club dates and allnighters as well as selling northern soul merchandise.

76. E.g., Frank Elson's "Check Out the North" column in *Blues & Soul*. More recently, another means through which the northern soul scene is sustained is through the internet. See K. Milestone, *From Detroit to Manchester to Berlin*, 9th Conference of the International Association for the Study of Popular Music, Kanazawa, Japan, 1997.

77. K. Hetherington, "New Age Travellers: Heterotopic Places and Heteroclite Identities", unpublished paper presented at the Alternative Political Imagination Conference, April 1994, Goldsmiths College, University of London; forthcoming in *Theory, Culture, and Society*.

78. R. Shields, "Spaces for the Subject of Consumption", in R. Shields (ed.), *Lifestyle Shopping: The Subject of Consumption* (London: Routledge, 1992), p. 16.

79. R. Shields, "The Individual, Consumption Cultures, and the Fate of Community", in Shields, *Lifestyle Shopping*, p. 99.

80. K. Hetherington, "Stonehenge and its Festivals: Spaces of Consumption", in Shields, *Lifestyle Shopping*, p. 93.

81. Ibid., p. 95.

82. G. Revill, "Reading Rosehill", in M. Keith and S. Pile (eds.), *Place and the Politics of Identity* (London: Routledge, 1993).

83. There are currently numerous northern soul compilations available on CD on which the liner notes emphasize "histories" of both disks and clubs. This is emphasized by the ways in which some compilations stress the "place of origin" of the disks, e.g., *The Sound of Detroit* – or the place in which they were consumed – e.g., *The Golden Torch Story*.

84. See A. McRobbie, "Settling Account with Subcultures: A Feminist Critique", in Frith and Goodwin, *On Record*, pp. 68–69. While on the subject of this chapter, we are aware of the gender blindness displayed here. However, it is worth noting that the ways in which we have conceptualized members of the northern soul scene does not presume a masculine identity in the same way as is evident in much subcultural theory. Indeed, activities such as dancing and listening to love songs are often demarcated as "feminine". Positions of power within the scene, however, are almost exclusively occupied by men. There has been little research into the ways in which forms of "cultural" and "subcultural" capital are not only distributed between classes but are also gendered, but this may offer a partial explanation of the predominance of men as DJs and record traders within musical scenes. See Thornton, *Club Cultures*.

85. Shields, "The Individual", p. 107.

86. Hetherington, "Stonehenge and its Festivals", p. 93.

87. Shields, *Places on the Margin*.

88. Cited in Jenkins, *Textual Poachers*, p. 51.

3 "Out on the Floor":
The Politics of Dancing on the Northern Soul Scene*

Tim Wall

Dobie Gray's 1966 US record 'Out On The Floor'[1] was taken up in the early 1970s by dancers in clubs in the English north and Midlands. As well as having the beloved Motown-esque beat that dominated the playlists at the time, the song itself was a paean to the cool and hedonism of the dancefloor that these clubs celebrated. The popularity of the record[2] coincided with the spread of the term "northern soul" to describe a dance scene and associated music. The scene is still active today, with club nights across the UK attracting a mix of the original participants (now over forty) with new converts to a community built on high-speed dancing to obscure records mainly recorded in the 1960s by African American singers.

The scene's development is chronicled in the pages of British specialist magazines from the 1970s like *Blues & Soul*, *Black Music*, and *Echoes*, and was first summarized in a mid-1970s review of popular music (Frith and Cummings 1975). More developed accounts appeared in the early 1980s (Cosgrove 1982; Chambers 1985) and a growing body of journalistic accounts of the scene (Winstanley and Nowell 1996; Nowell 1999; Ritson and Russell 1999) has been paralleled by academic explorations (Milestone 1997; Hollows and Milestone 1998). Dancing has a very minor role in most of these accounts, which is surprising given its centrality in the scene. More recent television programmes exploring the history of northern soul have given a visual prominence to dancing, but restrict such representations of dance to the "gymnastic" (see, for instance, Hepton 2001; Littleboy 2003). Moving and still images in these programmes are always focused on dancers doing "backdrops", "spins", and "dives". Academics share this emphasis, presenting northern soul dancing as a "distinctive, acrobatic style" and suggest a parallel with break dancing (Milestone 1997: 145). However, attentive viewing of the television images reveals that few dancers move in this manner, and then only

---

* Originally published in *Popular Music* 25(3): 431–55.

for a few seconds. There is far more to northern soul dance than the standard representation as gymnastic movement, and even these moves need to be understood in the wider context of dancing, music and culture.

Stuart Cosgrove, in an insightful article, emphasizes the way dancers "predict almost every beat and soul clap in a thousand unknown sounds", and argues for the importance of "the ritual elegance of a dance style that glides from side to side but refuses to adopt a name" over that of eye-catching moves (Cosgrove 1982: 38). Strangely, Milestone quotes Cosgrove but removes the "glides from side to side" phrase without ellipsis, and does not comment on his suggestion that there is more here than "acrobatic style". She does, however, offer a number of other interesting observations upon the competitive and display nature of the dancing rituals, and the applause of appreciation that accompany the fadeout of well-regarded records (Milestone 1997: 146). In this article I want to explore these rituals in their full cultural complexity by restoring the gliding movement to the centre of the analysis.

Using Dobie Gray's record as an exemplar of the "northern sound", and drawing upon participation observations of thirty years of soul dancing,[3] this article investigates the politics of the scene's dancefloors. I start with a short discussion of how the existing literature has tried to theorize dance. Building on Ben Malbon's approach to the cultural meaning of dance (Malbon 1999), I then analyse the movement and proxemics of the dancefloor routines, the relationship of the dancing to recorded music, and the way that the tension between individual display and solidarity are resolved. This approach is then extended to explore the role of gender and sexuality, and cultural identity with place and ethnicity.

Theorizing dance

There are few systematic methods for studying dancing to popular music, and little developed theory that could be used as a foundation for such a method. In this section, therefore, I aim to highlight the most productive contributions. In particular, I point to the importance of understanding the physical experience of dancing, and, making substantial use of Ben Malbon's excellent work in this area, I establish a template for analysing northern soul dancing. I end this review of literature with a consideration of issues of social identity that are undeveloped in Malbon's work.

At the outset, it should be noted that the marginalization of dancing within studies of northern soul culture reflects a wider lack of attention in the literature of popular music studies. In 1979 Richard Dyer felt obliged to write *In Defence of Disco* (Dyer 1979), and over fifteen years later Sarah Thornton was still noting the neglect of dance, dance music and dance spaces in pop scholarship (Thornton 1995). Like Thornton I see this as the result of the dominance of a "rock aesthetic" (Regev 2002) in studies which "tended to privilege 'listening' over dance musics, visibly performing over behind-the-scenes producers, the rhetorically 'live' over the 'recorded'..." (Thornton 1995: 1–2). Andrew Ward has suggested that this neglect reflects the response of rational scholarship when faced with non-rational activities (Ward 1997: 8). He argues for a focus on the embodied experience of dancing, rather than an attempt to understand dance as some form of externalized non-verbal message (p. 17). However, this approach simultaneously severs this experience from wider contexts of meaning created by our interaction with the music, other dancers, and the ambience of the dancefloor. When we dance we do so by making choices about particular ways to move from the many ways that are available. An analysis that excludes these factors is neglectful of the rounded whole of the experience of dance.

A number of writers have theorized just these interactions in physical experience. Richard Dyer argues that late 1970s disco dancing was characterized by a whole-body eroticism in contrast to the phallic focus of rock dancing (1979: 152–54), while Gilbert and Pearson emphasize the way that sound vibrates through our bodies (Gilbert and Pearson 1999: 44–47) and, along with Gill (1995) and Reynolds (1998), see dance as an exemplar of Barthesian *jouissance*. It is notable, however, that most of these discussions of the ecstasy of dance are located in drug-altered perceptions of music, and not primarily in the physicality of bodily movement. While dance (and drugs) are clearly linked to senses of such intrinsic physical pleasures, they are also part of wider extrinsic cultural activities.

Attempting a synthesis of these approaches, Ben Malbon formulates dancing as "a conceptual language with intrinsic and extrinsic meanings, premised upon physical movement, and with interrelated rules and notions of technique and competency guiding performance across and within different situations" (Malbon 1999: 86). For Malbon, dancing is meaningful through, and expressive of, interconnected cultural activities articulated by bodily movement and posture. He investigates these cultural meanings through concepts of identification, sociality and performability.

He relates identification to a construction of self, and notions built on the binary oppositions of the in-crowd/out-crowd, and coolness/mainstream (pp. 37–69). The concept of sociality explores the relationships within the club between the individual, the space of the club and the other clubbers (pp. 70–89). The final "situation" is focused on the performance of dance in these wider contexts. This is achieved through the study of the physical geography of the club; the environment created by music, lighting and other factors of ambiance; the density of the crowd and the spacing and orientation of individuals within it; the competencies utilized by dancers; and the emotional spacing (pp. 90–101). I use all these ideas and approaches in adapted form in the analysis that follows.

Malbon is particularly effective at recasting Ward's emphasis on embodied experience as a set of "intrinsic" meanings interacting with "extrinsic" meanings. However, he marginalizes other extrinsic meanings including the wider cultural context of power relationships of class, gender, sexuality, ethnicity, and geography. Largely, this reflects a shift in theoretical interests within the academy from the modernist politics of equality and liberation struggle to a postmodern focus of locality and individualized identity through practice. While the modernist theorizing ignored its embodied experience in order to emphasize its political significance, a fuller insight will not be secured by jettisoning wider power relationships. As I will show, power relationships are centrally important in the study of the northern soul scene.

As I have argued elsewhere (Wall 2003: 188–92), we need to be aware that at different times, and for different groups of people, to dance (or not to dance) has been a significant political position deeply rooted in ideas of race, gender and sexuality, and linked indelibly to the ideas of cool/not cool that Malbon discusses.

There are some helpful pointers in some existing work as to how these issues could be dealt with. The role of dancing for women in the late 1970s (McRobbie 1984), for gays (Dyer 1979: 136–80; Brewster and Broughton 1999: 135–80) and for different ethnically-based cultural groups (Boggs 1992; Vincent 1996; Reynolds 1998) has been effectively explored. Even more interesting has been Paul Gilroy's notion of the dancefloor as a real and cultural space in which the usual hierarchies of society are inverted, so that competencies of dance are more important than those that prevail outside (Gilroy 1991). He gives a dominant role in this space to the formation of a black British identity, to the formation of proto-feminist senses of empowerment, and to new possibilities for white, working-class, male identity. His historical narrative charts developments which significantly contextualize the birth and development of the northern soul scene outside, and in opposition to, the rock aesthetic.

In what follows, I build on these engagements with existing analysis and theory, and move on to explore how dancing is meaningful within the modern northern soul scene. I start this examination by concentrating on the physical movements of dancers as style, focusing on the relationship of these movements to the music used for dancing, their setting within the dancefloor as a physical space and a cultural crowd, and their cultural and historical location.

I give a central role to an idea of competence, a term which I use to mean the state of mastery over techniques and competencies of a particular dance culture. I will make particular use of Dobie Gray's record 'Out On The Floor' as a case study. In the second section I connect these practices to the politics of dancing and to the relationships of power and identity.

Dancing, northern soul style

Style refers to the *manner* of expression; it is the particular way certain actions are performed. In his semiotic investigation of style, Dick Hebdige suggests it can be understood as bricolage, homology and a signifying practice (Hebdige 1979). By this he means that style is the active use of available materials, in which each use is interconnected with other uses, to produce a meaningful whole. As such, I want to explore dance style as a process of meaning-construction, distinct in its usage of available moves, and linked to other practices that make it meaningful. It is, therefore, far more important to understand how, and in what context, dancers dance, than it is to simply record what they dance, or how it feels.

I start by identifying a central set of practices which were established in the early 1970s, and (mainly because of the continuity of many of the participants) have remained the predominant way in which dance is organized within the scene. These aspects of style constitute a narrow definition of how music can be danced to, expressed by the scene's participants as a shared set of dance techniques and an associated notion of competence.

Competence and dance technique
Malbon places competence within the realm of sociality, and drawing on Goffman (1959), identifies its aim of "successfully negotiating the trials of 'impression management'" (p. 97). That is to say, it matters what you look like when you move, and it matters what spatial relationships you produce in relation to other dancers. In fact, as I will show, on the northern scene the idea of competence orders the spacing of dancers and variation in style in a way that it does not seem to in the post-House club culture Malbon investigates.

I noted earlier that we will not find an understanding of dance within the scene if we concentrate on the "gymnastics" of back drops, spins and dives that impress the on-looker at a northern night. They are the most *obviously* distinctive features, and certainly they give a heroic appellation to the exponents, and a sense of the extraordinary to these dancefloors. However, even when (thirty years ago) we were younger, fitter and more practised, only a minority of dancers used these moves, and only at set places in certain records. Today it tends to be the older male dancers who execute them, rather than the large number of younger dancers. I would suggest that it is through this relationship that a sense of the heroic has been established.

Cosgrove tried to put his finger on northern style by noting that the dancer "glides from side to side" and dancers "predict almost every beat and soul clap" (1982: 38). The predominant "glide" style is achieved through some core characteristics of posture and movement: rigid upper torso, eyes up and looking forward; weight back and pushing down through the hips on to the heels; moving mostly with feet, with fairly straight legs, to propel oneself across the floor (almost always sideways); arms and hands tend to follow the shifting weight of the dancer, or push against it for expressive counter-point. It is this core competency that signals you as an insider, and not a dance tourist. Many – and at an increasing number of northern nights, most – dancers limit their dance to these core postures and movements. There are some who do not adopt this predominant style, and I will return to them later.

There are also a series of elaborations to the core style that are available to the competent dancer. The most common are to do with the dance steps. The standard steps of the side-to-side dance movement count out the four beats of each bar of the music as a basic repetition: four beats to the right, four beats to the left. This seems to be the easiest way to interpret the steady, even, lightly syncopated beat of the up-town sixties soul records that characterizes the music played at northern venues. This beat is the main drive of the dancing style because it determines the even time marking which underlies northern dance style.[4] However, by shifting weight across two beats from the heel to the toe the dancer can momentarily keep their balance on one foot. This allows dancers to undertake steps characteristic of a more practised participant. Primarily it allows a heavy use of the ankle, rather than leg, to propel the dancer, and to use their other foot for an action that does not require carrying their weight. It is this movement which makes the dancer seem to glide, while at the same time allowing leg and foot movements that counter-point the main beat. This puts considerable stress on the ankles and is the reason that northern dancefloors are lubricated with talcum powder by the dancers.

It is these pieces of footstep improvisation and elaboration that form the base for the other extended bodily movements. They mostly cover a range of small shifts which have significance within the scene. These would include changing direction, interspersing short and longer sideways strides, twisting the body in a counter direction to the movement of the feet, and shifting the weight around the centre of the hips. These moves are paralleled by hand and arm gestures which play with or emphasize other aspects of the song. This is most notable in the soul clap, an exaggerated wide-armed, communally executed clap, which marks out certain beats usually in the bridge of the record.

These relatively simple moves can then be built up into more dramatic moves that produce the acrobatic activities of spinning, falling backwards, or diving forwards. At their most elaborate these would be combined in the gymnastic mode. So, for instance, a spin ends in a backdrop, which merges into a kick from the prone position, and a return to the vertical ends with a spin to hit the first beat of a new stanza of the music.

However physically demanding such elaborated moves are, they are not in themselves valued. There are dancers who can do the gymnastic techniques, but do not dance with competence. Along with all movements, the judgement of competence is applied to the way they are executed. While dancers are allowed quite a degree of variation in the moves that are executed – in fact it is greatly valued – the times when they can be executed is strictly delineated. These structures of "what is possible when" are related to the musical and performance structure of the recordings themselves. Knowledge of the structure of individual records is therefore central, and unites two forms of competence: the ability to do the moves; and the knowledge of when, in a particular record, certain types of moves can be executed.

Competence and scene knowledge
Records have been, and are, valued on the scene because they provide opportunities for the competencies of style to be enacted. Dobie Gray's 'Out On The Floor' is such a record, and so an exemplar for analysing how musical and dancing competence relate. In many ways the recording is a basic song form, but not one strong on lyrical content. The introduction is based on a transposition of the lyrical and musical material of the song's chorus cut down to four three-bar stanzas. "Hey, hey, hey", sing the backing vocalists twice; "Yeah! Yeah! Yeah! Everything is out of sight!" replies Dobie, as we are called to the floor. This is followed by the first verse (four eight-bar stanzas), then the chorus (one eight-bar stanza), the second verse, chorus again (this time two eight-bar stanzas), and an extended bridge section built on multiple phrases of eight bars. Moving to the fade-out, the verse and one-stanza chorus are repeated, and then the lines of the extended bridge are used with new lyrics.

At a basic level, the recording's structure provides the framework for the execution of the dance: dancers use the core techniques described above during the verse; a flourish of extended techniques in the chorus; and quite developed versions of the extended techniques in the elongated bridge. This basic organization of the dance is then elaborated through movements that interpret the shifting textures of the song, its playfulness with time and changes of emotional intensity.

For instance, competent dancers use moments of rhythmic intensification in the recording to increase the speed of their footwork. The occasional use of melisma by the singer to spread a note over one or two bars is given a prominence in the dance through slides of the feet. Differences between the organization of the stanzas are used by dancers and echoed in the dance by visually different moves, and this is particularly apparent in the last two bars of the final stanza, where the most musically intensive section is matched by the most intensive dancing. Here the drums move from keeping steady time in the verse to double time, while the vocal holds a single word, "pushing" us into the chorus, and many dancers use this as an opportunity to display dexterous footwork, and an off-balance body movement.

Dancers also respond to the affective use of the piano in the recording. Towards the end of each stanza of verse (the song's secondary hook) the instrument plays a short musical motif matched by dancers with footwork or balance motifs. In the first three lines of a stanza, when the motif is played softly and with some improvisation against the vocal, the dancers use less intensity; in the answer section of the extended bridge, when the motif is played with full attack on the keys, dancers deploy their most energetic improvisations.

Competence in the northern scene, then, can be understood to relate to three necessary and interconnected competencies. Of course dancers must first know what range of movement is generally sanctioned within the scene. To dance in any other way is to reveal oneself as an outsider. Then they must be able to physically perform those sanctioned movements, and to be able to do so with style. That is, the dancing must look controlled and accomplished. "Giving it a go" is not competence. Finally, the dancer must have a detailed enough knowledge of specific records so that they can perform certain techniques at their appropriate place in the structure of the record.

The basic, but shifting structure and the subtle elaborations of the musicians and singer which characterize 'Out On The Floor' provide abundant opportunities for dancers to demonstrate all three of these competencies. It possibly explains its consistent popularity over three decades.

However, dance is more than a combination of posture and steps, it obviously also involves moving in a space used by other dancers and marked out for different activities. This constitutes Malbon's second "situation" of dance: the physical geography, ambience and spacing and orientation of dancers. Given what has preceded it, it will come as no surprise to learn that the scene also has a strong set of rules about how one moves in this space.

Moving in space
The dance spaces of the northern soul scene are not the mainstream clubs of youth nightlife, and they have never been so. They are based in a mixture of

old ballrooms, pub function rooms, halls, and social clubs, based in communities (mainly in the English north and Midlands) which have been increasingly marginalized by the shifting economics of post-war wealth creation. Many early venues did not even have a licensed bar. The most important element was a large wooden dancefloor, and contemporary northern nights are in venues dominated by the dancefloor. Bar and sitting areas usually surround the dance space on two or more sides and there is usually a space set aside for selling records and memorabilia, as watching the dancers and buying records and CDs are important secondary activities at northern nights. The DJ desk is usually raised on a stage at the other end of the room, and all these activities are orientated to the dancefloor and the dancers.

Few present-day venues are of the size, or have the scale of attendance, of the largest 1970s clubs like Wigan Casino or Blackpool Mecca. Typically, the numbers present at northern nights today will be in the low hundreds, with less than a hundred on the dancefloor at any one time. Even so, with so many enthusiastic dancers in a confined space some form of regulation is required. An etiquette of the dancefloor has developed to try and deal with the danger of clashing with another dancer. While some dancers will operate in an area as large as one or two square meters, this space will overlap with other dancers who seek to negotiate the use of the space through some sort of order to their dancing and a high degree of control over their techniques. Dancers with a developed technique and a high degree of competence hardly ever come into contact, and such incidents are usually followed by fulsome apologies. The sorts of orientations apparent in Malbon's account of 'post-House club cultures' are not present on northern dancefloors. Dancers do not face the DJ, or any other common part of the space. Dancers on the outer edges of the floor almost always face inwards, but on the inside of the dance space different dancers face different ways. Although friends often dance in a broadly similar part of the floor, they do not normally form a distinctive group, and dancing between couples is very unusual (and would produce comment by on-lookers).

There is a continual churning[5] of dancers, usually based upon preferences for certain records over others. A particularly popular record will quickly fill the floor, but the two to three minute length of the records means that there is a change in those dancing every three minutes or so. Dancing is therefore an activity defined not just by the physical relationship to the music, but also to the other dancers, and to the wider space through which the dancers shift their activity from dancing, to sitting, watching and offering comment. I estimate that dancers today spend far less time on the dancefloor than they would have in the 1970s – probably the product of our increasing age – and the composition and operation of the floor has shifted far more than the basic dance itself.

The most notable change is the role that women occupy. Once a minority of dancers, they now constitute a majority. Although one must be careful as the 1970s published photographic records of dancers tend to focus on the acrobatic dancing performed by men, the distribution of the dancing crowd supports the claim that it was men who predominated in numbers, in occupancy of space, and in the spectacle of dance. At a number of present-day venues I visited, a high proportion of the men occupying the floor kept to the outer edge, and women out-numbered men in the centre. Although men tended to be the ones who used the acrobatic elements in their dances, some women included spins and elaborated dance steps.

Secondly, there is far less cohesion to the dancefloor than there used to be. This is most obvious in the division between dancers in their twenties – who construct their dance identities around a revival of the dress and dance of the late 1960s Mod scene – and those in their late thirties, forties (and sometimes fifties) who link themselves much more to the northern scene of the late 1970s. The relative proportion of these groups varies from venue to venue, but there was not a venue I visited where the younger group were in the majority. For this reason the dominant meanings of the scene are still derived from the three decades of northern soul. There has been some antagonism to mod-revivalists in the northern scene since the early 1980s because it is perceived to lack authenticity and to be a youth fad (see St. Pierre n.d.; Winstanley n.d.), but this seems to have dissipated if my research sample is representative of the whole. Although there is some overlap in which records are danced to by different groups, the neo-Mods tend to dominate when certain records are played, and these are usually played within a themed set of early 1960s R&B, rather than the uptown soul style associated with Detroit or Los Angeles labels. During these sets there are few differences between dancers, as the older dancers curtail the more distinctive features of their style. At other times, though, the differences between styles often leads to bodily contact as it is harder to predict the patterns of different (northern dancers would say less disciplined) styles.

There is another sense in which the northern scene has expanded outside its former cultural territory of exclusion, and this has expanded the backgrounds of people at northern venues. The rare soul records which were collected and exchanged by DJs and dancers are now widely available on compilation CDs, and they have a wider circulation in radio programmes and on the soundtracks to adverts and TV programmes.[6] Further, the greater prominence of women dancers, and of dancers who do not share the traditions and history of the northern soul scene, have made the practices of the scene less excluding, and the notion of the in-crowd less pronounced.

My main point here is that northern soul dancers are not just involving themselves in a physically pleasurable activity. Of course ethnographic observation and participation reveals dancing as physically and psychologically pleasurable; and the sweat and physical flow of dance, the relationship to music, and physical communality are major reasons why dancers dance. However, these factors cannot explain the ordering of selected music nor the distinctiveness of dance movements. The major part of this chapter deals with the latter issue, and I will leave it to others to elaborate on the former issues.

Thus far I have followed Malbon's schema, using ideas of competence – and extending it from dance technique to dance style, and to competencies related to knowledge of rare records – as articulated through the "sociality" of dance, and the way that it relates to the physical geography of the dancefloor. I now want to turn to his idea of identification. In Malbon's work, this is focused on a post-modern sense of self, and particularly the binary of in-crowd/out-crowd and coolness/mainstream. It should be apparent from my analysis so far that, while these are also important themes in northern soul, other concerns not taken up by Malbon, especially the politics of place, of gender and of ethnicity, also play out in the scene. These are equally demanding of our attention, and they are the subject of the next section of my analysis.

The politics of dancing in the northern soul scene

While the localized practices of dance are centrally important to understanding its meaning, so too are these wider issues of power relations and identity. I therefore want to develop the earlier analysis into an attempt to place northern soul dancing in the wider context of the politics of gender and sexuality, and the relationship of cultural identity with place and ethnicity. I take each of these issues at a time, but try to connect each theme to the preceding observations, and to each other, as they constitute senses of identity for participants on the scene.

Over three decades the characteristic and consistent narrative in the discourse of the northern scene has been the idea that the scene is distinct from what is constructed as mainstream music culture. This idea is found in accounts of the scene in the music magazines from the 1970s through to the recent flush of web-based and printed historical accounts. Part of this narrative is the contention that, for "true" participants, the music and dancing are the central focus, rather than a means to another cultural or social end.

Most significantly, these accounts usually construct a binary opposition between the northern scene, focused on music and dance, on one hand, and the construction of a mainstream nightlife focused on the pursuit of sexual partnerships (see, for instance, Winstanley and Nowell 1996; Hepton 2001).[7] This discourse is echoed through the orientations of both the dancing and non-dancing participants on the dancefloor, and on the important place given to record buying at club nights. It may also explain why the scene has survived when the participants are now in long-term relationships, and the largest groups of attendees are made up of couples.

The relationship of masculinity to the dancefloor is more complex, however. It is certainly the case that male northern dancers operate in a cultural space which Angela McRobbie has argued provides a rare opportunity for women's self-determination and personal expression (McRobbie 1984). And in fact many of the reminiscences featured in recent documentaries on the origin of the scene carry a subtext that the individual male social dancing characteristic of northern soul did not fit with mainstream senses of masculinity, and sometimes that it was a transformation of usual male behaviours and identities.[8]

On the other hand, even an evening's ethnographic observation will reveal that there is a significant dimension of male competition and display which is central to understanding northern dance. Male dancers dance with more elaboration and more energy as the number and competency of other men on the floor increases. Male dancers orientate themselves to other male dancers, and they "compete" to demonstrate their control of physical movement and understanding of particular records. At one level this could be understood as friendly rivalry, or masculine showing off, and as such a simple reproduction of male activities elsewhere. However, while this is a superficially convincing interpretation, such practices also work within the subculture to emphasize mutual participation. The shared understanding of the musical structure of records and the possibilities for dance they allow unites participants; and to some degree operates across gender lines. The "soul clap" identified earlier is perhaps the best example of this phenomenon. Here the unison clap at agreed points in the music brings together the sense of communality of the scene and its shared competences by emphasizing the beat of the music, and the collective experience of the dance.

In spite of these constants through the history of the scene, there are a number of interesting but rather subtle shifts in gender identity and power relations in recent years. These are explained by the fact that women now dominate the floor numerically. Although the male-dominated dance rituals remain significant, they are now far more muted, and far more women participate in these practices of dancer orientation and dance synchronization I outlined earlier. I would interpret this as a general downplaying of the competitive elements and an increasing orientation towards cultural solidarity. This has not, however, led to a decline in the importance of technique and competence. While the acrobatic movements are less in evidence, the other competences remain significant in the dancefloor practices. The ideas of solidarity are produced through participation on the dancefloor, and essentially in relationship with other "good" dancers. Judgements of the quality of a particular evening are made using criteria which encompass both the music and the dancing of others. In other words, it is not sufficient to dance to "show off"; rather it is necessary to be part of a larger whole of dance competence and technique.

Joanne Hollows and Katie Milestone have raised these issues of solidarity in relation to geo-politics of England. In particular, drawing upon ideas of cultural capital (Bourdieu 1984), they see northern soul as "a refusal of the South's claims to legitimacy and distinction" (Hollows and Milestone 1998: 88). They produce a thoughtful mapping of the cultural geographic meanings of the relationship of the northern soul scene with the northern cities of the USA where the music was recorded. The authors note that by using imported records, participants in the scene could produce a culture independent of London, and negotiate the competing meanings of "North America" in English culture to produce a relationship with an "imagined" African American culture structured through an interpretative community which extends from the US cities in which the music was produced, through the dancefloors of the northern scene, and to the pop sensibilities of other consumers of soul records (pp. 87–94).

While these are important ideas for the understanding of this scene, their observations need some finessing. Firstly, the label "northern soul" was created in London to refer to something taking place to the north of the definer's "map of meanings".[9] The scene was not initially based upon a self-conscious articulation of a sense of "northern-ness" (the leading clubs of the scene in the early 1970s were to be found in the Midlands);[10] it grew out of a temporally- (rather than geographically-) located sense of modernism; and drew participants from the whole of Britain. It is also important to note that the significance of the term "northern" only became redolent in the discourse of its participants after 1975 when clubs in Blackpool and Wigan drew members from hundreds of miles away, and the term became a commercial genre for selling records in mainstream pop.

Secondly, the relationship of the scene to the black culture of northern cities of the US is even more complex than Hollows and Milestone suggest. While northern DJs play music recorded by African American artists from the 1960s to the 1970s, it is simplistic to even consider African American culture during this period as a single interpretative community. As a number of other scholars have demonstrated, there is a richness to the politics of culture, identity and music generated in African American communities in the 1960s and 70s, which requires sophisticated analysis (see, for instance, George 1986, 1988; Early 1995; Ward 1998; Smith 1999). Drawing on these readings of African American culture in the 1960s and 70s, we can see that the music played in northern clubs is selectively drawn from the historical moment in which the aspirations among black Americans for integration gave way to aspirations for a self-defined equality. Specifically, northern soul DJs most often play records from the earlier period in the 1960s when a self-consciously bi-racial pop sound was developed by white-owned record labels featuring African Americans and aimed at both black and white teenagers. A large number of these records were produced to meet the teen dance fads that developed around the international success of the Twist (Wall 2006). The records do tend to be the ones originally more popular in local black community, rather than those which featured on the 1960s national pop charts, and many feature qualities associated with the rising black conscious movement and the idea of "soul" as an articulation of black identity. Nevertheless, northern club playlists tend to systematically exclude records characterized by musical elements associated with the "funkier" music[11] which followed in the 1970s, and through which black Americans developed an Afro-centric identity.

This point will become clearer, perhaps, if we return to Dobie Gray's recording of 'Out On The Floor'. Lyrically and musically, the song is an interesting mid-point between the integrationist agenda in black politics and the civil rights movement; between Ward's cultural poles of Motown and James Brown (1998: 123–69). The early operation and music of Motown Records in Detroit exemplifies the internationalist cultural and political ambitions (Smith 1999) – and it is no coincidence that Motown's early records are often presented as key to the northern sound – while Brown's late 1960s and early 1970s music embodies both the move to a more conscious celebration of the distinctive qualities of black culture and the contradictions of trying to operate in a white dominated society and music industry (Ward 1998: 388–415).

On the one hand the lyrics of 'Out On The Floor' deal with hedonism and dancing, drawing upon a repertoire of black entertainment, and reference points from the broader sixties American youth culture which were apparent in much of the black pop produced by Motown and other independent record labels that were established after the success of rock and roll (Gillett 1971). Gray sings them in a style mid-way between the dominating influences of Sam Cooke and Jackie Wilson; two of black pop's biggest contemporary stars, who worked in Los Angeles[12] where Gray also recorded. The production reflects many of the pop experiments undertaken by Phil Spector at the time.

On the other hand the recording also features hints of the new developing music of soul and funk. Unusually for black pop the lyrics feature the sorts of African American phraseology increasingly apparent in the music of James Brown at this time (see Wall 2003: 138–41). As such, it is an example of what Brackett argues is the articulation of a new black "soul" culture (Brackett 2000). While his vocals do not feature the high key style which gives James Brown's singing its distinctive feel, he does use Sam Cooke's characteristic glissandi and the urgency of Jackie Wilson's blues gospel style with increasing prominence as the song progresses. Nevertheless, the song structure is characterized by the same sorts of developments found in Brown's music, where verses and choruses are increasingly dissolved into continual movement and delayed harmonic releases. The increasingly emotional black vernacular one-liners of the middle section are reminiscent of Brown's repertoire of the time, particularly the ground-breaking 'Papa's Got a Brand New Bag' from 1965.

The interpretation of the musical and cultural characteristics of Gray's record in the northern scene are instructive. It is not incidental to the popularity of the song that along with another Gray success ('The In-Crowd'), the lyrics seem to celebrate the world of dance culture that gave them a new life beyond the deletion racks. More interestingly, perhaps, even the lyrics (which draw on sixties black vernacular speech) are, I would argue, transformed by northern soul's discursive practices to articulate its own communality (rather than its connection to liberation politics). This is also apparent in the wider use of the African American-derived terms "right on", "keep the faith", and "brothers and sisters" which primarily index northern soul and its participants, and not African Americans.[13]

This lyrical content, then, is understood to stand for and articulate the scene as a whole, and many dancers sing these key lines as they dance. The sense of identity with northern soul is the product of a complex set of layered relationships: the musical structure of a record like 'Out On The Floor'; then performed as dance within a common set of competencies of dancers and shared techniques. That is not to deny that there is a sense of identification with African American culture, just that it is much more conditional, and relates more to the cultural possibilities it offers for an English alternative identity, than any consistent support for the liberation struggle taking place in the US at the time.

Conclusions

I have shown that dance within the northern soul scene has a sophisticated cultural function. The dance techniques available to the dancers involve a high degree of skill and practice, and are both ordered and limited by a particular disciplined style. The techniques themselves are part of a wider set of dance and musical competence that construct both the scene and the membership of individuals. Using the example of Dobie Gray's record 'Out On The Floor', and investigating how northern dancers perform their dances, I have been able to draw out exactly what those competences are, and how they relate to a sense of solidarity with other members of the scene and with wider issues of cultural politics.

The analysis also raises some important questions about how vernacular dance can be theorized and analysed. While work like Malbon's has significantly moved these two scholarly activities beyond the notion that dance is a totally intrinsic activity, or one that can be made meaningful through sociological polemic, there are important dimensions of dance which need to be linked to wider issues of gender, sexuality, ethnicity, geography and class.

I have, though, also highlighted important differences between the post-House dance culture Malbon examines and the northern scene. The meaning of dance is not, therefore, to be found in the essence of physical movement, but in distinct cultural practices and their historical and social locales. This suggests that there will be differences between other historical or contemporary dance cultures that cannot be understood without close analysis. This is an area that needs significantly more research if this aspect of popular music culture is to be illuminated.

I have also tried to show the importance of the relationship between the competences of music interpretation and dance movement. We need more worked-through examples of how music and dance relate, both in form and in performance. That there is so much to be understood through the analysis of one record and how it is danced to suggests that there is more to be revealed through further such work. Though music does not determine dance, the two things are related through a wider set of developments in which music is produced and selected for certain forms of dance culture and then transformed through specific dancefloor practices. In a scene like northern soul, where the music was produced outside the culture, this also reveals the importance of recording and distribution, and of the way that distant popular cultures can relate. In particular this study reveals how the meanings of the music of one culture are transformed in the cultural practices of another place and time.

About the author

Tim Wall is Professor of Radio and Popular Music Studies, and Associate Dean for Research in the Faculty of Arts, Design and Media at Birmingham City University. He undertook his doctorate on black music and radio at the

Centre for Contemporary Cultural Studies at the University of Birmingham. He researches into the production and consumption cultures around music and the media, mixing historical analysis with contemporary investigations. His publications include the second edition of *Studying Popular Music Culture*, and recent research as varied as the politics of dancing on the northern soul scene, US dance fads from 1955 to 1965, music radio online, the transistor radio, personal music listening, music on television, jazz collectives, and *The X-Factor*. He has been a devotee of northern soul since his teens in the 1970s, and can still be found on the dancefloor on some weekends.

Notes

1. Dobie Gray, 'Out On The Floor' was recorded in Los Angeles and released originally on the now obscure Charger subsidiary of the small independent label Crusader Records.

2. In a listing of Top 500 northern records produced by a leading DJ in the scene (Roberts 2000), the record is rated as number two. Robert's comments on Gray's record is: "The groove encapsulates the sixties 'full on' with a stirring LA production and DG controlled vocal and Spectoresque reverb. In terms of 'feel good' they do not come any better than this".

3. I first started dancing on the northern scene in about 1974, and over the decades since I have attended clubs in the Midlands, Lancashire, Greater Manchester, and London. I conducted additional formal research for this article over eighteen months at five regular northern club nights in the Midlands.

4. This contrasts significantly with the highly syncopated style of funk (up-town soul's 1970s successor in African American music), with its heavy emphasis on the first beat of the bar derived from New Orleans drumming styles and its requirement for different forms of time keeping. See Stewart (2000: 293–318).

5. By this I mean individual dancers move onto and off the floor continually throughout the night as different records are played. The numbers on the floor therefore varies.

6. For the last few years BBC Radio 2 has featured an irregular specialist music show playing northern; during 2003 the KFC fast food chain used northern soul records to promote its products; and several BBC TV programmes including *Hustle* and *No Angels* featured such tracks prominently.

7. Paradoxically, it has to be noted that these are at least equalled in the autobiographic accounts by the stories of how northern soul fans met their life partners.

8. I would cite the example of comments made by Pete Waterman, northern DJ-turned-music-producer, that his friends who danced all night in northern soul clubs were miners as operating within this discursive practice. Quoted in Hepton 2001.

9. The term is widely attributed to Dave Godin, who ran a London-based record shop and wrote a column in *Blues & Soul* magazine in the mid-1970s.

10. In particular the Catacombs in Wolverhampton, Chateau Impney in Droitwich, and the Torch in Stoke were all key clubs in establishing a distinctive scene in the period up to 1973.

11. Funk is an adjective derived from African American slang which is usually used to mean "redolent of the unwashed". It has a fairly long history in black music, and was

first used in the 1950s in jazz to indicate music that was understood to feature elements derived from "black" music.

12. Because the subbed-down histories of northern soul always highlight the importance of Motown Records to the scene, they not only neglect the equally important contributions of the music of other northern cities, but also the importance of the black pop of LA. It was here that Cooke recorded many of his cross-over pop hits and established a formula for post-rock and roll black music success. See Hoskyns 1996; DjeDje and Meadows 1998.

13. See the pages of *Blues & Soul* magazine during the mid-1970s.

References

Boggs, V. 1992. *Salsiology: Afro-Cuban Music and the Evolution of Salsa in New York City*. New York: Greenwood Press.
Bourdieu, P. 1984. *Distinction: A Social Critique of the Judgement of Taste*. Cambridge, MA: Harvard University Press.
Brackett, D. 2000. "James Brown's 'Superbad' and the Double-voiced Utterance". In *Reading Pop*, edited by R. Middleton, 122–39. Oxford: Oxford University Press.
Brewster, B., and F. Broughton. 1999. *Last Night a DJ Saved my Life: The History of a Disc Jockey*. London: Headline.
Chambers, I. 1985. *Urban Rhythms: Pop Music and Popular Culture*. Basingstoke and London: St. Martin's Press.
Cosgrove, S. 1982. "Long After Tonight is All Over". *Collusion* 2: 38–41.
DjeDje, J. C., and E. S. Meadows. 1998. *California Soul: Music of African Americans in the West*. Berkeley, CA and London: University of California Press.
Dyer, R. 1979. "In Defence of Disco". *Gay Left* 8: 20–23.
Early, G. 1995. *One Nation under a Groove: Motown and American Culture*. New Jersey: Ecco.
Frith, S., and T. Cummings. 1975. "Playing Records". In *Rock File 3*, edited by C. Gillett and S. Frith, 21–48. St Albans: Panther.
George, N. 1986. *Where Did our Love Go?: The Rise and Fall of the Motown Sound*. London: Omnibus.
—1988. *The Death of Rhythm & Blues*. London: Penguin.
Gilbert, J., and E. Pearson. 1999. *Discographies: Dance Music, Culture and the Politics of Sound*. London: Routledge.
Gill, J. 1995. *Queer Noises: Male and Female Homosexuality in Twentieth-century Music*. London: Cassell.
Gillett, C. 1971. *The Sound of the City: The Rise of Rock and Roll*. London: Sphere.
Gilroy, P. 1991. *"There ain't no Black in the Union Jack": The Cultural Politics of Race and Nation*. Chicago: University of Chicago Press.
Goffman, E. 1959. *The Presentation of Self in Everyday Life*. Woodstock, NY: Overlook Press.
Hebdige, D. 1979. *Subculture: The Meaning of Style*. London and New York: Routledge.
Hepton, B. 2001. "Pioneers: Wigan Casino". Channel 4 TV programme.
Hollows, J., and K. Milestone. 1998. "Welcome to Dreamsville: A History and Geography of Northern Soul". In *The Place of Music*, edited by A. Leyshon, D. Matless and G. Revill, 83–103. New York and London: Guilford Press.
Hoskyns, B. 1996. *Waiting for the Sun: The Story of the Los Angeles Music Scene*. London: Viking.

Littleboy, H. 2003. *Soul Nation*. Diverse Productions.
Malbon, B. 1999. *Clubbing: Dancing, Ecstasy and Vitality*. London.
McRobbie, A. 1984. "Dance and Social Fantasy". In *Gender and Generation*, edited by A. McRobbie and M. Nava, 130–61. Basingstoke, UK and Atlantic Highlands, NJ: Macmillan.
Milestone, K. 1997. "Love Factory: The Sites, Practices and Media Relationships of Northern Soul". In *The Club Cultures Reader*, edited by S. Redhead, J. O'Connor and D. Wynne, 152–67. Oxford and Malden, MA: Blackwell.
Nowell, D. 1999. *Too Darn Soulful: The Story of Northern Soul*. London: Robson Books.
Regev, M. 2002. "The 'Pop-rockization' of Popular Music". In *Popular Music Studies*, edited by D. Hesmondhalgh and K. Negus, 251–65. London: Arnold.
Reynolds, S. 1998. *Energy Flash: A Journey Through Rave Music and Dance Culture*. London: Picador.
Ritson, M., and S. Russell. 1999. *The In Crowd: The Story of the Northern and Rare Soul Scene*. London: Bee Cool.
Roberts, K. 2000. *The Northern Soul Top 500*. Todmorden: Goldmine/Soul Supply.
Smith, S. E. 1999. *Dancing in the Street: Motown and the Cultural Politics of Detroit*. Cambridge, MA and London: Harvard University Press.
St. Pierre, R. n.d. *The Mod Revival: Where will it End*. Available at: http://martins_box.tripod.com/id33_m.htm
Stewart, A. 2000. "'Funk Drummer': New Orleans, James Brown and the Rhythmic Transformation of American Popular Music". *Popular Music* 19/3: 293–318.
Thornton, S. 1995. *Club Cultures: Music, Media and Subcultural Capital*. Cambridge, UK: Polity Press in association with Blackwell.
Vincent, R. 1996. *Funk: The Music, the People, and the Rhythm of the One*. New York: St. Martin's Griffin.
Wall, T. 2003. *Studying Popular Music Culture*. London: Arnold.
—2006. "Rocking Around the Clock: Teenage Dance Fads 1955 to 1965". In *The Social Dance Reader*, edited by J. M. Malnig, 182–98. Chicago: University of Chicago Press.
Ward, A. 1997. "Dancing aound Meaning (and the Meaning around Dance)". In *Dance in the City*, edited by H. Thomas, 3–20. New York: St. Martin's Press.
Ward, B. 1998. *Just My Soul Responding: Rhythm and Blues, Black Consciousness and Race Relations*. London: UCL Press.
Winstanley, R. n.d. *The Mods Revival and Northern Soul*. Available at: http://martins_box.tripod.com/id33_m.htm
Winstanley, R., and D. Nowell. 1996. *Soul Survivors: The Wigan Casino Story*. London: Robson Books.

Discography

James Brown. 1996. 'Papa's Got a Brand New Bag'. *Foundations of Funk*, Polydor, 531165-2.
Carstairs. 2001. 'It Really Hurts Me Girl'. *The In Crowd: The Story of Northern Soul*, Sequel, CMEDD04.
Dobie Gray. 1990. 'Out On The Floor'. *Sings for In-crowders that "Go Go"*, Collectables, I97875.
Dobie Gray. 1990. 'The In-crowd'. *Sings for In-crowders that "Go Go"*, Collectables, I97875.

4 Beyond the Master Narrative of Youth:

Researching Ageing Popular Music Scenes*

Nicola Smith

Popular music has consistently been tied to youth. Stemming from the Chicago School studies of urban existence and delinquency, music was highlighted as a component in gang formation. Thus the entry of popular music into sociological study was contextualized in relation to urban youth formations, deviant behaviour and the social – as opposed to psychological – reasons for, and implications of, subcultural participation.[1] Subsequent Birmingham School subcultural studies focused more directly upon popular music yet continued to define music-related activity as a form of resistance and rebellion but also exclusively for the young.[2] The aim of academic popular music investigation has thus been contained within seeking to achieve an understanding of societal problems led by youth and to map deviant behaviour and alternative (i.e. non-mainstream, non-adult) style. In critique of the Birmingham School Centre for Contemporary Cultural Studies (CCCS) this chapter moves beyond notions of (youth) activity as fixed, spectacular and contained within the temporality of the cultural fad to enable recognition of active and meaningful *adult* scene participation.[3]

In response to the prioritization of the master narrative of youth within popular music studies this chapter explores how post-subcultural theorizations possess the potential to examine ageing popular music practice. Several post-subcultural frameworks currently exist,[4] yet it is the suitability of the neo-tribal paradigm that is discussed here in terms of its potential to embrace ageing participation and scene longevity. Here music is theorized as pleasure, as an aspect of everyday life and as a component for the construction of identity. Via an examination of the effect of time on a music scene, it can be argued that the appeal of participation is not dependent on age nor does it derive solely from a desire for community or a resistance to mundane existence, but

*   Originally published in Derek B. Scott (ed.), *The Ashgate Research Companion to Popular Musicology* (Farnham: Ashgate, 2009), pp. 427–45.

is instead tied to identity formation and reflexive agency. As such, the self of youth constructed in relation to scene affiliation need not diminish with age.

While the notion of a popular music scene shelf-life has been repeatedly implied in media representations, via music industry marketing strategies and by fans keen to experience the "next big thing", the instances of continuing music scenes are more common than we might first assume.[5] However, examples of continuing scenes with the same body of *continuing participants* are less frequent. The case of northern soul offers one such example. Northern soul is a British dance-orientated music culture primarily located in the Midlands and north of England. The scene originated in the late 1960s, reaching its heyday in the 1970s and continuing to the present day. The music of choice is 1960s black American soul. The 45rpm vinyl records that are fanatically collected and passionately danced to are predominantly rare, non-chart hits from often unknown artists and minor record labels. Still attracting the same body of fans to all-night dancing events, northern soul highlights the need for a theoretical paradigm that bridges the gap between the frivolity and temporality of postmodern experience and the static, homogeneous subcultural collective. I present my typology of the scene with this longevity in mind, emphasizing the postmodern fluidity of, and the complexities inherent in, performing continued fandom within a continuous scene in adulthood. From this we can focus on the self within a collective and unpick the significance of identity performance, thus being able to focus on ageing (and the related issues of subjective constructions of self and nostalgia). The passage of time is relevant to music scenes in two ways: firstly, in terms of the ageing of a scene and secondly, in relation to the complexities of ageing participation. In other words, theorizations of a scene *and* theorizations of the participants must be explored.

Ageing scenes

The aim of this section is to highlight the potential for post-subcultural theory to recognize ageing music cultures. Music participation is not about spectacular existence but everyday life; it can be conducted beyond the fad. With a nod to postmodern conditions of cultural consumption, participation is also not about fixed, static routines as the CCCS implied. However, postmodern fluidity need not mean engagement without celebration of specificity; there is a middle-ground. This middle-ground demonstrates that music cultures have the potential to possess lasting appeal for participants and a level of depth that enables identity synthesis, yet are fluid enough to be maintained throughout a participant's cultural career in an everyday sense. The need for fluidity *and* specificity leads us to post-subcultural theory.

The issues and flaws evident in the CCCS approach are well-documented.[6] As such it is not necessary to recount the limitations of this body of work.

It is sufficient to note that subcultural theory overstated the difference *between* groups and also the internal homogeneity *within* groups. It neglected women, ethnic and racial minorities and, I argue, the non-youth. With post-subcultural theory, there is acknowledgement that postmodernity allows for movement between identities, eroding the suggestion of a homogeneous collective and diluting the resistance reading of subcultures. To break away from the CCCS approach is to eradicate the unreflexive, passive subcultural participant. It is the potential for reflexive, active engagement in cultural practice that is relevant to post-subcultural theory and, as we shall see, to ageing scenes. A task of locating scenes with longevity, such as northern soul, within post-subcultural theory therefore involves understanding how performing within specific guidelines of scene membership is an expression of fluidity and how one individual's expression of specificity can occur alongside another's ephemeral experience.

Post-subcultural scenes
The passion, commitment and community constructed around northern soul by fans of the music are testament to the importance of communal interaction (sociality) as stressed by Maffesoli.[7] The idea that a "will to live" (*puissance*) and a human desire for belonging influence sociocultural participation are valid in relation to our understanding of the *initial* aspiration to become a member of a cultural group. However this, I believe, is not sufficient an explanation as to why people *continue* as members of a particular cultural group. In a postmodern world of choice, with ease of access and the frequency of movement in and out of cultural worlds, how can we explain individuals opting to remain as members of one collective for extended periods of time?

Northern soul is embroiled in desires for and methods of identity-construction. Individuals acquire an aspect of self via scene participation. The space of social interaction is a zone in which participants can perform displays of knowledge thus exhibiting passion and competency within that scene. By demonstrating to fellow participants the extent and proficiency of their membership, participants can perpetuate and improve their construction of personhood and as such affect their creation of selfhood.[8] Individuals become someone specific because of their involvement with(in) a scene. This presents an initial explanation as to why people continue to desire scene participation. But how does this intercept with post-subcultural (postmodern) constructions of frivolous, temporal and fluid cultural consumption? To answer this we must turn to the concept of the *tribus*.

With an aim of moving beyond positioning popular music as a study of deviant gangs and alternative collective practice for the disillusioned mass, and in an attempt to demonstrate postmodern characteristics of popular music consumption, many post-subcultural theses overtly foreground the individual and the frivolity, temporality and multiplicity of interaction.[9] In response to such and in recognition that consumer choice and individualism may produce a loss of shared sentiment of interaction, Maffesoli's Durkheimian focus centralizes the collective, thus challenging the isolated, selfish, ironic individual of postmodernity. The collective is the site in which the creation and maintenance of self is achieved. It is thus the individual's awareness of this and the subsequent desire for the continuation of the collective that neo-tribal theory must address in the example of northern soul and arguably in the case of all scenes with longevity.

Northern soul is competitive; it is constructed around the acquisition of identity, status and prestige as demonstrated by the overt and spotlighted performance of competency, skill and connoisseurship. As such, the pleasure of belonging of which Maffesoli speaks is tainted by the drive to construct selfhood derived from scene membership. To address this, we can follow Sweetman's conclusion that we can entwine the reflexive process of identity-construction and neo-tribal sociality.[10] Sociality therefore can be considered in relation to the pleasure derived *because of what it can offer self* rather than simply the pleasure of belonging within a collective. As Bauman states, neo-tribes for him are formed "by the multitude of individual acts of *self-identification*".[11] While examples of continuous and long-running scenes contradict Bauman's pessimistic view that an individual moves between neo-tribes because of frustration with the unrealized promise of cultural affiliation, it is true that in northern soul participants do *dance alone, together*. Is this an example of the greyness of postmodern isolated practice? This is arguably not the case if the centralization of self is read not as a display of isolation or disengagement but as a method of maintaining the purpose of collective interaction. The individual is celebrated within the collective and as such perpetuates the need for the collective.

While this postmodern approach to ageing scenes may provide a platform from which to explain the significance of an individual's understanding of their cultural participation, the temporality and fragility of neo-tribes does not immediately lend itself to an examination of scenes with longevity. Nor does the multiplicity of tribal engagement suggest the option of remaining within *one* cultural group. How does this temporality and fragility intersect with the commitment and longevity of the northern soul scene? As Hodkinson queries in relation to goth, the fluidity and ephemerality of neo-tribes is problematic.[12] However to place this fluidity and ephemerality in context, neo-tribes are fluid if we compare them to the prescriptive, fixed, social background-specific forms of affiliation exhibited within traditional anthropological tribes (in which membership is ascribed not achieved). However, membership in *neo*-tribes is a choice: one option from an array of cultural groupings selected by an individual. What complicates matters further is that the fluidity and ephemerality with which Hodkinson takes issue is based on a comparison with the fixity of subcultures. It is subcultural fixity and associated values that Hodkinson desires to keep when theorizing goth. A *tribus* is fluid and as such the freedom to move in and out of neo-tribes dilutes, for Hodkinson, the depth of engagement attainable through cultural interaction and as such does not accurately represent the commitment evident in the goth scene. To remedy such neo-tribal fluidity Hodkinson gives us "subcultural substance": a reworked version of subcultural theory. With empathy for Hodkinson's concerns, I agree that it is paradoxical to classify a scene with longevity as solely constructed around frivolous engagement. Yet subcultural theory (even if reworked) does not present sufficient scope to present the participants as reflexively engaged in their own scene-derived identity-construction. Not all participants may desire fixity, just as Hodkinson recognizes that not all goth participants desire fluidity. In response, I think it is vital that we highlight the distance between the concepts of frivolity and fluidity. I suggest all post-subcultural practice is fluid (but not necessarily frivolous). No fixed boundaries exist as participants can freely move between neo-tribes as, when, and – importantly – *if* desired. Participants can consistently return to a cultural group just as easily as they can participate in many. Individuals may opt to engage with frivolity or with specificity (or substance as Hodkinson terms it) or with any degree of both.[13] For me however, to engage with substance is not akin to spectacular displays to symbolize transgression, resistance and "'traditional' notions of stylistic unity and cohesion that have consistently been associated with the notion of subculture".[14] Such specificity is instead "post-subcultural subcultural play".

Post-subcultural subcultural play[15]
If variety of consumer choice and reflexivity are aspects of contemporary cultural practice why then can a participant not engage with cultural practice in a manner reminiscent of subcultural affiliation despite the absence of subcultures? Put simply, if every other option is available in postmodernity, why not the option to perform with "subcultural" intentions? Individuals knowingly opt for and consciously engage in whatever level of cultural activity they desire/deem necessary. For some there is a desire to perform *as if* in a subculture. Importantly however, this performative form of engagement is devoid of the possibility of magical solution: it is *playing the subcultural game*.[16] That the method of cultural interaction can be specific to a cultural activity creates – at least from an external perspective – the *illusion* of subcultural interaction:

situated in terms of rules, rituals and preferred modes of performance. Participants will knowingly interact with the pretence of subcultural specificity in order to create an identity but are aware that "subcultural" persistence, fixity and all-encompassing exclusivity are not essential (but can be performed, if desired). This is not subcultural as it is an option to repeatedly return to *one* scene. The links with longevity are evident here in relation to consistency of participation: a welcome alternative to the overarching postmodern post-subcultural presumption of ephemerality.

To perform with post-subcultural subcultural play is to perform seriously while knowing the limits of that performance (in terms of what that performance can achieve). Awareness of the illusory quality of cultural participation is not expressed as ironic or carnivalesque. Such play is not frivolous either but an expression of agency: it is "playing at" rather than "playing with".

Highlighting the reflexive potential of postmodern practice and drawing upon Sweetman's instructive fusion of the reflexive modernization thesis and neo-tribal sociality,[17] engagement with cultural commodities involves a *knowing use* of these commodities. To have a choice (to achieve a form of cultural involvement rather than to have it ascribed) situates the individual as reflexive. Those playing the subcultural game are aware of the limitations of participation, how they can mould their form of engagement and that subcultures are not solutions. This may appear to be a rhetorical method of overcoming CCCS theory while explaining northern soul's subcultural elements but I must stress that the unique feature is that the participants are aware that "subcultural" affiliation is an illusion. They are not, as the CCCS would have proposed, using northern soul as a magical solution to, or rebellious resistance of, the conditions of existence; scene participation instead involves pleasure, play and resultant identity-construction. For this reason, Maffesoli's religiosity thesis fails to step far enough beyond the idea that cultural practice is a solution. He sees the *tribus* as a solution to the disenchantment of contemporary society. This rather sanguine perspective fails to acknowledge that postmodern participants are (and arguably always have been) aware of the limitations of play and as such they are able to find a function of play that is not characterized as a sociocultural solution. In essence, the central feature of post-subcultural subcultural play is reflexivity:[18] it relies upon the individual knowing that this is a substitute for the traditional community now lost. That said, knowing such does not dilute the passion for the rituals performed. If anything, performing with subcultural play heightens the Maffesolian insistence that it is part of the human condition – especially within postmodernity – to desire belonging.

Post-subcultural subcultural play depends on three factors: an individual's passion for the neo-tribe (implicit in Maffesoli's thesis), the reflexive intention of an individual and a similar response from fellow tribal members (as it makes little sense to behave with post-subcultural subcultural play alone). You brush against people in the collective, feeling the pleasure of belonging implicit in the need to perform. This need to demonstrate self within the collective thrusts the intention of interaction beyond the basic appeal of togetherness (while still embracing it). It is worthy of note that it is not surprising that performing for each other and finding pleasure in this sociality creates networks (friendships). Yet this only occurs if performance translates into familiar interaction. Perhaps the only prerequisite for this is *prolonged interaction*. There is something paradoxical about Maffesoli's insistence of belonging and the ephemerality of the experience of belonging. Ultimately, to talk of belonging should not exclude the potential for longevity.

It could be assumed that, as the "sole *raison d'etre* [of the neo-tribe] is a preoccupation with the collective present",[19] longevity and constancy of neo-tribal association are irrelevant. Yet if the moments of aesthetics, shared sentiments, and sociality are experienced as the here-and-now, this does not eradicate the potential for continuous enjoyment of that "now", arguably lasting for many years. The subcultural adage of living for the weekend remains for as long as the working-week does. Similarly, the need for the pleasure of being-together fades only when the alienating conditions of (post)modernity cease. As Maffesoli notes, the solution to the isolation of contemporary existence is the solidarity of the neo-tribe. So why should we assume that participants always leave? Participants may and do move in and out and between neo-tribes but the need for a neo-tribe – in whatever form and in whatever quantity – does not necessarily cease. The thirst for solidarity can be quenched by experiencing a multitude of neo-tribes but this can also be achieved via sustained commitment to *one* scene. This is not exclusive affiliation but sustained interaction. Individuals within scenes with longevity desire not to have to keep moving and to invest effort into re-creating the sentiment of belonging with each fad. This is taking the search for the sentiment of belonging and togetherness to the point at which the knowing individual plays at a more grounded, less ephemeral version of neo-tribal association. The postmodern choice can be to remain active within adulthood and to do so within one music scene. This however produces a problem, as not everyone engaged in a scene will treat that scene as those participating with post-subcultural subcultural play. Some will participate within scenes such as northern soul with frivolity, the impact of which is a significant one. Who the participant-types are is therefore relevant and is examined below but first it is necessary to place ageing participation in context.

Ageing participation

The connection between popular music and identity-construction is often portrayed as solely a youth act.[20] Popular music is considered one method of separation, distinction and freedom from adult control and thus aids the life-course development from child to adult. As Sardiello states, "adolescents and youths become emotionally involved with their music as a way of distinguishing themselves from adults and from each other".[21] I do not refute this. However, there is little attention paid to the *adult* use of music cultures as the role of music scene involvement is rarely considered beyond this adolescent usage. Brake hints at the justification for the concentrated focus on *youth* practices:

> The relation of subculture and age is important, because adolescence, and the period of transition between school and work, and work and marriage is important in terms of secondary socialisation [...] actors enter into subcultural interpretations of the dominant hegemony, which presents them with a different perspective of social reality, or sometimes a different social reality [...]. They introduce the values of the world outside work and school [...] Youth culture emphasises a relation of unattachment, dislocation from the confinements of work and committed relationships, a genuine experiment with "free time" [...]. The attraction of subculture is its rebelliousness, its hedonism, its escape from the restrictions of work and home.[22]

However, such hedonistic exploration and the use of leisure to inform self and to achieve imagined escape do not necessarily have to cease as a consequence of maturity. The explorative necessity may become exhausted in adulthood, yet the identity acquired via this initial youthful exploration informs and continues to inform selfhood and personhood if allowed. The continued northern soul scene does allow for this as the behaviours practised within the scene are, in the main, the same today as always. What we are therefore presented with are youth actions originally considered as distinct from adult society being performed by adults.

There is a misguided assumption that adulthood brings about a rejection of, disinterest in, or even an inability to participate in a music scene. Andes states in reference to the punk scene:

> Individuals must *become* punk and they must also, in most cases, cease to be a punk eventually. There are very few participants in the subculture who are older than their early twenties. Those who do stay actively involved in the subculture into their late twenties and beyond are people who are somehow involved at a more organi-

zational level or creative level: musicians, promoters, fanzine writers, artists, etc. Most ... people ... eventually leave behind their punk identities.[23]

This implies a lasting rejection of identities achieved via pleasure-only participation. Yet identity is multi-faceted and dynamic with the most appropriate cultural identity becoming salient as and when required. Maturing fans that have moved away from scenes with longevity do not necessarily lose or discard their scene-derived identity but can opt to put these identities on hold. Other socio-cultural identities may become salient as marriage, children, and further life commitments occupy an individual's primary focus in place of music scene participation. Equally, a loss of interest in scene participation can cause an individual to put their identity on hold. However, if a music scene remains in existence the non-active fan can return to a scene and scene-derived identity can be recalled.

Participants have control over how, where and when they perform. This occurs throughout the life-course. The question is: if a scene ages, do the attitudes of the participants remain static? Do intentions of scene participation alter with age? Arguably they do if they have to. The conditions causing this alteration include the presence of newcomers who disrupt the illusion of scene stasis and physicality (actually being unable to perform as you did in youth).[24] Problems arise when a participant is unable to achieve the expected level of status via displays of fandom as a result of age. If all participants were maturing at an equal rate, competitive displays of membership would be unmarred as the reduction in competency because of age would be relative. It is the presence of *young* newcomers to a scene that causes tensions of competitive competency; hence the conflict noted below. For those ageing participants who have no issue with young newcomers age may still be an issue, but in terms of an internal struggle with self to overcome the limitations of ageing in the context of the physicality and endurance inherent in music scene participation. If the scene were changed to accommodate age, so too would the original context of belonging. The self-taught displays of competency and knowledge would lose meaning if the context of participation changed and thus the celebration of the specificity of a scene would be placed under threat. The definition of the scene therefore does not change and individual capacities to perform within this definition become a personal quest or reversely an expression of self.

As exemplified by northern soul, it is clear that attempts to recover scene-derived identity again in adulthood are pursued and also that ageing individuals do not have to eradicate music scene participation if continuation is possible. Ageing fans have continuously remained active in northern soul while some have returned. So what is the appeal of continued participation in a "youth scene" in adulthood? The answer is quite simple: the appeal of participation is the same in adulthood as it was in youth: to possess an identity and a form of cultural involvement that results in the achievement of scene-specific status, personhood and subsequent selfhood. The recognition of what scene-derived identity offered a participant in youth should be considered a major factor in the reasons why participants have returned to, or persisted with, a scene. A participant is aware of what cultural affiliation can offer them and they have experience of achieving this via past scene participation. Returning, or persistent participants, are using their return to, or persistence with, the scene as a process of regaining or maintaining a strand of self just as newcomers to a scene seek initial identity formation.

The adults within the current northern soul scene are not aiming to be deviant, rebellious or in opposition to the mainstream *per se*. It could be argued that ageing participants are trying to relive their youth as opposed to directly resisting society. The realization of this does not need to be an extreme one. Reliving one's youth via involving oneself in a pastime once undertaken in youth can be understood as a method of maintaining and supporting the aspects of your personhood and selfhood informed and constructed via music scene involvement. Despite identifying the appeal of adult scene participation as beyond desires for achieving rebellion, this identity *does* stand in opposition to the norm. The adult is being alternative but unwittingly so by re-initiating or continuing a form of youth identity. Participants can still be received as deviant irrespective of intention simply because they are no longer young. Holland discusses the act of "policing oneself" as an ageing, alternative female in terms of choice of dress and behaviour in reference to perceived appropriateness.[25] She situates the act of dyeing your hair pink at the age of fifty as more outrageous than doing this at a younger age. The older woman, via this alternative act, is not simply defying social norms but refuting the idea of women becoming less visible as they age. As Holland states, "[she] becomes far more visible than a young woman with the same".[26] Could it be that the act of membership within a music scene in adulthood is a greater form of supposed sociocultural rebellion than it was in youth? It is arguably regarded as socially less acceptable – or at least less expected – to be part of an underground dance scene at fifty as opposed to at the age of eighteen. Therefore a form of rebellion exists in adult-frequented scenes irrespective of whether it is intended by the participant or not. Looking again at the example of northern soul, the complexities of ageing participation will be investigated.

Ageing northern soul

For every northern soul fan who ever attended a Wigan Casino allnighter, the haunting Tobi Legend phrase "time will pass you by" will be all too familiar.[27] The warning of a fleeting present and the nostalgic consideration of the past that the song suggests was during the 1970s perhaps nothing more than a sentimental musical method of wrapping-up a northern soul dance event. However, listening to this record in the twenty-first century has altered relevance. For the present-day northern soul fans – many of them now in their forties, fifties and sixties – the realization of a past youth rings with different sentiments. Much of what is written about northern soul concentrates on the 1970s scene. This limited focus is somewhat predictable as this was the decade in which a definition of northern soul was cemented. This is the era during which the unique dance styles, "classic" records and majority of fans entered the scene. Over the scene's history the arrival and departure of fans is to be expected. To discuss present-day northern soul is therefore to discuss the complexities of the fan dynamic in light of the continuous arrival of new fans and the manner in which existing, consistent fans respond to both the presence of newcomers and their own mode of performing northern soul fandom while ageing. Fans that have been continually performing northern soul fandom have to cope with altered subjective constructions of selfhood and personhood induced because of age.

Longevity alters the participant dynamic: it matures the existing fan-base while simultaneously allowing a steady stream of new participants to discover the scene. Longevity and the different stages of fandom create an interesting and, at times, conflicting scene dynamic. To give an idea of some of the difficulties created because of scene longevity and the relevance this could have in terms of wider post-subcultural theorization, I present the "scene with longevity participant typology" (see Table 1). To surpass subcultural theorization this typology acknowledges cultural fluidity, the variations in modes of cultural membership and individual – as well as collective – significance of such variations.

The typology in Table 1 illustrates the potential for sociality in terms of offering wider modes of postmodern cultural fluidity and choice while also recognizing the possibility of specific scene involvement. Each participant-type is dependent on two factors: when and how the participant found the scene and also the intentions of that participation. So to briefly explain each participant-type, the passer-by embraces postmodern fluidity of cultural involvement. The passer-by experiences the fluidity of cultural affiliation but will be disinterested in or unable, at this stage, to experience northern soul membership.

After experiencing a scene as a passer-by, the individual may respond to the scene in one of three ways: they may reject the scene, adopt the role of a day-tripper,[28] or aim to be a potential member. The day-tripper desires merely to socialize in a club venue without any pursuit of membership and as such celebrates the possible insincerity of consumer selection and therefore the

4 Beyond the Master Narrative of Youth

Table 1. Typology of participants in a scene with longevity

Non-Established Participants			Established Participant
Non-Members	**Members**		
Passer-by	*Newcomer*	*Returning Participant*	*Constant Participant*

1. Day-tripper
2. Potential Member
	1. *Mature*
	  i. Access via friend/sibling/spouse
	  ii. Access via complementary music scene
	  iii. Access via affiliation after "passing by"
	
	2. *Young*
	  i. Access via parent(s) [soul children]
	  ii. Access via friend/sibling/spouse
	  iii. Access via complementary music scene
	  iv. Access via affiliation after
	  v. "passing by"
		1. Progressive
		2. Nostalgic
			1. Progressive
			2. Nostalgic

opportunity to compile dynamic collages of neo-tribal experience. The specificity of post-subcultural subcultural play would be unappealing to the day-tripper who regards too highly the frivolity and multiplicity of postmodern cultural consumption. So, although the boundaries between participant-types are permeable, the choice remains with the participant, and there is no guarantee that non-members will progress into the membership stage.

The potential member has a curiosity about the scene in response to participating from the margin.[29] To achieve membership[30] the potential member alters his or her intentions of cultural involvement by learning to perform to achieve peer acceptance and by displaying commitment to the scene (by increasing personal experience longevity). Such commitment will be embroiled in reflexive awareness of this performance of post-subcultural subcultural play.

Newcomers are those who have chosen to pursue an affiliation with a scene; they are learning about membership but are not yet established participants. This can occur via potential member status, or if an understanding of a scene has been granted via a friend, sibling, spouse or parent, or via a complementary music scene. The issue of age becomes relevant here. *Young* newcomers possess additional pressures in terms of performing fandom to achieve in-crowd acceptance (to become established). Such difficulties include the pressure from protective existing fans, especially those experiencing subjective disruption of cultural identity due to the presence of newcomers and the possible internal conflict of ageing. The *mature* newcomer is less visible due to "fitting-in" in terms of age and thus they experience fewer problems of access because they do not visually incite existing fans to question how suitable their own adult participation in the current scene is, as young newcomers potentially do. Aware of this, young newcomers may resort to retro performances of northern soul in an attempt to display their understanding of the history of the scene and to counter the issue of youth. Yet this somewhat paradoxically places the young newcomer as visibly separate to the constant (progressive) participant, who no longer dresses or dances in what has become a stereotypical fashion. Returning participants have quite obviously left the scene at some point and have decided to return. Constant participants have remained active on the scene. Returning and constant participants can be either progressive or nostalgic. The nostalgics are committed to reliving and maintaining scene involvement, as well as protecting the specifics of northern soul. The progressives are committed to exploration, discovery and development within the scene. Progressives and nostalgics are ideal types; they are extremes of experience. The majority of established participants will identify more strongly with one rather than the other type but may exhibit characteristics representative of that other type.[31] This reflects the idea that cultural identity is open to choice (at least in terms of intention).

The young newcomers are adventuring into the unknown by participating in something that not many of their peers are doing while also experiencing an adult world in everyday terms. This is an escape from childish things into something that "the adults do". The potential for northern soul to create distance between youth and parental authority – a trait often considered evident in youth cultural activity – is problematic for the soul children, however. The rebelliousness of partaking in cultures unknown to parents is severely limited for the soul child, especially if their parent(s) remain active on the scene. Perhaps parental first-hand knowledge of the deviant aspects of the scene and the heightened comprehension of scene specificity is rewarding, but ultimately being unable to create a cultural identity beyond parental influence may hinder the appeal of northern soul once it has been explored, understood and exhausted of the uniqueness that initially presented itself as an identity construct beyond that available to their peers. Living in a post-subcultural age aids the ease with which soul children can opt out of northern soul, with many looking to the nu-soul, modern soul, funk and acid jazz scenes for potential music membership that embraces the specificity of northern soul but without parental presence.

A survey of self-identified northern soul fans showed that 49.5 per cent of participants in 2005–2006 were aged 46–55 years.[32] No participants were over 65 years or under 18 years. One participant was aged 18–25 years (the daughter of a returning participant). 95 per cent of all survey participants were aged 36+ years, clearly illustrating that the current scene is adult-frequented. When asked in which year the fans originally participated in the scene, the highest number of people questioned entered the scene in 1973 (12.3 per cent). Sixteen per cent of people first participated in the scene in the 1960s, 66.7 per cent in the 1970s, 8.6 per cent in the 1980s, 3.7 per cent in the 1990s and 4.9 per cent discovered northern soul post-millennium. Notably, 16 per cent of people discovered northern soul in the 1960s and are still participating today. As expected, the 1970s saw the majority of these participants join the scene. As nostalgics tend to attend events with little routine and only when the opportunity arises (major events), it is interesting to note that 44.4 per cent of people attend on an infrequent basis, with 7.4 per cent of people attending events once or twice a year compared to 56.8 per cent attending current events regularly.[33] This supports the thesis of a divide on the scene between the nostalgics and the progressives while also demonstrating that northern soul is, for the majority, still an active (as opposed to a retro) scene.

Conflicting fandom: an issue of age
Age-related conflict within northern soul is two-fold. First, there is the internal conflict between the identity of the participant in youth and of that participant, still on the scene, having to rectify the contradictions inherent in an *aged* youth identity. The concept of nostalgia is relevant here. Second, there is the conflict between the established, older participant (either returning or constant) and the young newcomer. While such age-related conflict is not a condition of *all* participant experience it is a noticeable and talked-about aspect of the current scene. As a 19-year-old northern soul DJ told me:

> Northern soul's a scene that's very much stuck in its ways because obviously it's an older generation and although there's a lot that are accommodating to younger people there's a lot who aren't and jealousy rears its head. It's like it's always "oh he's only so young, what's he doing?" It's extremely difficult. [...] From the majority of people you'll get support and encouragement but from the minority you won't and it's very elitist [...] you have all these records and you can put a set together better than anybody else could but because of your age it doesn't seem relevant.[34]

Self is context-specific and develops via monitoring our own behaviour and by making social comparisons. Established participants are forced to re-evaluate personhood and selfhood in relation to northern soul based on comparisons they make between themselves and the young newcomers to "their" scene. This re-evaluation comes as an unexpected downside especially as the initial appeal of returning to, or persisting with, the current scene involves the assumption that past participants would not need to reassert themselves in an alien social context to experience a music scene in adulthood. The fears that younger participants produce among some existing participants has caused conflict to arise. The fact that older newcomers are not experiencing this level of conflict supports my claim that this tension is *age*-related rather than simply being an issue of commitment and exclusivity. This conflict exists, I believe, because young newcomers are problematizing the merits of ageing competitive display thus complicating the achievement of status and resultant personhood and selfhood for older, existing participants. This is combined with fears of losing ownership of the scene and subsequently losing what informs this strand of a participant's selfhood.

Current older fans, either constant or returning, have conflicting identifications as participants. This is a result of possessing (memories of) selfhood based in a youthful past and simultaneously possessing personhood on the present-day scene. This internal conflict of cultural identity is evident in the participant who has to re-evaluate because of the arrival of new, younger fans. Moreover, this is further complicated by feelings of reminiscence and the subsequent separation of then and now, in other words because of nostalgia. Nostalgia is relevant to the conflict of age in northern soul as it creates a unique subjectivity for the older participant that the newcomer cannot possess.[35] Beyond this separation, nostalgia impacts upon the subjective identity of the older participant. The older participant compares youth-derived selfhood with adult scene personhood that is now being applied to them, both from without and from within. The emotive response from existing fans to young newcomers, cumulating in conflict, mediates the personal relevance of nostalgia in relation to the formation of personhood and selfhood, as Tannock explains:

> Nostalgia [...] invokes a positively evaluated past world in response to a deficient present world. The nostalgic subject turns to the past to find/construct sources of identity, agency, or community, that are felt to be lacking, blocked, subverted, or threatened in the present [...] Invoking the past, the nostalgic subject may be involved in escaping or evading, in critiquing, or in mobilizing to overcome the present experience of loss of identity, lack of agency, or absence of community.[36]

Tannock goes on to say that nostalgia typically manifests itself within an "underlying suggestion that ... sources are not available in the present" and that "that was then, and this is now".[37] However, this is not true in the case of northern soul because the scene continues to exist. It follows therefore that participants are not nostalgic about the scene but about the loss of the youth experience of the scene. Nostalgia is thus an internal sense of separation: dividing what informs a fan's sense of cultural self by categorizing the source of that self as discontinued. Conclusively therefore it seems that while a scene may experience longevity and appear unchanged, the type of participant and the reality of participant experience do alter with the passage of time. With such complex networks of subjective identity-construction and the age-derived conflict evident in the scene the methodology implemented to observe and record such scenes with longevity requires careful consideration.

Researching ageing participation

As identity is central within northern soul it is essential to involve ethnographic methods to investigate the current scene and to access personal understandings of self expressed by the participants. The techniques of participant observation, focus groups and interviews grant access to participant interpretations of, and involvement in, a scene. Ethnographic methodology can thus penetrate the specifics of cultural participation yet the necessary inclusion of participant observation is complicated in light of the fact that access is problematic due to the visible distinction of age that potentially situates the researcher outside of the subject group.[38] Such a difference in age is an indicator that a young researcher could not possibly have gained first-hand experience of a scene with longevity. That researcher has to deal with the fan assumptions that they do not understand what has occurred throughout the history of the scene under study. To tackle the issue of "not knowing what went before", access to the scene and to fan accounts of the scene are essential. A covert researcher position is implausible because of the visibility of age, yet it is essential for the overt researcher to demonstrate some understanding of the scene to gain acceptance and thus access. Efforts should be made to locate gatekeepers to enable access to the present scene and to gain information from constant fans about the past. Data from the latter are open to narrative analysis.

Arguably the forced overt position of the researcher is not such a hurdle for the researcher who complements the age of the subject group, and acceptance may be more easily achieved as the possibility of "knowing the scene" exists. Interestingly the problems of gaining access and "not knowing what went before" are eradicated if the researcher is a fan of the scene under study. However, a fan-turned-researcher may potentially fix investigative research within (biased) fan discourses and, while they may know the scene, they must consciously keep a check on subjective interpretations. To separate personal comprehension derived from the experience of being a fan from the information gained via ethnographic research may be impossible. Moreover, the fact that fan-researchers have to deal with the ethics of recording a scene consisting of their peers for academic gain is not easily dealt with. Of course, scholars cannot choose the researcher position they possess: they are either fans of the scene under study or not. If the fan-researcher can successfully and in an unbiased manner manage their duality, then the consequent data will have depth of historical understanding. The researcher new to a scene has to learn the rules of behaviours and as such does not have access to comparative experience of then and now. However, they do possess details of the experience of gaining access to a scene. They can tell the illuminating story of the process of becoming a fan.[39]

The issues inherent in ethnographic research of scenes with longevity are thus:

- Access for the researcher who belongs to an age group visibly distinct from the group under study
- Interpretation of participant observation when the subjective issue of identity is central to such investigations
- Not knowing what went before, because researching a scene with longevity means missing aspects of that scene
- The complexities of recording biographies of all participant-types
- Coping with the duality of a fan-researcher position.

In response to such issues, the technique of narrative analysis offers the researcher of ageing music scenes an insight into a fan's scene career with scope to span all eras of participation and to include issues of subjective identity-construction, nostalgia and sentiments towards self and others without having to delve into discussions of scene politics and value judgements. The implicit innocence and personal sentiment of one's own story-telling dilutes the need for the researcher to openly and directly probe sensitive areas of cultural involvement. This – for a scene in which members continue to participate and have participated in for many years – is a welcome method of qualitative analysis.[40]

Concluding thoughts

The fact that northern soul consumption centres upon already-aged vinyl records has meant that the passage of time has not impacted upon this scene to the extent that we might witness in live (as opposed to record-based) music scenes. The lack of relevance of the performing artist, chart positioning or major industry input has enabled northern soul to continue for five decades without being pushed to "move with the times". But while all else remains in stasis, the fans still age. In fact, the only visibly ageing dimension of the scene is the fans. This would not be such a pertinent issue if it were not for the constant arrival of younger participants highlighting the passage of time and as a result disrupting the illusion of stasis: reliving your youth through northern soul has become more difficult. Age and scene longevity have altered the subjective conceptualization of being a northern soul fan for continuous and returning older participants. This initiated a confusion of identification and expectations of the role of fan when performed in adulthood. The presence of young newcomers to the contemporary scene forced older participants to question the appropriateness of performing youth-derived actions in adulthood and also acted as a reminder to these older fans of a past youth.

The fact that we do not have a term in popular music for an adult-frequented music culture is very telling. Even apparently innocuous terms such as "music scene" imply youth association. The adult scene I recognize in northern soul is not independent of the original youth culture but serves to give recognition to adult participation. The prioritization of the master narrative of youth in popular music studies can therefore be placed into question and subsequently age – *not merely youth* – should be considered a relevant element within the construction of popular music identities.

About the author

Nicola Watchman Smith is Head of Higher Education at Newcastle College University Centre and a cultural sociologist and researcher. A Masters graduate of the Institute of Popular Music at the University of Liverpool, her PhD from the University of Salford was an ethnographic investigation into youth/ageing and cultural performance on the northern soul music scene. Ageing, adulthood, and the master narrative of youth within popular culture was the focus of her post-doctoral research, and her current research interests include: audiences, fandom and spectatorship; post-subcultural theory; the performance of identity; and pedagogic practice, studentship, and higher education. Nicola has previously published on northern soul in chapters in *The Ashgate Research Companion to Popular Musicology* (2009) and *Ageing and Youth Cultures: Music, Style and Identity* (2012).

Notes

1. Merton 1957; Matza and Sykes 1961; Becker 1963.
2. Hall and Jefferson 1976; Hebdige 1979.
3. Here the use of the term "scene" is not tied to scene theory as explored by, for example, Straw 1991. The choice of terminology instead reflects the northern soul participants' own use of the term to describe their cultural world. This is more akin to Goffman's (1959) use of the term "making a scene".
4. Post-subcultural theorizations stem from Redhead 1990 and Muggleton 1997. Alternative approaches include scene theory, neo-tribes, lifestyles and numerous reworked versions of subcultural theory.
5. For example goth, punk and heavy metal.
6. See Bennett and Kahn-Harris 2004: 6–11.
7. Maffesoli 1996.
8. Jenkins (1996: 30) makes a distinction between selfhood ("private experience") and personhood ("what appears publicly").
9. For example, Chaney 1996.
10. Sweetman 2004: 88–89.
11. Bauman 1992: 136, original emphasis.
12. Hodkinson 2002.
13. This potential to perform with a fusion of frivolity and substance reflects the postmodern experience and is as such distinct from Sweetman's fixed categories of Tourist *or* Traveller. Mine is a post-subcultural option; Sweetman's a depiction of both subcultural and post-subcultural activity occurring alongside one another. See Sweetman 2004: 80.
14. Bennett and Kahn-Harris 2004: 17.
15. The use of the term "subculture" in the current post-subcultural climate is frowned upon. Yet I have opted to use the phrase "post-subcultural subcultural play" in a paradoxical manner as this highlights the recognition of the inappropriateness of the term; just as the post-subcultural subcultural players are reflexively aware of the limitations of such play, post-subcultural theorists are reflexively aware of the rhetorical limitations of subcultures.
16. A useful analogy is that of a church wedding for a non-religious couple. This is a desire to perform a marriage ceremony under the guise of what is expected of a wedding yet with full awareness of the illusion of religiosity as no belief system is in place. This is "playing the wedding game". This is not ironic or carnivalesque as this would disrupt the impact of the ceremony but the significance of this experience is merely one of choice, one of aesthetics and one of doing what is desirable. Yet getting married in a church may generate a sense of appropriateness, correctness and depth of engagement. From this the ceremony, the day (and indeed the marriage) may gain additional meaning/kudos. The appeal is to hold a wedding in a traditional sense but not in relation to the symbolism of faith. Many thanks to Derek Scott for this analogy.
17. Sweetman 2004: 79–93.
18. It is worth noting that the postmodernity versus reflexive modernity debate, while not pivotal here, is discussed in detail by Sweetman 2004: 80–85.
19. Maffesoli 1996: 74–75.

20. I am defining "youth" as simply as Bennett defines it: "a specific age group, typically 15 to 25 years old" (Bennett 2001: 152). Discussion of the complexity of terms such as "youthful", that consider youth an entity beyond age, is not pivotal here.

21. Sardiello 1998: 123.

22. Brake 1985: 15–17, 191.

23. Andes 1998: 218–19.

24. This was a theme repeatedly addressed by ageing northern soul fans in a scene in which dancing is central to the majority of participants' experience.

25. Holland 2004.

26. Holland 2004: 26.

27. Tobi Legend, 'Time Will Pass You By', Gomba Music Inc. (BMI) 8453, 1968. A popular northern soul record; one of the "three before 8" at the Wigan Casino club (the three tracks played at the end of every Casino allnighter). The Wigan Casino was arguably the most celebrated and popular of all northern soul nightclubs. It ran allnighters (all-night dance events from 8pm to 8am) from 1973 to 1981 in Wigan, a town in north-west England.

28. This is the term used by northern soul fans for those participants who visited the scene in response to the heyday peak in popularity.

29. Interestingly this is often the position of the non-fan researcher at the initial stages of participant observation.

30. To move from column 1 to 2 of Table 1.

31. For example, those who consider themselves progressives may have a fondness for a classic (nostalgic) record, although this will not shape their weekly experience of the scene.

32. Author's PhD findings: 81 quantitative questionnaires were completed by self-identified northern soul fans in the UK, 2005–2006. Pilot questionnaire results are not considered.

33. Infrequent attendance is defined as those attending less than twelve times in one year (less than monthly). Regular attendance is defined as those attending northern soul events monthly, fortnightly, weekly or several times a week.

34. Interview with author, Salford, 3 November 2005.

35. This begs the question: are newcomers entering the scene for northern soul of today or in response to the golden age of the scene? Are young newcomers nostalgic for the myth of northern soul? The answers may well be unique for each participant, so narrative analysis would be a useful tool here.

36. Tannock 1995: 454.

37. Tannock 1995: 456.

38. There is a barrier between older researchers and their access to (new) youth cultures and also between younger researchers attempting to conduct ethnographic explorations of cultural groups frequented by notably older participants.

39. Drawing from personal experience, I consider my initial outsider status to northern soul as an advantage because I experienced first-hand the issue of gaining access to a scene shrouded in exclusivity. I was able to better understand the issues involved in joining a music scene as a younger newcomer.

40. See Coffey and Atkinson (1996: 56–57) for the merits of narrative analysis.

References

Andes, Linda. 1998. "Growing Up Punk: Meaning and Commitment Careers in a Contemporary Youth Subculture". In *Youth Culture: Identity in a Postmodern World*, edited by Jonathon S. Epstein, 212–31. Oxford: Blackwell.
Bauman, Zygmunt. 1992. *Intimations of Postmodernity*. London: Routledge.
Becker, Howard S. 1963. *Outsiders: Studies in the Sociology of Deviance*. New York: Free Press.
Bennett, Andy. 2001. *Cultures of Popular Music*. Buckingham: Open University Press.
Bennett, Andy, and Keith Kahn-Harris, eds. 2004. *After Subculture*. Basingstoke: Palgrave Macmillan.
Brake, Michael. 1985. *Comparative Youth Culture: The Sociology of Youth Cultures and Youth Subcultures in America, Britain and Canada*. London: Routledge.
Chaney, David. 1996. *Lifestyles*. London: Routledge.
Coffey, Amanda, and Paul Atkinson. 1996. *Making Sense of Qualitative Data: Complementary Research Strategies*. London: Sage.
Goffman, Erving. 1959. *The Presentation of Self in Everyday Life*. Harmondsworth: Penguin.
Hall, Stuart, and Tony Jefferson, eds. 1976. *Resistance Through Rituals: Youth Subcultures in Post-War Britain*. London: Hutchinson.
Hebdige, Dick. 1979. *Subculture: The Meaning of Style*. London: Methuen.
Hodkinson, Paul. 2002. *Goth: Identity, Style and Subculture*. Oxford: Berg.
Holland, Samantha. 2004. *Alternative Femininities: Body, Age and Identity*. Oxford: Berg.
Jenkins, Richard. 1996. *Social Identity*. London: Routledge.
Maffesoli, Michel. 1996. *The Time of the Tribes: The Decline of Individualism in Mass Society*, trans. Don Smith. London: Sage.
Matza, David, and Gresham M. Sykes. 1961. "Juvenile Delinquency and Subterranean Values". *American Sociological Review* 26/5: 712–19.
Merton, Robert K. 1957. *Social Theory and Social Structure*. New York: Free Press.
Muggleton, David. 1997. "The Post-subculturalist". In *The Clubcultures Reader: Readings in Popular Cultural Studies*, edited by Steve Redhead, Derek Wynne and Justin O'Connor, 185–203. Oxford: Blackwell.
Redhead, Steve. 1990. *The End-of-the Century Party: Youth and Pop Towards 2000*. Manchester: Manchester University Press.
Sardiello, Robert. 1998. "Identity and Status Stratification in Deadhead Subculture". In *Youth Culture: Identity in a Postmodern World*, edited by Jonathon S. Epstein, 118–47. Oxford: Blackwell.
Sean. 2005. Interview with author, 3 November 2005, Salford, UK.
Straw, Will. 1991. "Systems of Articulation, Logics of Change: Communities and Scenes in Popular Music". *Cultural Studies* 5/3: 368–88.
Sweetman, Paul. 2004. "Tourists and Travellers? 'Subcultures', Reflexive Identities and Neo-Tribal Sociality". In *After Subculture: Critical Studies in Contemporary Youth Culture*, edited by Andy Bennett and Keith Kahn-Harris, 79–93. Basingstoke: Palgrave Macmillan.
Sykes, Gresham M., and David Matza. 1961. "Juvenile Delinquency and Subterranean Values". *American Sociological Review* 26/5: 712–19.
Tannock, Stuart. 1995. "Nostalgia Critique". *Cultural Studies* 9/3: 453–64.

Musical Bookmark 2

Sean Chapman photographed at Chapman Records, Stafford, November 2016
Jonathan Capree, 'I'm Gonna Build Me A Mountain'. US Ox Bow Records – RI3109A

> "It was played on the mod scene for some time and about four years ago I managed to get a copy of it. Now, at this time there was only three known copies, which to me was a bit of a coup because, although I've DJed over thirty years, nearly all the records have always been spun by somebody else. So, to be associated with a particular record – to break it onto the northern soul scene – that's always appealed to me."

Sean Chapman is a record dealer, collector, and DJ. He currently DJs on both the northern soul and mod scene, at the King's Hall Allnighter in Stoke on Trent, Rugby Soul Club All-Niter, and Out of Time in Wolverhampton, amongst others.

5 Acquiring Rights and Righting Wrongs?

Ady Croasdell

In 1970, I hitchhiked from Market Harborough to Leicester to visit Jeff King's record stall in the market. He sold mainly old singles with an emphasis on soul, especially discs that were getting played on the burgeoning "old soul" scene, of which I had become a part as a keen soul fan and dancer. On a previous visit, I had been bedazzled by Jeff producing a UK Capitol copy of the Human Beinz, 'Nobody But Me', and telling me it would sell for £10 as it was the biggest record on the scene at that time. That was staggering news: old records were usually much cheaper than a new record. It was way above my price range, so I settled for some obscure Motown and Stax. Then I was told that they had copies of the Poets, 'She Blew A Good Thing' in stock for fifteen shillings (75 pence) on a US label, appropriately called Old Soul; I should have twigged then. That was crazy: that record fetched upwards of a fiver though I only knew it as by the American Poets on the UK London label. Knowing its worth, I said I'd buy a copy and Jeff asked me how many did I want? I was on a very limited student grant so I put the other records back and bagsied three of the Poets. I knew I could move them on at the Lantern allnighter in my hometown later that evening. Nobody had ever seen the Old Soul label before and I got 25 shillings each for my spares. I had become a bootleg dealer without knowing it.

As a lifelong advocate against bootlegging, that would be an embarrassment if I had not been an unwitting teenager, caught up in what would become a major interest of my life, and of the rare soul scene to come. What started as a hobby would turn into a passion and a career. I have attended rare soul dances since 1969 and my record collecting would see me being one of a handful of full-time rare record dealers in the early 70s. My love of the scene saw me turn first to promoting dances, then to DJing, and finally to working in the record business re-releasing the music that I have enjoyed. I initially followed the words and credo of soul music journalist Dave Godin, and later was taught the correct way to re-release the music by the directors of Ace Records – an established leader in the reissue market. I came to understand the morality and legality of recompensing the music makers for the work that we enjoy. On the scene for nearly 50 years, I have been fortunate to work at the different branches of the industry for a substantial time, nearly forty years as a promoter and DJ, and thirty-five with Ace Records. The morality and acceptability of bootlegs has been a constant discussion and argument on the northern soul scene since that first Old Soul label disc in 1970, and still rages to this day.

Soul Sounds: the development of a bootlegging economy

Bootlegging in the music industry usually refers to the reproduction of recorded music for sale without having the mechanical rights licensed from the owner to do so, or without the publishing rights being paid for the song. The reason bootlegging started within the soul scene was one of demand and supply. There was a small but dedicated demand for the old soul records that were being played on the scene by DJs with good collections. The fans of the music wanted to buy copies to hear at home, or possibly to include in their own DJ set lists, but the record companies who owned the master rights were unaware of this demand or uninterested. It may have been Jeff King himself who started the Old Soul label. It only lasted for three releases, but was followed soon after by a new Soul Sounds imprint, again probably set up by King. It featured the revered and super-rare 'Baby Reconsider' by Leon Haywood as its debut disc; and in most stories about its origin, a top northern DJ supplied the records to dub the sound from. Soul Sounds went on to have thirty releases, all of which except the Haywood 45 had been issued in the UK in the 60s. By 1970–1971 they were deleted by the licence holders and hard to find as they sold poorly on release. The pressing plant for Soul Sounds was alleged to be the same one that manufactured the legitimate President and Jay Boy re-releases of old soul records. It would undoubtedly have to have come about as a cash deal with one or more of the employees at the plant; bootlegging was known to be a serious offence so the rewards had to be secretive and worthwhile. Jeff King was reputedly jailed for his nefarious activities when the British Phonographic Industry (BPI) eventually caught up with him, at the behest of the big record companies whose product he had been reproducing. King disappeared from the scene, never to return.

Apart from the higher prices these newly pressed discs could command, there were significant cost savings for the bootlegger not paying any licensing or publishing fees, including any royalties for the artists or songwriters themselves. The sales were small but virtually guaranteed, as the demand had already been established from DJ spins of the rare originals. Needless to say, the DJs and collectors were livid when one of their cherished possessions was duplicated and made available at a much lower price to the discs' then-current value. Through this process, the record lost its exclusivity and was available to anyone with the cash, avoiding the need to scour record lists and junkshops for hours as those pioneering collectors had done.

Other smaller labels popped up from that point onwards. BJD and Magic were reputedly pressed at the Lyntone plant in Upper Holloway, London, whose main work was producing thin plastic flexi-discs for magazines and fan clubs. BJD was a label of the Selecta Disc record shop in Nottingham. The initials were of Brian Selby the owner, John Bratton the manager, and Dave Whymark (aka Dave Williams) who ran the Soul Cellar part of the shop. The shop had been implicated in the Soul Sounds case as one of the main outlets for the bootlegs and they became wary of getting too involved after that. Ironically, given this, they chose to bootleg a Chubby Checker 45 on BJD from the Cameo Parkway label, which by then was owned by Alan Klein, one of the most litigious men in the business. In a story often told, Selecta worked with two veterans of the American music industry. One was Bernie Binnick from Philadelphia who had ties with that city's Swan label and a business interest in the Global record shop in Manchester. He would eventually run a UK Swan label and the Cream label from that shop. The second, Bill Buster, ran the Eric reissue label out of New Jersey and cottoned on to the northern soul scene in its early days, reissuing the likes of 'I Got The Fever' by the Creation and 'Time Will Pass You By' by Tobi Legend. He noticed that some of his re-releases for the American market were selling in the UK, saw a business opportunity and was directed by Selecta Disc to get in-demand titles pressed up from original US labels like Brunswick, Columbia, Okeh, MGM, and others. Those were largely legitimate represses.

Around that time, the out-and-out bootleg label Out Of The Past began. It was strongly rumoured to have been run by a major scene promoter. There were over twenty releases on labels of various hues before they changed to an abridged OOTP on a plain white label for a similar number of releases. They pressed the hugely popular 'Landslide' by Tony Clarke at the same time it was being re-released on the UK Chess label. These bootleg imprints ran from around 1973 to 1975 and, with their large centre holes and US type of vinyl, seemed to be American pressings. The rapidly growing scene was insatiable in its appetite for new discoveries from the DJs to dance to. The DJs had long since realized that the UK mid-60s releases were the tip of the iceberg of great uptempo soul music issued in America, and it was to US releases that they now devoted their detective work. By 1973, the attendances at rare soul events had burgeoned, with the increased demand meaning the financial rewards of bootlegging were even bigger. Some records would gain a following, becoming a new "monster" sound, as the records were colloquially known. The allnighter-going public craved these discs, with many eventually purchasing them through the illegal pressings. The DJs were generally innocent cogs in the machine, but some were inevitably complicit in the bootlegging process, and likely directly involved in getting the latest big tunes to the bootleggers for financial reward.

Some northern soul fans were vehemently against bootlegging on moral grounds. The scene's top journalist, Dave Godin, was experienced in the ways of record companies having helped Berry Gordy set up the Tamla Motown label with EMI in the UK, and having advised many labels on the records they should release, either because of demand or because of musical merit. Above all, Godin was a critic and a promoter of the black music he adored. He had his own legitimate imprints running in these early days of the northern soul scene. His and his partners' (David Nathan and Robert Blackmore) Soul City and Deep Soul labels ran from 1968–1970. Godin then helped his *Blues & Soul* magazine editor, John Abbey, to advise Polydor on the releases on their new soul music label, Mojo. Though the scene was not at its peak by 1971, Mojo managed Top 40 entries by The Fascinations, The Formations and Tami Lynn who reached number 4 in the national music chart; all were 1960s recordings played on the old soul scene. Other labels followed suit and MCA subsidiary Probe had a number one national hit with The Tams' 'Hey Girl Don't Bother Me' recorded some seven years earlier. Seven years felt a lifetime away in the fast moving 60s and 70s. Motown scored big with The Contours' 'Just A Little Misunderstanding' and The Elgins' 'Heaven Must Have Sent You', neither of which sold well when first released in 1966. It was in this early 70s period that the term "northern soul", commonly believed to have been coined by Godin, became widespread, superseding the "old soul" tag.

State side: bootlegging soul in America

It seems odd to me that the major labels did not put more effort into their re-release programmes at this time. With the recordings already in the can, the profitability of these potential hits was considerable. However, they were not really clued into the developing scene and its demand for the northern soul sound and, as reported by Dave Godin in *Blues & Soul*, the London-based music business could not initially understand the phenomenon which was spreading around the country to just about everywhere but the capital. The DJs, promoters and operators of the all-night dances had their ears closer to the ground than the employees of the record company giants; that is when the bootleggers seized their chance. The profits were worth the risk, particularly as the BPI was not as attentive to this activity at the time. They were more interested in stopping the live concert LP bootlegs of the industry's biggest breadwinners – The Beatles, Bowie, Stones, and Led Zeppelin. By then the bootleggers had realized it was safer and cheaper to press in the USA.

Apart from shifting most of their illicit pressing operations over to the United States, bootlegs began to appear on facsimiles of legitimate labels such as Los Angeles music producer Bobby Sanders' Soultown logo. This can be seen as an attempt to make the releases look authentic to British collectors. By then the man who is widely seen as the most infamous of all the bootleggers, Simon Soussan, had infiltrated the Los Angeles soul music scene. As most versions of the Soussan story attest, on arrival in the city from his home town of Leeds, and through a winning combination of flattery, trickery and cash, he allegedly won the trust of several of LA's major soul music players. These included Randy Wood of Mirwood Records, the Bihari brothers who owned Modern records, Anthony Renfro who had several northern "hits" on Renfro, Madelon Baker who owned the Audio Arts label, as well as Sanders himself. There were, in most interpretations, different degrees of illegality to Soussan's deals. The Soultown pressings certainly included several releases owned by the massive Columbia Records company. Tracks by The Sweet Things, Johnny Moore and The Glories came out under that banner, with the correct credits, as did Renfro and Veep label singles. Though these were blatant bootlegs, the lack of knowledge about this obscure side of the US soul scene would mean that most fans would not be certain about the legitimacy of the records. It was also not easy for an executive of a major record company to prove that these discs were breaking the somewhat untested copyright laws. A later bootleg of The Charmaines 'Eternally' from the same Columbia group of labels, Date Records, was pressed as 'Love You Eternally' by The Sweet Things on the entirely fictitious Jade Owl label. The extra secrecy could have been prompted by US Columbia repressing several of their big titles for the English market: misinformation became commonplace on the bootlegs' labels.

DJs with a desire to keep their discoveries big for longer (or maybe even a conscience about bootlegging) were motivated to cover up the labels of their rare discs, and to give them fictitious titles and artist names. That way, the logic went, the bootleggers would not know which records to hunt out in the USA to bootleg. Simon Soussan was a very proficient hunter of records and it seems had a genuine admiration of the music he exploited. Many of the big early "discoveries" on the scene are said to have emanated from him. He was the first to come across what is regarded by many as the greatest northern soul record of them all, Frank Wilson's 'Do I Love You ('Deed I Do)' on Motown's Soul label subsidiary. Wishing to avoid the glare of Berry Gordy or EMI in the UK, he decided to adopt an alias for the singer and attributed it to Eddie Foster, a legitimate Bay Area singer, instead of Frank Wilson. He used

Foster's imprint In Records, on which he had a big northern hit 'I Never Knew' and changed the writers' and producers' names to put others, including in all likelihood the authorities, off the scent.

Soussan was nothing if not an entrepreneur; he knew northern soul dancers had a lust for instrumentals, particularly those of well-known and well-loved records. We know that Soussan visited the studios and record companies where the master tapes were kept. By the mid-1970s, the 60s records that hadn't made a commercial impact had been largely forgotten by the label holders. No doubt flattered by Soussan's interest and the prospect of a pay day, Randy Wood at Mirwood, the Bihari brothers at Modern, Madelon Baker at Audio Arts, and others either copied the multi-track tapes for him and mixed them into instrumentals, or allowed him to borrow the tapes to arrange the same process at one of the Los Angeles studios. In any case, a number of copies of instrumental versions of popular records became available to collectors, allegedly through the activities of Soussan in the United States.

The Biharis were more cautious and worked with Soussan pressing up instrumental versions of Mary Love's 'Lay This Burden Down', Vernon Garrett's 'If I Could Turn Back The Hands Of Time', and Jackie Day's 'Before It's Too Late' at the record plant that was part of their office building. Soussan would have been charged a fee for the pressings which he sent over to the UK to be sold in the shops with a northern soul clientele. If that speculation is correct, these Modern records were not bootlegs but pressings, neither were they re-pressings as the instrumentals were new to disc, even though they had been laid down ten years or so earlier. The Audio Arts Strings' instrumentals on a lookalike Audio Arts label were a different matter. Madelon Baker, the Audio Arts owner, told me that Soussan had stolen tapes from her and she knew nothing of the records. They were made to look like authentic 60s releases by the fictitious act The Audio Arts Strings. Soussan passed them off as new discoveries of old records until they were mass imported and the ruse became too obvious.

He did more than cover up The Checker Board Squares' 'Double Cookin'' instrumental on Villa records. Knowing he had discovered the first copy, Soussan cut an acetate for some of the Wigan Casino DJs (with whom he had close contacts) to play. He called the group The Bob Wilson Sounds – Wilson had had an earlier northern "hit" with his 'Suzy's Serenade' instrumental – and claimed the publishing and the writing and producing credits for himself. He renamed the recording 'Strings A Go Go'. The superb instrumental went massive and its soon-to-follow bootlegs, at the height of the scene in 1974/75, reputedly sold in the tens of thousands. With no artists or writers paid, Soussan is likely to have made a small fortune. Encouraged by this, he later recorded a vocal over the track and presented it as The Del Satins, a rare original according to him called 'Baby You're The Fire'. Oddly, by then the true artist and title of 'Double Cookin' had been revealed and the flip featured the correct credits on its re-release. The songwriter credits on the new vocal were the correct Villa records' owner and producer, so it is possible that this mid-70s vocal of a mid-60s instrumental may have been released in conjunction with its creators.

Other tailor-made recordings for the scene from this time included The Charades' 'Dreaming Up A World Of Fantasy' (a poor vocal over the in-demand Warner Brothers-owned 'Afternoon Of The Rhino' by the Mike Post Coalition). Mirwood songwriter Sherlie Matthews' name was usurped for a session-vocalist's take on her song 'My Little Girl', pressed on a lookalike Mirwood label and renamed 'My Sugar Baby'. Tracking Soussan's activities accurately is virtually impossible. He re-recorded Bob Relf on his northern classic 'Blowing My Mind To Pieces' for the Selecta Disc-run Black Magic label, which also issued a female singer's version of Eddie Parker's 'Love You Baby' over the instrumental side of the original disc, passed off as by its Detroit originator Lorraine Chandler. The label had the gall to put the original recording of 'What Can I Do', Lorraine's debut single for the Giant label, on the flip. During this time of avid bootlegging and re-recording of records, the lines of legality were increasingly blurred.

I happened to be touring the US on a record-buying trip just as the new list of super-rare records at high but affordable prices started to come out. I had bumped into Soussan in one of the Flash record stores in Compton and mentioned I had picked up a copy of 'Broadway Sissy' by Rosco & Friends on Tec. This was one of the current big sounds that Soussan was desperate to acquire, no doubt to press up to sell in the UK. He arranged to visit me in my hotel and promised he would trade me some unbelievable gems for it. When we met, he produced brand new copies of big records like Eddie Foster's 'I Never Knew', The Salvadors' 'Stick By Me Baby', and Billy Prophet's 'What Can I Do?'. I noticed they were far too new to be authentic and examined them closely. I saw that there was a "pb" stamp etched into the run-out grooves on each record and as the titles emanated from right across the USA, I surmised correctly that they would not have been pressed up at the same record plant. On telling him that I believed they were fakes, he virtually admitted it and advised me to scuff them up as originals stating that I'd be a rich man. Having now become acquainted with the West Coast record manufacturing process, Soussan would be well-placed to use his knowledge and contacts to counterfeit rare in-demand records and sell them at a premium. Bootlegs were selling for around £1.50 each, but these pressed-up limited editions, probably around

100 of each, were sold as originals on record lists to the UK for around £15 to £20 each. I was in contact with Ian Clark, one of the main DJs and collectors in the UK, and told him the story, warning him not to buy any and to pass the message on to others. However, the lure of the titles the DJs were so desperate for, may well have led to many DJs buying the counterfeits at the high prices. They did not complain until a long way into the affair once others had corroborated my story by studying the records. The incident speaks volumes about the scene at that time.

With his experience of recording studios, Soussan did make a legitimate record. He updated The Rivingtons' early-60s doo-wop rocker 'Papa Oom Mow Mow' into a mid-70s disco hit for The Sharonettes. The group had two Top 50 UK hits in 1975, but Soussan seemed to soon return to his nefarious ways. He is often alleged to have re-recorded the Earl Wright instrumental 'Thumb A Ride' with studio session guys and called them the Soul Fox Orchestra; Soul Fox being his vainglorious nickname for himself. As the Wigan Casino reached its peak of popularity, more dubious releases continued on Black Magic throughout 1975 and 1976. Soussan's other operations also thrived. In 1977, a deal with the big US TV show *Soul Train*'s producer saw him record a disco medley of ten Motown songs with a studio group he named Shalamar. It was a top ten R&B hit in the States and Soussan became an in-demand disco producer, often using his old northern soul records for inspiration or material, as with his 1979 hit for Arpeggio on Patrice Holloway's 'Love and Desire'.

Others may well also have been dipping into the lucrative trade in unlicenced vinyl. Yorkshire DJ Tony Banks was proud of having bootlegged US singer Jimmy Thomas (who by then resided in West London) on his UK-only Parlophone release 'The Beautiful Night' on Banks' T. B. label; a one-off, almost a vanity, project. The bootleggers were desperate for new titles. Some records were even being counterfeited before they had a chance to gain popularity. Soussan had a detrimental effect on the scene in this and in other ways. He was so obsessed with the instrumental that he created his own cheesy versions in the Los Angeles studios using session men. Apart from the desired beat, to my ears the records have virtually no musical merit and certainly no soul quotient; however, these were mainly legal pressings, but whether the publishing was being paid correctly is a moot point.

By then back in the UK, some record companies had responded to the demand for their old masters by forming reissue labels. Pye was the first of the mid-70s successes, with Disco Demand and RCA following suit with their Grapevine label. EMI reissued several titles on Capitol, Liberty, United Artists and, of course, Tamla Motown. However, their executives were not *au fait* with the scene; often a release would come out after it had been bootlegged and the demand had dissipated. The pressings could be in the shops a couple of weeks after the record's first spins; a contributing factor to the "killing" of some titles and another nail in the coffin of a scene which by the late 70s was shrinking. Many of the smaller US labels had no major affiliations, and pre-Internet the chances of contacting the owners were low.

Wigan closes, the scene goes back to basics, and new record companies emerge

For many people, the traditional northern soul scene symbolically finished with the closure of the Wigan Casino in 1981. Over the three previous years many fans had moved on to the modern soul scene where newly available releases were played next to rare original discoveries. Others embraced disco, while some decided it was time to settle down and try the straight life. Potential new recruits were probably lured away from a tired scene to the excitement of post-punk and indie rock.

The northern soul scene returned to the underground, at least in terms of press and public visibility. The eighties saw regular allnighters in Morecambe, Stafford, Blackburn, Rotherham, Leicester, Scotland, and London among other places. The numbers were not as big as in the heyday but attendances were healthy, and the scene reinvented itself to a large degree. Many venues continued to play the classics, but spurred on by the Top Of The World Allnighters in Stafford, new discoveries and a constant turnover of sounds was deemed essential for a thriving and vibrant scene. This demonstrated that there were hundreds of great records lying undiscovered, or that had never had their time in the spotlight. Additionally, there were new categories of music that were increasingly acceptable to be played on the scene, namely beat ballads, bluesier R&B sounds, some Latin, mid-tempo, very soulful sounds, and 70s and early 80s tracks that were a little too fast for the increasingly mellow modern scene. Running parallel with northern was the originally mod-scooterist scene which took their pick of oldies and newly discovered rarities and the post Quadrophenia and Jam new traditional mod scene who took to classic soul, northern, Latin, jazz and more R&B with some British beat group music thrown in. After a short lull in titles being bootlegged, a new random set of labels like Joker, Mafmon, SOS and counterfeit J&W and Cortland emerged. The revival mods even got into it, releasing Maximilian's 'The Snake' on a Time label bootleg.

During this time demand for black American music began to increase in the UK. The British music scene had begun to appreciate its musical roots in the mid-70s with the arrival of the pub rock bands and the soon-to-come punk scene which also looked back to classic 60s sounds for inspiration. Record collecting took off and old rockers, mods, teds, soul boys, and others sought to buy the originals they cherished and to add to those with new compilations of vintage music from record companies in the know. London-based Charly Records was one of the first to issue intriguing, new LP collections of seriously obscure (but great) tracks most fans had not heard. Ace Records was quick to follow with its first reissues at the end of the 70s. Grapevine and other northern soul labels like Inferno were either gone or stuttering. In 1982, I proposed an LP of US Modern and Kent label soul recordings from Los Angeles to Ace Records, who I knew had access to the recording masters. They agreed and formed a separate subsidiary label for the first soul release and named it Kent after the label that featured on this first disc. It was later often referred to as UK Kent to distinguish it from the US original label.

The Kent LPs sold well from the outset and I was asked to compile further albums. After three US Modern and Kent-sourced albums, Ace approached MCA records for a series of Impressions LP re-releases. That led to access to the huge catalogue which included ABC, Duke, Kapp, Decca, Coral and many more. The LPs from those sources continued the rise of the label and I continued to work as label manager and compiler for Kent through the 1980s. With the advent of digital music, the record business became my full-time job and I was employed by the company as Head of A&R (Artists and Repertoire) with a brief to source music from US licensors.

At the time of the first Kent LPs, Ace was a licensee of music, obtaining the rights for these tracks from the original owners: the Bihari brothers. The accepted business method in place then and now was that Ace would pay a percentage of the wholesale price in a royalty to the master owners. It would then be down to those licensors to pass any artist or producer (rarely in evidence contractually until the 70s at the earliest) royalties to those concerned. A contract would be made allowing the reproduction of the master by the licensee with the agreed royalty stipulated (usually 16 to 26 percent for these types of recordings) and a cash advance would be paid upfront to seal the deal. The advance was important as it represented a concrete reward to the licensor for passing on their rights. It would be a guarantee of at least the minimum amount of money they would get from the deal. The record business is familiar with fly-by-night companies with poor accounting; the advance was a guarantee that the licensors would at least get some of their dues. Sales of the records should have been accounted regularly, usually at six-month intervals for the duration of the time-limited contract. Before the contract expired it could be re-negotiated if needed. When the advance in royalties was matched by earned royalties, further cheques would be sent out to the licensor and again it would be their duty to pass on the artist royalty.

On pressing a record, there would also be a separate additional payment for the use of the song which would go to the publishing firm that controlled the song at the time of release. The publisher would be obliged to pass on the individual writer's share of that fee to the correct parties. One of Ace's three owner/directors was (and remains) Trevor Churchill, who entered the music business in the 1960s and worked for EMI records. There, he was schooled in the correct ways of licensing masters. Having somebody so experienced with the process proved to be an advantage in securing rights and licensing from major record companies. To this day, his accurate accounting system and payments keep licensors happy to do business.

Churchill, along with Roger Armstrong and Ted Carroll (the other Ace owners), entered the music business as fans and always wanted to pay their dues to the artists, songwriters and label owners. Soul music journalist Dave Godin was of a similar ilk, putting the music's producers on a pedestal and demanding that record companies pay these people their full worth. He took a strong line against bootlegging on the northern scene which he had originally championed and unwittingly named. It was a major factor in his disillusionment that eventually led him away from the scene, once the illicit bootleggers had become part of the northern soul economy. Aside from any moral debates, it was a relative handicap to be paying royalties and acquiring rights while bootleggers simply dubbed a record and had it pressed up ready to sell in the shops and by mail order in a matter of days. The BPI (master rights) and MCPS (publishing rights) that regulate the record industry did achieve some victories against the bootleggers and the shops they sold their pressings through in the early 70s. By the mid-70s the bootlegging of the LPs by major artists like Bob Dylan and Pink Floyd seemed to take up all their resources, and northern soul bootleggers usually managed to stay below their radar.

However, there were many benefits to playing the game correctly. Offering proper contracts and decent advances against royalties meant that the understandably wary label owners were prepared to find their master tapes and search back in their lofts and memories to find other examples of their work from which they could belatedly earn money. Some of these licensors had done earlier deals with UK companies, received a cheque for the advance and never heard from the company or individual again. When further statements and cheques arrived from a reputable firm, they were pleased and slightly shocked. This goodwill often led to recommendations to other label owners they knew from "back in the day" and subsequently an increase in available material. Ace also has the advantage of being a broad musical church with releases of R&B, doo wop, jazz, rockabilly, garage rock and, in the soul field, ballads, funk, disco and early soul as well as prestigious northern soul tracks. That meant they could offer advances and releases on far more recordings than most other specialist reissue labels and benefit from that proportionate increase in access to the tapes.

Soul from the vaults

My first road trip for Ace in 1984 made me aware of the potential of master tapes. Ace was licensing from Columbia Special Products, a division of Columbia Records which specialized in getting third party licensing deals for their clients. Among the music they controlled were the Brunswick/Dakar and Scepter/Wand/Musicor catalogues. Top sound quality was an important aspect of Ace's success; they had invested in master tape copying in a big way, even developing their own system of digitally copying to Betamax tapes for best results and sound economy. The Modern vaults had already yielded great unissued and alternate takes on some of the blues artists, and Ace were planning a trip to Nashville where those tapes were stored. Coincidentally, the Scepter vaults were also in Nashville and an advance list of recordings held there, including mouth-watering titles on Maxine Brown, Chuck Jackson, Tommy Hunt, The Shirelles and others. I was taken along on the trip to help with tape research and song identification.

The tapes were stored in a huge warehouse on the outskirts of town and it was a pleasure to see what a master tape looked like for the first time. I pulled out anything of soul interest to be copied, and in the process we ended up with The Platters' version of the Johnny Hampton "monster" 'Not My Girl', Tommy Hunt's 'The Pretty Part Of You' and 'New Neighbourhood', Judy Clay's 'I Want You', and a slew of Chuck and Maxines. Biggest of them all was the third track recorded for Melba Moore's sole Musicor 45 in 1966, and unheard since its recording. It was a dynamic production of 'The Magic Touch', originally issued as a rock record by the Bobby Fuller Four. Musicor Records chose to go with the other two tracks on the 45. Its discovery came at the right time for the northern soul scene. In the early 80s forward-thinking members of the scene were desperate for "newies", having rejected the constant regurgitation of the same old classic "stompers". These Young Turks jumped on this new take of the classic soul dance formula. The success of 'Magic Touch' at the 100 Club, Stafford, and Leicester allnighters swept across the country once it was made available as the second 100 Club Anniversary commemorative 45 with a limited 400 copy pressing. It had an even bigger impact in Europe, where the DJs were not so hung up on spinning solely original 60s vinyl.

People had known about occasional, unissued soul tracks but these were usually in the form of one-off acetates, and often Motown-related. Nobody had realized the wealth of material that had been cut and abandoned. Philly producer Billy Jackson told me that when he was with Cameo-Parkway in the early 60s, they would record four songs in a three-hour session and cut acetates on them all. The label owner would then take them home and play them to his pre-teen daughter to ask which were best for release. They usually went with her first choices. It is not surprising that many of the unissued numbers appeal to our more mature tastes when they finally emerged.

On the same field trip, unissued Jackie Day, Johnny Copeland, Other Brothers, and Willie Gauff recordings were found among the Modern and Kent tapes and eventually released. It was the same in the Brunswick and Dakar vaults where previously unheard gems from Lavern Baker, Erma Franklin, Gene Chandler, and Cicero Blake were revealed. These finds enhanced Kent's reputation in the soul world and gave us excellent material to compile from. The label owners were happy that we had found enough material for further Chuck Jackson, Shirelles, and Maxine Brown LPs and many extra Various Artist compilation tracks in addition to singles. Apart from these sources, Ace were dealing with major companies like Universal, Sony, EMI, and Atlantic. Undoubtedly our accounting accuracy and established track record helped the licensing process. Occasionally the odd unissued tape came through, usually by accident, but it was hard to get a foothold into the tape vaults of such large and bureaucratic organizations.

In the CD era, newly accessed catalogues like Carnival, Swan and Excello augmented the repackaging and further researching of the Scepter, Wand, and Musicor sources. The mid-90s saw a departure from traditional re-releasing of old soul recordings when the GRC/Moonsong catalogue became available. Those tapes revealed a large amount of Sam Dees' demos of his own songs. Many had become hits for other artists; there were originals of those and some gems that had never been heard before. They were mainly Sam on piano, backed with bass and drums and, though relatively sparse, Sam, who was a revered artist and vocalist, gave his all.

When released the eventual three CDs' worth of material was received with acclaim and eventually would lead on to similar packages from George Jackson, Dan Greer and Dan Penn. In the late 90s Kent finally accessed a major label's vaults when Paul Williams, a sympathetic Englishman, was put in charge of reissues at RCA. Knowing there were tracks we could use in the UK, which meant nothing in the US, he invited me over to NYC for an A&R expedition. That visit led to exemplary unissued soul from the likes of Lorraine Chandler, Roy Hamilton, Willie Kendrick, Sharon Scott, and Johnny Nash among others: doing things the right way had paid off again.

The CD market

Nowadays soul collectors from all over Europe travel regularly to the US where they are augmented in the charity shops, flea markets and record fairs by a new breed of US aficionados. They are looking for rare discs or acetates and even master tapes that they can either reissue themselves or get a company to handle for them. Most of these music fans idolize the artists and music-makers and want their finds to be represented professionally and ethically. In the 1990s, two such UK enthusiasts, Ian "Gilly" Gilbert and Andy "Tats" Taylor, found a venerated Detroit producer called Dave Hamilton who reputedly had a studio basement in his house filled with hundreds of tapes. Dave was a brilliant guitarist (an original Motown Funk Brother), songwriter and producer, but a less successful businessman. Of his several hundred recordings, less than ten percent were released at the time. He was either running out of funds or failing to place the tracks with other labels. Gilly and Tats were friends of mine and knew that Ace/Kent had a good reputation for looking after the artists and producers. They set up the contact for us to purchase the songs and recordings from Dave's wife Alice. Sadly, Dave died mid-way through the deal. Though there was only estimated to be enough tracks for a couple of CDs at the time, the tapes proved to be so extensive that currently the equivalent of at least twelve CDs' worth of black music has been issued. Many of those tracks are now considered to be black music classics, though they were not heard until the compilations came out.

When CDs began to take off on the soul scene around 1990, it initially had the effect of splitting the market between CD and vinyl buyers. By this time several other companies had entered the marketplace and sales were down from the early 80s. It was not possible to issue compilations in both formats (if you paid your dues properly) and turn a profit for a year or two, until the majority had accepted the switch to the shiny disc. In this new era of CD technology, a new type of company emerged in the form of Goldmine Records. Run by three luminaries of the northern and rare soul scene, it can be seen as semi-legitimate in that it paid its publishing dues (publishing is better protected by law than performance) but was, I would argue, fast and loose with licensing. For instance, their first release in 1990 detailed the records' original labels but gave no mention of any licensors. By the time of their *Torch Story* release in 1995, they were confident enough to mix legitimate deals from companies like Nestshare who owned the Scepter/Wand material, Demon who controlled Invictus in the UK and even majors EMI and RCA, along with vaguely attributed licensing deals for individual tracks, of which some at least were unbeknown to those licensors. One of the licensors credited was Harem Records Inc, a company owned by Simon Soussan. Needless to say, Soussan did not own the rights, but by crediting such a company, Goldmine linked the track back to a US company. Later releases did not detail each of the individual labels in their licensing credits, and linked them back to legalistically-sounding entities like Toller Licensing, which would have needed to be responsible for "licensing" a large array of unconnected recordings from all over the USA; a highly unlikely scenario.

Their packages were usually low on information and accuracy. However, if a company like Goldmine Records failed to acquire the licences through the correct means, soul fans alike never got to hear the full stories of the recordings from the participants. It would require dubbing a master from old discs, where the sound would be noticeably inferior to proper mastering from the original tapes. Such CD releases did give record buyers who did not know, or did not care, how their music was sourced, a large selection of rare tracks they could not access themselves. Goldmine eventually folded in the mid-2000s but not before they had issued approximately 200 CDs and LPs. Any company that did not acquire proper licences could not pay royalties to the original artists, and the record buyers would inadvertently deprive their soul heroes of their rightful recompense.

Forty-five years of bootlegging: what next?

After forty-five years of bootlegs, many soul fans are resigned to their inevitability. With even what they thought of as legitimate companies being shown to operate unfairly, record and CD buyers have become cynical as to whether artists receive any remuneration from reissue labels. However, many companies do operate correctly and it is heartening to see that most of the newer companies who aim their releases at the rare soul scene seem to have got the message. Several have approached Ace to license masters we control.

Being able to approach your musical heroes in the knowledge that they will get a fair and, more than probably, the best deal from the company you are working for is very satisfying. The financial details of contracts are private, but I know that many acts have benefited from having their work released by legitimate companies and for some it has been a life-changing amount. For others, it has reaped very limited rewards, but often these lesser selling artists appreciate receiving proper accounting and a cheque. For many it represents the first money they have earned from their artistry. The interest and acclaim they have received, so many years after their work was forgotten about in their home country, validates the talent, effort and emotion they put into it at the time.

The Internet has made people more aware of the arguments against bootlegging but has also opened up a bigger market for its output. The vinyl resurgence of the past decade has seen more titles counterfeited and vinyl carver machines have made it possible for people to run off copies to order, for a relatively low price. The British Phonographic Industry (BPI) has been more proactive of late and there have been some successful prosecutions with more apparently in the pipeline. Some of the felons have even served time for their crimes. At the time of writing there are an estimated 45,000 confiscated bootlegs awaiting use as evidence against their manufacturers.

Current bootlegging practices include the selling of USB memory sticks with thousands of soul tracks ripped from legitimate CDs. Some recent vinyl bootlegs are extremely well-copied lookalike labels that can easily confuse an online buyer. Others are happy to pay well above the odds for illegal represses, building a great collection of "originals" for the uninitiated. One bootlegger offers to reproduce any single label through a vinyl carver – a one-off pressing, similar to an acetate but more believable as a record – creating tailor-made boots. There are even bootlegs of legitimate reissues (a practice that first started in the USA with newly released Motown hits in the 60s): ingenuity and gall of the highest order. Even the aforementioned Grapevine label has fallen foul of this practice. Similarly, some of the recently released Motown unissued tape finds have been put out on lookalike Motown labels. Understandably, these have brought a lot of attention on the culprits from legitimate collectors and reputedly the BPI.

The relaxing of the copyright laws concerning music reproduction in the EEC in recent years meant that recordings issued over fifty years ago went out of copyright, and anybody could therefore reproduce them in any format as long as the publishing was paid; this remained protected by law. That relaxing in the legal protection of recordings was closed in 2013, meaning that only records released before 1 January 1963 can be reproduced without paying royalties. Many companies sprang up to take advantage of this window of opportunity. Not only were their products free from paying musical royalties, there was no legal discussion or paperwork to be undertaken. It severely affected the licensing and re-releasing of music from this era by companies such as Ace who do not recognize the no-royalty period, continuing to pay licensors and artists royalties. In the case of Kent Records, with soul fans looking back to the black music roots of the soul sound, OOC (out of copyright) companies can manufacture these CDs much cheaper by eschewing royalties. The same is true of compilations for the R&B scene, some of which are spin-offs of the mod and northern scenes which have accepted and appreciated recordings of the late 50s and early 60s on their DJs' playlists.

Ace's access to original tapes, by virtue of being a properly run company, keeps them ahead of the game in this field too. Unreleased recordings from before 1963 do not go out of copyright until fifty years after their first issue; it is only the ones that were issued before 1963 that are royalty free in Europe. Ace has been able to present CDs of previously unheard 1950s and early 60s recordings from acts of the calibre of BB King, Wynonie Harris, Etta James, and Jackie Wilson that, though recorded before 1963, do not go out of copyright until 50 years after the date they were first issued for commercial sale. Improved sound from the master tapes is also a big advantage in keeping these sales buoyant. Though some artists and record makers are dying as the record business gets older, they frequently leave families who benefit from their work. Most weeks I am contacting an artist, producer, or their relatives with a view to a new licence, or arranging for an account to be switched to the estate should they die.

Bootlegging is an appropriate term for a practice that echoes the gangsters of the depression who were "only supplying what the people wanted". With nearly fifty years of research and education within the soul-loving community, one would have hoped it would have withered away. That would only happen if collectors stopped buying bootlegs, but there is little sign of that; it is sadly ingrained within the scene. It is heartening, though, that younger music fans, who will eventually take the music's appreciation forward, seem to have got the message.

About the author

Ady Croasdell is a CD compiler and researcher for the Kent label, part of Ace Records, and has written more than 200 booklets tracing the musical history of particular record labels, artists, producers, or genres. Having been involved in the northern and rare soul scene since 1969, Ady promotes the longest running northern soul events, allnighters at London's 100 Club and the Cleethorpes Northern & Rare Soul Weekender.

6 (Re)Marking Old Records, Making New Meaning:

Debating the Questionable Home of Northern Soul

Nicola Watchman Smith

Introduction

> The devotees of Northern Soul were carrying on a long-established tradition whereby British music fans have embraced American black music often far more enthusiastically than the home base (Shapiro 2003: 248).

> Northern Soul need only exist if you want it to. Putting on the Soul. The musicians who make the recordings might as well be on another planet. They probably are by now (Walters 1975: 455).

Northern soul records originate from a place and time separate from the scene in which they are enjoyed. The fact that the scene (of the 1970s, in particular) situates itself firmly within a north of England locality while the music originated from across the Atlantic – and (often) produced a decade earlier – poses a variety of questions, most notably in relation to the tensions and significance created by placing an adopted music into, what can be considered, an alien locality. Of interest within this chapter are the issues surrounding the direct adoption of original music (i.e. not tailor-mades[1] or records that found the northern soul scene via the reissue market), raising questions concerning the implication that local musicianship is rejected in favour of what could be deemed *alien authenticity*. Soul fans choosing records from a locality distinct from their own is significant: the resultant scene is not simply homage to the alien locality (i.e. US culture, reproduced at distance) but it is distinctly British. Northern soul is arguably unique in its primary *dislocation*, in both the *dislodging* of music from its place of production and in the *disturbance* of the oft-cited academic argument that location and sound are intrinsically linked. This dislocation is not only relevant in a scholarly sense in its request for reconsideration of theories of musical geography, but it is vastly relevant to northern soul fans; the soulies. The relocating of (northern) soul vinyl records signals a fracturing of the soul music genre. The breakaway fracture of northern soul is (re)built into a youth culture in its own right, possessing little of the infrastructure of the original; UK-based soulies consider themselves the architectures of this new build.

The fact that North American soul music became labelled as a reflection of the tastes of northern English youths complicates the notion of authenticity, ownership, and locality as an origin of identity. This chapter therefore discusses the role of American soul music in the synthesis of (an initially) northern English cultural identity and unpicks the significance of the separation between the USA home of soul music and the UK locality in which this music is enjoyed.

Before we begin, it is worth stating that producing any account of northern soul is not a simple process of telling *the* story of the scene. There are many stories and just as many variants of each of these stories; assumed and retold by soulies and subsequent media in its numerous forms, as Raine and Wall illustrate in Chapter 8. As such, it feels appropriate to add a caveat (perhaps several) to this chapter to both contextualize what I am presenting here but also to scratch that academic itch to demonstrate that I am aware of the exceptions that sit beyond the rules depicted here. For instance, I have discussed in my earlier work (Smith 2006, 2009a, 2009b, 2012) how the scene has remained active from inception to today and, as a condition of this longevity, scene participant demographics have varied across its lifespan (beyond the UK, beyond youth). Yet the context for this chapter is the formative years of northern soul (late 1960s to mid-1970s) when it was very much a youth culture.

In fact, I use "shorthand" for many of the specifics of northern soul. Take the music, for example: I suggest here that the music is *rare, original, commercially unsuccessful 1960s black American soul music*. Every one of these adjectives – and I include "soul" within this – can be contested, as can similar shorthand for the British scene as *white, working-class and from 1970s northern England*. This shorthand is a writing device for the purpose of efficiency but also acknowledgement of scene participant musical preferences and an allowance for the musical "trial and error" of an organic youth culture. Other examples of shorthand (or "symbolic indicators", if you prefer) that I employ include: using Wigan[2] to signify the UK scene; Detroit to signify the USA musical home of soul; Motown to signify chart successful US soul music;[3] and northern soul to encompass the northern and rare soul scenes. With this in mind, let me begin.

The questionable home of northern soul

In order to explore the relevance of the original locality of the music upon the UK-based scene, I ask what impact does the USA-based musical production of this music have on the British northern soul scene? The argument presented here differs from previous academic considerations of northern soul, which draw a link between Wigan and Detroit as a result of cultural empathy or because of shared industrialized social experience (Hollows and Milestone 1998; Browne 2006). The northern soul scene has a distinct identity. This identity was (perhaps still is) predominantly read as a working-class youth identity, and this construction of a particular type and era of northern soul fandom is relevant. I aim to show that the desire for a distinct (youth) identity is the reason for the soulies' selection of rare and obscure (and thus exclusive) American records, not an empathetic socio-economic alliance with American Rust Belt cities, as is suggested within existing literature on northern soul.

Kev Roberts' 2003 book, *The Northern Soul Top 500, Special Edition* lists the author's pick of five hundred pivotal northern soul records. By taking note of the label locality of the records within the "Top 500", it is clear that high numbers of record labels were located within Detroit, Chicago, Philadelphia, and New York. Such localities, I will argue, are not direct factors in the choice of music by northern soul participants. Instead, soulies wanted music that was unknown in the mainstream, uncommon in terms of chart presence and, subsequently, a music format upon which they could stamp their own identity. Rare, obscure, commercially unsuccessful American black soul records – those often ignored by the public and the music industry[4] – offered soulies all of these desired components. The records from Detroit, Philadelphia, Chicago, and New York were far enough removed from Wigan, Stoke on Trent, Cleethorpes, or Blackpool (or any place the northern soul scene was situated) to appeal to soulies. The records were obscure enough to avoid mainstream attention and music industry presence in the UK, at least until the 1970s heyday. They were also rare enough to intrigue northern youths who deemed these records worthy of adoption. Importantly, it was not merely a case of rarity; these records could be re-contextualized as a UK scene because they were not too alien a music form to deny understanding nor so removed from UK travel networks to restrict the purchasing of such vinyl. These songs made sense to, and elicited an impassioned response from, UK audiences. As Joe Street notes in Chapter 7, and as Iain Chambers (1985) stated in relation to the appeal of the USA for 1970s working-class youths (from the north of England), there is a tradition of UK engagement with black America; northern soul is a (unique) part of this.

Keith Negus (1996) suggested that the pushing of American records onto another country's culture or market could be considered a form of cultural imperialism. However, the fact that the movement of American soul records into the British northern soul scene was a largely covert, organic pursuit by British soul fans, and therefore not (initially) driven by the music industry, suggests something other than cultural imperialism. It, in fact, goes further than this, with the resultant northern soul scene positioned as British. As one soulie commented on a YouTube video of northern soul dancing: "This is what makes me proud to be British. Our fantastic music culture, even though the tracks are American, the movement was ours".[5]

This transplanting of music might be considered an attempt to strip black cultural heritage from this music, by creating a predominantly white subcultural practice. This is not how soulies interpret the initial intent of the scene, however.[6] Instead, for soulies, northern soul was one example of the appreciation of black American music; a process which begins with Dave Godin's *Tamla Motown Appreciation Society* (TMAS). This appreciation highlighted a batch of 7-inch vinyl soul records that had otherwise been ignored or forgotten. From this obscure forgotten music and the niche interest it generated, an identity was formed in peripheral UK towns. Northern soul fans expressed a level of interest in this music that had not been expressed by USA audiences. For soulies, this unique engagement with forgotten records set the northern soul scene's taste and practices beyond those of mainstream music fans and, significantly, beyond the recognition of the intended USA audiences. Such distinction provided the northern soul scene with the potential for unique participant cultural identities.

That northern soul borrows from black America is not unexpected. Chambers (1985) shows that popular dance for white youth is typically borrowed from black music culture. Paul Gilroy's recognition that dancing "is regularly identified as one of the most reliably and authentically African elements in the black vernacular" (1997: 21) situates northern soul – as a dance culture – as borrowing from black cultural practices. Andy Bennett (2000) positions such appropriation "a long established tradition" for northern English youth.

The appropriation of black music within a UK working-class scene is clearly not uncommon. In the case of northern soul, however, the scene relies on the direct acquisition of recorded music from an unknowing (perhaps uninterested) source. The scene thus has to construct its own ideas of how to consume this borrowed music, thus emphasizing the fact that musical appropriation is a route to socio-cultural identity formation. This creates an interesting dynamic, one hinged on celebratory respect towards the home of the music and the apparently paradoxical intention to create something unique from this borrowed music. It is true that, over time, the music has become synonymous with an aspect of British culture. As such, to the audiences that acknowledge the music (soulies or otherwise) and the media that document the use of this music, the owners are considered to be UK soulies who have the vinyl records in their possession. The soulies are considered the protagonists in this scene to the extent that the industry looked to soulies for guidance. As Tim Brown (2001) suggests, northern soul dictated Motown's choice of reissues (at least, that was until supplies of "newies" ran dry. Then Motown held the reins in terms of dictating which previously unissued material they would release from their vaults). Hollows and Milestone (1998) remedy the implication that the UK took US culture without asking, by suggesting that there is an imaginary identification with the USA. However, while I agree there is a connection with, or appreciation for, North American culture, I question whether this is self-reflective identification.[7] The choice in records, I argue, is not so much an indication of a shared transatlantic empathy but instead UK soul fans desiring an association with *something beyond* their locale and using distant cultural artefacts (vinyl records, deemed unwanted) as a vehicle to achieve this. It is not about the USA *per se*, but about distance.

Creating distance

When the northern soul label was coined, publicized, and adopted by those on the scene, this signalled the birth of a distinct soul music subgenre and a unique youth culture. Soulies had removed themselves from commercial sounds, rejected popular soul and R'n'B (as popularized by the Beatles and others) and had their own identity, as desired. This is evident in the unique dance styles, dress code and the formulation of "sacred" venues. Therefore, while America was a focus that led to an initial interest in such music, soulies generated their own subgenre with a specific musical blueprint and therefore no longer considered Detroit the home of this music. The home became Manchester, later Stoke on Trent, Blackpool, and Wigan, and it was held within the DJ boxes of the local northern soul record collectors not with the American studios, artists or indeed with American soul audiences. The significance of the source became less relevant when the scene was cemented as belonging to northern England.[8]

Soulies wished to distance themselves from *all* mainstream music. This, as we know, was translated into the search for rare/obscure soul. Selecting commercially unsuccessful songs suggests northern soul was not necessarily about expressions of taste, but more about an expression of distinction. Prioritization of musical rarity and obscurity was therefore about creating distance. This was, first, distance from the mainstream, achieved by avoiding well-known chart successful soul. Second, distance from London or "the national" as Hollows and Milestone (1998) suggest. Third, as linked to both of the above, distance from pre-existing UK scenes (Merseybeat for example), thus meaning soulies did not have to grapple with pre-existing identities attached to such scenes. Ultimately, distance was achieved by selecting records from across the Atlantic, and then, in response to the UK mainstreaming of R'n'B and soul sounds (post-Beatles, post-Mod and post-Motortown Revue), looking for something rarer still. While I agree with Hollows and Milestone that northern soul bypassed and rejected the national (1998: 91), cities such as Detroit were places distant from northern English towns. Therefore, the records originating in Detroit did not represent a connection "between the urban American North and the urban English North" (p. 92) but they were instead representations of *distance*; far-removed from the mundane. The appeal for soulies was novelty, exoticism, and a break from the norm that America symbolized.

The idea of soulies desiring a relationship with the USA is prevalent yet the appreciation for American music is not an obvious indicator of an allegiance to the USA by soul fans. Soulies were concerned with developing notions of self and original scene practice rather than politicized solidarity as Godin's TMAS seemed to embody. Moreover, a reading of the scene suggests that soulies were not intentionally ignoring or eradicating the American heritage of the music. From the fans' perspective, this was discarded music, something that Browne (2006) – an American himself – recognizes when he terms the vinyl records that became northern soul, "throw away" cultural artefacts.

Hollows and Milestone (1998) grapple with the problem that identifications with America appear contradictory. They situate the northern soul aspirations for American records as contradictory because the "pop cultural myth" contrasts with the northern scene's appreciation for rarity and the niche. Hollows and Milestone state that the representation of "true place", as represented via the discs, contradicts the cultural myth of America (not a Real America, but the America of the escapist dream). This is an interesting notion, something I see mirrored in the contradictory musicological reading of Motown music as discussed below. However, I suggest that the reality of the USA and the myth of the American Dream are less relevant when we recognize that soulies do not know the former, only the latter. As such, they are one and the same: a distant unknown place. Whether real or imagined, America equates to the same thing for a soulie – something other than their peripheral UK town. This further problematizes the suggestion of transatlantic empathy.

Transatlantic empathy?

Milestone positions the choice of American music as intrinsically tied with big city representations of industrial living, stating,

> it is no coincidence that black soul music, which emerged from the huge US cities of Detroit and Chicago, should be used for this purpose – a music which not only came from the city (and was industrially produced), but whose lyrics also constantly referred to the experience of living in the city (1997: 137).

Here Milestone is inferring that this music is the music of choice for soulies because of the similar economic climates of the mid-twentieth-century industrial United States and the industrial north of England, thus implying an empathetic allegiance to the industrial cities in America via this music. Youth cultural motivations would be, in this scenario, driven by considerations of economics. As such, any connection between the UK and the USA is impacted by the (lack of) knowledge soulies possess about the USA (in terms of audience reception). Later, soulies would possess a great wealth of knowledge about the recorded music they fervently collect but here the concern centres upon the amount of information the soulies had of places like Detroit during the era in which northern soul was conceived (late 1960s/early 1970s). We should question whether soulies knew enough of Detroit's economic status to realize an empathetic connection.

There is a connection between the industrial living standards of the mid-twentieth century in both Wigan and Detroit. We see this connection now – with access to socio-economic data and with hindsight – but the 1960s/1970s soulies arguably would not have done. If it is debatable whether soulies were aware of the socio-economic status of Detroit, it follows therefore, that it is unlikely that soulies were in a position to compare the economic status of Detroit with their experiences and social situation. When my interviewees were asked what they knew of Detroit, they all identified Detroit as the home of Motown and a few (three) had visited Detroit (or its surrounding areas) for holidays or business. Beyond this, interviewees struggled to give further details. When asked if they knew of Detroit as connected to the music played on the scene when they first became interested in northern soul, most replied that they did not. The three interviewees who had travelled to Detroit had all done so recently (rather than at the time of their early engagement with the scene). This presents a hurdle to the notion of participant self-reflective identification linking the place of the scene and of place of music production.

If soulies did not know of Detroit directly then perhaps they knew of Detroit via possessing knowledge of the records played on the scene. However, many of the soulies I interviewed suggested that they had known very little about the records they danced to in the 1960s and 1970s. A minority (five) claimed that they had known the labels the records were on, and even fewer (two) claimed to have known the town or city from which the label came. This is not surprising given that northern soul saw the introduction of vinyl cover-ups. Therefore, soulies would not have had access to basic information such as song title or artist, far less the record label. Achieving an empathetic connection to the USA can thus be considered restricted because soulies did not know the specifics of the location of records, nor did they know of Detroit personally during the early scene. Achieving empathy via connection with the artists singing the songs was also severely diminished as many artists were unknown on the UK scene, as shall be explained below. In sum, the less soulies knew of the records, the less likely it was that an understanding of the socio-economic setting of the records could be read and empathy shared.[9]

Does music code for place?

Detroit, and the USA, does hold weight in terms of northern soul's ideas of the authentic because of its association with Motown, and soul music, respectively. That said, the popularity of records can be explained in terms of the appeal of rarity and a specific soul music variant, not because of the identity of a place. Is place therefore merely coincidence in the case of northern soul?

Connell and Gibson state that Motown is an example of a "wider geographical region in which musical production and consumption occur" (2003: 90), meaning it clearly has an articulation of place through consumption, but can the music be read for these articulations? The big question therefore is whether industrial Detroit is coded for in the music: does Motown code for Detroit? The records clearly code for America, as soul music, but whether there is a regional identification that could allow for interregional alliance is still questionable, especially when we bear in mind that Berry Gordy intended to produce the Sound of Young America not the sound of Detroit, via Motown Records. Perry and Glinert stated,

> As rock myth has it, the growth of the Motown sound has explicitly related to the industrial focus of the city [... Holland-Dozier-Holland] developed a rhythm based on the clattering mechanical beat of Detroit's assembly lines [...] and created rudimentary sound effects with chains, hammers, and planks of wood (1996: 191).

In contrast, Connell and Gibson note, Motown was "always a commercial venture: Motown artists were expected to conform to standards of deportment, performance (including rehearsed dance moves) and common marketable sound" (2003: 99). Moreover, this sound is "a combination of sweet vocals, dramatic themes of love and loss and exuberant arrangements" (p. 99). A comparison of Connell and Gibson's and Perry and Glinert's readings of Motown demonstrates the contradictory sentiments of the Motown sound. The assumption that industrial sounds are represented in Motown – the clatter of machinery and the pounding of hammers – do not echo Gordy's intentions to create a polished, smooth, and highly marketable product. It might parallel the techniques of production (Fordist, in nature) but the resultant sound is sweet and exuberant, according to Connell and Gibson. Furthermore, the myth of the machinery-inspired production techniques of Holland-Dozier-

Holland suggests a level of audience codal incompetence (Tagg 2012) if we are to assume that audiences on either side of the Atlantic found escape from their industrial everyday life via Motown songs. It is clear that the sentiments of the music have proved difficult to pin down by academics and authors and, as such, it is problematic to suggest that all within the northern soul scene will read Motown-esque records in any one manner. Therefore, we cannot conclude that the music successfully and undoubtedly presents the experience and actuality of life within industrial Detroit. It is equally as problematic to assume that an audience would want to hear the industrialized character of Detroit in this music, if we are to recognize that the (initial) northern soul participants stem(med) from working-class, industrialized, peripheral towns.

It could be the case that soulies knew of Detroit via Motown performances. There was opportunity for this during the Motortown Revue. Yet soulies did not witness Detroit *audiences* reacting and interacting with Motown music. Therefore, the soulie was not influenced by face-to-face familiarity with local Detroit's response to Motown. If soulies were to gather notes on consumption practices (and therefore notes on Detroit) via the Motortown Revue, then, soulies had to rely on the displays presented to them by the performing artists.

The Motortown Revue used glitzy and glamorous costumes. The choreography was smooth and organized. The artists were polished professionals thanks to Gordy's insistence on finishing school-style lessons (Brown 2001). The Motown artists looked and acted every part stars. This is a far cry from real-life 1960s Detroit. It follows, therefore, that while soulies would have seen Motown as representing an alluring form of stardom around which to build an escapist fantasy, they would not see the reality of Detroit. Remember, Gordy, pre-1971, was trying to appeal to mass America. It could be argued, therefore, that Motown was not intending to be overtly black, overtly working-class, nor overtly Detroit. When soul fans saw the glamour of the Motown stars they were seeing black artists being granted Hollywood-esque status. This display of success for a socially marginalized group could arguably be seen as a reason why soulies were drawn to Motown sounds. Soulies arguably saw potential, possibility, and hope when they saw the glamour of Motown. This supports my positioning that soul music was initially appealing to British working-class youths because it represented something different and distant from the north of England. It is not a case of industrialized connections between Wigan and Detroit, but between working-class kids and a distant locality to fuel fantasy.

The glamour of Motown, with all of its commercial success, would have been an initial attraction to the general soul fan. However, northern soul took the records that *sounded* like Motown[10] but the important difference was that the records chosen by soulies were those that had not gained commercial success (originally). This adds an interesting dimension to the relationship soulies have with the rare/obscure sounds of American black soul music, because when soulies retrieved these records and, thus, rescued them from obscurity, the soulies made successes of forgotten artists and their songs.[11] Therefore, the glamour of the commercially successful strand of Motown is not applicable to the songs chosen within northern soul. As such, soulies are seeing tried-but-*failed* attempts at making it out of the margins, rather than the hope and possibility recognized in acts like the Supremes, for example. Therefore, the suggestion that soulies chose records for inclusion on the northern scene because of a desire to witness escape from working-class lifestyles is limited. Yet what we may have is a representation, via commercial failure, of the difficulty of escaping the confines of life on the margin. It was the soulies who retrieved these records and subsequently made these records popular. It was therefore soulies who gave the artists and their songs the popularity that the industry failed to grant. Subsequently, the choice of northern soul records should be considered as more than an understanding of working-class limitations. The soulie is positioned, via the roles of retriever and tastemaker, as *the reason* that a record has become loved by many people and the reason an artist has a career, however belated. By doing what the label originally failed to do, the soulie is responsible for creating the lasting relevance of a (northern soul) record.

It is therefore not the case that soulies sit in awe of an artist, nor, incidentally, of North America as the creator of this sound, because North America (from the soulies' perspective) failed to recognize the potential of these records. The façade of fame and glamour exhibited by successful Motown acts does not affect the manner in which soulies read a northern soul record because fame and glamour do not apply to many northern soul artists as they failed to be successful originally. Scene-specific status and fame were granted to the collector, northern soul DJ or vinyl retriever as it was these tastemakers who were responsible for giving vinyl records their on-scene (and later more mainstream) popularity. The commanding position gained by soulies eradicates the potential for a rare soul record to indicate the same hope, via glamour, as commercially successful Motown records. This also means that any sentiments of marginalized struggle evident in the northern soul story are judged by soulies (from their heightened position as the grantor of success) to be of muted relevance. The northern soul record retriever grants success to numerous soul artists so has little reason to mull over the limitations of working-class capacities, in a cultural sense at least. Soulies do not need music to demonstrate these ideas when they are dispelling such ideas through their participation on the northern scene as a retriever of records. This, therefore, dilutes a record's potential to represent marginalized lifestyles and with it further dispels the possibility of an empathetic relationship between soulies and Detroit.

Perhaps soulies build associations, and thus empathetic connections, with black American soul music via song lyrics? Hollows and Milestone (1998) and Stuart Cosgrove (1982) suggest that songs such as Eloise Law's 'Love Factory' illustrate industrial representations. Yet Roberts (2003) shows that the dominant theme within northern soul songs is that of love. Moreover, soulies potentially associate empathetically with commonly understood love songs, but this is not soulies empathizing with the supposed pain of actual singers. Soulies are simply becoming lost in the compelling story of love and loss. It could be argued that this is because soulies know very little about the artist and, therefore, the potential to relate to the artist as an individual from a similar economic background is limited. I am dispelling the idea of empathy between performer and audience on the grounds that the *artist is absent* in northern soul. What we have is soulies becoming engrossed in the emotion of a song and using this as a vehicle for indulgence in something other than the concerns of the everyday.

The absent artist

The separation between, first, commercial success and northern soul and, second, the home of the music and the home of the scene creates a situation in which the *artist is absent*. The fans on the scene in their various guises (collector, DJ, promoter, dancer, record dealer) consider records to be of greater relevance than live performance. Adulation is expressed for the vinyl before it is expressed for a performing artist. In fact, there is a distinct lack of interest shown for the *current* careers of the artists noted by the scene. Most fans will know more of a record, a record label, or a soulie who dances competently than they will of the biography of a particular soul singer. Soulies know the back catalogue of a particular artist and this level of knowledge will exceed what they know about the artist themselves.

The artist is thus, I argue, absent in northern soul because soulies do not celebrate him or her as they do the vinyl disc. Live performance is secondary to the recorded format. When live performance does occur, soulies expect to hear northern soul songs in the live repertoire, showing little interest in the other (i.e. non-northern soul) songs recorded by that artist. A case in point here is a Dean Parrish live performance at the Blackpool Boardwalk in December 2004. The attendees only danced to Parrish's known northern soul songs (of which there are three); his Wigan classic 'I'm On My Way'[12] was played twice. Dancers danced to this song but did so as if Parrish were not in the building; there was no adulation towards the stage. In fact, at one point Parrish stepped off the stage and walked amongst the dancers. The dancing crowd did not alter their step; they continued to perform as if the original recording of the song was being played. The crowd wanted the songs they favoured and in the format that they knew. Parrish, as well as all other live acts on the scene, had very little scope for artistry, embellishment, or creativity when performing northern songs live.

Furthermore, as noted above, many soulies do not know of the artists because they know very little about the rare/obscure records that are played on the scene. The covering-up of records further muddied the connection soulies might have made with an artist. The secrecy of the songs favoured on the northern scene was prevalent to such an extent that even some artists were/are unaware that they are "famous" on the northern soul scene (Winstanley and Nowell 2000). Soulies frequently sing the lyrics aloud to prompt the singer, who has most often been flown in from the USA to take part in a northern soul weekender event, by singing a specific northern soul song (not merely any song from their back catalogue). Often the singer will not remember having ever cut the record (Nowell 2001) and therefore soulies may know more about the record than the actual artist does. Thus, the artist is absent in terms of influence because the power lies with the knowing soulie and not with the artist.

Some soulies are interested in the biographies of artists but this occurs in a manner akin to the search for vinyl records. The information is sought to add context to a vinyl collection and to embellish connoisseurship, not initially out of adulation towards an artist. The possibility of the northern soul artist being considered "a star" is tainted by the fact that soulies played a hand in the resurrection of many artists' careers and, thus, it is known that the artist's original attempt at fame failed. Therefore, unlike the successful Motown acts, a large proportion of those singing northern soul songs do not possess the glamour that comes with, what Nicholas Abercrombie and Brian Longhurst (1998) would describe as, the air of the unobtainable that fan adulation is informed by.

This begs the question, is there an active artist – present, not absent – in northern soul? Most recorded music scenes place the DJ in the role of the artist (or, at least, as the musical *auteur*). As Tony Langlois states, the DJ is "simultaneously the performer, marketer and composer of the music" (1992: 229). This is not the case in northern soul, in which an authenticity discourse dictates that the DJ cannot alter the original arrangement of the music. Records are not mixed but kept true to the original. The northern soul DJ is therefore not an artist, nor *auteur*; he (and it is usually a he) is simply the vehicle by which audiences hear records. That said, however, the DJ is granted scene-relevant status based on the records in his possession, his knowledge of the records he plays, and knowledge of the scene as indicated by the records he chooses to purchase. Deejaying in northern soul is thus about possession (of records, of knowledge and of status) rather than proficiency within the art of deejaying. When playing a record, the northern soul DJ does not possess the opportunity to express personal sentiments equal to a live performance, but is given the opportunity, through record selection and by talking to the participants between records, to express self in terms of his personality and his scene knowledge.

Musical reimagining: authenticity and the act of (re)marking

Returning to the wider concept of the interplay between geography and authenticity within northern soul, the separation of the location of music and cultural (symbolic) ownership of that music is both interesting and loaded. What is happening here, namely the application of new meaning to existing cultural artefacts, is a process of reimaging musical identity without distorting the original artefact nor removing the original link to the place of production (in this case, the USA).

The connections between identity, locality and the scene in its original guise are clear. It is assumed that ideas of fandom will be maintained throughout the lifespan of the northern scene because the records, if protected by collectors and DJs, will continue to exist in an unchanged format. The transition of northern soul records, both in terms of geography and definition, is complex when we consider the expected modes and displays of popular music-related authenticity. As food for thought, Roy Shuker notes that:

> Authenticity assumes that the producers of music texts undertook the "creative" work themselves; that there is an element of originality or creativity present, along with connotations of seriousness, sincerity, and uniqueness; and that while the input of others is recognized, it is the musicians' role which is regarded as pivotal. [... authenticity is also considered as] a series of oppositions: mainstream versus independent; pop versus rock; and commercialism versus creativity, or art versus commerce (2017: 23–24).

It is thus clear that the music consumed on the northern scene does not possess *obvious* authenticity. The dichotomies of mainstream versus independent; pop versus rock; commercialism versus creativity, or art versus commerce would situate northern soul music *in its original context* as inauthentic (mainstream, commercial, pop soul). It should possess none of the creativity, originality or sincerity of which authentic popular music is expected to embody. Yet, the specific variants of scene consumption practices, the re-contextualization of music and the aura of the vinyl record (Benjamin 1936) alter this.

Northern soul *does* possess discourses of authenticity because of the source of the music (the authenticity of the USA as the home of soul music) and, somewhat paradoxically, authenticity is evident in the modes of consuming this music. This is paradoxical because the authenticity derived from locality is relevant only to the vinyl artefact. Scene authenticity is thus UK-bound and devised by the scene tastemakers. In other words, northern scene authenticity is generated without approval, or *direct* input, from the home of the adopted soul music. The re-contextualization of the music (from the USA to the UK) means that the songs are no longer merely American soul but they are now *northern soul*. This enables the scene to conjure elements of the authentic around what was, originally, an inauthentic pop product.

As we have heard, northern soul adopts forgotten/commercially unsuccessful records from American cities and re-contextualizes these vinyl artefacts in northern England. This process of adoption, re-contextualization, and alteration of cultural significance I call (re)marking. (Re)marking can occur if, firstly, the records were unreleased or unsuccessful and therefore unknown or forgotten in their original context and, secondly, if the records were geographically relocated and consumed in a unique and culturally distinct manner (i.e. distinct from intention). This allows for the records to be (re)marked as belonging to the scene locality, not the production locality.

The term (re)marking, with parentheses, indicates that meaning is applied to recorded music by an audience *other than the anticipated audience*. Reception of the music, rather than intention, is clearly the issue here.[13] John Fiske (1989) proposed that cultural texts only gain meaning when used by audiences, through circulation and appropriation. This is relevant to the concept of (re)marking in that the potential to place a new and a distinct significance on music which had a strong original identification was possible because initial release of this music (or lack of) did not gain widely acknowledged success. The lack of widespread involvement of these records in American culture meant that British youths could claim the records via unique modes of scene-based consumption. These records have subsequently become synonymous with northern England, not (merely) North America.

Northern soul embodies the cultural specifics of the scene above those of the industry. The scene consciously opts to maintain authenticity by selecting records from minor record labels or subsidiaries and, perhaps more than any other scene, by selecting the commercially unsuccessful records as the musical foundation of the scene. The rarity, exclusivity, and obscurity of such records aids claims of authenticity: the records are largely unheard of except on the scene. Connell and Gibson allude to this when they suggest that, "In the 'northern soul' scenes ... particular credibility is attached to music that has 'come a long way' to the final consumer" (2003: 107). By choosing records from America but the records rejected by Americans, soulies are maintaining authenticity via the selection of sounds yet simultaneously assuming a form of one-upmanship over the unknowing originators. This suggested "knowing" takes northern soul adoption of the American sound beyond a celebration of American consumerism. As the myth would have it, northern soul sees something that mass America missed. They saved records from extinction by taking these records out of America. With a nod to, but a movement beyond, America, the northern soul scene is authenticated and original.

The authentic in relation to classification of suitable northern soul records relies, predictably, upon clear ideas of what the inauthentic is, in terms of scene-relevant discourses. For example, blue-eyed soul is not favoured and nor are records made after a certain date (for some only pre-1964 will do, for others it is okay if the record is simply a sixties record). Chart success might mar a record's authenticity, as might a non-American record label or artist. The grey areas touched upon here mean that there is scope for particular members to claim distinct levels of connoisseurship. Blue-eyed soul, British soul and post-1960s records are played on the (wider) scene but they are in the minority, and they are guaranteed to generate discord between fans. Authenticity is a subjective notion strengthened – but not confirmed – by majority agreement.

The construction of the authentic northern soul identity, and, as such, the fan search for connoisseurship, knowledge and status are formulated, in part, by the (re)marking of 7-inch 45rpm rare soul vinyl records. Modes of (re)marking include the application of a blueprint for the northern soul sound and, subsequently, the scene-relevant canonization of certain record labels, records and eras of production. Once tastemakers established the blueprint for northern soul, all soulies had a platform from which to perform scene-based status and to exhibit scene-relevant knowledge. This recorded music scene *creates* authenticity via the production of rituals of musical selection and the (re)defining of a musical (sub)genre.

DJ-led culture is problematic when we consider the originality versus imitation aspect of authenticity. If northern soul were a live music scene, then the use of the Motown sound would be an imitation of black American soul; it would be situated outside of its original context and, thus, be an inauthentic (retro) re-creation. Northern soul, however, does not favour the production of new music tailored to the scene but instead relies on the actual sound of sixties American soul. This creates a platform from which soulies can generate original cultural practice and, via that practice, weave definitions of authenticity in acknowledgement of the fact that the music is original.

The playing of recorded music is preferred over live performance on the northern scene. That said, artists do sometimes perform live, as described above. When they do, it is expected that the songs remain true to the recorded version. There is therefore no room for improvisation or musical adaptation. This lack of expression and subsequent restricted form of performance can be interpreted as prioritization of the vinyl record. Thus, in the case of northern soul, where the vinyl record is granted an aura, a strict re-creation of the recorded version of a song is deemed more authentic than if the artist were to perform a new arrangement of the song. The artist, holding to such requirements, does not have the scope to convey extra sentiment to the audience in a personal exhibition of artistry. The authenticity of the vinyl record is maintained and displayed within the live performance. This contradicts the assumption that live music is the authentic expression, while the recorded format is an attempt to capture – crudely and unsuccessfully – that authentic moment. Interestingly, live music is commonly considered more authentic than recorded music because the former is deemed to be the "one-off". For northern soul, the likelihood of an artist performing a song is often greater than finding an original copy of a rare vinyl record. Thus the "one-off" on the northern scene is predominantly the recorded format.

Somewhat paradoxically, therefore, authenticity in northern soul is reliant upon recorded music: a format commonly deemed to be inauthentic. When UK northern soul aficionados or the wider music industry try to produce new "correct sounding" soul records for the scene, the scene questions the suitability of such tailor-mades. Tailor-mades lack authenticity because part of the process of a record being defined as northern soul is the search and retrieval of pre-existing material. The vinyl is identified based on ideas of suitability, criteria that are defined and understood by soulies. This is not about producing music (musicianship) but about knowing music (connoisseurship).

Concluding comments

The authenticity evident in northern soul differs from wider understandings of musical fan representations of the authentic. Northern soul music *in its original context* was arguably inauthentic due to being a mainstream commercial pop soul sound. However, the re-contextualization of the music, the absence of the artist, and the (re)marking of the record as synonymous with the British scene, have meant that this same music can be considered as embodying authentic elements. The participants who can identify these elements are, in turn, granted scene membership.

Via the (re)marking of American records, northern soul takes an alien music and re-houses it in the locale of the fan. Soulies then build traditions, codes of identity, status, knowledge, and rituals around these adopted records. The (sub)genre classification of the music changed, *without the sound altering*, because of the emergence of a scene and the identity created within it. The soulies – as connoisseur, retriever and tastemaker – are elevated from a basic level of fandom to the active originator of a soul music subgenre, therefore challenging the concept of locality as a musical indicator within popular music.

As the definition of northern soul is set from within, and this definition has altered over the six decades of the scene, there is some disagreement among northern soul fans as to what the authentic northern soul sound, vinyl record, and form of membership should be. This debate has produced conflicting performances of northern soul fandom. However, this has allowed fans to claim and perform variants of authentic northern soul expression. The result is pockets of soulies performing *their* most authentic variant of northern soul, yet, in each case, the authentic is created via the consumption of the 7-inch 45rpm vinyl record.

About the author

Nicola Watchman Smith is Head of Higher Education at Newcastle College University Centre and a cultural sociologist and researcher. A Masters graduate of the Institute of Popular Music at the University of Liverpool, her PhD from the University of Salford was an ethnographic investigation into youth/ageing and cultural performance on the northern soul music scene. Ageing, adulthood, and the master narrative of youth within popular culture was the focus of her post-doctoral research, and her current research interests include: audiences, fandom and spectatorship; post-subcultural theory; the performance of identity; and pedagogic practice, studentship, and higher education. Nicola has previously published on northern soul in chapters in *The Ashgate Research Companion to Popular Musicology* (2009) and *Ageing and Youth Cultures: Music, Style and Identity* (2012).

Notes

1. A tailor-made is a record produced, usually in the UK and typically during the 1970s, with the intention of selling to the British northern soul scene. This is quite separate from pre-existing soul records which are celebrated on the scene. Winstanley and Nowell describe tailor-mades as "not genuine, obscure American recordings from years

gone by but recently pop-orientated dance records using all the ingredients of the northern soul sound" (2000: 45).

2. It should be noted that, although the northern soul scene did not begin in Wigan, for the purpose of this chapter I use Wigan as an example of its UK locality. Wigan is the choice here because the Wigan Casino club is still considered as the heart of heyday northern soul due to its mass popularity, as expressed by high club membership numbers in the 1970s.

3. I recognize that Detroit is not the only home of soul music but I follow the lead of other authors on northern soul that highlight the significance of Detroit (and other Rust Belt cities), namely Winstanley and Nowell (2000), Milestone (1997), Hollows and Milestone (1998), and Browne (2006). There is also a shared perspective amongst those on (and writing about) the scene that many northern soul songs were aiming to emulate the Motown sound and/or success.

4. This is not to say that the music favoured within northern soul is second-rate; it merely goes some way to acknowledging the high quantity of soul records produced in 1960s America, especially in light of the success of Motown, Stax and Atlantic.

5. https://www.youtube.com/watch?v=M-xoxh9yfXI (accessed 18 June 2007).

6. Based on interviews with northern soul participants, conducted by the author between 2005 and 2011 (n=91). Interviews were predominantly face-to-face but some were conducted electronically. I should note that my reading of the choice of American soul music (from my outsider perspective as researcher, later fan) does often differ from the perceptions of soulies themselves. Mirroring Raine and Wall's suggestion of the mythologizing of northern soul, there is a blurring of actual and hindsight; many people had not thought through their reasons for youthful musical choice (which I do not think is unusual) but, when contemplating this in later life, answered such questions based on the mediated version of northern soul. So, Ian's Levine's access to the US becomes relevant to fan stories, as did Godin's TMAS. For me, there is a disconnect here: liking the music is different from knowing where it came from.

7. Perhaps this is not as simple as "taking without asking" but not knowing (who) to ask permission (of). Many of the specifics of the music's origin were hidden as I note below (cover-ups etc.) but there was also a general "if you don't want it, we'll have it" mentality; the USA were positioned as not wanting this music so northern soul adopted it. Keeping with the adoption analogy: soulies looked after this music; nurturing it, giving it a new home and a new name (to represent its induction into a new family). In the care of soulies, this (assumed) unwanted music thrived and found its own identity, something the scene continues to respect, protect and celebrate.

8. This raises questions about whether this has continued throughout the lifespan of the scene to date. Arguably, given the US interest in northern soul within recent years, we now see this in an international context too. The USA looks to the UK for a style guide on consuming the American soul music now defined as northern soul. I saw this first-hand during an ethnographic research project in Chicago in 2014 when attending the Windy City Soul Club. Youths in this club danced (and dressed) as they would have done in heyday UK-based northern soul venues and to largely the same playlist. This blurring of retro performance, borrowed youth cultural activity and notions of musical ownership warrants further future investigation.

9. Those on the current scene know more of the artists but, in keeping with scene discourses established in the 1970s, current soulies predominantly want to search for information relating to the vinyl rather than information about Detroit specifically.

10. Or rare/obscure/unsuccessful/unreleased Motown records.

11. A case in point here is the magnitude of Ian Levine's *Strange World of Northern Soul* project.

12. Dean Parrish (1967) 'I'm on My Way' (Laurie).

13. This raises more questions, namely concerning the scene recognition of this process and the implications of such. It also presents a chicken–egg scenario: which came first, the new meaning or the new scene? Youth cultures are not so clear-cut as to allow a pinpointing of the formation of engagement and music attachment but a further study, which unpacks the mediated storytelling of northern soul, might be useful in shedding a little light on this.

References

Abercrombie, N., and B. Longhurst. 1998. *Audiences: A Sociological Theory of Performance and Imagination*. London: Sage.

Benjamin, W. 1936 [2008]. *The Work of Art in the Age of Mechanical Reproduction*, translated by J. Underwood. London: Penguin.

Bennett, A. 2000. *Popular Music and Youth Culture: Music, Identity and Place*. Hampshire: Macmillan.

Brown, T. 2001. "The Northern Soul of Berry Gordy". In *Calling Out Around the World: A Motown Reader*, edited by K. Abbott, 223–54. London: Helter Skelter.

Browne, K. 2006. "Soul or Nothing: The Formation of Cultural Identity on the British Northern Soul Scene". PhD thesis, UCLA.

Chambers, I. 1985. *Urban Rhythms: Pop Music and Popular Culture*. Hampshire: Macmillan.

Connell, J., and C. Gibson. 2003. *Sound Tracks: Popular Music, Identity and Place*. London: Routledge.

Cosgrove, S. 1982. "Long After Tonight is All Over". *Collusion* 2: 38–41.

Fiske, J. 1989. *Reading the Popular*. London: Routledge.

Gilroy, P. 1997. "Exer(or)cising Power: Black Bodies in the Black Public Sphere". In H. Thomas, *Dance in the City*, 21–34. Hampshire: Palgrave Macmillan.

Hollows, J., and K. Milestone. 1998. "Welcome to Dreamsville: A History and Geography of Northern Soul". In *The Place of Music*, edited by A. Leyshon, D. Matless and G. Revill, 83–103. New York: Guilford Publications.

Langlois, T. 1992. "Can You Feel It? DJs and House Music Culture in the UK". *Popular Music* 11/2: 229–38.

Milestone, K. 1997. "The Love Factory: The Sites, Practices and Media Relationships of Northern Soul". In *The Clubcultures Reader*, edited by S. Redhead, 134–49. Oxford: Blackwell.

Negus, K. 1996. *Popular Music in Theory: An Introduction*. Cambridge: Polity.

Nowell, D. 2001. *Too Darn Soulful: The Story of Northern Soul*. London: Robson Books.

Perry, T., and E. Glinert. 1996. *Rock & Roll Traveler USA: The Ultimate Guide to Juke Joints, Street Corners, Whiskey Bars and Hotel Rooms where Music History was made*. London: Fodor's Travel Publications.

Roberts, K. 2003. *The Northern Soul Top 500, Special Edition.* Nottinghamshire: The KRL Group.

Shapiro, H. 2003. *Waiting for the Man: The Story of Drugs and Popular Music.* London: Helter Skelter.

Shuker, R. 2017. *Popular Music: The Key Concepts*, 4th ed. London: Routledge.

Smith, N. 2006. "Time Will Pass You By, A Conflict of Age: Identity on the Northern Soul Scene". In *Perspectives on Conflict*, edited by C. Baker, E. Granter, R. Guy, K. Harrison, A. Krishan and J. Maslen, 176–95. Manchester: University of Salford Press.

—2009a. "Beyond the Master Narrative of Youth: Researching Ageing Popular Music Scenes". In *The Ashgate Research Companion to Popular Musicology*, edited by Derek B. Scott, 427–45. London: Ashgate.

—2009b. "Performing Fandom on the British Northern Soul Scene: Competition, Identity and the Post-subcultural Self". Unpublished PhD, University of Salford.

—2012. "Parenthood and the Transfer of Subcultural Capital in the Northern Soul Scene". In *Ageing and Youth Cultures: Music, Style and Identity*, edited by Andy Bennett and Paul Hodkinson, 159–72. London: Berg.

Tagg, P. 2012. *Music's Meanings: A Modern Musicology for Non-musos.* New York and Huddersfield: Mass Media Music Scholars' Press.

Walters, I. 1975. "Is Northern Soul Dying on its Feet?" *Street Life*, 15-28 November 1975. Reprinted in H. Kureishi and J. Savage, *The Faber Book of Pop*, 443–56. London: Faber & Faber, 1995.

Winstanley, R., and D. Nowell. 2000. *Soul Survivors: The Wigan Casino Story, 30th Anniversary Edition.* London: Robson Books.

Musical Bookmark 3

Emily Jane photographed at Rubber Soul Records, Stoke on Trent, February 2017
High Voltage, 'Country Road'. Columbia 7 inch single – 4-45701

> "It's special to me because it says something. It was recorded in 1972, so round then it was the Vietnam war ... everything that was going on ... Black Panthers, you know, Civil Rights. So that's why it means a lot to me and it's a good dancer as well. It's an uptempo tune."

Emily Jane is a record collector and DJ. She DJs regularly at Go, Go Children in Bristol, Black Bee in Manchester, and the Rugby Soul Club All-Niter, and as a guest DJ at Los Chavales in Santiago de Compostela (Spain).

7 Dave Godin and the Politics of the British Soul Community[1]

Joe Street

Dave Godin emerged from the fan club scene to become Motown's UK representative and was a driving force behind Motown becoming a significant commercial proposition in the British charts. In 1966, he established the first specialist retail outlet for soul music in the UK, Soul City – which traded for five years and only sold soul, R&B, and blues – and through his knowledge of the soul market, defined what became known as "northern soul" (Brewster 1998). More importantly, his personal warmth ensured that he became admired and loved in almost equal proportions. The outpouring of grief at his death in 2004 was unprecedented in the soul community (Williams 2004; Anon 2004, n.d.; various authors 2004, n.d.; Nathan n.d.). But Godin was more than a nice man who knew a lot about soul music. He was finely attuned to the political subtext that accompanied soul music and to the political economy in which most soul artists worked. He felt very strongly that awareness of these issues was fundamental to being a true soul fan. As he lamented in 1971, "I am ... distressed that people apparently reap great pleasure from buying records by black artists and musicians, and at the same time do not apparently wish to concern themselves with the fate of black people en masse beyond that point" (Godin 1971c: 18). He told purchasers of his indispensable 1997 compilation album *Dave Godin's Deep Soul Treasures* that "the music of Black America ... [emerges from] the collective experience stemming from what a race's cultural and sociological development has had to undergo in its own history" (Godin 1997: 5). As this quotation suggests, Godin was insistent that listeners attempt to understand the background of soul music as well as enjoy it for its own sake.

This chapter examines Godin's role in forging the British soul community and in attempting to define the purpose of this community. It is particularly concerned with Godin's understanding of the relationship between soul music fandom and the historical and political circumstances of black America, and his insistence that soul fans understand the economics that underpinned the production of soul records. These ideas also relate to Godin's belief that such a thing as a soul community existed, one that had certain parallels with the vision of community expressed by 1960s civil rights activists in the United States. Before evaluating Godin's thought, it is necessary to understand his early life, particularly his emerging political sensibilities, immersion in soul music, and understanding of the racial politics of the 1960s. This contextualizes Godin's later ideas about the politics and economics of soul music, which forms the basis of the chapter's second section. A particular concern here is Godin's understanding of the centrality of exploitation of artists to the popular music business, and his insistence on the importance of fans and consumers in tackling the economic imbalance that resulted from this exploitation. A final section concentrates on Godin's understanding of community among soul fans and the importance of interracial brotherhood to his understanding of soul fandom, an aspect of his thought that unconsciously reflected similar feelings that developed among 1960s civil rights activists. Whether Godin was alone in believing this is less the point than his preparedness to use his position as a leading light in the British soul community to articulate ideals that transcended mere music and that were, in his view, fundamental to any understanding of black culture.

Godin's life and early activism

Godin was a radical from a very early age, and remained so until his death. Born in Lambeth during 1936, he grew up in Peckham before his family house was bombed in World War Two and the Godins relocated to Bexleyheath. He attended Dartford Grammar School, an experience that he did not enjoy, in part because he was one of only a small number of working-class children in a fee-paying school which attracted children of more affluent families. One such pupil was Michael Philip Jagger, who achieved fame and fortune courtesy of a band that he formed not long after Godin introduced him to the music of black America (Williams 2004; Savage 1995: 1). Godin himself was turned onto black American music courtesy of a chance encounter with Ruth Brown's still astonishing 1953 rhythm and blues hit '(Mama) He Treats Your Daughter Mean' at a local ice-cream parlour. "I'd never heard a record like that before. It was so earthy, so real", he later told the music journalist and historian Jon Savage (1995: 2). It is no exaggeration to state that he found his calling in life in that Bexleyheath parlour. Hooked, Godin set about collecting as many R&B 45s as he could, and his burgeoning fandom further isolated him from his more mainstream peers.

An avid reader as a young man, Godin quickly developed strong opinions, a trait that would remain through his life. By the early 1960s he had developed a set of principles including pacifism, vegetarianism, a staunch opposition to apartheid, and an interest in the ideas of Wilhelm Reich, all coupled with an anarchist, left-wing streak. This latter belief occasionally surfaced in slyly humorous ways. Prior to a visit to the United States, Godin was asked to attend an interview at the American Embassy in London. When questioned whether he was a communist or a member of the Communist Party, he declared that he was not but when his interviewer asked him whether he was an anarchist, Godin claimed that he replied, "what's that?" Always a truthful man, Godin did not want to lie but his faux naïveté was enough to hoodwink the official (Street 2011b; see also Godin 1970a: 16). This gentle approach to others was a defining feature of Godin's personality. A member of an anti-conscription league from an early age, he developed a lifelong conviction in treating every human being justly and fairly, a principle that he extended to all living animals (Street 2011b; Blackmore 2014; Ritson and Russell 1999: 36; Savage 1995: 3, 5–6; Nathan 2006; see also Godin 1977b).

Godin's interest in black American music was deepened through his avid readership of Norman Jopling's work in *Record Mirror* – he especially appreciated Jopling's willingness to champion unknown and obscure records recorded by black American artists – and regularly listening to a French radio show named *Salut les Copins* (Savage 1995: 2, 6). Without a large network of similarly-minded friends, Godin described the experience of being a soul fan in years prior to the soul explosion of the 1960s as like being an "orphan ... in a storm" (Savage 2015: 450). He went "potty" over The Marvelettes' 'Please Mr. Postman', which was a Motown record released on the Fontana label in the United Kingdom, and became convinced that Motown was in the process of developing a new, distinctive sound (Savage 1995: 7; see also Wilson 2009: 35–36). As is well documented, various distribution deals meant that Motown records appeared in the UK under numerous labels, including Fontana, Oriole, and later Stateside (Wilson 2009: 34–44). At once charmed by Motown's music and irritated by its almost haphazard distribution amid this mélange of labels, Godin wrote to Motown's owner Berry Gordy with a plan to unite the disparate group of Motown fans in one organization to be titled the Mary Wells Fan Club (which morphed into the Tamla Motown Appreciation Society when Godin heard rumours that Wells was planning to leave the label [Savage 1995: 8]). He hoped to publicize Motown and give the label a cohesive identity in Britain. The creation of the Society was also an outlet for his frustration at the failure of British radio to give airplay to Motown's acts. Motown was frequently reaching the high echelons of the United States charts and was developing a small but fervent following among music fans across the Atlantic, but had yet to make the breakthrough into the mainstream British charts that Godin felt the music warranted. The BBC's control of radio meant that fans could not hear certain forms of music and consequently would not buy it. This, he concluded, resulted in the charts being full of conservative music which was considered safe by the BBC and bought by people who knew no better. In forming the Society, Godin said that he wanted to "put down some sort of marker, no matter how humble, that would affirm the fact that some of us over here [in the UK] knew a damn fine record when we heard it" (Hewitt 2003: 21).

Not long after the Mary Wells Fan Club took off Godin received a five-page telegram from Berry Gordy inviting him to Detroit for further discussions about Motown's future in the UK. Gordy had been impressed with Godin's chutzpah in writing to him in strong terms about Motown's shortcomings and with his plans to address these problems. Godin encouraged the establishment of the proprietary Tamla Motown label, on which all future Motown records were released. His stroke of genius was to market the label as a unified whole – the "Tamla Motown" sound – rather than through individual artists (*Independent* 2004). Aware of the relatively unified sound of the records, dominated by the instrumental backing of Motown's in-house band, the Funk Brothers, and the songwriting of Smokey Robinson and the Holland-Dozier-Holland team, Godin thought that a single Motown image would enable fans unfamiliar with individual artists to spot records instead by their brand identity.

His first engagement at Motown's headquarters, Hitsville USA, was a reception in his honour, followed by dinner at Detroit's Playboy Club and an evening at the Gordy household during which he and Harvey and Gwen Fuqua discussed the African American struggle for civil rights and Godin told them of his support for its ideals. Godin so impressed Gordy that he was invited to become Motown's British representative and to select his favourite of Motown's upcoming records by Martha and the Vandellas. Gordy thought all were good but apparently asked Godin to choose which one the label should release first. Godin selected 'Dancing In The Street', the record that became Martha Reeves's signature song. Not long after his return to the UK toting advance copies of the Supremes' 'Where Did Our Love Go', Motown's British fortunes began to improve. Vicki Wickham, a producer of British television's regular pop music show, *Ready, Steady, Go!* and a TMAS member, started booking soul artists whenever possible, which gave Motown's stars indispensable exposure to British teenagers (Godin 2009; Savage 1995: 11; Savage 1997: 6; Savage 2015: 454–56; Street 2011c; Hewitt 2003: 20).

Perhaps as important, the TMAS was a channel through which Motown artists could meet their British fans. Godin frequently organized informal meetings for touring Motown stars above various pubs in east London. The stars would occasionally mime to Godin's collection of singles and then have a chat with their small audience (Street 2011b, 2011c; Nicholls 2011). This in itself was a hugely significant act: in rejecting segregation, both formal and informal, Godin and his friends were making important political statements both about the artists and themselves. While racial segregation was not pursued with as much zeal in the United Kingdom as it was in many American states, integration was far from a fact of life. Although a small number of groups existed which wished to promote integration, there was not yet a legal basis under which integration could be officially enforced. Pubs could still impose a "colour bar" if they wished, and many Londoners expressed concern at the prospect of a multiracial future. Even the passage of the 1965 Race Relations Act failed to bring any convictions for racial discrimination in public places in its first two years (Davis 2015: 126–27, 129; Street 2015: 178). Godin, then, must have scouted appropriate pubs which did not object to an interracial gathering on the premises. And while it seemed perfectly natural to all of the participants, observers of a group of well-dressed black Americans accompanying a gaggle of young white Britons might well have had them raising an eyebrow or muttering into their pints of mild that things weren't what they used to be, and perhaps even verbally objecting. Such folks would have been further outraged to hear that Godin's raffle winners might receive a kiss from a Motown star upon receiving their prize (Street 2011b). Yet that very intimacy was a further indication of the ease with which TMAS members and Motown stars mixed: as TMAS member Graham Moss recalls, "it was just – what do you talk about? You just talk about *shit*! You know!" just as if they were long-time friends chewing the fat over a pint at the end of the week (Street 2011b).

As suggested by this informal activism, Godin championed the African American civil rights movement which was then pushing for an end to legal segregation in the United States and receiving international attention for its mass demonstrations and marches. In May 1964, he wrote a letter to the Congress of Racial Equality (CORE), expressing his hope that the TMAS could become an affiliate. Godin's selection of CORE, rather than the more famous Southern Christian Leadership Conference headed by Dr Martin Luther King, Jr and the more radical Student Nonviolent Coordinating Committee (SNCC) is itself significant and offers further insight into Godin's politics. CORE's roots were in the Fellowship of Reconciliation (FoR), a pacifist group that had roots in the United Kingdom but that operated most successfully in the United States. CORE emerged from a Chicago FoR cell in 1942 and quickly attracted numerous pacifists who were committed to ending racial discrimination in the United States (Morris 1984: 157–58). In 1961, it achieved international renown after organizing a series of 'freedom rides' which sent interracial groups of bus riders on journeys through segregated states in an attempt to test a recent US Supreme Court decision that declared segregated facilities in interstate bus terminals unlawful. The experiment was met with mob violence in Alabama which forced the Kennedy administration to intervene and protect CORE's riders, its first major intervention in support of the civil rights movement (Cook 1998: 123–24). At the time of Godin's letter, CORE was working in conjunction with SNCC to plan a major project in Mississippi for later that summer. Meanwhile, the US Congress was in the midst of a Senate filibuster of a civil rights bill that had been proposed by the Democratic Party in tribute to John F. Kennedy. Senators who were opposed to the bill, which proposed to desegregate public accommodations across the southern states, had successfully stalled it since 26 February and were to do so until 10 June (Guéron 1994–1995: 1219–221).

Aware that he and his fellow soul music fans could do little other than offer "moral support and admiring blessings", Godin thought that sending 12 dollars in return for membership, 100 "Freedom Now" buttons, and two "Equality" pins plus postage would make a start towards showing their solidarity in the struggle to fight racism. "We are all personally pledged to combat racial tension here in Britain too and to spread understanding and tolerance through the conduct of our own lives", he wrote, before declaring that the members of the TMAS were "beside you all in spirit" (Godin 1964). He clearly considered these buttons to be a display not only of political solidarity with the civil rights cause, but also as a way of publicly linking soul music to the political struggle of the civil rights movement. He and the other members of the Society placed these buttons on their jackets alongside those declaring their love of Mary Wells, Martha and the Vandellas, and other Motown acts (Street 2011b). As this suggests, for Godin, as for many of the core members of the TMAS, listening to soul music was part of a more complex political struggle in which young white Britons were engaging during the 1960s. He saw their enthusiasm for the music as a way of expressing their political support for the movement, and as a way of proving their commitment both to soul and to racial equality. Clearly, being a fan of the music could be only one part of a complex political identity that encompassed youthful rebellion, political maturation and transatlantic identification. The letter suggests that Godin believed that it was not enough merely to be a fan of the music; a true soul fan also had to be in support of black equality. Indeed, one of Godin's friends commented that even the music was secondary to the politics – that racial inequality was being challenged, and possibly broken down, by white kids getting into black music (Street 2011b, 2011c).

The politics and economics of soul

A November 1966 letter to *Record Mirror* offered further evidence of Godin's understanding of the close relationship between soul and the political world from which it emerged:

> because American Negroes can only enter the musical field, and are denied opportunities to enter other fields, this pent-up talent will dominate the one area where they are allowed artistic expression ... A Glasgow orphan doesn't find doors closed in his face just because he is an orphan but this is just what does happen to the American Negro, day in and day out (Godin 1966: 2).

Through the 1960s he impressed on fellow soul fans the importance of the social and political context that gave rise to soul music, urging them to make similar connections: "I feel that *everyone* who buys and enjoys R&B records should be fervently concerned with race relations, and should be engaged in action that will prevent the American tragedy from ever repeating itself in this country" (Godin 1968: 324, emphasis added; see also Croasdell 1997: 3).[2] After all, Godin admitted, "were I faced with having to choose between the demise of R&B and Soul, and the advance and surge upwards of full integration, then I'd choose the latter every time" (Godin 1968: 326). This kind of thinking was not necessarily popular with his *Blues & Soul* readership, as reflected in *Blues & Soul*'s founder and editor John Abbey's public admission that he "tried to steer B&S away from the political implications of Soul music" because he felt that they did not pertain to the music's British listeners (Abbey 1970; see also Anon 1972). Godin, meanwhile, continued to promote his political interpretation of soul. In 1971, he ended a column by urging his readers to "do what's right – not what's white". Within context this was a fairly innocuous statement: Godin was keen for readers to put aside notions of race in favour of pursuing the higher cause of justice for all. Many of his readers took umbrage, however, feeling that he was being needlessly ideological. This prompted an extraordinary response in Godin's next column which took a number of his correspondents to task personally (Godin 1971c; see also Godin 1970a; Street 2011b). Hurt by the lack of empathy shown by his readers, Godin told them that it was "selfish and unimaginative" to be buying records by black people while refusing to take an interest in the political and social situation facing black people en masse. "I'll do all I can", he promised, "to ensure that the younger generation ... does not grow up to be ... racial bigots" (Godin 1971c: 18). So concerned was he about the impact of his words, that he asked the Race Relations Board and the pressure group Christian Action for their opinion on the controversy. Unsurprisingly, neither took issue with

Godin's phraseology. His sign-off that issue simply exhorted his readers to "do what's RIGHT! O.K?" (Godin 1971c: 19). The omission of the "not what's white" clause might appear to be concession, but the implication was crystal clear.

This discussion reveals a major difference between Godin and his readers. For many soul fans, the music could be divorced from the socio-political contexts in which it was produced and experienced. As Jeremy Gilbert and Ewan Pearson (citing Roland Barthes) have written about late twentieth- and early twenty-first-century dance music, music (sub)cultures "are almost all – one way or another – about the pursuit of *jouissance*" – a joy on the dancefloor that is almost sexual in its intensity (Gilbert and Pearson 1999: 65). *Blues & Soul* occasionally reserved space for its readers to opine on "My Idea of Soul", in which reflections on politics were very few and far between (announced in Anon 1973). While some soul fans wore black gloves to nightclubs in homage to the famous Black Power salute given by American sprinters Tommie Smith and John Carlos at the 1968 Mexico Olympic Games, others wore them simply because the gloves protected their hands when they touched the floor (which could harbour splinters or even shards of glass from broken pint pots or bottles) during particularly daring dance moves (Godin 1971a). Some were even less enlightened. In 1974, *Blues & Soul* columnist Frank Elson declared that one of the major problems with the John Peel-fronted *Top Gear* radio show was the "drivel" that Peel played, which supposedly included recordings of "New Guinea natives doing a chant to celebrate having caught a white BBC man whom they are about to eat!" Elson's attempt at humour revealed the racial stereotyping and primitivism that ran underneath his love of black American music (Elson 1974a: 15). Thankfully, such comments are as notable for their rarity as for their racism.

To give Godin his credit, he acknowledged that *jouissance* was central to northern soul dancefloors, arguing that "one must always bear in mind that the northern scene is largely a discotheque one, and when people go to a disco, they want to *dance*. They don't want to sit and listen and launch into a pseudo type conversation" (Godin 1971f: 18). He knew that "Soul appreciation springs from the heart rather than the brain", but his understanding of the relationship between soul and black politics threatened to bring political thought into an arena that many fans felt was better reserved purely for the pursuit of pleasure (Godin 1971f: 18). Yet he was also disgusted that many middle-class white gatekeepers of soul, "knew all of Howlin' Wolf's flipsides, but nothing at all about Emmett Till" (Godin 1999: 19, 20 [quote p. 20]). Emmett Till, of course, was a fourteen-year-old boy who was lynched in Mississippi in August 1955. His "crime" had been allegedly to flirt with Carolyn Bryant, a twenty-one-year-old white woman who owned a grocery store. Till's death and the subsequent acquittal of his killers caused uproar across the United States, although the British response was relatively muted (*Times* 1955a-b; *The Guardian* 1955a-i).

The second aspect of Godin's position stemmed from his awareness of the economic exploitation of many soul artists. According to his friend Graham Moss, Godin had a clear understanding of economics (Street 2011b). He regularly reminded his *Blues & Soul* readers that soul artists deserved full payment of royalties and clearly understood that unfair business practices riddled the music industry (see, for example, Godin 1975d, 1975h). He hated the petulant attitude of British soul fans who "are only interested in artists who have never seen the inside of the Hot Hundred ... [and who] drop them and almost sneer at them just because they make the top ten and make a commercial hit" (Godin 1968: 325; see also Godin 1970b). Such elitism, he later opined, was a hangover from the colonial mentality that dominated the UK prior to World War Two. This attitude led to a certain form of African American rhythm and blues being accepted only if it was "authentic" and was unconcerned with achieving chart success. The desire of these elitists to keep the music as the preserve of the in-crowd led them away from actively publicizing the artists, and their ignorance of the political realities that faced African American people led them towards an exoticization of the music created by these very same people.

Godin's response was not merely rhetorical. In 1966, he was instrumental in establishing the first British record shop that specialized in selling black music. Not insignificantly, it was formally opened by Godin's friend, the writer, feminist, animal rights campaigner, and tireless activist Brigid Brophy. Her speech at the event made explicit links between soul music and political freedom (*New York Times* 1955; Ritson and Russell 1999: 101). Godin became a champion not only for the music but also for the artists whom he felt were being exploited, not only by their managers and record labels but also by British groups who made careers out of covering their hits. One incident is reflective of his attitude: his old schoolmate Mick Jagger bumped into him on the set of *Ready Steady Go* not long after Jagger's band hit the big time. The Rolling Stones were appearing on the show alongside Motown's Marvin Gaye, who had become friendly with his label's British representative, and Jagger was keen to meet an artist whom he regarded very highly. Godin dispensed with the usual pleasantries. "Why the fuck did you record 'Time Is On My Side' and steal the limelight from Irma Thomas?" he demanded. Jagger responded that he considered it a tribute. "Fuck off!", came the reply, "and you can introduce your fucking self to Marvin Gaye" (*Independent* 2004; Hewitt 2003 [Jagger quote p. 20]; Savage 1995, 1997).

Godin had been annoyed with Jagger for some time and continued to be for many years. Earlier in the 1960s, he often hosted Jagger and Jagger's friend Keith Richards at his parents' home, where he would play them numerous records from his extensive collection. In return, they picked the best ones to cover in their band and would continue to ask him for favours into 1963 (Jones 1963).[3] More importantly, Godin soon worked out that the Rolling Stones, along with other visitors to the Godin home, like Dave Munden of the Tremeloes, were exploiting both him and the music, so he refused to host them anymore. This antipathy for Jagger lasted throughout Godin's life. In a 1975 *Blues & Soul* column, he denounced Jagger as "a perfect example of an upper-middle-class yob who waxed fat off the backs of black people whilst he was telling us all the while that he was interested and keen to help them gain recognition" (Godin 1975f; see also Godin 1976c). To *The Guardian* he denounced Jagger's band as plagiarists (Godin 1975i) and later in his life declared, "I loathe to the marrow in my bones such people as the Rolling Stones. To me they are as reprehensible and exploitative as the very people who owned the slaves. They have done exactly what American slave owners did", which was slightly hyperbolic but perfectly conveyed Godin's deep enmity (Brewster 1998).[4]

Godin was acutely aware that the Rolling Stones and their ilk were not only depriving artists like Irma Thomas of the limelight but also of their careers. As he pointed out in his 1966 letter to *Record Mirror*, African Americans were denied opportunities to enter other employment fields (Godin 1966). Music was, for many, the only field in which they were able to achieve. Thus, they were being deprived of a regular career, and forced into a murky and exploitative business with little guarantee of success and economic reward for their talent. This in part explains why he expanded Soul City to encompass a record label. The label would give a British release to original versions of hit covers or soul records that had not received the success they deserved, such as Gene Chandler's 'Nothing Can Stop Me'. Most famously, it issued Bessie Banks's definitive version of 'Go Now', which had been mangled by the Moody Blues a few months after the original was released. The cover version, of course, was a huge hit, and Banks feared that it would spell the end of her career (Nathan 2006; Savage 1997). Godin's encouragement and championing, however, spurred her to continue and ensured that she received proper monetary returns for her talent. The Soul City record label, which was run as a worker's cooperative, was also a manifestation of Godin's antipathy for the music industry's exploitation of African American artists whose careers were in the hands of unscrupulous or plain ignorant label managers and licensees – or, indeed, victims of bootleggers who pressed up illegal copies of their recordings (Croasdell 1997; Godin 1971b; see also Anon 1971).[5]

Godin was a staunch critic of the bootleg culture that emerged in the 1970s. Obscure and often forgotten tracks that DJs rediscovered and brought to popularity in nightclubs like the Wigan Casino or Blackpool Mecca, occasionally found their way into the hands of bootleggers. Their repressings of these records would be sold to 1970s fans, with the bootleggers taking all of the profits that should rightfully have been diverted to the producers of the original. This bootlegging culture was a capitalist response to the cult of exclusivity and elitism that increasingly surrounded northern soul during the 1970s when DJs began crate-digging for ever more obscure releases, and started to remove the labels on the discs to prevent others discovering the identity of particularly rare and special records. The reason for this was twofold: to ensure that rival DJs might not identify "killer" tunes and adopt them for their own sets in a competitive market where one's standing was related to the quality and obscurity of the records they championed; and to deter bootleggers from identifying the record, purchasing their own copy and repressing it to sell to fans. Mecca DJ Ian Levine charged that the "welfare of the scene" could be compromised by such unscrupulous people pressing new editions of the rare records he played (Elson 1974a: 14; see also Nowell 2011: 101–102; Hooton 1976; Elson 1974b: 16; Godin 1976a). Godin, naturally, was aghast. Again, the black artists found themselves "anonymously waiting empty-handed, as usual, at the back door. Where Blackamericans [sic] had generally been kept waiting ever since the days of 'emancipation'" (Godin 1999: 20; see also Godin 1977c). The inverted commas around "emancipation" were a bitter reminder of his feelings about the African American experience since the American Civil War.

Barry Doyle argues that the privileging of the rare and often unattainable produced "an anti-consumerist form of consumption ... which ... allowed the maintenance of an aura of authenticity in a culture of mass production" (Doyle 2006: 323; see also Winstanley and Nowell 1996: 1). Katie Milestone points to the theorist Walter Benjamin in noting that the records played at northern soul nights are "reactivated" in the particular situations of the nightclubs and thus are "given new life and meaning" (Milestone 1997: 144). Part of Godin's slight alienation from the northern soul community in the mid-1970s revolved around these issues. Godin was extremely upset whenever he discovered a DJ playing a record that had no label. He disagreed that the lack of a label meant that the ritual of playing the record became all about the music. He wanted to ensure that the artist, and not the DJ, received proper recognition for the music: "I was very into de-mystifying records", he said in 1998. "[I]f I went somewhere and some DJ had some exclusive cover-up I knew, I would immediately blow the whistle and review it. Fuck it. Because they were putting their own ego above the singer, the composer, and everyone else and I couldn't abide that" (Brewster 1998; see also Godin 1999: 20, 22, 24; Godin 1974; Dean and Godin 1976). If a record was unidentifiable by the crowd, its inclusion in a DJ's set became more about the DJ elevating his own status rather than that of the artist. Moreover, if people were unable to buy the record themselves, then the artist would not benefit financially from the popularity of their record. For Godin, the aura of authenticity that swirled around these unidentified records was not only false but was dangerous since it involved depriving artists of reward for their talent. In this, he points to a more orthodox Marxist analysis of northern soul: the new life and meaning is nothing for the artists without the economic base to this superstructure. Ultimately, the artists deserved economic as well as symbolic support.

The DJs, for Godin, had what he termed "a vested interest in control" (Brewster 1998). They would stop playing records once they had been reissued, for example, which Godin considered abhorrent. Did The Tams's 'Hey Girl, Don't Bother Me' become a bad record because it was popular, he asked rhetorically (Godin 1971f). In the same 1971 column – one of his most important and well-argued – he accused people like *Record Mirror*'s Tony Cummings of wanting soul music "to remain the exclusive territory of the elitist cult who expect an army of Black Americans ... to endlessly perform and create for them so that they can earn two bucks from the sales of their records to this precious band" (Godin 1971f; see also Riston and Russell 1999: 129–31). This, he declared, reduced black American singers to the status of court jesters: minstrels, even, fated to sing for their supper before a coterie of soul fans who had little interest in ensuring that the artists whom they loved received the economic benefits that their talents deserved. Godin's enmity toward Cummings reached its peak in May 1977 when he compared Cummings to Stalin and other authoritarian dictators for his supposed attempt to control the development of soul in his critical appraisal of the music played at northern soul venues, which was perhaps more illustrative of Godin's occasionally frenzied hyperbole than anything else (Godin 1977d).[6]

The feud with Cummings perhaps obscured Godin's own previous culpability in developing the cult of the DJ. In 1971, he acknowledged that "good DJ's need just a few 'specials' to get a following" in his report from his first visit to the Blackpool Mecca (Godin 1971e: 19). By then, he was well known for the breadth and depth of his knowledge of soul music, an image that he was prepared to cultivate. He confessed to his *Blues & Soul* readers in summer 1971 that he spent part of a train journey north fashioning his own white labels with which to mask the identity of "a few secret sounds" he was taking to play at a club in Manchester (Godin 1971d). One *Blues & Soul* correspondent picked up on Godin's apparent hypocrisy, pointing out that the magazine had previously printed complaints from soul fans about a certain DJ who wanted to keep particular records to himself and wondered whether Godin was jealously attempting to do the same. "Dave lad, try a little harder", it concluded ("Yorkshire Soul Lover" 1971). By autumn, Godin clearly was trying harder: the white-label policy was publicly renounced and Godin became ever more critical of what might be termed the "DJ-centrism" of the soul scene, where the men who played the records achieved greater renown in the community than the people who actually made the records themselves. He later admitted that he "only ever kept any side secret for twelve months", which does not quite absolve him (Godin 1972d).[7] For Ian Levine, this was evidence of Godin's ego: Godin couldn't bear the fact that some DJs had records that even Godin had not heard, which drove him to distraction and thus explains why he wanted to keep a few specials to himself, even if temporarily (Brewster 1999).[8]

The soul community

As the debate over obscure "specials" suggests, for numerous soul fans, the attraction of the music was in part its qualities that separated fans from the mainstream. Soul fans were identifiably different, and in separating themselves from the mainstream they were able to claim a higher status than the average music fan. This exclusivity was itself a badge of commitment (Street 2015: 184). Even though Godin often protested that a good record was a good record, irrespective of its commercial success, part of the appeal of northern soul was the fact that it separated connoisseurs from the general herd. Northern soul fans knew their stuff, and often preferred the obscure over the popular (Street 2011a). This itself was fundamental to the sense of community among some northern soul fans. Godin himself was keenly aware of the relationship between the music and these bonds. He understood that that dancers rarely, if ever, consider politics and economics while dancing, but also that their decisions on whether to buy certain records were likely made on that dancefloor. Their subsequent purchases could make an impact, however minor, on the artists' economic and political situation, which itself enables a reading which envelops soul fandom in the political struggles of the epoch.

As important, his now-legendary first visit to the Twisted Wheel club in Manchester towards the end of 1970 offered conclusive proof that the music itself forged bonds between disparate people in a way that was not dissimilar to the brotherhood that helped to define the African American civil rights movement. His first meeting with a gang of pen-friends was reflective of these bonds: "We were soon talking like we'd known each other for years (a common experience amongst Soul people since we always have so much to talk about which bores the pants off your average non-Soul fan), and the time flew by" (Godin 1971a). Upon entering the club, Godin observed that:

> Anyone is welcome to get up and join in, and soon the place was alive with sounds and movement! ... And talk! I thought I'd never stop! Everyone was so friendly and kind, and I truly felt quite humbled that so many people knew who I was, and who came up and introduced themselves and had a kind word to say about my writings ... There was no undercurrent of tension or aggression that one sometimes finds in London clubs, but rather a benevolent atmosphere of benign friendship and camaraderie. Everyone seems to know everyone else, and if they don't, then they don't stand on ceremony about getting to know each other, for one thing they know they all have in common is a love and dedication to Soul music, and it is this common factor that links everyone there, and makes everyone a potential friend of the other ... Live and let live is a rather worn out well intentioned cliche these days when life seems to be coming more and more restricted and uniform, but you would have to search a long way to find a setting where that theory was put into such real practice as Manchester's Twisted Wheel club, and I shall always remember with gratitude that I was taken to its heart, and allowed to be part of that scene even if I could only stay for such a short time (Godin 1971a: 18–19; see also Lawson c.1990: 36).

If he was less ecstatic about the atmosphere at the Blackpool Mecca in 1971, the themes of brotherhood and community remained strong:

> I reckoned that a good 2,000 were in the Highland Room! And by 11:30 it seemed that I'd spoken to and shaken hands with a good 90 per cent of them! If there is one thing we Soul fans like doing next to listening to Soul Sounds it's talking about them! ... I can honestly say that I felt completely at home ... the Soul way is a definite way, and I think this is an element of our music that does bind us all closer together far more than non-Soul people could ever realise or appreciate (Godin 1971e: 18–19; see also Godin 1977e).

For Godin, soul bound the clubgoers together and created a sense of both unity and community; senses which he thought were not merely evanescent but remained in all aspects of soul fans' lives. There was, he later wrote, "a Soul ethic and way of life" which emerged from the shared experience of listening to the music (Godin 1972b). He was particularly impressed that one Twisted Wheel regular took time to welcome any newcomers and ensure that they settled in. Such acts demonstrated that the Wheel created a community of equals defined by a spirit of brotherhood. This was not far from SNCC's often-quoted declaration that it was a "band of brothers, a circle of trust" which aimed to bring about what it termed the "beloved community" in the United States (Forman 1964 [quotes]; Street 2012: 116–20). At times, he witnessed dancers expressing their own interpretation of solidarity with African American political protest: "Between records one would hear the occasional cry of 'Right on now'! or see a clenched gloved fist rise over the tops of the heads of the dancers" (Godin 1971a). Yet Godin was aware that, for many soul fans, this was no more than an empty gesture designed to ingratiate themselves with their fellow dancers, as opposed to an expression of political spirit. He was scathing about the DJs and fans who adopted such slogans as "keep the faith" without any awareness of their relationship with the African American freedom struggle and yet even in his younger days he must have been conscious that most soul fans were less politically inclined than him (Godin 1999: 20). Indeed, his regular admonishments to his readers to keep their minds open, whether it be towards black people in general or white people singing soul music, suggest such awareness. For Dave Godin, soul was all about community and not profit, about sharing love for records for their qualities rather than their obscurity.

In a broader sense, for Godin, the soul scene was a bottom-up phenomenon, led and defined by its grassroots supporters rather than the nominal "leaders" of the scene: hence his enthusiasm for *Blues & Soul*'s letters page and the fact that he only coined the phrase "northern soul" in order to create a shorthand for the music that appealed to northern visitors to Soul City. "When records came into the shop", he recalled, "in order to help my team sell them, the term Northern Soul was used to make us aware that this record would be the type of record that people in the north would like" (Nowell 2011: 49; see also Godin 1999: 24; Lawson c.1990: 37; Godin 1975b, 1975c). Northern soul's status as a marketing tool was almost incidental. More importantly, it reflected the demand created by the fans themselves. As he pointed out in his short-lived fanzine *Rhythm & Soul USA*, "We are out to popularise R&B and Soul music – to rescue it from the realm of rarefied pseudo intellectualism that prevents it from gaining a popular following here. Our motto is that 'it's what's in the grooves that counts'" (Ritson and Russell 1999: 61). The fans' response was, he felt, an important part of the music's development, and he was clearly proud of his ability to compel people to buy particularly important records, perhaps those on Soul City, which ensured that artists received appropriate remuneration for their labour (Godin 1976b). Their response, rather than the diktats of writers like Cummings (and presumably himself), was central to a song's success, and hence to the development of an artist's career and, indeed, the music itself. While he hoped for soul to become universally accepted and popular, he also could not help stroking his readers' ego by pointing out that, sometimes, soul records were "too deep, too heavy and too esoteric" for popular ears (Godin 1972c).

Of course, as Godin's shifting stance on disguising records suggests, there were lacunae in his thought. For example, as Motown's British representative in the 1960s, Godin played a key role in developing an overseas market for artists who were subject to exploitative and restrictive recording contracts by Berry Gordy. Further, his original enthusiasm for protecting the identity of certain records must have been an expression of his own ego (note, for example, Godin 1977a). By the 1970s Godin clearly relished the attention he was given and the esteem in which he was held. More than one of his columns included commentary on nightclub dancers parting before him as he entered on his periodic visits: the biblical allusion here simply cannot be ignored (Brewster 1998; Godin 1971a, 1971e; Street 2011c).[9] While he was a naturally self-effacing man, he knew that his knowledge of the soul scene was rivalled by very few and was certainly aware that his patronage could help bring a record to the soul cognoscenti's attention. He must also have felt that he needed to maintain his image as a leading light of the soul scene, and so bringing some unknown gems to the attention of other fans must have delighted him. Yet once he thought deeper about the economic reality of this process, he rethought his decision. Similar thoughts must have been in his head when he constructed his long and controversial "'Northern Soul' Is Dead!" column in September 1975. Lambasting members of the scene for chasing their tails in ever more desperate attempts to find ever more obscure 1960s songs which were increasingly deservedly obscure rather than lost classics, Godin also took aim at artists attempting to record new songs in the "northern" style. Such attempts to jump on the bandwagon were folly, for they relied on such a small market that success was unlikely. Moreover, these records were often made by neophytes with no awareness of what actually constituted soulfulness. This attitude had its roots in Godin's antipathy for the Rolling Stones' exploitation of blues records made by often-impoverished black Americans: "it seemed that they were working on behalf of themselves. This is why I've never forgiven them", he spat to Jon Savage (1995). His last target was the cult of the DJ, which he suggested was a perverse development which again withdrew attention from the artists (Godin 1975e; Brewster 1998). Much of this, he later reflected, was rooted in the power held by white people. As happened in the civil rights movement, white interlopers entered the soul music business and attempted to gain control and dictate the future direction of the movement. "In a sense we are all guests at the wedding", he reflected, "and it ill behoves the guests to decide how the bride and groom should organise the party, what tunes the band should play and so forth ... in a sense I've always had that very clearly in the back of my mind" (Savage 1997).

Ultimately, he saw spreading soul to the masses as part of the quest for equal treatment of black people by white people. As early as the first few months of Soul City's operations he was aware that the soul market in the UK was almost exclusively white. The role of proselytizers like him, then, was to improve the awareness of soul fans as to the circumstances that produced soul music. He was, as he later told Bill Brewster (1998), as much an agitator as a fan. He lamented the impact of market economics on the northern soul scene. After hearing an obscure record that one trader was hawking for £1,000, Godin concluded, "This is the trouble with capitalism and art: when art takes on value" (Brewster 1998). Towards the end of his life, his views arguably became even more vociferous. He used the privilege of his foreword to Mike Ritson and Stuart Russell's history of the northern soul scene to discuss his political interpretation. Where most book forewords offer a bland encomium to the book's contents, Godin's lambasted numerous unnamed northern soul DJs, bootleggers, and journalists for their egotism and failure to comprehend the social milieu from which soul music emerged (Godin 1999, esp: 19–20, 22–24). This doubtless did not endear him to those who were less politically-minded than him, but it also reveals the strength of Godin's feelings and his willingness to court controversy, even if such bad-tempered comments clashed with his belief that soul was a healing force for society, an expression of emotions and sexuality that the "dominant white ideology" hoped to suppress (Savage 1997).

The emotional freedom afforded him by the music, he thought, placed him in a position where he felt compelled to bring others into the fold. "If I have got a lot of pleasure from something", he told Jon Savage (1997), "I don't want to keep it to myself. I want to share it". As important, Godin was alive to the political milieu from which this music emerged and wanted others to understand that this politics was as much about brotherhood, understanding, and equality as the music. Godin thus touches on one of the key areas for dispute within the academic study of dance music and dancing: namely whether it holds any meaning beyond the pursuit and expression of pleasure. Godin was of the opinion that dancing should have a direct economic impact beyond the dancefloor, namely for the artists who made the sounds. This he wrapped up in the political context of the black experience in the United States, which underlined his trademark sign-off to his columns: "keep the faith – right on now!"

About the author

Joe Street is Associate Professor in American History at Northumbria University, Newcastle. His research concentrates on the nexus between politics and culture in the twentieth century, with a particular focus on African American radicalism in the 1960s and 1970s and the San Francisco Bay Area after World War Two. His publications include *The Culture War in the Civil Rights Movement* (2007) and *Dirty Harry's America* (2016), and articles on the Black Panther Party, Malcolm X, and the 1967 Stax/Volt Revue. He loves soul music but cannot dance to save his life.

Notes

1. My thanks to Jon Savage for kindly sharing his interview transcripts, to Mike Tyldesley for his enthusiasm, inspiration, and contacts, and to all my interviewees for sharing memories of their lives.
2. According to Clive Richardson (2010: 52–53), this article was rejected by *Blues & Soul* for its political content.
3. Others who sat in Godin's room listening to his records include Graham Moss and Clive Richardson (Street 2011b; Richardson 2010: 18; Nicholls 2011). The Stones' attitude to Godin is perhaps exemplified in Keith Richards's memoir: he is referred to as Dave Golding (Richards 2010: 81). Godin is referenced correctly by Richards in Jagger *et al.* (2003: 28), leading to the possibility that "Golding" was a mistake by Richards's ghost-writer and editorial team.
4. Godin was certainly well-read enough to comment on slavery with some authority: in 1976 he recommended that his readers obtain a copy of Eugene Genovese's *Roll, Jordan, Roll*, one of the most important studies of slave life in the American South, and one that he considered "highly relevant to the music of today"' (Godin 1976d). That Genovese's book applied a Marxian lens to the history of slavery surely added to its appeal to Godin.
5. 'Go Now' was released by Soul City in May 1968. Information at http://www.45cat.com/record/sc105 (accessed 10 September 2018).
6. Part of Godin's ire was his perception that Cummings gave poor publicity in *Black Music* to certain artists because of an association with Contempo – a company linked to *Blues & Soul* – rather than the quality of the records (for example Godin 1975g, h). Cummings later regretted the spat, although he held firm to his opinion that some of Godin's work for *Blues & Soul* was "absurdly OTT" and pompous (Ritson and Russell 1999: 134).
7. This was Godin's last column before his temporary retirement due, he said, to his legend becoming a burden to him; he appeared on the masthead as an editorial contributor until December 1972 and returned as a columnist in March 1975.
8. Levine and Godin became antagonists in 1975 after Levine issued Godin with a solicitor's letter claiming that Godin defamed him in a column. Godin was unmoved; the feud lasted until Godin's death (Godin 1975a; Street 2016).
9. As David Nathan later recalled, Godin was widely recognized as "the godfather of R&B in England" (Nathan 2006; see also Nathan 2000: 3).

References

Abbey, J. 1970. "Thoughts…". *Blues & Soul* 44 (9-22 October): 18.
Anon. 1971. "Editorial". *Blues & Soul* 57 (16-29 April): 3.
Anon (presumably Abbey). 1972. "Comment". *Blues & Soul* 87 (30 June–13 July): 3.
Anon. 1973. "Comment". *Blues & Soul* 102 (2-18 February): 3.

—2004. "Sad News Dave Godin RIP". 30 October post at: http://www.soul-source.co.uk/articles/soul-artists-sad-news/sad-news-dave-godin-rip-r318/ (accessed 22 January 2016).

—n.d. "Dave Godin, 1936–2004". Available at: http://www.soulfulkindamusic.net/dgodin.htm (accessed 22 January 2016).

Blackmore, R. 2014. "DG and Soul City III". Unpublished document, 2014 copy in author's collection.

Brewster, B. 1998. "Interview with Dave Godin". *DJHistory.com*, September. Available at: http://daily.redbullmusicacademy.com/2018/01/dave-godin-interview (accessed 10 September 2018).

—1999. "Interview with Ian Levine: Northern Soul Legend". *DJHistory.com*, March. Available at: http://daily.redbullmusicacademy.com/2016/01/ian-levine-interview (accessed 15 December 2015).

Cook, R. 1998. *Sweet Land of Liberty?: The African-American Struggle for Civil Rights in the Twentieth Century*. Harlow: Longman.

Croasdell, A. 1997. Liner notes to *Dave Godin's Deep Soul Treasures*, vol. 1 (London: Kent, CD).

Davis, J. 2015. "Containing Racism?: The London Experience, 1957–1968". In *The Other Special Relationship: Race, Rights, and Riots in Britain and the United States*, edited by R. D. G. Kelley and S. Tuck, 125–46. New York: Palgrave.

Dean, S., and D. Godin. 1976. Letter from Simon Dean, and Dave Godin's response, *Blues & Soul* 187 (6 April): 26.

Doyle, B. 2006. "'More Than a Dance Hall, More a Way of Life': Northern Soul, Masculinity and Working Class Culture in 1970s Britain". In *Between Marx and Coca-Cola: Youth Cultures in Changing European Societies, 1960–1980*, edited by A. Shildt and D. Siegfried, 313–30. New York: Berghahn Books.

Elson, F. 1974a. "Checkin' It Out". *Blues & Soul* 130 (12-25 March): 14–15.

—1974b. "Checkin' It Out". *Blues & Soul* 132 (9-22 April): 16.

Forman, J. 1964. "A Band of Brothers, A Circle of Trust: What is the Student Nonviolent Coordinating Committee?" Internal SNCC document, c. November at: http://www.crmvet.org/nars/forman1.htm (accessed 20 January 2016).

Gilbert J., and E. Pearson. 1999. *Discographies: Dance Music, Culture and the Politics of Sound*. London: Routledge.

Godin, D. 1964. Letter to Jocelyn Jerome (Congress of Racial Equality), 22 May, Records of the Congress of Racial Equality, Wisconsin Historical Society, Madison WI Series 5, Box 30, folder 4.

—1966. Letter to *Record Mirror*, November 26, p. 2.

—1968. "R&B and the Long Hot Summer". *Soul Music Magazine* (March) reprinted in *The Faber Book of Pop*, edited by Hanif Kureishi and Jon Savage, 324–27. London: Faber & Faber, 1995.

—1970a. "Dave Godin Column". *Blues & Soul* 44 (9-22 October): 16.

—1970b. "Dave Godin Column". *Blues & Soul* 47 (20 November–3 December): 16.

—1971a. "Land of a Thousand Dances". *Blues & Soul* 50 (8-21 January): 18–19. Copy at: https://tinyurl.com/y6uolus8 (accessed 16 December 2015).

—1971b. "'Dave Godin Column". *Blues & Soul* 55 (19 March–1 April): 18–19.

—1971c. "Dave Godin Column". *Blues & Soul* 57 (16-29 April): 18–19.

—1971d. "Dave Godin Column". *Blues & Soul* 62 (25 June–8 July) in *The Gospel According to Dave Godin* issue 3, p. 45. Available at: https://tinyurl.com/page2-issue-3-PDF (accessed 20 January 2016).
—1971e. "Dave Godin Column". *Blues & Soul* 67 (10-23 September): 18–19.
—1971f. "Dave Godin Column". *Blues & Soul* 68 (24 September–7 October): 18–19.
—1972a. "Dave Godin Column". *Blues & Soul* 77 (4-17 February): 19.
—1972b. "Dave Godin Column". *Blues & Soul* 86 (16-29 June): 18.
—1972c. "Dave Godin Column". *Blues & Soul* 87 (30 June–13 July): 12.
—1972d. "Dave Godin Column". *Blues & Soul* 90 (11-24 August): 18.
—1974. "The Dave Godin Page". *Black Music* 1, 3 (February): 44.
—1975a. "Dave Godin Column". *Blues & Soul* 159 (29 April–12 May): 18.
—1975b. "Dave Godin Column". *Blues & Soul* 163 (24 June–7 July): 18.
—1975c. "Dave Godin Column". *Blues & Soul* 164 (8-21 July): 14, 18.
—1975d. Responses to letters, *Blues & Soul* 167 (19 August–1 September): 30.
—1975e. "Dave Godin Column". *Blues & Soul* 170 (30 September–13 October): 14, 16.
—1975f. Review of *The Soul Book*, *Blues & Soul* 171 (14 October). Available at: http://www.soulfulhorwich.org.uk/godinbs171.html (accessed 1 June 2012).
—1975g. "Dave Godin Column". *Blues & Soul* 173 (11-24 November): 14, 16–17.
—1975h. "Dave Godin Column". *Blues & Soul* 174 (25 November–8 December): 12, 14, 16.
—1975i. Letter to the editor, *The Guardian*, 31 December, p. 10.
—1976a. "Dave Godin Column". *Blues & Soul* 183 (9 March): 26.
—1976b. "Dave Godin Column". *Blues & Soul* 187 (6 April): 10.
—1976c. "Dave Godin Column". *Blues & Soul* 190 (27 April): 8.
—1976d. "Dave Godin Column". *Blues & Soul* 205 (10 August): 23.
—1977a. "Dave Godin Column". *Blues & Soul* 220 (1-14 March): 16.
—1977b. "Dave Godin Column". *Blues & Soul* 221 (15-28 March): 40.
—1977c. "Dave Godin Column". *Blues & Soul* 222 (29 March–11 April): 20.
—1977d. "Dave Godin Column". *Blues & Soul* 225 (10–23 May): 33, 34, 37.
—1977e. "Dave Godin Column". *Blues & Soul* 236 (11–24 October): 42.
—1997. Liner notes to *Dave Godin's Deep Soul Treasures*, vol. 1 (London: Kent, CD).
—1999. Foreword to Ritson and Russell, *The In Crowd: The Story of the Northern & Rare Soul Scene Volume one*. London: Bee Cool Publishing.
—2009. "The Detroit Report". In *The Sharper Word: A Mod Anthology*, revised and updated edition, edited by Paolo Hewitt, 105–115. London: Helter Skelter.
The Guardian. 1955a. "Negro Boy Killed in Mississippi". 2 September, p. 7.
—1955b. "Murdered Negro". 6 September, p. 7.
—1955c. 'Murder of a Negro Boy". *Manchester Guardian*, 7 September, p. 7.
—1955d. "Death Penalty Not Demanded", 20 September, p. 7.
—1955e. "Alleged Murder of Negro", 23 September, p. 9.
—1955f. "Alleged Murder of Negro Boy", 24 September, p. 1.
—1955g. "American Civilisation on Trial", 26 September, p. 7.
—1955h. "Grand Jury to Meet", 28 September, p. 7.
—1955i. "Emmett Till Case", 10 November, p. 1.
Guéron, N. L. 1994–1995. "An Idea Whose Time Has Come: A Comparative Procedural History of the Civil Rights Acts of 1960, 1964, and 1991". *Yale Law Journal* 104: 1201–1234.

Hewitt, P. 2003. "The Soul Pioneer". *Manifesto*, June. Available at: http://www.soulwalking.co.uk/%A5Dave%20Godins%20File/Dave-Page-1.jpg; http://www.soulwalking.co.uk/%A5Dave%20Godins%20File/Dave-Page-2.jpg (accessed 4 November 2010).

Hooton, A. 1976. "North versus North". Letter, *Blues & Soul* 204 (3 August): 24.

The Independent. 2004. Dave Godin obituary, 20 October, p. 34.

Jagger, M. *et al.* 2003. *According to the Rolling Stones.* London: Weidenfeld & Nicolson.

Jones, B. 1963 (2005). Letter to Dave Godin c. January in Mark Paytress, *The Rolling Stones Off the Record: Outrageous Opinions and Unrehearsed Interviews*, 21. London: Omnibus Press.

Lawson, P. c.1990. Interview with Dave Godin, *The Gospel According to Dave Godin* (an independently-published fanzine), issue 1 p. 36 at: https://tinyurl.com/page2-issue-1-PDF (accessed 20 January 2016).

Milestone, K. 1997. "The Love Factory: The Sites, Practices and Media Relationships of Northern Soul". In *The Clubcultures Reader: Readings in Popular Cultural Studies*, edited by S. Redhead, D. Wynne and J. O'Connor, 134–49. Oxford: Blackwell.

Morris, A. 1984. *The Origins of the Civil Rights Movement: Black Communities Organizing for Change.* New York: Free Press.

Nathan, D. 2000. Liner notes to *Dave Godin's Deep Soul Treasures*, vol. 3 (London: Kent, CD).

—2006. Interview with David Freeland, September. Available at: www.davidnathan.com (accessed 11 May 2011).

—n.d. "My Friend, the Godfather of R&B in the UK", *6T's: Rhythm and Soul Society*. Available at: http://www.6ts.info/dave/ (accessed 22 January 2016).

New York Times. 1955. Brigid Brophy obituary, 9 August. Available at: https://preview.tinyurl.com/1995-08-09-brophy (accessed 22 January 2016).

Nicholls, R. 2011. "The Tamla Motown Appreciation Society", *The Mod Generation*. Available at: http://www.themodgeneration.co.uk/2011/01/tamla-motown-appreciation-society.html (accessed 21 January 2016).

Nowell, D. 2011. *The Story of Northern Soul.* London: Portico.

Richards, K. 2010. *Life.* London: Orion.

Richardson, C. 2010. *Really Sayin' Something: Memoirs of a Soul Survivor.* New Romney: Bank House Books.

Ritson, R., and S. Russell. 1999. *The In Crowd: The Story of the Northern & Rare Soul Scene Volume one.* London: Bee Cool Publishing.

Savage, J. 1995. Interview with Dave Godin, 11 February. Copy courtesy of Jon Savage.

—1997. Interview with Dave Godin, 13 June. Copy courtesy of Jon Savage.

—2015. *1966: The Year the Decade Exploded.* London: Faber.

Street, J. 2011a. Telephone interview with Brian Lovegrove, 29 March. Notes in author's collection.

—2011b. Interview with Graham Moss and Mike Tyldesley, 16 August. Transcript in author's collection.

—2011c. Telephone interview with Chrissie Charlton, 22 August. Transcript in author's collection.

—2012. "From Beloved Community to Imagined Community: SNCC's Intellectual Transformation". In *From Sit-Ins to SNCC: The Student Civil Rights Movement in the 1960s*, edited by I. Morgan and P. Davies, 116–34. Gainesville: University of Florida Press.

—2015. "Stax, Subcultures, and Civil Rights: Young Britain and the Politics of Soul Music in the 1960s". In *The Other Special Relationship: Race, Rights, and Riots in Britain and the United States*, edited by R. D. G. Kelley and S. Tuck, 173–95. New York: Palgrave.

—2016. Telephone interview with Ady Croasdell, 4 February. Notes in author's collection.

Times. 1955a. "Negro Boy's Death", 24 September, p. 6.

—1955b. "Negro Boy's Death", 7 December, p. 9.

Various authors. 2004. *Soul Music Forum*. Available at: http://www.soul-source.co.uk/soul-forum/topic/58194-dave-godin/#comment-600644 (accessed 22 January 2016).

—n.d. Tributes at "Dave Godin". Available at: http://www.soulwalking.co.uk/Dave%20Godin.html (accessed 22 January 2016).

Williams, R. 2004. Dave Godin obituary, *The Guardian*, 20 October. Available at: http://www.theguardian.com/news/2004/oct/20/guardianobituaries.artsobituaries (accessed 19 January 2016).

Wilson, T. 2009. *Tamla Motown: The Stories behind the UK Singles*. London: Cherry Red Books.

Winstanley, R., and D. Nowell. 1996. *Soul Survivors: The Wigan Casino Story*. London: Robson Books.

"Yorkshire Soul Lover". 1971. Letter, *Blues & Soul* 64 (23 July–5 August): 2.

8 Myths on/of the Northern Soul Scene

Sarah Raine and Tim Wall

A history of the northern soul scene is comprehensively set out in a range of books, films and websites which give a rich picture of the scene's past. They tell a story of the background to the scene's formation and its early and later incarnations, all expressed through the strong sense that the scene has survived and flourished, welcomed new members and renewed itself, while always remaining true to its origins and traditions. Many of these mediated histories are stories produced for an insider audience by authors and media producers who themselves have personal experience of the scene. We see this as part of an extensive process of self-documentation and myth-making which has become a central cultural practice of the northern soul scene.

We argue that the histories of northern soul represent a shared narrative; held as a common point of reference, widely distributed, and used as a locus for personal identity. Above all, these stories are testaments to an insider identity: a sense of what it is to be a member of the scene and, by contrast, what lies outside. In unpicking the strands of northern soul storytelling, it soon becomes clear that these are tales of a mythologized past full of heroes and villains, moments of self-affirming valour, adversity, and threatened extinction. In this chapter, we are particularly interested in the way participants on the scene have recorded and communicated such narratives about the scene's development, and how these stories are woven into their involvement in the scene today. We seek to explore how the story of the northern soul scene is told through these media and how they relate to processes of scene self-documentation. We tease out the differences between self-documenting processes and the more mainstream ways in which the scene is represented.

At the heart of all these stories is an origin myth, the veneration of the point from which the scene emerged as a collective culture and established its sense of itself, its way of being and behaving: the point at which it was named "northern soul". We focus in particular on the origin myth connected to *Blues & Soul* journalist Dave Godin in the first years of the 1970s, who is credited as coining the phrase "northern soul" in the London-based magazine and, as we show, is responsible for establishing the main mythologized themes apparent in the books, films and websites which continue to memorize the scene.

In seeing northern soul self-documented histories as mythologies, we do not seek to say they are factually wrong. The accounts we explore in this chapter go into enormous detail about the dates, events and people which constitute the scene's past. However, we do point to the way that such mediated histories are built upon a series of dominant stories of the scene as a linear "history" that streamlines the multiple and sometimes discordant individual experiences into a logical, memorable and mythologized history. There are interesting factual differences between what constitutes the standard story of northern soul and what the primary evidence shows, and we do identify a number of these below. However, our purpose is not to construct an alternative history of northern soul, or offer an academic truth in opposition to the mythologized stories, but to explore how the existing stories are the creation of processes of self-documenting and mainstream representation.

In this chapter, then, we see northern soul scene participants as organic historians producing a vernacular history of their scene, and the histories as a highly codified set of representations of the scene's past, most often produced by people with detailed and personal knowledge of the way that the scene evolved and how it works. As insiders, these producers usually have strong psychological and cultural investment in both the scene and its past. As we detail, these collective processes of self-documentation embrace the collecting of mementoes and records, curating them alongside other tangible and intangible pieces of the scene's history. Such artefacts are also interwoven with nostalgia, memory, and the power of recall. This material, and the stories that organize its meaning, have been woven into commercially produced books, structure and illustrate the scene in documentaries and, more recently, have been forged into feature-length film fictions. The representations captured in this primary material have then been recirculated as iconography in pop videos, feature films, television dramas, and adverts. At the same time, they have been reused by northern participants themselves to create new artefacts that memorialize, celebrate and reproduce the scene's past through fan-produced YouTube videos, Facebook posts and web forum discussions.

The production of such stories and the media texts that carry them are part of a process of cultural authentication, through which participants call on detail that would only be available to those who had experienced the scene first-hand. In this chapter, we explore in greater detail the degree to which the position of insider or outsider is apparent in the very form of the mediated histories, and we illuminate the way scene participants apply this authentication process when new examples of the scene history are tested in online discussions. We show that the strength of a history producer's claim to be an insider is a major factor in determining the value of a particular mediation of the scene's past by and to the northern soul community. The authentication process is also apparent in the way scene members use these materials to articulate their own identity as insiders, and the way these histories are utilized as forms of power to define who is an authentic insider. As with other insider DIY scenes, these mythologized self-documented histories are a structuring and stabilizing force, capable of subtle yet essential changes to suit a continuing, multigenerational and international scene, facilitated by the very form of self-documentation and the role that it plays in individual claims to scene membership.

In what follows, then, we explore some of the self-documented histories of the scene, draw out core myths, explore how they operate over a range of media as a key part in the mythologizing process of self-documentation, and identify the ways in which they act as a stabilizing and legitimizing force. We start with an examination of then contemporary representations of the early scene, including a key origin myth to which almost all other histories point. This is followed by an exploration of the burgeoning body of self-documented histories that have been produced since 1990 in both traditional published and broadcast media, and increasingly on more informal online platforms. In noting that a major part of the cultural activity that define today's scene is dedicated to documenting and accounting for northern soul's past, we contrast published, filmic, and online histories and examine the mythologized senses of belonging they generate. We conclude by opening up the implications for a multigenerational scene which expects an affinity with the scene's history as a requirement for membership.

Northern soul material culture and the origin myth

It is worth starting with two central ways to engage with the mythological processes that take place on the scene. Firstly, in thinking about mythologizing processes, we summarize the material out of which the stories of the development of the scene are constructed, and make some simple points about the relationship between access to the scene, and a sense of insider or outsider status often applied to them. Secondly, reflecting on one key mythologized story, we explore the origin myth of the scene. Like other origin myths, it encapsulates the idealistic nature of the society such myths bring forth, and it stands as the foundation for all other myths of such a society. As we will see, the story about the origins of northern soul interestingly grows out of one of the first attempts to name and mythologize the scene.

Anyone interested in constructing a history of the northern soul scene can draw upon the material culture that has survived since its 1970s origins. The pre-internet age documents that were produced as part of the cultural practices of the scene survive mainly due to both conscious and accidental archiving activities, which in itself demonstrate the commitment of its participants and the importance of participation in their lives. Over the five decades of the scene, its adherents have hoarded the photographs, membership cards, and flyers which memorialize their participation and form the visible tangible heritage of the scene. As a record-based music culture, collecting the physical seven-inch 45rpm discs is a central activity, and these collections also document the shifting popularity of individual records and index the venues in which they were first played. This historicizing of individual records is apparent in the way records are discussed online and the way they are introduced within a DJ set at a northern night.

At the same time, glimpses of the scene are apparent in more formally archived media coverage of its activity. Sometimes this involves the specialist journals that capture events, profile the people and articulate the values of the scene. In the 1970s, the richest account is to be found in two regular columns that appeared in the widest circulation magazine aimed at soul fans, *Blues & Soul*, the most noteworthy being the column authored by Dave Godin. Parts of the scene gained a notoriety that led to coverage in local, and occasionally the national press, when "moral panics" about a venue's place in the locality or police activity around drug taking became issues of public debate. There are also a couple of early self-conscious attempts to produce a serious documentation of the early scene. The first, Tony Palmer's 1977 television documentary *Wigan Casino*, was part of a British social documentary series and remains accessible as a commercial DVD today. An article on northern soul, Stuart Cosgrove's 1982 piece (also reprinted in this book as Chapter 1) appeared in a low-circulation cerebral music magazine of the time and tries to convey something of the specificity of the scene.

Northern participants, especially in their online discussions, most often judge the value of such stories using the notion of scene insider and outsider. However, in reflecting on this material as the primary texts of the scene's past, it becomes obvious that such categories are not as straightforward as they seem, and we can discern two dimensions of importance for its place as historical document. The first dimension involves the degree of access to the scene; the second the degree to which the material is given a narrative order by those who present it. In the first dimension, while the photographs, membership cards, flyers and records only exist because of the insider status of the owner, the insider credentials of those who narratize this material move along a sliding scale. We raise these points to demonstrate that the simplifying narratives of northern soul myths function less as historical truth, and to point out that more important issues of belonging and the right to speak about (or even, for) the scene need our attention.

For instance, in thinking about the dimension of access, the insightfulness of Cosgrove's 1982 article is in part a result of an insider status perhaps not apparent when he wrote his article, and only fully shared publically in his 2016 book. By contrast, the early 1970s *Blues & Soul* journalism of Dave Godin, while clearly very committed to understanding the scene, required access to scene participants as source material as, in reality, he was at best an onlooker. It is also clear from the 1977 documentary that Tony Palmer gained a similarly substantive access to Wigan Casino, but his representation of the late 1970s club is still contested as that of an outsider today. As the interview with Palmer reproduced in Chapter 13 of this book shows, it is possible to construct a plausible argument that Palmer gained greater and more diverse access than Godin, who nevertheless is featured in the origin myth as central to the formation of the scene. And the journalists who produced the news coverage of scene drug dealing and complaints against different clubs clearly cared little about understanding the scene itself, and even less about addressing its participants.

In narrating the raw material into media texts, the position of the authors within the mainstream media becomes pertinent. The Palmer and Cosgrove media texts, as professionally produced forms, organize the meaning of the early scene in a much more orderly form than the often random collections of the horded ephemera of participants and the sensationalized coverage of the news media. The skills of media professionals may make northern soul more comprehensible to those outside the scene; for those who memorialize their participation through the records and keepsakes they accumulated, the meanings of these objects are to be found in their place in their autobiographical stories of their participation. Collectively, these autobiographical stories form an intangible heritage of the scene, which during the 1980s and 1990s remained relatively obscure, indexed by equally obscure objects which only survived because of the personal commitment of individuals.

In the late 1990s, in a noteworthy index of interest in the scene, the number of magazines, television documentaries, and serious journalistic and academic articles on northern soul increased exponentially. The number of media texts documenting and celebrating the scene is many times greater in the twenty-first century than it was in the origin days of the 1970s. At the same time, the media documenting or referencing the scene and its music has also expanded to include fiction feature films, music videos linked to a range of "outsider" artists, and adverts for commercial products unrelated to the scene's cultural practices. It is to this material and the way that it is used as a mythologizing cultural practice that we turn in the next section.

Before examining contemporary representations of the scene, though, we need to understand how individual myths of northern soul are ordered, and there is no better way to do this than to start with the very earliest documenting of the scene. As most histories of northern soul attest, it is in the pages of Dave Godin's column in *Blues & Soul* that the scene was first identified and named. Godin's place in northern soul lore is so strong that even the Wikipedia page that explains the scene starts the history with the claim that the phrase northern soul "was first publicly used in Godin's weekly column in *Blues & Soul* magazine in June 1970". The fact that this is not actually the case has not stopped the story being given prominence on the Wikipedia page, and in just about every published account of the origins of the scene (including some of the other chapters within this book). Like all origin myths, the importance of the story of the naming of the scene is not to be found in its factual accuracy but the way it functions within the scene community. As we show, Godin's widely cited, but infrequently read, column is important in constructing a set of foundational myths about northern soul even before its name crystallized into the now widely used term.

It is apposite that the key origin myth assigns the naming of northern soul to a man named Dave Godin. The ordinary Englishness of his diminutive forename is matched with the mythological-sounding surname. Godin's column in a specialist music magazine for British soul fans actually represents not only one of the first detailed accounts of the scene, but also the first codification of most of the mythological tropes that followed. Like Tony Palmer's 1977 televised documenting of the scene, Godin's representation is that of the onlooker from outside – in Godin's case, the perspective of a London-based journalist and record shop owner with left libertarian views and a long track record as a UK advocate for the value of black American music. Joe Street considers Godin's background at greater length in Chapter 7 of this book.

Godin's column, in the leading magazine for what was in the 1970s contemporary black music, was usually based on lists of records (which displayed his mastery of the music's past and present), together with homilies on the value of soul music and the fraternity of soul fans. Issues 36 and 37, published in 1970, deviate from his normal approach in focusing entirely on what he terms "the up-North soul groove". Of course, to a Londoner, most of Britain is "up-North" and, in Godin's narrative, it is presented as the counter to a London "jaded by a surfeit of novelty and sensation" (Godin 1970a: 16). It is in issue 50, in "Land of a Thousand Dances", that Godin takes a strikingly different journalistic approach to the one he routinely used, adopting a distinctly ethnographic descriptive style to recount his adventure by train and taxi beyond London to the Twisted Wheel soul club in Manchester (Godin 1970b). While he may not have coined the phrase "northern soul" in the article, he does call on a longer history of a mythologized English "northcountry", setting the precedence for the ways in which future stories of northern soul places are narrated. Godin evokes a place free of the "tension or aggression" and the "social stand-offishness" that "plagues" the south. Something of Godin's prose can be discerned by the third paragraph:

> Somewhere out in that back night gloom – in this city of what looked like perpetual night – there was an oasis known as the Wheel. It was as if all the life energy of the great city was channeled into this spot and hidden away under the ground for fear of disturbing the respectable citizenry, because looking out from the cab windows on this dank and murky night, Manchester looked like a ghost town. How wrong first impressions can be was to be shown by later events and happenings (Godin 1970b: 18).

In the company of friendly "brothers and sisters" in soul at a local pub, Godin moves on to queue outside the Wheel and then enters the small, two-level venue. In his account, he is always an observer, approached to discuss his *Blues & Soul* column, offering records to be played and watching the dancing he considers "the highest and finest ever seen outside of the USA"; he is noticeably never a participant. His commitment to a soul fraternity, often expressed in earlier columns, is liberally applied to those at the Wheel, joined by their "love and commitment to Soul music" which he contrasts with "the lifeless pulp of the manipulated hit parade".

For Godin, Manchester and the Twisted Wheel represented "the North" in terms of its vestiges of traditional working-class community, re-imagined through a common interest in soul music. The club on that autumn evening (and in his imagination on many evenings before and after) represents a specific, "northern" and "truthful" expression of soul music enjoyment, embodied in the dancers, bounded and made secret by the walls of the venue. Godin's prose narrates the myths of unbelievable nights, records and dancers that are at the root of every other northern soul story. While the "Land of a Thousand Dances" may change location and spatial specificities over the years, its northern-ness, communality, and separateness from everyday life permeate all subsequent versions of the story.

Godin, now sadly no longer alive, has become a mythologized character himself in northern soul lore; some aspects of his life disregarded (such as his sexuality and political beliefs) and others exaggerated in accordance with his role as the godfather of northern soul. Godin emerges time and time again in the self-documented histories of the scene, a dominant expert (yet at times cantankerous and opinionated) voice, his foreword in Ritson and Russell's *The In Crowd* (1999) and frequent quotes throughout many other publications representing a continuation of his mythologizing influence, even after his death. Origin myths and mythologized tropes are common within all music scenes, acting as a consolidating story of belonging and shared beginnings (see, for instance, Bennett 2002; Forman 2013; Gebhardt 2015). Given that, for insider societies, the task of recording scene history must only take place within the scene itself and must function as another platform for the public demonstration of scene membership, the role assigned to Godin – the personification of an outsider – is contradictory at best. It is in the way he establishes the mythological tropes that follow, and the role he performs in a mythical naming of the scene, that his ideological position is so important.

As we show next, self-documented histories simplify and make heroic dominant stories and voices in the same way that they do in this origin myth. The insider value of such later documents, and the retrospective critical evaluations of every other 1970s documentarian except Godin, are both dependent upon the perceived insider/outsider status of the creator. As we show, to be deemed acceptable authors must be able to demonstrate insider status within the text itself through reference to the detail of the scene's past, through personal connection to key individuals who testify to the authenticity of the tale, and repetition of the approved origin myths. These stories bind the scene, determining who is inside and who outside. While a passion for the music, dedication, and a desire to develop one's knowledge are seen as the fundamentals of authentic membership, and this allows a degree of flexibility in who can become a member, the ability to connect to the scene mythology is central to full acceptance. While the mythology is determined by a strict timeline, membership is afforded through an adherence to fundamental scene values.

Self-documenting as a process of myth-making

As we have already shown, in the last twenty years the original documents of the early scene are overshadowed by the even greater quantity of material produced within the scene today. This culturally organic media most often takes the form of histories that both return to the origins of the scene to explain where it comes from and seek to tell its history through to the present. As forms of media they usually draw on the conventions and styles of the journalistic article, the video documentary, or the historical account, or they use aspects of these in more diffuse forms of online media where digital technologies and online platforms are utilized to produce splintered elements of a larger historical project. In fact, a major part of the cultural activity of today's northern scene is dedicated to documenting and accounting for northern soul's past. There is not always a clear distinction between material which can be understood as entirely produced within the scene, solely for other scene participants using vernacular forms, and that produced outside the scene using professional conventions for wider audiences. Nevertheless, the notion of insider narratives and outsider positions are central to understanding both how this material is constructed and how it is used and valued within the scene itself.

The hoarded and professionally-ordered material represents two senses of the process of documenting: two sets of sources that document the past; two sets of historical document. For both the academic cultural historian and the scene participant these historical sources constitute a way at getting at and representing the origins of the scene and its unfolding story. They provide clues to what happened, who was involved, and how things looked and sounded. They also provide versions of how the events, people and cultural bricolage are made meaningful through the narratives that organize them. These two connected activities of documentation (hoarding tangible fragments of "being there" and setting out what happened) produce a wealth of representations of northern soul that can be circulated, selected from and formed into new representations of the scene's past, or used to signify the scene's present as rooted in its tradition.

The power of the narrative to organize the tangible heritage of music culture within professionally-produced music documentary is something addressed in our earlier work (Long and Wall 2013, 2010; Wall and Long 2010), and elsewhere we have critiqued how academics have engaged with this documented past to frame their investigations of different aspects of the contemporary scene (Raine and Wall 2017). In the latter, we sought in part to raise interesting questions about the insider and outsider positions of academics who study popular music culture. Here, though, we want to focus on a vernacular form of historiography to understand the increasingly large body of media material produced by members of the scene. In doing so, we draw upon the themes of this earlier work to explore how the process of self-documenting has generated narratives about the scene, and how the tangible heritage is utilized by the organic historians of northern soul, especially the way that narrating the history is used to make a claim to insider status. As we will show, these processes of historicizing northern soul are built around ideas of the scene's intangible heritage. Unlike the physical documents that constitute the tangible history of northern soul, the ideas, values and commitments that comprise the scene's intangible heritage can only be shared through participation in the scene. The complex social rules, rituals and hierarchies are not always discernible to anyone who enters the scene from outside, and the commonly distributed images of the scene that are in wider circulation often focus on the superficially striking cultural practices, such as the gymnastic dancing or dress style, rather than the subtle codes of belonging which are so valued by members (see Wall 2006 for an exploration of the politics of northern soul dancing). Equally, ownership of the tangible heritage or primary documents of the scene, from personal photographs, membership cards, and flyers through to original pressings of records or vintage clothes, are central to claims of being an authentic scene member. It is access to this material culture that enables authorship of self-documenting media and the opportunity of insider display.

For these reasons, the self-documentation label we apply does not indicate a category of products or activities, but more specifically refers to the relationship of the media product to the scene's participants, to the scene-defined intentions behind the production, and to the scene members who constitute these media products' primary audience. That is not to say that some examples of these self-documenting texts have not been produced with wider commercial objectives in mind, nor that they might be bought by a wider audience or be understood differently outside the scene. As we show below, however, they are often different in form from the professional media products that are primarily produced for audiences outside the scene, even if the producers of the latter have a connection to the scene. They are also significantly different from media products that signal a connection to the scene, or use its iconography for purposes other than self-documentation. Most of the feature films set on the scene, and the adverts or music videos that call on "northern soul cool", therefore fall outside this type of media. In fact, as we explore later, such products are widely discredited and often ridiculed by scene members, and significant debates take place about the authenticity of particular media artefacts. The line between scene insider and outsider is rigorously guarded.

Of course, the use of self-documented texts is not unique to the northern soul scene. They are central activities within most popular music fan communities, particularly those who engage in DIY practices, and often a primary way in which the scene defines itself. In an earlier analysis, we argued that this self-documenting process is one of the characteristics that define northern soul as a DIY culture, the narratives of these DIY products articulating a mythical history which establishes the authenticities of the scene (Raine and Wall 2017). The self-documenting books, videos and websites represent the insider construction of the scene, usually in starkly contrasting ways to those representations produced by outsiders. The testaments to the scene in the pages of early 1970s issues of *Blues & Soul*, for instance, are sharply different to the sensationalized press coverage produced in the same years, as later self-documenting texts almost always point out.

In exploring the self-documenting narratives as myths, or discussing all texts about northern soul as mythologizing, we draw on the notion that myths are stories developed by particular cultures to explain who they are, often pinpointing origins, traditions and norms or morals of behaviour. In particular we have been influenced by the work in anthropology and cultural and media studies which uses notions of myth as active cultural processes and ideologies pervasive within media texts. The stories of the northern soul scene exhibit many of the characteristics assigned by theorists of myths in traditional societies, and those adapted to look at contemporary industrial society more generally. Certainly, Sahlins' (1981; 1985) argument that we can see the mythologizing process as one of simplification and symbolism which naturalizes power relationships and cultural change, and resolves contradictions, is manifest in the self-documenting narratives of the scene. They certainly highlight the relationship between the heroic "inside" culture and the mundane "outside" inauthentic experience. As stories, they feature the repetition of familiar tropes of hero, the testing challenge, and restoration of community values that Propp identified in the folk tales of Russia (1958). And in Barthesian (1972) terms, such stories not only justify, legitimize and maintain the current form of the scene, they also act to demonstrate and legitimize the "insider" identity of the author, ensuring compliance with dominant narratives of scene past and present.

These self-documented histories, then, offer a means of recording significant moments in the scene's past, often dealing with its origins and founding period. They also usually make significant use of the author's personal experience, or draw on the testament of named individuals. At the same time, though, they all tend to reproduce a pre-existing narrative; one that is itself in wide circulation within the scene, and often articulated as an oral history, shared and passed on to younger members in order to explain both the origins of the scene and its continued existence. Through the construction of a logical and linear narrative of the self-documented history, the many stories and experiences of the scene are simplified and made symbolic, key events representing key scene discourses and acting to remove the northern soul scene from the mundane mainstream and subcultural "other".

For instance, one of the central myths of northern soul relates to the importance of "rare" soul records. The music played on the northern soul scene comes from a wide range of African American and other pop music genres, and is most strongly associated with sounds established in the early 1960s. As such, it is not a genre of music, but rather a scene-specific canon of records, regulated by dominant narratives concerning musical form, an "uptempo" beat, and the mythologized idea of the expression of "soul". In fact, the predominant sounds of records played have their origins in what Brian Ward (1998) has called bi-racial pop of the early 1960s, rather than the soul sound of late 1960s African American music. In articulating the sound of northern soul, then, it is most often associated with the notion that it is based upon musical qualities characteristic of records released on the UK Tamla Motown label which provided European releases for records on the independent US Tamla and Motown record labels. Again, though, this original Tamla sound shares far more with the polished, highly-produced bi-racial pop sound than the more gospel-influenced soul sound that supplanted it culturally and commercially. A high proportion of 1960s bi-racial pop was produced to serve the dance fads of the same period, and the televised youth culture dance parties and the increasing prosperity of the postwar younger generation led to a rapid expansion in independent record labels generating a high volume of short-lived record releases (see Wall 2009, for a discussion of this phenomenon). It is from this massive pool of recordings that northern soul has been primarily built.

Although there are sometimes references to the cultural context in which these records were produced, the narrative of northern soul histories never use the sorts of ideas set out by Ward, let alone go into the nuanced detail he uses. In the northern soul myth, it is the music's rarity that challenges the record-collecting hero and allows the scene to be constructed in opposition to the commercial, mediated abundance of mainstream 1970s pop culture. The recorded black American music at the heart of the scene is most often dealt with through a simplified version of the historic experiences of the music's originators which is then reframed into a story built around the sustained values of an oppositional community. In the mythologized narrative of northern soul records there is an almost overwhelming detail about the physical form of the record itself and the small marginal record companies who produced them. In the myth, the standard ubiquity and availability of music as a capitalist commodity is subverted by the scene to emphasize an alternative community driven to discover the unique great sound lost in the general functioning of commercial record company systems. One version, articulated by David Nowell, uses Motown records as an explanatory exemplar:

> By 1966 the hits were so prolific that Berry Gordy decided at his make-or-break quality-control Friday meetings ... that no singles would be released that weren't guaranteed Top Ten hits! ... This ensured that only the most commercial-sounding recordings were

> ever released, while thousands of superb-quality master tapes never saw the light of day. At least it gave the Northern Soul fans of the future something to hunt for (Nowell 1999: 24).

Nowell here outlines his own version of the mythologized creation of a UK northern soul culture made out of the discarded outtakes of US black popular music industry, stored away in dusty warehouses for their heroic liberation and inclusion within the northern soul canon. By placing the story within the wider history of Motown's infamous owner, Berry Gordy, Nowell demonstrates a legitimizing access to not only scene-specific knowledge but also general music history, yet in doing so he perpetuates the dominant scene association between the records of northern soul scene and the Motown genre. Through such stories, the origins of the music and the scene are made heroic, the liberators of records endowed with the ability to pick out rare gems for soul enthusiasts back home, the records themselves a marvellous accident. These stories are self-celebratory and valorize the unlikely and the underground, positioning northern soul records and participants as enlightened and enjoying exclusive access to a "true" music rejected by the ignorant masses.

In terms we will explore next, Nowell, *Too Darn Soulful*, has an interesting relationship to our notion of a self-documenting culture because it adopts a standard professional journalistic history mode of writing. It is, though, widely referenced in northern soul social media communities, either used to warrant a particular position in a discussion or recommended to those seeking answers to questions about northern soul's past. In its 2011 edition, it claims to be the "definitive history" of the scene "that refused to die", and it remains a common reference point for outsider writers, from journalists to online commenters, academic researchers to fan authors. Like the other books we look at below, Nowell draws upon a standard narrative about the rise and fall of key venues and the roles of heroic and demonized characters in the creation (and at times destruction) of the scene. He articulates a dominant view of the scene and its participants as musically and culturally enlightened, on the periphery of respectable society, yet bound together through a sense of community and their truthful passion for an authentic music. Quite strikingly, as we go on to demonstrate below, these narratives are central to the very earliest documenting of the scene we have already discussed, undertaken by Dave Godin, the slightly estranged godfather of northern soul.

The documents and their myths

We have already indicated that the histories of the northern scene can be found in books, films and the online activities of scene participants. It is productive to take each of these in turn. They interestingly relate to the issues of material culture and mythologizing self-documentation in different ways and are positioned along the dimensions of insider/outsider culture and professionalized order in very different ways.

I know about being there: book-length histories
There are over twenty books published about northern soul and the scene, and most offer a history of the scene. Interestingly, given the scene's 1970s origins and strong continuing life through the 1980s and 90s, these books are mostly a twenty-first-century phenomenon. At the time of writing, examples were consistently to be found in the top 20 of best-selling books on dance or soul music. While Nowell's book has remained the best-selling over two versions (1999 and 2001), Mike Ritson and Stuart Russell's (1999) *The In Crowd*, Elaine Constantine and Gareth Sweeney's (2013) film tie-in *Northern Soul: An Illustrated History*, and Stuart Cosgrove's (2016) *Young Soul Rebels* demonstrate the main mythologized tropes and offer very interesting points of comparison.

Nowell, Ritson and Russell, and Cosgrove all in their own way make the claim for an insider narrative, even when they adopt more standard forms of journalism and writing apparent in other areas of music culture. Certainly, such accounts dominate the written histories of northern soul, offering readers access to the "key" events and personal histories of the writers and their scene. The specific contexts of each author's scene participation are subtly evident within the books, often set out in the biography, and always coded in the implicit claim they make to be "authentic" accounts. As we have seen, Ritson and Russell even draw upon Dave Godin's position of mythical signifier, celebrating him as author of the book's foreword writer and acknowledging him as a guide to the book's contents.

All these authors seek to establish an origin for the scene and provide a detailed account of its development, usually through moments of disruption and a continuing theme that northern soul sits, mainly hidden, in the margins of mainstream popular culture. These are common features of all popular music histories (see Wall 2013 for a discussion of these tropes). They all also include certain key elements: a common geographical and chronological trajectory; a curatorial author role; an informal tone and rejection of academic research form and method; a valorization of the scene as distinct from the mainstream and subcultural "others"; and the construction of the "true fan" as hero. These five fundamental characteristics act to (re)draw the scene boundaries, placing the author firmly within its precincts as an insider scene historian and the embodiment of the "true fan", defined by their own experiences and the dominant narratives of the scene.

Interestingly, while Elaine Constantine could probably make a greater claim to longevity on the scene, she makes no such explicit statement in the book that positions her in that way. Perhaps the fact that she cannot claim to have "been there" in the 1970s disallows such an authorial narrative, and leaves her to pay homage to Wigan Casino through the personal experiences of others. There is an equally strong strand of autobiographical publishing within the scene's self-documentation tradition (see, for instance, Reg Stickings [2008], Paddy Grady [2001] and Brian Waterhouse [2012]). Such an autobiographical style also appears in the scene history books, and any attempt to express an objective, journalistic account in the early pages of a book often break down as the author takes on the myth-making role, the narrative becoming dominated by the authorial experience, and the rite of passage into the original scene, not now available to the reader, is foregrounded as the defining quality of scene authenticity.

In these published scene histories, the complex network of venues, records and DJs of the historic scene has been simplified into a common geographical and chronological trajectory of the "northern soul story"; beginning with Dave Godin's origin myth of the Twisted Wheel in Manchester, moving to the Midlands for Tunstall's brief and infamous Golden Torch, and then back up to the north-west to the combative relationship between Wigan Casino and the Blackpool Mecca. These myths relate strongly to tropes that mythologize northern English cities as strong industrialized communities of open people, and the positioning of northern soul as a marginal culture is set through a binary opposition with the UK capital city and the south as a dominant British culture. Within these publications, key mythologized original venues are narrated through heroic tales reminiscent of, and at points directly quoting, Dave Godin's personal experience as detailed in *Blues & Soul*.

There are differences: Cosgrove looks at the scene in 1970s Leeds, and Ritson and Russell provide a substantial diversion from the established narrative, possibly reflecting their London base, by beginning in the London-based Mod scene and tracking the emergence of rare soul events. However, even when northern soul is seemingly placed within a longer (and southern) narrative of engagement with black American popular music, the differences between the two scenes are considered to be substantial, innately related to geography and associated cultural differences. Similarly, Cosgrove's time in London is presented as being "in exile" from the scene homeland of "The North" (2016: 227–31). These temporary deviations represent an authorial attempt to establish self as central to the "true" northern soul story, tempered by a desire to align oneself with the dominant scene myths of key venues and events: a balancing act of self and scene.

The role of the insider historian is that of a curator, forging a communal history from participant voices (collected through generally undeclared means), newspaper and magazine articles, photographs, records, and the personal experiences of the author(s). Highlighting this patchwork of memories and sources works at a scene level to warrant the authenticity of the history as an insider account, bringing together influential voices from within the scene and placing the author as "one of us" through both their knowledge and their impressive social networks. Men dominated many dancefloors and DJ decks of the 1970s and have since been immortalized through the following years of DJ sets, nostalgic CDs, websites and indeed scene histories. It is therefore unsurprising that the histories of northern soul are recounted through a male-dominated narrative, supported by a cacophony of male voices and memories (a point developed by Katie Milestone in Chapter 11). Constantine and Sweeney's book represents a notable deviation in this, giving voice to those who are normally provided in pictorial form alone or the named "girl-friends" of other scene histories, and Cosgrove singles out significant women participants, though mainly through his own relationship with them.

The complex discussion of comparative record rarity or labels, and the "breaking" of particular records at certain events, assumes a knowledgeable insider reader. Similarly, the masculine authorial voice genders the audience: a reader/author "like me". The informal tone of an insider conversation is further emphasized by a rejection of academic research form and method. The many voices of the scene converge at curated points of common experience to form the backbone of this scene-legitimized "history", yet they are detached from the processes of secondary source research and primary data collection. The outsider skills of research and academic writing form are erased from the narrative, the author expunged of all pretension and positioned for the reader as not only "one of us", but one of the best of us.

I'm still here: the scene online

One of the most striking aspects of the contemporary northern soul scene is how much of its communal activity takes place online. Insiders publically amass and share their tangible and intangible history through websites and social media platforms, often requesting or prompting the critical input of others (for a wider discussion of this phenomenon, see Long and Collins 2016). In addition to sharing, archiving and critiquing existing texts, northern soul insiders also produce short videos, hosted, shared, and in turn critiqued on YouTube, Facebook and scene-specific discussion forums. While part of wider online practices, from promoting events to buying records, it is the processes of archiving, production and critique that play a central role in the construction of a self-documented history of the scene. These texts demonstrate the key elements evident in fan publications, (re)drawing the scene boundaries, placing the producer, archivist or critic at the centre of the scene through their ability to replicate the dominant narratives of the scene and call upon their own experience to validate their claim to be an authentic insider.

Paul Long and Jez Collins (2016: 107) have highlighted the use of "closed" Facebook groups as a platform for the archiving and sharing of both tangible and intangible scene heritage by soul fans; many of these online groups are dedicated to memorializing venues now lost to car parks and council development. Brought together through their participation within the scene, group members post pictures and scans of physical objects, such as ticket stubs or membership books, old photographs (with the encouragement to others to "tag" those in the picture), as well as accounting memories and stories of the people, places and events of the historic scene. Similarly, YouTube offers a platform for the archiving and sharing of historic and previously inaccessible videos that captured some aspect of the scene, to be discussed and interrogated for their ability to authentically capture the reality of the scene.

Alongside the mainstream texts archived and shared on YouTube are a range of fan-produced texts. The number is staggering, with some fans producing tens of videos each week. In mapping out these videos, three key categories emerged: the amateur video (recording events, dance competitions, dance tutorials); the professional film (made by scene members in association with mainstream magazines or films); and the video montage. Both amateur and professional videos focus primarily on an engagement with the contemporary scene, documenting the events, people, places and dance moves of the scene today. It is, though, in the video montage where the self-documenting processes of the scene's history are most apparent. These online fan texts bring together a range of media that have over the years visually documented the scene, from mainstream documentaries to fan photographs (available on sites such as YouTube or accessible through search engines), and all set to a northern soul soundtrack. Most of the source visual elements used within these videos were originally created during the 1970s and are chosen to illustrate key, mythologized practices (such as dancing), places, and the mundane yet retrospectively heroic stages of the historic allnighters.[1] These inclusions bring together symbolic illustrations, to be decoded by knowledgeable insiders but, once again, based upon a collective knowledge and pool of materials and not rooted in original research of sources or information. Like the semi-autobiographical fan publications, these online texts follow the locations and events of the widely understood "northern soul story", the producer curating the images, videos and music available to them online to memorialize the historic scene as the pinnacle of authenticity, and to illustrate the "true fan" through the dancing bodies of the scene past, demonstrated also in the curator who brings together these disparate parts and in the understanding viewer.

Scene participants also use website discussion boards on Facebook and especially on the scene's key website, *Soul Source*, to debate a range of scene-related topics, including the successes and limitations of books, films, television documentaries, adverts, and journalistic coverage, as well as fan texts which claim to document the scene. These online platforms offer a space for a community "testing" of mediations. Platform members offer up these mediations and their creators for discussion, or as part of individual claims that they signify a "true" representation of scene experience.

The acceptance of a particular media text as an "authentic" contribution to scene history is therefore the final stage of the self-documenting process and further cements the myths of the northern soul scene. To successfully pass muster within these fora, publications or cinematic interpretations must demonstrate both a mastery of scene knowledge and the revelation of factual information from the scene's past, and the ability to reproduce the central scene origin myths. In doing so, the producers make claim to be an insider who understands the meaning of membership for other insiders and can accurately account for where the scene and its music originated. Deviating too drastically from these myths leads to texts being rejected by members of the scene as an outsider interpretation. Through this process of online community critique, the myths of the scene are systematically and more deeply engrained into the story of northern soul and the senses of identity within the contemporary scene.

Northern soul mythologies and identity in a multigenerational scene

In this chapter, we have examined the way that participants on the northern soul scene have drawn upon the material culture and personal narratives that have been used to construct a mythologized northern soul story. We identified the origin of these powerful myths in one of the documents that itself has ironically been mistakenly constructed as the moment in which the scene was first named. We have also sought to understand the processes of self-documentation through which a range of books and websites have been created to serve the interests and passionate consumption of scene participants. We have been careful to think about the mythologizing process as one of simplification and symbolism, rather than misunderstandings or misrepresentations, and one that constructs a heroic "inside" culture against a mundane "outside" inauthentic experience. A process that in turn demonstrates and legitimizes the "insider" identity of the author. We have also compared the formal differences between insider histories and those produced by non-participants, and highlighted the indeterminate position that commercially or professionally-produced feature films and documentaries have occupied when their author/producers have some personal relationship to the scene. Finally, we have shown how the equally important online activity of scene participants has simultaneously reused the material culture and scene representations to create new memorializing texts, and debated issues of professional production and insider status as a means to test the authenticity of a range of media texts produced on and of the scene.

There is an equally interesting investigation to be made of how different groups of scene participants have used and positioned themselves in relationship to the histories generated within and about the scene. These processes are just as apparent within a range of self-documented histories as they are in the discussions about their authenticity. An "authentic" or "real" experience is felt to be only possible through a rejection of mainstream technology, mediations, behaviour, and places. By extension, histories written from within the scene make a claim to greater authenticity and they receive greater scene support. As we show, the scene insider knowledge is demonstrated by an adherence to the dominant form of the scene "history" and by one's central position and performance within the key social networks of the scene.

As we see in Chapter 15, older members most commonly turn to the written histories of northern soul to redevelop or reaffirm their knowledge of the historic scene. Online critique of self-documented texts provides another opportunity for public demonstrations of scene membership, evaluated through the frame of the dominant, mythologized history of the scene. In this sense, scene myths provide the yardstick of insider experience, and self-documented books offer the reader precious and detailed knowledge of these myths to be performed in conversations (off and online) with scene others. For the older generation, *personal* experience of the historic scene is central to the placing of oneself within the mythologized scene past, and in critiquing the insider knowledge of others.

By contrast younger generations, and especially those who engage with the scene outside the UK, cannot reasonably make a claim to the same authentic connection to the scene's history. They cannot claim to have been there in the (mythologized) past. However, that is not to say that this history is not important to them. Feature-length films and the use of older footage in online fan mediations, or on YouTube, are common sources of initial introduction to the scene. In addition to recruiting new participants, online videos of the historic scene are used by the younger generation to access the scene past and to develop skills, particularly dancing. Most importantly, though, for these younger participants is the ability to master and reproduce the mythologized stories as a means to secure, as best they can, a substantial place on the scene. We return in greater detail to this research in Chapter 15, but here it is important to stress that this reuse of mythologized histories is as important as the reuse of the material culture to memorialize.

Of course, none of these processes is unique to the northern soul scene, and there is much value in understanding other popular music cultures in terms of the processes of mythologizing the past. We make this very argument at greater length in other published research (Raine and Wall 2017). However, the nearing fifty-year history of northern soul, the sheer quantity of self-documenting histories produced, and the multigenerational nature of today's scene make this a distinctive and fascinating way to understand exactly what northern soul culture means to its participants.

About the authors

Sarah Raine is a Research Fellow at Birmingham City University. Her research into the ways in which the younger members of the northern soul scene negotiate their place in a multigenerational community that values "original" participation has been published in a range of journals and books. She is co-managing editor of *Riffs: Experimental Writing on Popular Music*, review editor and special issue guest editor (2018) for *IASPM@Journal*, and the network coordinator for *Jazz & Everyday Aesthetics*. She has been attending northern soul events in the UK and Spain since 2012.

Tim Wall is Professor of Radio and Popular Music Studies, and Associate Dean for Research in the Faculty of Arts, Design and Media at Birmingham City University. He undertook his doctorate on black music and radio at the Centre for Contemporary Cultural Studies at the University of Birmingham. He researches into the production and consumption cultures around music and the media, mixing historical analysis with contemporary investigations. His publications include the second edition of *Studying Popular Music Culture*, and recent research as varied as the politics of dancing on the northern soul scene, US dance fads from 1955 to 1965, music radio online, the transistor radio, personal music listening, music on television, jazz collectives, and *The X-Factor*. He has been a devotee of northern soul since his teens in the 1970s, and can still be found on the dancefloor on some weekends.

Note

1. For example, the swimming pool that was frequented by Casino attendees for Sunday morning showers, or the buses from across the UK that were organized by scene members from points across the UK, as shown in Tony Palmer's *Wigan Casino* (1977).

References

Barthes, R. 1972. *Mythologies*. New York: Hill and Wang.
Bennett, A. 2002. "Music, Media and Urban Mythscapes: A Study of the 'Canterbury Sound'". *Media, Culture & Society* 24/1: 87–100.
Constantine, E., and G. Sweeney. 2013. *Northern Soul: An Illustrated History*. London: Virgin Books.
Cosgrove, S. 1982. "Long After Tonight is All Over". *Collusion* 2: 38–41.
—2016. *Young Soul Rebels: A Personal History of Northern Soul*. Edinburgh: Polygon.
Forman, M. 2013. "Kill the Static: Temporality and Change in Hip-hop Mainstream (and its 'Other')". In *Redefining Mainstream Popular Music*, edited by S. Baker, A. Bennett and J. Taylor, 61–74. New York and London: Routledge.
Gebhardt, N. 2015. "'Let There be Rock!' Myth and Ideology in the Rock Festivals of the Transatlantic Counterculture". In *The Pop Festival: History, Music, Media, Culture*, edited by G. McKay, 49–59. London: Bloomsbury.
Godin, D. 1970a. "The Dave Godin Column: The Up-North Soul Groove Part One". *Blues & Soul* 36 (December): 16.
—1970b. "Land of a Thousand Dancers". *Blues & Soul* 50 (December): 18–19.
Grady, P. 2001. *That Beatin' Rhythm*. Self-published.
Long, P., and J. Collins. 2016. "Affective Memories of Music in Online Heritage Practice". In *Music, Memory and Space*, edited by J. Brusila, B. Johnson and J. Richardson, 96–116. Bristol: Intellect.
Long, P., and T. Wall. 2010. "Constructing the Histories of Popular Music: The Britannia Series". In *Popular Music on British Television*, edited by Ian Inglis, 11–26. Farnham: Ashgate.
—2013. "Tony Palmer's All You Need is Love: Television's First Pop History". In *The Music Documentary*, edited by B. Halligan, K. Fairclough-Isaacs and R. Edgar, 25–41. Abingdon: Routledge.
Nowell, D. 1999. *Too Darn Soulful: The Story of Northern Soul*. London: Robson.
Propp, V. 1958. *Morphology of the Folktale*. Bloomington, IN: Research Center, Indiana University.
Raine, S., and T. Wall. 2017. "Participation and Role in the Northern Soul Scene". In *KISMIF Conference 2016: Book of Proceedings*, edited by P. Guerra and T. Moreira, 75–86. Porto, Portugal: University of Porto, Faculty of Arts and Humanities.
Ritson, M., and S. Russell. 1999. *The In Crowd: The Story of the Northern and Rare Soul Scene*. London: Bee Cool Publishing.
Sahlins, M. 1981. *Historical Metaphors and Mythical Realities*. Ann Arbor: University of Michigan Press.
—1985. *Islands of History*. Chicago: University of Chicago Press.
Stickings, R. 2008. *Searching for Soul*. London: SAF.
Wall, T. 2006. "Out on the Floor: The Politics of Dancing on the Northern Soul Scene". *Popular Music* 25/3: 431–45.
—2009. "Rocking around the Clock: Teenage Dance Fads 1955 to 1965". In *Ballroom, Boogie, Shimmy Sham, Shake: A Social and Popular Dance Reader*, edited by Julie M. Malnig, 182–98. Urbana: University of Illinois Press.
—2013. *Studying Popular Music Culture*, 2nd ed. London: Hodder & Stoughton Educational.

Wall, T., and P. Long. 2010. "Jazz Britannia: Mediating the Story of British Jazz on Television". *Jazz Research Journal* 3/2: 145–70.

Ward, B. 1998. *Just My Soul Responding*. London: UCL Press.

Waterhouse, B. 2012. *Going Back: Memories of a Soul Boy*. Self-published.

Musical Bookmark 4

John Manship photographed at John Manship Records, Melton Mowbray, December 2016
Darrell Banks, 'I'm The One Who Loves You'. US Volt VOA-4014 1969

"On so many levels it's my favourite. It's a B side which is great because it's hidden away from the general public, it's been left to the English collectors and European soul fans to turn it over and play it and unleash a piece of magic. It's a great record; instrumentation wise it's superior to most records I've ever heard, vocally it's emotional and Darrell Banks is a great artist. This is for a maturer ear and it's become my favourite over the decades and remains so, I don't imagine I'll ever hear another record that'll affect me like this."

John Manship is a record collector, DJ, and record dealer well-known on the scene.

9 Soul Survivors

John Barrett

Keeping the faith

In 2004 I published my book *Keeping the Faith* which collected together photographs documenting the late 1990s soul revivals throughout the north of England. This chapter explores the background and motivation behind that book. In the late 1980s it felt like the scale of the northern soul scene was in "decline" and the choice of venues was becoming fewer. At that time, I was a freelance illustrator and designer based in West Yorkshire, and used to travel past the Ritz Ballroom in Brighouse. One day I noticed that Tony Banks was the resident DJ for the Friday Tamla/soul nights. Tony had been a seminal DJ around Leeds from the mid-1960s, and was making plans for a northern night. I made contact, and he convinced me that he needed some photographs taking for publicity. Tony invited Ginger Taylor to DJ, as this would attract large numbers from all over the north of England. Ginger was a great supporter of my photography, seeing the potential for capturing the new emerging venues.

The place was packed from the first night. The mix of memory, nostalgia and even melancholy written across the faces of the dancers was matched by the celebratory happiness that they could hear their music once more in a decent venue. The sense of *déjà vu* made me quite emotional about being part of a group of people wishing to regain a form of togetherness that had existed a decade before. I initially decided that these events were a brave attempt at a temporary revival that most subcultures experience, and that this momentary rebirth of the UK soul scene should be recorded before it disappeared permanently. My initial photographs using a range of 35mm film cameras were technically raw, as much of the venues were so poorly lit and many images were not satisfactory. With practice I developed gritty, monochromatic reportage outcomes that suited the urban nature of the scene, engendered through the visceral qualities of film. I surrendered to the idiosyncratic nature of film and soon realized that it suited the subject matter perfectly.

As a photographer, I realized I needed to gain the respect of the soul fraternity and follow these conventions and protocols of the dancefloor, while being creative in the interpretation of those codes of behaviour. It was not uncommon for photographers to be thrown out of northern venues for a lack of scene-specific knowledge, and while I was welcomed at some venues, at other places I would not shoot as it might not be appropriate to the situation. Invitations to take photographs at that time were few, and most soulies questioned my motives. Despite facing distrust and scepticism I compiled a catalogue of images as the scene grew throughout the country. I realized that a structured method of recording the changes to the scene was vital. As the era of the digital cameras emerged, the soul scene became more confident and more accepting.

In 1999, I was invited by Paul Welsby to record the opening of the Hideaway club in Manchester. The Hideaway was central to the Mod revival, its connections to the rest of the soul scene were considerable. The clothes, small dancefloor venue, music policy, and overall ambience of the Hideaway were reminiscent of the original Twisted Wheel, and established Manchester once more as the leading light in the UK soul scene. For me, the Hideaway was imbued with all the amazing qualities and richness of the soul culture, and, in bringing the many tastes of the soul scene under one roof, predicted the future of venues to come. Its eccentricity, eclectic fusion of music and cosmopolitan style made this venue one of my favourite places to photograph.

After conversations with Dave Godin and friends at the Twisted Wheel reunion during the summer of 2001, I realized that rather than a final huzzah, the scene was once again rising in popularity, and that my new focus should be to document this growth. A book was the obvious choice knowing that the scene would appreciate a printed document that could be part of their desire to collect memorabilia. Up to this point, documentary evidence of the scene had been scant and intermittent. Dave agreed that the meagre evidence of ephemera via battered and torn membership cards, posters, and faded photographs did not reflect the rich visual cultural heritage that emerged over the years. He suggested that no detailed photographic record had been compiled previously. We agreed that few people on the soul scene were interested in spending their precious (dancing) time recording what was happening around them. Dave also believed that in order to visually communicate my research, consideration was needed to capture the stunning aesthetic visual qualities of the soul scene. The photography, design and typography of the book would be an integral part of the outcome. In his foreword to the book, Dave encapsulated our discussions and the process through which the photographs were realized:

> As someone who has earned a living by writing, it perhaps seems strange that I should affirm the old adage that "one picture is worth a thousand words", but, just as a piece of recorded music (which is fundamental to this work) can trigger a hundred different emo-

tional responses and reactions, so too this splendid collection of photographic images will trigger a hundred loving memories. What we see here is the phenomena of the Northern Soul scene made visual (Godin 2004: 10).

My initial, self-created brief had been to document these "survivors" of an inimitable subculture that had defied the media and remained staunchly concealed from the establishment. However, by 2002 I was going out two or three times a week, taking photographs at an increasing variety of venues. Thirty-one years since the Twisted Wheel closed, thirty years since the Torch opened, and twenty-one years since Wigan Casino closed, who on earth would have thought that the interest in the northern soul scene would once again be running at fever pitch? Completing my project was going to be costly both financially and personally as I grappled with a full-time job and home life. Sometimes I would return from a weekender to the normality of my job, attempting to answer the common office question, "So, what did you get up to over the weekend?"

R.E.S.P.E.C.T

From the outset, my intention was to include the most positive aspects of the soul scene, those rooted in working-class communities. Traditional political and social class attitudes such as camaraderie, solidarity, unity, thrift, loyalty, respect, and pride in community (and nation), inclusiveness, cordiality, integration and support, were all clearly a part of the scene of which I was a part. During the eighties and nineties, the North particularly had witnessed the dramatic decline in working-class employment in mass industries. I realized I was photographing a social group in transition. As Dave Godin, talking about the scene's participants, put it in the foreword to my book:

> And those people were predominantly working-class, and, to the surprise often of those who made and produced the records in America – white males. This characteristic, which has seldom been recorded, does have a political dimension, because just as the records were made by the predominantly black, disenfranchised, urban working-class of America, so the resonance of recognition found a response in the hearts and souls of their UK equivalent at that time – the white, working class of Britain (Godin 2003: 10).

One of my aims was to seek out the longevity of those belief systems from a previous political and social era, and to explore whether they were still prevalent within the soul scene in the new millennium. In the past, it wasn't unusual for working-class culture to have been denied a voice. This "underground" scene was a unique phenomenon and reflected the idiosyncratic behaviour of the British. I wanted to articulate the taste, language and wit of this culture. Notions of loyalty, community, struggle, and opposition to authority are all evident in the soul scene: the parallel between the African American in the 1960s and 70s and white working-class had a resonance then and now.

The unity of black and white communities was central to the "unofficial" soul ethic, and the soul scene was naturally anti-racist, with the affinity between the African American soul performers and the mixed working-class communities in the UK often articulated by David Godin. Through my photography, I sought to record the sincere friendship and unity of the scene. Integration, inclusion, and diversity were quite natural at a soul night and I set out to record the theme. Themes of blackness and whiteness were naturally embedded in the clothes and pattern of the fashion. A sense of pride is also captured in the photographs, as the clothes are invariably handmade and unique to each individual, creating a style and taste that were deeply underground and rarely seen in the mainstream culture. These images articulate the unity of true friendship and a deep respect for each other born out of loyalty and shared identity. I also sought to capture the progressive attitudes of inclusiveness and integration so evident within the soul scene.

The central challenge was to negotiate the central "soulie" attitude and ethic that avoided the mainstream and endeavoured to maintain a sense of purity within the scene: ultimately the desire for it to remain "underground" indefinitely. The balance between popularizing the soul scene through photography and keeping the distinctive principles and appeal of the soul fraternity was to be demanding.

Storytelling

My intention as an artist and photographer is always to impart some form of observational narrative. The notion of the photographer as storyteller and narrator engenders creative encounters and challenges that eventually established core themes. The depiction of the range of various classes and "tribes" that made up the soul scene at that time required some clarification, and the written element of the book suggested an overlap and unity between soulies, skinheads, mods, scooterists, all connected to northern soul. Using the notion of the photographer as "story teller" and narrator facilitated the emergence of an organic thematic within the project.

Many images sought to encapsulate the stunning combination of the soulie individual style and message. The words on their vests, dresses, and accessories told stories about the wearer, and northern soul signs, icons, and symbols were everywhere in the form of patches, slogans, flyers, and personalized clothes. Creative communication of individual narratives were available through these myriad shapes and formats, often customized graphic images designed by non-designers. For me, this was the most striking and original form of visual expression of northern soul, and the book reflected my interest in the vernacular of signs. I was intrigued by the low tech, arrogated handmade visual culture at that time, and many people were able to relate to my interest in recording all aspects of the soul scene. I was keen to capture the visual diversity and yet recognizable personality of people within the scene. Many of the participants within the soul scene wore recognizable brands, such as Fred Perry, but I also found so many were committed to a unique dress code that was completely inimitable and inventive. This appropriation, customization, and combination of well-known brands encapsulated the irreverent and light-hearted aspects of the soul scene.

Through the process of photographing members of these northern soul scenes, the stories, anecdotes, and memories of participants were naturally integrated, due in part to the enduring values of the scene. The photographs explored this fraternity and the places, music, objects, words, thoughts, and actions that surround their identity. In particular, I was fascinated by the allure of the music and the interpretation into a unique form of dance. The diverse social backgrounds appear to collide in a creative way on the dancefloor, combined with a great sense of dignity and mutual respect for the soul community.

My involvement in recording the soul scene grew out of my personal experiences, knowledge, and memory of the subjects I was trying to capture. I had been socializing at soul events intermittently throughout my life but had lost touch with the scene for twelve years. When I first began to explore recording the scene in the late 1990s, I was interested in revealing the over-looked and often-forlorn places and spaces where soul dances were held. The lack of glamour and glitz, the banal, forgotten towns such as Morecambe and Cleethorpes, were fascinating visually as they were often abandoned and suspended in time, and in documenting them I discovered that northern soul was as British as fish and chips, and was warmly and fondly respected in such areas that were familiar with its heritage.

As a photographer, these "soul" images represent a moment in time and a fantastic insight into the lives of a massively diverse range of people that congregated in sites familiar or unknown throughout the country. Some of the places were so obscure and off the beaten track that I was sometimes unable to find them, returning home after many hours of driving around. Finding certain venues in the middle of the night without a map, provided on a battered flyer, led to a lot of wasted time and frustration. The Wilton Ballroom allnighter was particularly problematic to locate despite being near to the M62, and I had to depend on the directions from a man walking that was completely blotto, who insisted it was best if he got into the car to take me to the venue. I had no choice as I had been driving around for some hours.

For those that I photographed within the scene, I believe that they came to trust my judgement to capture the spirit of the soul scene. At that time, I was gradually accepted as a serious documentary photographer and, unusually, an inside member of the scene. Gradually my relationship with scene members became unique as they began to realize that I was collating a dossier of the scene rather than just taking an occasional "snap". I covered a huge range of their experiences of northern soul including the expected events of dance competitions, live performances of soul singers, weekenders in the UK and abroad, and the myriad of backgrounds and interests of the participants. This unexpected content included soul weddings, soul funerals, scooter runs, soul fashion shows, charity fundraising events, and soul "cruises" on the river Thames.

Through this grounded and familial networking approach, the images gradually became accepted within the community as capturing the spirit of the soul scene, and provided the basis for an on-going dialogue between photographer and the photographed. The eventual warm acceptance of my project was in part due to my enthusiasm for the music, fashion, and identity of the scene's participants. My fascination for dance within the soul scene also motivated the need to record the characteristic social and personal identities of the dancers. I already knew the music and dance so well that I could predict the movement on the dancefloor to capture the decisive moment of the dancers. I would invariably print selected images and take them to show the soul dancers to gain their confidence.

Just as many aspects of the soul scene are unpredictable, the participants and organizers of the various soul gigs continue to re-invent themselves anew, and the humour and goodwill of the scene always provided new and exciting narratives. Intentionally avoiding sentimentality, I had encountered a lot of love and respect amongst soul brothers and sisters. Regretfully, with an ageing soul grouping, there was also a resignation about their limitations on the dancefloor but nevertheless a great tenacity to creatively make adjustments to this very challenging dance routine. I observed a potent mix of pride, surprise, and humour during the serious business of a dance competition. Some images captured the sense of dedication to be "out on the floor" despite the physical demands of the ageing dancers at that time. Subsequent dance competitions introduced fresh, younger legs, sons and daughters that had grown up with the driving beat of northern soul. I also realized that a group of middle-aged men participating in a dance competition was truly rare within British culture and underpinned the idiosyncrasies of the scene. At all times, I tried to avoid a sense of posing for the camera as that would have taken away the energy of the moment and often the results were quite raw and the composition of the images invariably cropped and immediate. The speed with which I took the photographs ensured that I was not imposing on their space and indeed much of the soul fraternity had not realized I had taken their photographs. Nevertheless, I nearly always sought permission, from each individual, before taking a photograph to prevent any antagonistic responses and negative attitudes to my presence.

The book

As I accumulated a range of subject matter for the book, I worked with graphic designer Tim Rowe to ensure that its design would be a square format and imitate the format of a 45 or LP vinyl, reflecting the passion for memorabilia within the soul collectors, and affordable for my intended audience. All of the photographs were taken with a Canon EOS 35mm film camera. My aim was to capture the timeless "grittiness" of the soul scene utilizing film to enhance documentary and reportage visual methodologies. There are many technical problems associated with photographing on crowded dancefloors with poor lighting conditions. Most of the photographs were taken using flash photography techniques and the results are often grainy and have a sense of immediacy. This, and the rich monochromatic qualities of film, perfectly suited the subjects I encountered.

My fascination for the subjects within the soul scene was tempered by the need for sufficient images in creating distinctive subjects, which would populate the book. My guiding principles for the book were also stimulated by a need to record characteristic social and personal identities of the soul fraternity. The basic premise of the photographic lens base was to record a "moment in time" in sufficient depth to accumulate a portfolio of documentary evidence. There was also a natural need to celebrate those individuals that were still "keeping the faith" in the soul scene, despite the many years that had passed. I stopped taking photographs in early 2003, scanning and cleaning up all the film I had taken. This took over a year due to the number of images and having to do this at night after my "day job". Another six months and personal funding budget was needed to get the book to publication.

The book was finally printed in 2004 in Birmingham by Jones and Palmer Ltd. I was delighted that I had self-published and subsidized the whole project by myself. With no financial backing, I could only afford to print 500 copies. On the 15th of October 2004, I collected the books from the printers and I set off to South Yorkshire to deliver the first issue in person to my friend and mentor, Dave Godin. I stopped at a service station to call him just in case he was out and was devastated when his partner informed me that Dave had just passed away. I felt that Dave needed to see the design and appearance in context of the images he was clearly so fond of and written about so eloquently. His personal support for my project was undeniable: he was a true soul brother and is sadly missed.

My launch night was held in Wolverhampton at the Civic Hall a month later, and I sold all of the thirty books I had brought within an hour, not thinking that anybody would be that interested. I also had a mini exhibition on the walls of the bar of forty A1 images and these too were in great demand, forcing the bouncers to try and protect them from eager hands. However, by midnight the walls were bare and I was signing both images and books. The level of interest was amazing, and within a week of publishing, Waterstones had offered a key point of sale positioning for the books. Needless to say, all of the books had been sold within a month and there were calls for a second edition.

Within a few weeks of the launch of the book there were a lot of negative reactions surrounding the book publication, namely how I had "pictured" many participants within the scene. Many felt the images denigrated them and everybody looked "ugly" and "aged". For a while I felt it would be better if I stopped taking photos. That was until Chris Waterman, promoter of the big soul events in the north such as the New Century Soul Club, reminded everybody that they were not sixteen anymore and "nobody was officially a fashion model". Almost overnight many people acknowledged that Chris was correct, and I was eternally grateful for his intervention.

Forwards into the twenty-first century

From 2004 onwards there were soul nights in virtually every town and city, allnighters, soul weekenders, soul cruises, soul holidays, BBC reports of the soul revival, feature films, and a host of nights offering every shade of the music, with multiple dancefloors to bring together different sub-genres of soul dance music. Tribal differences didn't seem to matter and attitudes seemed to light up with a new breed of younger followers. After the completion of the book, I photographed everything from gay skinheads (in Bridlington) to the Rimini Soul Weekender in Italy. The soul crews were allaying their traditional view of the scene, becoming less conventional and purist in their outlook and musical tastes. I quickly realized that this scene was a very different one from those nights I had experienced in the mid-1990s, moving towards a global, mass participation movement. There was a passion to reinvent the soul scene, bringing together a disparate range of viewpoints about the re-emergence of this once disappearing phenomenon. In an age of accelerated culture, the soul scene kept the pre-digital era central to everything they organized. Vinyl was still king, although better speakers and mixing decks added to the northern soul DJ set-up. The younger generation had a desire to go where the "real thing" happened, and Mod clubs such as the Hideaway were a perfect example of this new flair in fashion, alluding to retro styles in music and venues. The older soulies were also bringing their children to events, with whole families congregating at weekender events, extending the social grouping. The younger soul rebels burnt up the dancefloors with fresh young legs at soul weekenders in the UK and in a range of European countries with their own soul following.

While documenting northern soul, I had brought together stories and memories of the followers of the scene. In its longevity, this photographic project represented the energetic experience and compulsive behaviour of participants from a complex range of backgrounds and social classes. Over the years the unity of the participants was almost a form of brotherhood, and the rallying cry of "keeping the faith" united soulies in a unique and compelling manner. I am still fascinated by the intertwining of a bond of friendship that covers the whole of the UK and beyond. My initial involvement in recording the soul scene was inspired and guided by my own previous experiences, knowledge and memory of the subjects. Through my research I completely regained my passion for northern soul and using the medium of photography I was able to contribute to this amazing sub-culture. This endearing, quintessential British subject encapsulates the best of the predominantly (white) working classes and shows warts and all their desire to be true soul survivors.

About the author

John Barrett is a graphic designer and photographer who has been documenting the UK soul scene since the 1970s. His book, *Keeping the Faith*, which collected many of his striking images, was self-published in 2004. He aims to capture the personal identities and obsessions of this endearing sub-culture. His gritty images of the northern soul artistes, dancers, fashion and lifestyles provides a fascinating insight into one of the most idiosyncratic dance scenes, which continues to survive, uninterrupted, since the 1960s. His photographs of the soul scene are naturally autobiographical as he has been part of the soul scene since 1966.

References

Barrett, J. 2004. *Keeping the Faith*. Birmingham: Jones and Palmer Ltd.
Godin, D. 2004. Foreword. In J. Barrett, *Keeping the Faith*. Birmingham: Jones and Palmer Ltd.

Photographic Dossier

John Barrett

The gents' toilets, King's Hall Allnighter, Stoke on Trent, 2006

Photographic Dossier 175

DJ Dave Evison, King's Hall Allnighter, Stoke on Trent, 2006

The Cloakroom, King's Hall Allnighter, Stoke on Trent, 2006

"Billy Back Drop", King's Hall Allnighter, Stoke on Trent, 2006

These photographs of the soul scene are naturally autobiographical as I have been part of the soul scene since 1966. My own personal artistic practice covers a wide range of visual communications, including illustration, printmaking, artists' books, and typography as well as lens-based image making. As a visual artist, I have included dance and the expression of the body in much of my artwork. This fascination for the subjects within the soul scene has also been stimulated by a need to record idiosyncratic social and personal identities of the soul fraternity. The basic premise of the photographic lens-based project was to record a "moment in time". I set out to celebrate those individuals that were still "Keeping the Faith" in the soul scene, despite the years that had passed since its peak in the 1970s.

About the author

John Barrett is a graphic designer and photographer who has been documenting the UK soul scene since the 1970s. His book, *Keeping the Faith*, which collected many of his striking images, was self-published in 2004. He aims to capture the personal identities and obsessions of this endearing sub-culture. His gritty images of the northern soul artistes, dancers, fashion and lifestyles provides a fascinating insight into one of the most idiosyncratic dance scenes, which continues to survive, uninterrupted, since the 1960s. His photographs of the soul scene are naturally autobiographical as he has been part of the soul scene since 1966.

10 Searching for the Subcultural Heart of Northern Soul:

From Pillheads to Shredded Wheat

Andrew Wilson

The focus of this chapter stems from my position as a university lecturer in criminology, a status that owes much to the nature of my involvement in the 1970s northern soul scene. I use insights from academia and my own personal experiences to explore the way we currently understand the 1970s scene. I also draw on my own published research, which was informed by interviews with fifty-five members of the 70s scene (Wilson 2007: 27; Wilson 1999), but I also take the opportunity to fill in detail about my own involvement in drugs and crime omitted from those accounts on the advice of others in academia. I specifically focus on the period from 1968 to 1974, which was significant in encapsulating a move from a discreet soul scene to one with a distinct regionally-coded identity as "the northern scene". This process began before 1968, and the scene obviously continued after 1974. However, in this period the scene first emerged without a clearly defined identity, with membership drawn primarily through word-of-mouth and its shadowy existence only reported in niche magazines. By the end of the period there were reports in the national tabloid and music press hailing the emergence of a sound and style that entered the public domain branded as "northern soul".

The image of northern soul presented in the recent Shredded Wheat advertising campaign has revealed a set of tensions within the contemporary scene that rest on emotionally charged matters of opinion. For some, the advert represents the wholesomeness of the scene; for others, it is a distortion of high ideals set in the grooves of original vinyl records. This chapter won't resolve those arguments, but I want to get behind the advertising image to the subcultural aspects of the scene – the drugs, crime, and policing – to explore how they defined a moment that was fundamental to shaping the scene as an underground movement. This chapter is directed by my personal experience of involvement in the scene from 1972, and while the drug focus of my research gives some indication of the nature of my involvement as a chemist burglar, that activity did not define my experience of the scene, as the chapter will illustrate. However, involvement in stealing, using, and selling drugs, as well as the premature deaths of many old friends, offers insight to a side of the scene that is at odds with the homely image of northern soul presented in the Shredded Wheat advertisement.

The argument made here is that the combination of drug prohibition and proactive policing played a vital role in generating cohesion, subterfuge, and excitement as a subcultural activity. I build on my earlier argument that outgroup identity – based upon law breaking, drug use, or beliefs – are the basis of subcultures (Wilson 2016). While it is clear that socioeconomic factors can play a significant role in shaping outgroup status it is not a prerequisite. This challenges the idea that subcultures offer resistance on a symbolic level (Hebdige 1979; Cohen 1972; Hall and Jefferson 1976) or that music-based scenes are not subcultures (Hesmondhalgh 2005), by arguing that social reaction (whether real or imagined) plays a central role in shaping the subcultural meaning of style. I suggest that once a style is accommodated into the mainstream repertoire the wearer cannot invoke or reimagine the subcultural prerequisites: for that reason, no amount of attention to stylistic detail will move it from pseudo-subculture to the realities of subcultural life. I focus on the way the criminalization of amphetamines in 1964 was fundamental to shaping the scene's "underground" subcultural status. To illustrate this, I draw on my personal experience of involvement in the scene from 1972 to 1981; specifically, on my involvement in the burglary of chemist shops to obtain and supply amphetamines – an activity that was valorized within the scene. While the changed legal status of amphetamines may have pushed the drug supply to mods into the hands of criminals looking to exploit the new market, supplies to the soul scene between 1968 and 1974 were primarily obtained by members of the scene. This form of internal exploitation was consistent with the nascent do-it-yourself ethos of the scene, with its members playing an active role in DJing and promoting clubs.

The mainstream media coverage of northern soul from 1974 onwards, and the baggy-trousers-and-badges image it created, came to define northern soul as graphically as the drape coat for the teds, the parka coat for mods, or Dr Martin's for skinheads. While these artefacts provide useful props for adopting a pseudo-subcultural image, taken out of context they evacuate the intensity and vibrancy created by the contextual dynamics of the scene. Many see the commercialized baggy trouser image of northern soul as symbolic of the low point of the scene, when the quality of the music was sacrificed in the pursuit of dance beats that filled the floor; a baggy-trouser time-stamp marking the point where the scene became victim of its own success.

10 Searching for the Subcultural Heart of Northern Soul

This chapter takes a closer look at the interaction between commercialization, the supply and use of stimulants, and policing. The accessibility of northern soul in mainstream culture meant the subcultural elements became less visible among the surge in numbers that diluted the intimacy of the scene, and in doing so changed the fabric of the relationship. The relative importance of the strands that formed the fabric of mid-1970s "northern soul" is not central to this chapter. Nor am I interested in whether the period prior to commercialization constituted an "authentic" moment in the history of the scene, if only to avoid contributing to the banal narratives that turn the joy of participation into theoretically-informed categories of action imbued with meanings that were invisible in their original moment. The account I set out draws on the detail of my personal journey for two main reasons: first, to use the personal to illustrate the relationship between the criminal aspects of the scene and the legitimate activities, and show how this contributed to the sense of excitement and embattlement; and second, to offer an account of the way that the accommodation of deviant activity within a scene offered opportunity for marginalized young people to gain a sense of belonging and purpose.

Deviant leisure

All-night dancing to records, when the nation closed down in the evening and on Sundays, may have deviated from the norm, but the amphetamine use that made the activity a policing concern was, in 1963, "normalized". The widespread use of "pep-pills", whether by prescription or buying them in the grey market, was not subject to the kind of stigma that came with its later criminalization. As I have argued elsewhere, there is little doubt that young mods, wandering around London's most seedy area in the early hours of Sunday morning in a state of elation from their session at the allnighter, played a crucial role in the criminalization of amphetamines early in 1964 (Wilson 2008). La Discotheque ("the Disc") in Soho was an important club, and not just because it was reputed to be the first to replace live dance music with a records-only policy in 1960, but it was the all-night dancing at clubs like the Scene in Ham Yard that called upon Soho's long history of Bohemian and deviant activity. The first mod allnighters thrived in settings that repelled young people who harnessed conventional views about sexual deviation, drugs, and gambling, in an area that had a risky reputation from earlier in the century, and was the site of the "battle of Ham Yard" between four London gangs in 1927 (Morton 2000: 137). These Soho venues did not have the glitzy façades that characterized many clubs that sprang up in the area, occupying an interstitial (Thrasher 1927) leisure space set in a kind of "no-man's land" hidden behind the showbiz façade of the city. For Gerald Suttles (1968: 35) in such spaces "the usual guarantees of social order and control are lacking. Ordinarily they are viewed as dangerous, and people cross them 'at their own risk'".

If the changed legal status of amphetamines created an opportunity for criminal exploitation in the mod scene, there were enough working-class delinquents involved in the nascent northern scene to make it a form of "internal" criminal enterprise. By the late 1960s the Home Secretary, the Royal Pharmaceutical Society, and Her Majesty's Inspectorate of Constabulary all raised concerns about burglaries for controlled substances in the first six months of the year (Wilson 2008: 11). The custom of burgling chemist shops directed police attention on the members of the soul scene as being at the "root of the problem", and there was increasing recognition that the clubs played host to the burglars. This coincided with drugs becoming a prime policing concern, reflected in the rise in drug offence arrests from the end of the 1960s into the early 1970s. Film footage of police officers storming clubs and premises in drugs raids regularly appeared on television news in this period and I recall seeing London police officers leading lines of long-haired hippies out of events. Away from the gaze of the national media, similar raids were taking place at clubs attended by smartly dressed young people described in one local newspaper as members of a "soul sect" (Leeds Evening Post 1971). The frequent raids on soul clubs often resulting in mass arrests as well as the withdrawal of the club's licence, or the threat of it if they allowed similar events to take place, had a significant effect on the psyche of the scene. Members of the scene carried a cultural memory of a time when use of amphetamines to aid all-night dancing was a legal activity, neutralizing the stigma associated with drugs.

However, it was no safeguard against arrest and this ever-present threat defined a subcultural underground status of the scene shaped by fear of social and/or legal censure. This outgroup status is essential for subcultural formations that lack the shared history, cultural ties, and experience concentrated within territorial boundaries (Wilson 2016). This "pressure of censure" on the cohesive qualities of groups formed outside the accepted normative framework can be regarded as a form of resistance, though not the symbolic resistance through style as some have conceptualized (Hall and Jefferson 1976; Hebdige 1979). Such status was also at play in the creation of a gay subculture in Britain that included dance clubs before homosexuality was legalized. The reality of outgroup status, the threat of imprisonment, move such groups beyond the symbolic of resistance theorized in notions of subculture that give too much emphasis to style and too little to actions and responses. The overlap between the different conceptualizations blur such distinctions, and while subcultural styles may have a generic image, they play out differently by locality (as in the case of skinhead) or over time (as it has for northern soul).

The commercialization of northern soul transformed a subcultural activity into one that was available to the mainstream, and it moved from being an underground policing problem with an outgroup status to something that was embraced by the media. The real dynamics of the northern scene expose the weakness of the theoretical treatment of subcultures as a literal reading of style that presents the wearers as caricatures. The interpretation of skinheads by Phil Cohen (1972) is a good example of this tendency: model workers, lumpen proletariat, reactionary youth attempting to magically resolve the loss of community. The temptation to create narratives around style results in a form of theorizing that fails to capture the dynamics of subcultural life. Seventeen of the fifty-five people in my study were skinheads before joining the scene, and this is reflected in my own move between subcultures.

Shaping subcultural allegiance: a personal account

I was seventeen years old with a bad reputation ten years in the making. By the age of nine all of the children in the street were banned from playing with me. For good reason: I was a persistent truant who attracted the attention of the police and was responsible for the firework accident that killed my best friend. Before moving from Sheffield at the age of six, I hung around with older boys, sometimes in a "gang" that staged battles with our neighbouring rivals, usually involving stone throwing, catapults, and air guns, but no serious violence. By the time I moved to secondary school, the image of gangs was styled mods and rockers; the former associated with the town and the latter with rural villages. By the third year of school in 1968 the mod presence in the town coffee bars had waned, but symbols like Tamla Motown and Lambretta were scrawled across my textbooks and I was counting down the days to owning a scooter. The local youth clubs and attending football matches at Leeds formed a bridge between mod and the nascent skinhead style. By 1970 skinhead ruled. It was, as far as my friendship group was concerned, the only option.

The process of becoming a skinhead is captured by David Matza's (1969) concept of affinity but its attraction as a force emerged by adding a specific style to the activities that we were already involved in. We were the "lads" that hung around the coffee bar, attended a secondary modern that we occasionally smashed up. I was the boy remanded to a secure home at the age of ten, and again at twelve, and sentenced to approved school just after leaving school without any formal qualifications at the age of fifteen. In East Moor approved school, I had a natural allegiance with the skinheads drawn from around the Midlands and Yorkshire. East Moor also created opportunity to associate with other mod influenced lads with a similar enthusiasm for Tamla Motown and an appreciation of my Lambretta SX200. At times these themes led directly to the Twisted Wheel. I recall, for example, Steph Koslicki while he was in East Moor telling me about the club in Manchester that his brother, Dick, used to attend. On one home leave, I travelled on my SX200 to a club in Bradford where I heard they played soul music. But none of these strands of information were enough to shape an image that invoked the possibility of involvement in "something". The same was true of the hometown soul scene influences of what I later recognized as "the Wheel Boys": the DJs at the youth club and under 16s dances that played the best music and gave spinning, back-dropping, dancing displays in the centre of a circle of clapping onlookers. One of the DJs organized an allnighter at a seedy local club that failed to generate much interest beyond the gang of skinheads, stood in an awkward cluster watching the DJ go through a routine of dancing to his own records, spinning with jacket splayed out. It was an impressive show of individual enthusiasm and skill but we had no way of linking it to a wider movement. The actions we witnessed were a legacy of mod contained in the moment. Even this was not enough to activate a link to Dick attending the Twisted Wheel; although by this time drugs and an over-zealous chief constable had closed the Wheel so, it could be, that I saw it as something else I had missed out on. At this stage I was buying and shoplifting soul records whenever possible, but that was set within the framework of a scooter-riding skinhead attending football matches to engage in violent disorder.

Within a couple of months after release from East Moor the skinhead activities invariably ended in another sentence. While Matza's concept of affiliation, conversion to activity established by others, is particularly useful for appreciating the way participants in the scene with no prior history of delinquency became willing (explicitly or implicitly) participants in the criminal activities around amphetamine use, it is also useful for explaining redirection. I arrived at Stoke Heath Borstal as a skinhead with a strong anti-hippie (so anti-drug) attitude; by the time I left these values had been recalibrated by affiliation to the soul scene.

Soul scene on the inside

Borstal is an unlikely setting for conversion to a music scene. Stoke Heath was built as a category C prison in 1964; the institution I was held in was converted to a Borstal in 1966. It was divided into four self-contained units, each with its own recreational facilities that included a music room with a record player. Inmates were allowed to receive ten records from a visitor that could be exchanged on subsequent visits, as well as buying records out of their meagre earnings by an order slip at the Borstal canteen that was passed on to the local record shop. Under the tutelage of Jeff Clarke from Widnes, the records I ordered now reads like a Radio 2 playlist: Fontella Bass; Joy Lovejoy; Homer Banks; Jimmy Conwell; Bobby Sheen; Willie Mitchell. But in 1972 this back catalogue of re-releases offered a rich source of music that was rarely heard on the radio or mainstream discos. The mod DJs had provided a taster to the music, style, and dancing, but introduction to a group of lads drawn from around the north and Midlands that had made the music and style the centre of their universe was the catalyst. I had all of the pieces that bound them together in one coherent scene. It was an epiphany: a revelation supported by the friendships formed with the soul boys in Borstal.

Manchester's Twisted Wheel may have closed in 1970, but it remained a major reference point for conversations about all that was good about the soul scene: the best of the music, dancing, and "doobs" (amphetamines). All of the records I was introduced to were "Wheel sounds", each demanding tailored dance moves. It was the closest I had seen to the brilliant dancing of the Nicholas Brothers, and included footwork I later recognized in the performances of artists like Jackie Wilson and James Brown, feet shuffling from side to side, gliding across the floor one way and back again, punctuated with the kind of fast spin or back drop in time with the beat, just as I'd seen the hometown DJ perform. Sometimes this was performed to an imaginary record that they all held in their minds that carried them beyond the high wire walls of the Borstal. Whether with eyes closed or with them bulging out of their sockets through reliving the drive of amphetamines, it was clearly an emotional experience that words alone fail to convey.

Away from the emotion of the music the soul boys formed an impressive array of characters. It was more than impressive, it was revolutionary to find a group of lads drawn from across the north of England who shared the same outlook and experience. The black jumpers they wore were highly symbolic. At the time, the uniform in Borstal consisted of blue and white striped shirt, jeans or grey trousers, grey jumper, and black slip on shoes. There was also a limited number of black leather soled shoes and black V-neck jumpers. These were cossetted items that provided opportunity to stand out from the crowd, and in doing so they became a statement of status. It would be too simplistic to suggest that the jumpers were worn by the most dominant characters in the Borstal (Austin and Bates 1974) but the group included lads like Bimbo from Nottingham and Frank from Harrogate who could be described the "daddies" of their wing. A Manchester gang, for example, later attempted to recruit Frank as an enforcer. But the cohesion of the grouping in those days papered over cracks that time revealed as fatal weaknesses for the relatively high proportion that went on to make the journey from amphetamine use to opiate dependency and premature death. I have outlined the background factors that help to explain this transition elsewhere (Wilson 2007). My emphasis here focuses on the way this network fed into and from the subcultural heart of northern soul.

I left Stoke Heath at the beginning of 1973 with a good education on the soul scene that included disdain for the use of the term "northern". Johnny Curtis from Wakefield was the soul music aficionado. His love of the wide range of musical styles stacked under the general term "soul" explains why he resented the introduction of "northern" as an attempt to limit his scene to one specific genre. There was universal disdain for the term among the lads from the soul scene: they did not need a label to identify what they owned. For them, being on the scene may have meant attending allnighters and dancing to records with an on the fours beat, but it did not exclude listening to other forms of soul music; I recall Curtis making a strong argument for including Jimi Hendrix as a soulful artist. I was not just leaving with greater knowledge of soul, I had also added many records to my collection of Tamla Motown, Stax, and Atlantic records. The additions included a Soul Sounds pressing of 'Nobody But Me' by the Human Beinz, posted to me by one of the Wheel boys, Jeff Clarke after his release. This turned out to be one of many records that I was given or bought from the Stoke Heath soul boys through meeting up with them at the allnighters. It is worth mentioning this trade, in part because it says a lot about both the value placed on the music by the delinquent soul boys, as well as saying something about the nature of the "old boy" network; if only to help disrupt the image that the relationship was simply one based on drugs and criminal activities. There is little doubt that amphetamine knowledge was a key pillar of our culture, though. Drug use was not a feature of Borstal life – apart from the occasional whiff of cannabis drifting down the corridor from the cell located at the outer extreme of the wing. All of the drug talk in the record room was about the "gear", that is, the pills and caps(ules) obtained from "canteens" (chemist shops). When it came close to my release, Paddy McKenna told me the names of his friends who would sort me out for some gear at the Torch allnighter. He, along with some of the other lads, also offered an education on chemist shop burglary: specifically, where to find the amphetamines. This meant ignoring the subcultural names for the array of tablets and capsules and learning the trade names, because at that time amphetamines were stacked on the shelves of the pharmacy among the hundreds of other branded medicines.

From soul scene to subculture

While I started and ended 1973 in custody, it turned out to be the year I enjoyed the most months of freedom than I did for any other year of the decade. Ironically the reason for successfully moving away from offending involved becoming more of an offender: drugs. On release from Stoke Heath, I returned home to find my friends sitting in the same pub I had left them in a year earlier. Their sullen greeting offered a stark contrast to the burning enthusiasm of the Borstal soul boys. But this did not lead to an on the spot detachment from joining the town lads at the Leeds United football matches. Within a few weeks I persuaded a friend, Chris Bolton, to make the train trip to the Torch in Stoke on Trent. If there were any doubts about the accounts of the allnighters, they were blown away by the experience of wandering around the Torch like a couple of tourists feasting on the new culture. The enthusiastic stories of the Borstal soul boys may have given a hint of the allnighter experience, but had not prepared me for the steamy, seedy atmosphere I encountered; it exceeded all expectations. The friendliness was striking, but we were still among strangers feeling our way around, that was until the moment when the soul singer Major Lance appeared on stage. Only the glory moments experienced at the most emotive football matches, the winning goal for a league title for Leeds United, could compare with the communal clapping and wild-eyed excitement. I didn't try to find the lads Paddy McKenna assured me would "sort me out". I wanted the gear I could see in the faces of the packed crowd, but as a tourist it seemed too difficult to access the "in-crowd". It was enough to find someone from Leeds that managed to get us a lift on the coach they travelled on. This was a crucial development that came to offer a foothold into the scene. Many of the coach passengers from around Leeds later became friends through attending the Central, the soul club where I would go on to take my first step to amphetamine use.

At the time, the move towards the scene seemed slow. Within a few weeks of attending the Torch, the allnighter had its licence revoked following objections by the police to the drug use and the uncooperative response of Chris Burton the club owner. I had started to attend the Central on a Friday and the Hypnoteque in York on the Monday. It was a time of naïve exuberance, as anyone that witnessed me dancing on stage with Major Lance in Scarborough would testify. The summer of 1973 seemed an endless quest to attend as many soul clubs as possible. The carefree attitude is illustrated well by the start of a midweek excursion to Blackpool and Wigan. I was working as a building labourer when two friends turned up in mid-morning saying they had time off work so were going on a tour. Without hesitation, I downed tools and without a word of explanation set off on the excursion to the Mecca, giving Ian Levine a lift home, and then on to the Everymans at Wigan where Russ Winstanley gave us a flier for the new allnighter opening in September. This was no big news because allnighters were springing up all around the north and Midlands in an attempt to fill the void left by the closure of the Torch. I had developed a sense of belonging for the Friday allnighter at Va-Va's in Bolton, so I was cautious about the effects of the new club on the Va-Va allnighter.

The demise of Va-Va's was not related to the opening of Wigan Casino. In fact, the opening night of the Casino combined both clubs in a high point of the scene. The weekend began as usual at the Central in Leeds where we loaded up on "back street" (illicitly manufactured) amphetamines. Chemist or pharmaceutical versions were preferable but the illicit pills were reliable enough. Then on to Bolton for the allnighter. Then to the public baths for a shower ready for the Pendulum in Manchester, then on to Blackpool Mecca on Saturday night before heading to Wigan for the 2.00am opening of the Casino then on to Sheffield for the alldayer at Samantha's and back home to Harrogate.

It is worth pausing to reflect on whether this constituted subcultural activity or simply participation in a scene. As I have argued elsewhere (Wilson 2007: 52), 1973 was a turning point for the soul scene. It marked the year when the term "northern" came of age. It gained a clearer meaning as promoters began to draw on it to define the scene from other forms of soul leading to the point where, as Frank Elson commented in his piece in the October issue of *Blues & Soul* (no. 121), "there was no better way of putting it". There is little doubt that the Casino opened a wider door to commercialization, if only for the fact that the relatively big space and stability combined with creative marketing helped to package a saleable image. While 1974 marked the year when northern soul seeped into the public consciousness, it probably needed a band that had nothing to do with the scene, and a record that had as little to do with soul to promote the now commercialized image of *the* northern soul scene. As far as I am aware, the cover record by Wigan's Ovation was never played at the Casino, but 'Footsee' was a floor shaker. This transition from a relatively small, tight-knit underground scene to a badge of identity worn by people that had never attended an allnighter at the Casino is both revealing and deceptive.

This sense of exclusivity is common in any subcultural grouping that feels it has privileged knowledge along with a degree of intimacy from the shared belonging. The change process produces common sense narratives expressed by those who shared the special moment when the group was formed and bound by their interest. It may reflect a reality, but when claiming the pioneer status there is a tendency to exaggerate the differences between what it was, and what it became. This takes place at both ends of the continuum: the limited level of participation does not mean all participants were as committed as the pioneers that stayed the course. I vividly recall, for example, seeing people at the first night of the Casino that I never imagined would attend an allnighter, and who I never saw at another one. At the other end, it was equally clear that beneath the layer of badge-strewn young people dancing to the soulless theme tune to Joe 90, the passion for rare soul records was growing stronger. And while the amphetamine culture of the scene may have been diluted the supply networks with its links to the "rogue" subculture of the scene remained.

It would, though, be wrong to think of the "rogue" element as a criminal subculture that existed within the scene but detached from the central activities of record collecting and dancing. In many cases the individuals that formed the rogue element of the scene were likely to be immersed in the cultural life of their home town or regional friendship grouping. The interconnection between the rogues varied from close hanging around – at the Casino the corridor between the main dance hall and Mr M's was the most likely place – to fleeting handshakes and the occasional conversation about business. These friendships draw heavily on criminal subculture sensibilities about trust and betrayal.

It is important for those unfamiliar with the context of the early 1970s scene to appreciate that criminal attributes were shared by the majority of participants in the scene as a matter of necessity in response to the heavy-handed policing of drugs in this period. The tales of police raids of clubs is embedded in the folklore of the scene for good reason: the immediate drama of dancing disrupted by a swarm of police officers rushing through the doors; the trauma of having a police officer shine a torch light in your eyes to decide whether pupil dilation meant you received a sticker for the all-clear, or were sent to join the queue for the coach to the police station; and the arrests, convictions, and drug seizures that had a direct impact on scene participants, as well as affecting clubs that frequently lost their licences. It was also to be found in the road blocks and the ever-present threat of arrest from undercover police officers operating at the allnighters and motorway service station stopping-off places. When the police objected to the renewal of the Torch licence, they claimed that seventy-seven percent of the club-goers used drugs. That sounds an underestimation given that all but two participants out of the fifty-five in my study went on to use amphetamines (Wilson 2007: 181). More significantly, amphetamine use was contextually normalized in that the drugs were available, offered, and the use of the drug was accepted by the abstainers. The story of Shirley and her friends' pretence to have used amphetamines to "fit in" with the crowd shows that rather than tolerance of drug use being an issue it was more likely that abstainers were perceived as the "outsiders" (Wilson 2007: 98–99). The proactive policing of drugs, the raids, searches, club closures, bound members of the scene together, abstainers and users, in a defensive pact that not only offered sanctuary to the rogue elements but also set the rules of the game in their favour, as the next section will illustrate.

The making of a chemist burglar

It is worth adding a little more biographical detail to help to illustrate the points made as well as to throw light on a hidden aspect of the scene. While a commercial burglary conviction contributed to my sentence to approved school, I had no inclination to draw on the knowledge passed on by the lads in Borstal. There was no need to disrupt the ritual of ordering a quantity of backstreet blueys and dexies at the Central on Friday evening and picking them up at the Birch motorway service area later that night on route to Va-Va's. There, pills were a reliable source of stimulation. That changed when the drug squad busted the supply network and I was arrested after a girlfriend from Selby, the town at the centre of the supply, told police that I had given her some pills in place of the £5 I owed her. Still on licence from Borstal, I expected a six-month recall for the offence and, this, combined with the loss of the stable supply of amphetamines, made burgling a chemist shop appear a good idea. It was not a success. By 1973 the new regulations on amphetamine storage in pharmacies removed them from the shelves to newly-installed secure cabinets. Ironically, this failed attempt, along with the signification afforded by my reputation, produced another opportunity. On a Sunday evening two lads (one from the town, the other from the scene) were after some help in finding the white cabinet in a Bradford chemist shop, and opening it. My enthusiasm for burglary had been tempered by the police chase from my earlier attempt, and I was worried that the break-in may have been discovered, but these reservations were outweighed by the thrill and opportunity to obtain supplies, and being seen as the person that could solve the problem. The satisfaction from the success of this burglary was relatively short-lived, and conviction for the burglary and another sentence of Borstal appeared lenient. The return to Stoke Heath in 1974 as a member of the scene meant that I was among friends – soul brothers – as well as a hometown friend, Frank, a key figure in future chemist shop burglaries. The shared experience of Borstal cemented relationships and extended networks that became a valuable resource after release for selling the "unwanted" opiates.

10 Searching for the Subcultural Heart of Northern Soul

The dependence of non-delinquent members of the scene on the rogue elements for the supply of speed stolen from chemist shops was created by the criminalization of amphetamines in 1964. The many other methods of obtaining amphetamines – from prescription seepage, factory thefts, importation, and illicitly manufactured forms – did not resonate as strongly with the subculture of the scene in the way that chemist shop burglary did. A point well made by Ian Dewhirst (2017) in an interview with Bill Brewster:

> some of the bad lads must've reconnoitred all the different ways into Wigan and looked at the chemist shops that didn't look like they had the greatest security. There used to [be] bunches from all around the country and you'd have people like Andy Wilson from Harrogate, Psycho from Leeds, whoever the nutter was from Nottingham. And whichever way they came in, you could almost bet your life that a chemist would be broken into and done.

It is a nice expression of the folklore of the bad lads picking up supplies along the way, but only one of the hundred and odd burglaries I committed happened on the way to an allnighter, as Thursday offered a Friday pay packet's cash bonus. This quote does, though, point out how being a "bad lad" was not detached from other aspects of the scene. I recall selling Ian my copy of Frank Beverly 'If That's What You Wanted' on Sassy, the same copy I passed to Kev Roberts after the first three records in his first DJ session at the Casino cleared the dancefloor. I was also in with a good shout to claim the spot DJing at the Central when Ian took over from Roger Banks; I had enough top sounds but, when asked, I suggested Ian as the best option. I did DJ at the hometown events I organized and hired minibuses for the weekend soul excursions. Like many of the other "bad boys" that were fully immersed in the culture of the scene, I was not just a chemist burglar, though that status had benefits that went beyond a supply of amphetamines and money to buy or exchange for records, and folklore stories about the record shop Select-a-disk in Nottingham had more than a grain of truth to them. The centrality of amphetamines within the culture of the soul scene, along with the scarcity of pharmaceutically pure supplies, contributed to a wide-level acceptance of chemist burglary. This may have been uneven across the scene, but the fact that demand for the substances outstripped supplies inevitably raised the social status of the chemist burglar. When I made this point at a symposium in Manchester in 2012, a former member of the scene agreed that "burglars were like Robin Hood" figures. Once the early mod dance scene was effectively "outlawed" by the criminalization of amphetamines those activities were shrouded in a veil of secrecy, and the proactive policing contributed to the elevation of the status of the chemist burglar, making burglary an excusable venture for a few individuals with no prior experience of the criminal justice system.

An often-neglected part of this process is the way the scene introduced delinquents like me to individuals drawn from a wide spectrum of society. There is no doubt about the working-class credentials of the scene, but it was not a narrow range within the working class. Nor was participation limited to just the working class, as prominent figures like Ian Levine illustrate. The wide social mix offered an expansion of horizons, and undoubtedly helped people like me to see the options open to "people like me". Sometimes that came in the form of direct encouragement, as it did when the graduate chemist burglar gave me his old economics books when he heard I was studying the subject at A-Level. Clearly, these forms of reciprocity, whether dealing in drugs or books, are common features of social life; though the commodity of exchange may vary. News of a chemist burglary raised expectations that there would be some "good gear" around. This produced tensions because demand for branded amphetamines would always outstrip supply creating the potential for disappointment. It is worth noting that this form of "internal exploitation" (Wilson 2007: 27) was in direct contrast to the then popular image of drug dealing as a predatory activity carried out by dispassionate criminals as a form of "external exploitation" (Wilson 2007: 27). That is not to say that external exploitation was completely absent from the scene: it could be argued that the selling of illicit pills at the Central was a form of external exploitation because the supplies were obtained from dealers in London driven by a profit motive. However, the move to obtain the pills stemmed from a search of supplies, a form of internal exploitation by providing insider goods and services to fellow participants and it was just another good that made up the commerce of the scene. There was little distinction between promoting venues, DJing, selling records, and selling drugs, in that the activities were carried out by traders with an interest in the scene and not by external profit seekers looking for a market to sell their records or drugs. Commercialization alerted "disinterested" outsiders to a market for goods, whether records, clothing, or drugs. That is not to suggest that the use of, and trade in, amphetamines was embraced by all members of the early soul scene; in that respect the activities have some differences to record collecting – though it is equally true that a greater proportion did not "collect" rare records.

The growing commercialization of the scene from 1974 increased the number of people attending the allnighters and with it came greater pressure on amphetamine supplies. From the early 1970s, a number of pressures reduced the amount of central nervous stimulants held in chemist shops: a turn away from prescribing amphetamines; the police actively encouraging reduced stock levels; and installing new cabinets providing opportunity to throw out outdated substances (though we once came across cocaine dated 1913, so the de-stocking message was not universal in its effect). But the 1,000 canisters of Dexedrine tablets had become a rare find by 1974. Most often, one chemist shop would provide enough speed for any immediate needs; sometimes two burglaries were needed to achieve that. Only once did we burgle three shops in the one night, though that was motivated by the challenge of burgling all of the three shops in one town, rather than any instrumental considerations. The geographic spread of the burglaries ranged from north Yorkshire to the south coast, to Cornwall, to Wales with by far the majority centred in Yorkshire. The haphazard nature of the enterprise made it difficult to police. The case involving thirty-three individuals drawn from Yorkshire and Greater Manchester threw a spotlight on the way the storage of amphetamines with class A drugs moved chemist burglary from the activity of pillheads to service personal needs to a commercial activity, involving trade with opiate users for money and/or amphetamine powder. As I explain elsewhere, the contact with an intravenous drug user culture led to a cross-pollination that proved fatal for many members of the northern scene (see Wilson 2008).

Subculture and scene

By the mid-1970s, the commercialization process I have described gradually altered the balance of the scene, changing the amphetamine culture, the playlists of some DJs to conform to the uptempo "stomper" image of the dance scene and, in doing so, moved away from the founding rare soul ethos of the soul scene. At its height, northern soul could be conceptualized as a dance or music scene inhabited by collections of strangers. There is little doubt that some of these were "in the know" about the roots of the soul scene and the amphetamine ethos (by that I mean a deeper appreciation of the place of each of them within the culture), and that some of those "in the know" followed a similar subcultural pathway to the Borstal boys I met in 1972. There is little doubt, however, that by the height of northern soul the policing of drugs was beginning to change the scene. This was certainly evident by 1978 when drug squads became aware of the challenge posed by the plentiful supplies of cheap heroin that was beginning to show up through arrests and seizures. By the time Wigan Casino held its last allnighter in 1981, the heat had long gone from policing amphetamine users at allnighters. It is difficult to determine the extent to which that perception is coloured by comparing the allnighter experiences of a teenager with those of a more mature young adult; though I was not far removed from chemist shop burglary prior to the last Wigan allnighter in September 1981. However, the scene was in the process of contracting to a core of rare soul enthusiasts that would go on to keep the northern scene alive in what returned to a small and intimate scene, not dissimilar to its late mod evolution in the late 1960s.

This begs the question whether the size and extent of the collective shapes the distinction between the more intimate gathering as a subculture and the larger more impersonal entity as a scene. Clearly it is an important aspect, but excludes the possibility that the wider loss of intimacy is experienced in the same way by all members of a scene. Or, to put it another way, that subcultures do not coexist within a scene. But the loss or weakening of external pressures towards secrecy, something captured well by people turning up at soul events in 1980 in Pil (Public Image Ltd) t-shirts, changes to amphetamine supply, and softer policing all contributed to undermining the significance of subcultural knowledge. This does not apply to knowledge about the music but, as I have argued, this aspect cannot be regarded as "subcultural". In fact, these mundane aspects, though enormously significant for members of the scene, constitute the kinds of social links and specialist knowledge that is a common feature of the many long-established clubs that form around specialist interests. As with any process of change the messy fragmented process makes it difficult to pin down a specific moment or event that marked a metamorphosis from one state to the next. This does not obscure the fact that the scene moved from being a hidden underground movement to something that was available within the mainstream repertoire of leisure options. In doing so it could be argued that the subcultural elements were simply hidden by the weight of numbers and their activities shielded by the media attention. The massive influx of stimulants like Tenuate Dospan (chalkies) was helped by the fact they were Class C substances so being legal to possess (as a legal high) meant they were subjected to laxer controls in places of manufacture. In fact when recounting how he was stopped by police on his way to an allnighter at Cleethorpes with thousands of the tablets in his bag, the respondent said he wasn't too nervous because it would have just been a handling stolen property offence.

So the threat of the drug squad was still present. In fact, I was busted at Wigan in 1977, but by then heat had gone from policing drugs. However, it is important to recognize that the context had changed beyond recognition.

This is not to argue that this working-class lad freshly released from Borstal would not have found a sense of belonging from the scene in 1977; I am sure I would have. The difference was that I would have been less likely to have found myself burgling a chemist shop with a public school-educated health economist. By that I mean the proactive policing and situational normalization of drug use provided fertile ground for the acceptance and elevation of criminal attributes. As I set out above, this was a two-way process that in my case helped to pave my way out of crime. However, at the time the policing created subcultural allegiances that had a powerful effect on shaping the scene, and added excitement to the vibrancy of newly discovered sounds.

Looking back from my perspective it is easy to see how a working-class lad with no prospects could be dragged into the socially marginal activities that became the increasing focus for police activity, but also how this subculture offered a home, acceptance, and a space for me to grow. In some respects, the subcultural status of the scene may be seen by others as an irrelevance, even more so to those that have stayed with it over the long haul. I have been able to show, though, that the ebb and flow of subcultural influences can be seen to match the changes in popularity of a scene, and that to key members of the early culture it was a central way that they found and sustained an identity and sense of purpose.

About the author

Andrew Wilson is a Senior Lecturer in Criminology at Nottingham Trent University. His PhD research at the LSE was published as *Northern Soul: Music, Drugs and Subcultural Identity*. He began buying Tamla Motown and soul records in the late 1960s but his introduction to the "soul scene" came in 1972 in the unlikely setting of Borstal. His journey on the northern scene began at the Torch allnighter in Stoke on Trent, extended through his attendance at many of the soul clubs across England, promoting clubs in his home town, and occasionally DJing. He was perhaps better known on the scene for his youthful involvement in the burglary of chemist shops in pursuit of amphetamines. He is currently a member of the Advisory Panel on Substance Misuse to the Welsh Government.

References

Austin, W., and F. L. Bates. 1974. "Ethological Indicators of Dominance and Territory in a Human Captive Population". *Social Forces* 52: 447–55.

Cohen, P. 1972. "Subculture Conflict and Working-class Community". *Stencilled Occasional Paper*. Birmingham: Centre for Contemporary Cultural Studies, University of Birmingham.

Dewhirst, I. 2017. "Interview: Ian Dewhirst, Northern Soul DJ". *Red Bull Music Academy*. Available at: http://daily.redbullmusicacademy.com/2016/01/ian-dewhirst-interview (accessed 8 January 2017).

Hall, S., and T. Jefferson. 1976. *Resistance Through Rituals: Youth Subcultures in Post-war Britain*. London: Hutchinson.

Hebdige, D. 1979. *Subculture: The Meaning of Style*. London: Methuen.

Hesmondhalgh, D. 2005. "Subcultures, Scenes or Tribes? None of the Above". *Journal of Youth Studies* 8: 21–40.

Leeds Evening Post. 1971. "Sect Calls for Legal 'Pot': A Night with the Soul Devotees in Leeds". *Evening Post*, 17 May.

Matza, D. 1969. *Becoming Deviant*. Englewood Cliffs, NJ: Prentice-Hall.

Morton, James. 2000. *East End Gangland*. London: Little, Brown and Company.

Suttles, G. D. 1968. *The Social Order of the Slum: Ethnicity and Territory in the Inner City*. Chicago: University of Chicago Press.

Thrasher, F. M. 1927. *The Gang: A Study of 1,313 Gangs in Chicago*. Chicago: University of Chicago Press.

Wilson, A. 1999. "Urban Songlines: Subculture and Identity on the 1970s Northern Soul Scene and After". PhD, London School of Economics and Political Science (University of London).

—2007. *Northern Soul: Music, Drugs and Subcultural Identity*. Cullompton, UK: Willan Pub.

—2008. "Mixing the Medicine: The Unintended Consequence of Amphetamine Control on the Northern Soul Scene". *Internet Journal of Criminology*. https://docs.wixstatic.com/ugd/b93dd4_bedb3571105b41999ac2fd0087c892d2.pdf

—2016. "The Same Old Song? The Contemporary Relevance of Subcultures". In *Mischief, Morality and Mobs: Essays in Honour of Geoffrey Pearson*, edited by D. Hobbs, 102–118. Abingdon: Routledge.

11 Soul Boy, Soul Girl:
Reflections on Gender and Northern Soul

Katie Milestone

In this chapter I discuss gender and northern soul with a particular focus on women. Little attention has been paid to women and their experiences of participation in the various incarnations of this scene. This is partly because the high status, high profile roles within the soul scene are dominated by men, and it is the opinion and experiences of these key players that tend to be highlighted in accounts of the northern soul movement. The DJ line-up of a soul night is usually entirely male dominated, and this was certainly the case during the heyday of the northern soul scene (the early 1970s through to the early 1980s). Record trading, event promotion, music journalism, and music distribution are key roles of the scene and where women are sparsely represented. Yet women have been active attendees of northern soul events and participants of the dancefloor since the scene began. This chapter aims to shine a light on women's relationships to northern soul and outlines the gender structures that exist within the scene. The chapter draws on archive data such as media documents, existing research on northern soul, ethnographic research, and data from interviews with women[1] who attended key northern soul clubs such as Manchester's Twisted Wheel and the Wigan Casino. The chapter looks at gender in terms of key aspects of northern soul: vinyl culture (DJ culture, record trading/collecting), dance, style, drug taking and travel to northern soul events. All of these features are particularly important within the northern and rare soul scenes, and originated and dominated the structure of the northern soul scene from the late 1960s to the early 1980s. This period saw the birth and "heyday" of northern soul which centred around the Twisted Wheel, the Golden Torch, Wigan Casino and Blackpool Mecca nightclubs. When these key clubs were no more (the Casino and Mecca both closed their doors in 1981) the scene became more geographically fragmented, but continued and continues in a variety of spaces and places. Northern soul has been somewhat reinvigorated in recent years by the Internet and social media revolution (see Cosgrove 2016) which has enhanced opportunities for promotion of soul events and social interactions between soul fans.

Gender and vinyl culture within northern soul

We begin our discussion with the sphere(s) that women tend to be most distanced from within northern soul – record trading, record collecting, and DJing. The scene(s) that came to be placed under the umbrella term northern soul maintained a focus on stirring and highly danceable 1960s US-produced soul music. Because the music of choice was not part of the commercial mainstream, it quickly became a specialist and underground music scene where attending a nightclub was the most effective way of consuming this music as it was not available on the radio and the vinyl was difficult to obtain (see Hollows and Milestone 1998). The 7-inch vinyl soul singles became a central focus of northern soul culture. With a huge value placed on rarity, a competitive atmosphere soon developed. With its emphasis on recorded rather than live music, the role of the DJ quickly became central. A small but significant number of DJs came to dominate the scene (as can be seen by the names that frequently reappeared on flyers and adverts for soul nights in *Blues & Soul*). During the heyday years of northern soul, at the key clubs such as the Golden Torch and Wigan Casino, the DJs were all men. As the first significant example of DJ culture in the UK, we have to ask why women did not enter the DJ booth. Indeed, for many decades the figure of the female northern soul DJ was non-existent in the popular and most celebrated clubs. It is only in the past decade that women have made in-roads as DJs and journalists, as Stuart Cosgrove recently noted:

> For the first concerted time in the history of northern soul, women DJs began to assert themselves ... Even the last bastion of northern soul maleness – the fanzine writer's bedroom – has been invaded by Julie Molloy, one of the scene's most consistent female reviewers and critics (2016: 261).

The gendered inequalities of the DJ culture of northern soul have parallels with later club cultures. An assumption that knowledge and expertise about music is a male domain persists (see Straw 1997). The DJ booth is one space that has not been particularly open to women in most club-based scenes. Rebekah Farrugia's (2014) research about women and electronic dance music traces a long heritage of the gendering of music and music technology. She cites research about women being driven out of the radio industry in the 1930s and subsequently data from the 1960s, which saw the arrival of hi-fidelity as technology aimed squarely at men. Farrugia's experience of discovering electronic dance music (EDM) in Detroit in the 1990s was one which saw her encounter the distinct gender boundaries:

> men would often dominate the area in front of where the DJs performed ... Women were often distanced – physically and at times even aurally – from the music and the technology so central to dance music and culture. For the most part they were relegated to the sidelines, encouraged to participate primarily as patrons on the dance floor (2014: 4).

This experience certainly echoes the gendered organization of space at the majority of northern soul events. An ongoing problem within club culture is the absence of women in the DJ booth, and in high status roles such as "remixing" and club promotion. Although there are examples of females in those roles, they are few and far between. As the first UK DJ focused club scene, northern soul did not break away from the patriarchal conventions laid down in British pop radio. The pirate radio stations such as Caroline and London that launched in the 1960s, and Radio 1 which launched in 1967, were dominated by male disc jockeys.[2] Likewise, the band masters and DJs in post-war ballrooms and nightclubs were almost exclusively male.

Aside from DJing, another aspect of northern soul vinyl culture where women were severely under-represented during the scene's heyday was in terms of trading and collecting vinyl. Photographic evidence of the Wigan Casino record bar[3] predominantly shows images of young men huddled around looking at the records sold by male traders. This is clearly a male-dominated space and activity. Andrew Wilson argues that female participation in central activities of the scene, such as collecting rare records, was non-existent: "It may have occurred but I found no evidence that female record-buying extended beyond purchasing the readily available records" (2007: 76). An explanation for this links to the powerful cultural ideologies about "appropriate" gender roles which begin to circulate in childhood. For example, the music fandom practices of young girls are a standard source of amusement and ridicule (see Garrett 1990), whilst boys' fandom and interest in music is frequently characterized as a worthy activity – marked by avid collecting and accumulation of information. Will Straw has identified the ways in which the "nerdish homosociality" of record collecting reinforces the machismo of popular music culture (1997), and this trait appears to be particularly intense within northern soul given the high status and intense spotlight on collecting rare vinyl. Yet there were women consumers and collectors of northern soul even during the scene's heyday, as a recent discussion on Soul Source made clear.[4] Likewise, all four of the women interviewed for this chapter collected vinyl. Two of them (Jody and Lisa) were keen collectors. Jody spoke of going to specialist record fairs and having over 5,000 records in her loft. Lisa said she regularly bought and swapped records with the Casino record traders. She also reported that the traders were friendly and helpful, and that she never felt "out of place" sifting through the vinyl. Although a small but significant number of women did buy vinyl there is scant evidence of women selling records in a comparable way to men. Cosgrove refers to "April the Mod" who ran a record shop in Huddersfield, and cites the example of Mary Chapman who established a highly successful northern soul venture in Cleethorpes along with her husband (2016: 139) as examples of women engaging in practices usually undertaken by men. Women were not actively obstructed or excluded from DJing or record trading, but the wider and almost insurmountable cultural rules about what men and women can and cannot do defined disc jockeying, expert knowledge about soul music, and record trading as a masculine realm. Women are largely invisible in the activities surrounding vinyl culture in northern soul. Why? The answer may lie partly in the lack of mobility afforded to women during the 1970s.

Women were not able to travel around and seek out the vinyl in the same way that some young men could. The expectations of the time for young women were dominated by what Angela McRobbie (1977) defined as the "ideology of romance". Basing her work on the teenage girl comic *Jackie* (which was the biggest selling girls' comic throughout the period in which northern soul developed and flourished) McRobbie highlighted that girls and young women were repeatedly informed, through the ideologies dominating popular culture, that their *raison d'être* was to find a mate and settle down. Work, friendships, and interactions with the public sphere were not aspects that were encouraged in publications such as *Jackie*. In terms of music, these magazines compelled girls to interact with mainstream and often manufactured and benign pop idols and teen heart throbs rather than the more underground and innovative music of the era. Expert knowledge about vinyl was very much a male preserve during the heyday of northern soul. Only in the last few years has the situation really started to change. There are now a small but growing number of female soul DJs, which is a development highlighted by Cosgrove in his recent (2016) publication on the scene.

Dancing and the dancefloor

The arrival of soul music in the UK coincided with the establishment of solo dance styles amongst young people. This had a profound impact on both male and female dancers. For men, it liberated them from the pressure of needing to ask a girl to dance. For women, however, the arrival of solo dancing was particularly emancipating. No longer did girls have to wait to be asked to dance: they could dance alone or with groups of friends. In his detailed and extensive discussion of teenage dance styles, Tim Wall (2008) highlights the trajectories and flows of dance practices emerging from the USA (usually with origins in African American communities before being emulated by white youths) that gradually trickled over to Europe (mainly via youth cultural films in the 1950s with the addition of television sources in the 1960s). A particularly revolutionary dance craze was The Twist – a dance craze inspired by Chubby Checker's hit song of the same name that topped the US charts in 1960 (and again in 1963) that had been a central focus of the dance culture of New York's *Peppermint Lounge* nightclub. As Wall argues, "the Twist seems to be a move towards the individualistic dancing of the later 1960s and the first move from couple-based dances" (2008: 194), although he goes on to note that the Twist was often carried out with reference to other dancers. Being able to dance on your own was revolutionary for both teenage boys and girls. A 1963 report from the *Bradford Telegraph and Argus* highlights a significant schism in dance history (albeit a moment that would have happened in different ballrooms in other cities around the same era). The report notes that:

> Shy boys invent a solo dance. Odd, isn't it, that in these days there are teenage boys in Bradford who are too shy to ask girls for a dance. But it's true. And these shy, so very shy, boys have found they don't have to be wallflowers ... They've invented a dance which doesn't demand the nerve to ask a girl to dance – because girls aren't needed! It's known simply as the Solo Bop. "It first started at Teenbeat nights, at the Locarno Ballroom of Mecca Dancing, Manningham Lane", said DJ Barry Goodwin, "and it just caught on".

Having to ask, or be asked to dance, was a pressure that was now dispensed with. This was an exciting new freedom for everyone. Notably there is a reference to the term DJ in this newspaper article, and it is clear that it was recorded music, rather than a live band, to which young people started dancing alone to. So, it would seem that around 1962 and 1963 was when young people began performing entirely new solo dance styles. 1963 has famously been identified by the poet Phillip Larkin in his poem, *Annus Mirabilis* (written in 1967) as a significant year that heralded the birth of new forms of youth culture, music, and sexual freedom. The difference in terms of the leisure pursuits of young people compared to their parents was striking.

It is apparent from the documentary evidence from this time that these massive social and cultural changes were being embodied in the way young people moved on the dancefloor. Indeed, the dancefloor is the ultimate space where young people can express their newly socially permitted youthful rebellion. Gone are the formal rules of ballroom dancing. Here it is germane to call on sociologist Pierre Bourdieu and his ideas about habitus. For Bourdieu (1984), habitus refers to the experience of markers of identity (such as class position, gender, sexuality, and ethnicity) becoming embodied. It is all about the way people walk, move, and occupy space. Newly relaxed attitudes to sex and youth culture are expressed through new dancing styles. Ballroom dancing, lovely as it is, is formal and rule-based. It is heteronormative. A male and a female dancing together was constructed as normal and any other combinations were constructed as deviant (notably men dancing together, which was frequently criminalized). Young men and women were free to dance alone if they so desired. With the arrival of more informal dance styles where no partner is required, the gendered codes of partner dancing where men "lead" has been dispensed with. However, subtle yet ubiquitous gender distinctions sometimes remain. Nadine Holdsworth notes that in dance styles such as northern soul, "there is a significant tradition of men asserting their skills and physical prowess on the dancefloor" (2013: 170). So even in dance styles which on the face of it might be regarded as unisex or gender neutral, individualized and free from social rules, this is rarely actually the case. On the dancefloor at least, young women no longer had to be given permission to enter. Standards of "appropriate femininity" changed dramatically and rapidly. On the dancefloor women's freedom and right to individual expression progressed rapidly compared to in other social spaces. Revolutions can happen on the dancefloor before they happen anywhere else. As McRobbie argues, regarding the role of the dancefloor for women, "[d]ance is where girls were always found in subcultures. It was their only entitlement" (1994: 168).

There are countless numbers of women who are passionate soul fans and skilful dancers but their stories are rarely explored in any depth. As Wall (2006: 439) argues, there may be a skewed impression about women's participation in the soul scene as media reports tended to focus on the "spectacular" male competitive dancing. Drawing on his own ethnographic experience, Wall suggests that women now outnumber men on the northern soul dancefloor:

> Once a minority of dancers, they now constitute a majority. Although one must be careful as the 1970s published photographic records of dancers tend to focus on the acrobatic dancing performed by men, the distribution of the dancing crowd supports the claim that it was men who predominated in numbers, in occupancy of space, and in the spectacle of dance (Wall 2006: 439).

In northern soul, much has been made of the "spectacular" dance styles such as spins, backdrops, and martial arts style kicks. Wall highlights that most northern soul dancers do not do the spectacular dance moves: "we will not find an understanding of dance within the scene if we concentrate on the 'gymnastics' of back-drops, spins and dives that impress the on-looker at a Northern night" (2006: 434). However, we cannot ignore the fact that at any given allnighter, you are likely to see a handful of dancers performing conspicuous and ostentatious dance moves. Take this account from an interview with Jody, who used to attend the key northern soul clubs in the early 1970s: "[t]he dancing became a big thing. If you didn't know how to dance you felt out of place. I could put my hand behind my back and spring down ...". Cosgrove highlights the serious and dedicated approach to dancing that some young women took when describing his friend Pat Wall from Rochdale: "She often practiced in the kitchen of her mum's council house, mastering the smooth sliding style across uneven linoleum, and within a matter of weeks she could compete with any of the Twisted Wheel's young men. Her dance tricks were mesmerising and her unassuming smile, whispering the lyrics as if she were praying, as if there were no greater music in the world, made her stand out in a crowd of older, brasher men" (2016: 32). Some of the female dancers moved on the northern soul dancefloor in ways uniformly attributed to men. This suggests that there was a good deal of flexibility around the spectrum of masculine and feminine dance styles. These female dancers were not inhibited or restricted by their gender in terms of expressive dance moves. Unlike the DJ booth, the northern soul dancefloor was a much more open and dynamic space in terms of gender.

For women, the dancefloor offers a space where they can be alone amongst the crowd and free from the "male gaze" (Mulvey 1975). This almost sounds contradictory but the dancefloor is both a communal space where feelings of togetherness are important, and yet is also a space where individuality can be expressed. This point has been discussed in detail by Nicola Smith (2009).

Whilst participating in street-based leisure was not deemed as an appropriate activity for girls, going out dancing was a more legitimate reason for young women to be in the public realm. The spaces of the early northern soul scene, notably the Twisted Wheel and the Golden Torch, were conducive to new embodied freedoms as they were busy, often crowded spaces. Jane recalls the original Twisted Wheel on Brazennose Street as being incredibly dark – indeed with black, sweat covered walls. She noted that a lot of clubs in Manchester in the mid-1960s had a similar décor. In this sort of cramped, dark space the view is obscured. The Wigan Casino ballroom was a more spacious structure with balconies that allowed for spectatorship. However, the immense popularity of the club rarely allowed for an uncrowded dancefloor. Just as women could express their individualism on the dancefloor, young men could engage with a more emotional self-identity, as investigated by Kimasi Browne (2005). Soul music is highly emotional, and both men and women lose themselves in the pain and drama of both lyrics and the stirring emotion evoked by the voices, strings, brass, and melodic keyboards of the quintessential northern soul tracks. For men, dancing and getting lost in the music allows for engagement with emotions that are typically defined as feminine, such as the expression of the pain of rejection or unrequited love. In terms of gender the northern soul dancefloor is in many ways a radical and innovative space. Whilst there were overt displays of masculinity via dance, a whole range of alternative gender positions were also available for both male and female soul fans.

The gender freedoms of northern soul

The 1977 Granada television documentary (directed by Tony Palmer) on the Wigan Casino focuses on a male and female participant in some detail and provides an insight into some interesting and unconventional gender patterns. The male interviewee[5] highlights what is a frequent narrative within the scene: that there is an emphasis on friendship rather than romantic courtship. A memorable part of the interview is when he explains that his non-soul loving friends are deeply surprised that the Wigan Casino is not focused on sexual liaisons. This highlights an important key feature of the scene for both men and women. In contrast to the expectations of nightclubs of the time, there is an escape from the emphasis on courtship and sex. Andrew Wilson makes important observations about male/female relationships on the northern soul scene: "the allnighter provided a context that freed behaviour from conventional constraints, while at the same time introducing normative standards based on the central values of the Scene. The centrality of dance, for example, was one reason why the conventional courtship expectations found in discos was shunned" (2007: 65). Wilson does also highlight, however, that in other scene spaces, notably travel related spaces, intimate relationships were formed. Wilson cites the work of Geoffrey Mungham (1976), who defined the mainstream as being dominated by the pursuit of sex, drinking, fighting, body taboos (a reluctance to touch friendly others), clumsy male dancing, and the control of individuality on the dancefloor, as "diametrically opposed to that found at a Northern Soul event. There was no pursuit of sex (not at the allnighter); the solo dancing included elaborate footwork and shows of individuality through 'spins' or 'back-drops'; and any accidental touching, as frequently happened on the dancefloor, was met with an acknowledgment, a raised hand and a mouthed 'sorry' or apologetic touch" (Wilson 2007: 54). The northern soul night, then, presents a space for men and women alike that is not dominated by the gender rules of the majority of nightclubs. It is also a scene that fostered male and female friendships. Indeed, a response from all my interviewees was that friendship rather than courtship was the dominant ethos. As Smith (2009) has highlighted, northern soul is a realm which men and women can continue to participate in, regardless of age, although life events may force people to put their soul identities on hold from time to time.

Gender, style, and creative labour

An important aspect of the ritual of going clubbing is the preparation beforehand (see Malbon 1999). Dress, choice of footwear, and hairstyle are all aspects that need to be taken into consideration. There are of course preparation activities that impact on men as well as women. However, women's preparations often involved more labour than that of men because there was a great deal more "off the peg" clothing available for men. We take it for granted now that fashionable clothes can be easily obtained, but until the late 1970s there were only limited options for getting hold of clothes specifically aimed at young people. Outside of London, for much of the 1960s, spaces comparable to London's Carnaby Street and shops such as Biba were simply not present in small towns and regional cities. Cities like Manchester had just started to become the base for a few youth culture focused shops by the latter part of the 1960s, but if you did not live in a big city then obtaining the relevant clothes was not always straightforward. Thus, young people were often forced to be resourceful and creative.

In my interviews with female northern soul fans who attended soul clubs in the late 1960s through to the late 1970s, there is evidence of a good deal of DIY culture in the form of home-made clothes and hairstyles. Take this account from Jane, who attended soul clubs in Manchester during the mid-1960s and described herself as a mod at this stage of her life: "[i]n my case I'd go around Stockport market, buy some fabric and make a dress to wear on Saturday night. Might have had a basic pattern. That's what you did. Some people used dressmakers. Crimplene was an exciting new fabric that was easy to work with". This trend of making clothes extended into the 1970s scene. In an interview in Elaine Constantine and Gareth Sweeney's book, Judith Searling describes making skirts on a sewing machine (2013: 147). Likewise, Jody (from Telford), who describes herself as a mod who became a northern soul girl, also talked about the efforts required to get the right look. Jody alludes to the DIY culture amongst young clubbers in the late 1960s and early 1970s:

> 1969, my mother knitted, well, crocheted me a dress. It was fantastic. It had flowers sticking out. I thought I was the bee's knees, it was amazing. It was the best dress I ever had – until it rained, and then it would get longer and longer.

The most distinctive style for women at the Wigan Casino was the long, flared skirt. Interviewee Lisa said these were often home-made and that the girls put weights in the hem lines so that they flowed well and didn't rise up too high during spins and high kicks. Costume designer and northern soul fan, Yvonne Duckett (cited in Constantine and Sweeney 2013) reflected on the fact that many women from the heyday of the northern soul scene went on to work in fashion related jobs. This phenomenon can be linked to McRobbie's (2002) argument that subcultures and club cultures are training grounds for the creative industries. It certainly seems that engagement with northern soul opened up new and innovative possibilities for cultural entrepreneurship and career options.

In addition to the home-made clothes another notable aspect of female northern soul style was the adoption of masculine clothes. Lisa, who started going to the Twisted Wheel in 1967 when she was fourteen, observed that by this time mini dresses were out of fashion and that she wore jeans (which were always Levis or Wranglers). By 1967 the Wheel was centred on DJs playing records (as opposed to the live music element of a few years before). Dancing was the reason for most people to attend the club. Lisa describes the club as a series of small, dark, cramped rooms with little or no provision of seating or tables. Sitting down and observing from the side-lines was not an option. Drugs were rife and taken to aid the stamina required for the late-night dance marathons. Lisa talked about wearing jeans as a practical choice due to being comfortable and durable. She also emphasized that flat leather-soled shoes were worn by girls to aid dancing. She talked about the girls wearing very similar clothes to the boys at this time and about "wearing a tight bra to minimize my bust". Her hair was short, she applied Miners pan stick[6] to her face and lips to make them pale and wore eye makeup in a style "similar to Twiggy". That she physically downplayed her bosom in order to appear more androgynous emphasizes the value she placed on dancing and friendship as opposed to attracting sexual attention. Lisa talked about this period as being a "time of androgyny". Whilst the concurrently developing hippy culture and then glam rock culture allowed men to physically express a more feminine appearance, mod, skinhead, and northern soul style offered women the opportunity for boyish modes of identity construction. Lisa's 1967 style contrasts starkly with the hyper-feminine style for women in hippy culture where long flowing hair, long flowing clothes and natural, makeup free faces were the norm. 1967 was the "summer of love". As such it could be argued that the Wheel was a space where girls could reject the conventions of the day, bend gender, and wear whatever they liked. That these young women were rejecting feminine clothes in favour of practicality and comfort suggests that they were breaking free of conforming to constructions of ideal femininity.

Jody first attended soul nights in local youth clubs before travelling to clubs further afield as she got older. By 1969 she was regularly travelling to the Twisted Wheel. For Jody and her peers, a lack of funds was a considerable constraint (alongside geographical hurdles) to obtaining fashionable clothes and shoes in the late 1960s and early 1970s:

> Nobody had any money. No shops locally sold decent clothes. The first two tone Trevira suit[7] I had I had to go to Birmingham to get. I saved up to get the train and the suit. I used to order the Polyveldts from the local shoe shop and he used to order them in.

Polyveldts were a shoe produced by Clarks Shoes; Jody wore them to clubs such as the Wigan Casino. She spoke about their comfort as well as style and that they were practical for all-night dancing marathons. Again, like Lisa, Jody is prioritizing the ability to dance over the female footwear fashions of the day. Platform shoes that were the dominant fashion in the early to mid-1970s were not conducive to the safe and smooth execution of northern soul dance styles.

As with clothing, hairstyles were often "home-made". Jody reminisced that: "I used to cut my own hair. We cut it with scissors, nail scissors. We feathered it. We didn't go to hairdressers". The hairstyle Jody is referring to was popular with northern soul and skinhead girls in this period. Like Jody, Lisa also talked about cutting her own hair using a bladed comb. Both Jody and Lisa cited singer Julie Driscoll as the inspiration and original source for this look. This hairstyle was radical and striking and in stark contrast to the trend for white British women to have long, straight hair.

As we can see from these recollections, a good deal of creative labour was expended on preparations for going clubbing. This ranged from having to travel some distance to metropolitan fashion boutiques to making clothes by hand. Home-produced hair-cuts were clearly important in the formative decades of youth (sub)cultures. For working-class women this bottom-up creativity is exciting and inventive. There are examples of creative labour amongst young men but this manifests itself in very different ways. For example, it is clear that young men within mod culture expended vast amounts of energy sourcing appropriate clothes. However, it is also fair to say that young men were able to access a lot more "off the peg" clothes than women were in the 1960s. There are many adverts in the pages of early 1970s magazine *Blues & Soul* for men's "northern soul" clothes but absolutely none aimed at women.

Amongst men there was a scene-specific tattoo culture during the scene's heyday. Often tattoos would take the form of references to record labels and recording artists, but there were also more obscure northern soul tattoos, as Cosgrove observed: "it was the men's tattoos that mystified me. Crude Indian ink etched into the forearms and knuckles spoke in hieroglyphics: SKF, ZTSC,

2648, CEN1179 and RIKER. I learnt that 2648 was Motown's address ... that CEN1179 was the Twisted Wheel's phone number, that SKF was the abbreviation for the pharmaceutical company Smith, Kline and French who manufactured the amphetamine drug Drinamyl, and that Riker was a rival company who manufactured Durophet" (2016: 44). These tattoos give a sense of the status levelled at the (masculine) expert and insider knowledge on the soul scene – not only about the music but also the drug culture that surrounded the scene. These "hieroglyphics" that so intrigued Cosgrove were "home made" and deeply symbolic. Photographs and film footage of the Wigan Casino era recurringly show young men wearing vests that display their tattoos. Dedication and passion were emblazoned on the body. Women on the other hand were tattoo free. This contrasts starkly with the contemporary state of tattoo culture that has seen the mainstreaming of tattoos for both men and women. Whilst young men felt able to (subtly) expose their drug taking via tattoos, women were far more guarded about open acknowledgement of drug taking. For example, in an interview with a woman who was a regular at the Twisted Wheel she claimed that she never took or saw anyone else taking drugs. This entirely contradicts most eyewitness accounts of this club.

McRobbie's (1977) work puts forward the idea that "bedroom culture" was important for young women who were not free to access the male, street-based subcultures of the 1960s and 1970s. However, the working-class women I interviewed did not refer to bedroom culture as an aspect of their experience but rather the lengths they would go to escape the limitations of home-based leisure. On this front McRobbie may well be guilty of making class-based assumptions that children had their own individual bedrooms. This particular theory overlooks the fact that as Deborah, a Manchester clubber in the late 1960s to mid-1970s, observed: '[i]t wasn't bedroom culture because you shared your bedrooms with siblings". Indeed, it is clear that for girls, going out to nightclubs offered a significant opportunity to escape the domestic sphere.

Travel and mobility

Because northern soul was an underground club scene focused on rare vinyl it was necessary for fans to travel to the handful of clubs where the music was played. For those located some way from metropolitan centres, travel was an essential element that had to be factored into a night out. During the peak years of northern soul, people would travel significant distances to attend clubs such as the Wigan Casino and the Blackpool Mecca. Before the age of the mobile phone, the organizational logistics were less straightforward than they are now. Jody gives an insight about how a night out might have been arranged: "I remember waiting at the phone box at the end of my street waiting for calls to arrange where to meet or to see whether we were going or not. We'd arrange to phone each other at certain times". What Jody describes was echoed in the late 1980s in the early rave scene where, for different reasons, people would phone a central contact to find out where the (illegal) rave was taking place. Aside from the pragmatic need to get from A to B, the act of travelling is an important symbol of escape and social mobility. Take this comment from Jody about hitchhiking from the village where she lived in Shropshire to visit clubs in Blackpool and Manchester: "We thumbed it, hitch hiked. Me mother didn't know where I was. I went to the Mecca, Twisted Wheel, all over". For people living in rural places in the late 1960s and early 1970s, hitchhiking was a common practice; young women engaged in this practice as did young men. It is a mode of travelling that has fallen out of favour due to increased car ownership and fears over safety. "Thumbing it" was an important, and sometimes the only, means of travel for young people in this period. However, for young women, there were additional fears over safety. Cosgrove adds an additional factor hindering women's full access to the scene, reminding us that during the height of northern soul the Yorkshire Ripper was on the loose and that, "[a]nxiety swept across the nightlife of West Yorkshire touching pubs, clubs, bingo halls, taxi ranks and, inevitably, the world of northern soul" (2016: 114).

Irrespective of public concern about women's safety, female soul fans continued to travel to soul events. Jody describes how her mobile lifestyle was a force of great fascination amongst the women she worked with in a toy manufacturing factory, who waited with great anticipation to hear about her weekend clubbing exploits:

> It was the whole package. The in crowd. People round here didn't go to Birmingham, Manchester, and the like. I used to work at Chad Valley and then go to the clubs at the weekend. The women there thought I was amazing. They'd never left Oakengates. I used to come in on Monday and tell them what I'd done all weekend and they thought it was fantastic. They couldn't comprehend that you'd go that far to go out.

This highlights the contrast between the lifestyle of the majority of working-class women in the early 1970s and Jody's more unusual leisure pursuits. The northern soul scene opened up new possibilities and opportunities for some young women. The vicarious pleasure Jody's colleagues gained from her captivating recollections of her weekend antics were repaid frequently when having to cover for the sleep-deprived soul girl who often arrived at work on a Monday morning having had no sleep, and sometimes resorted to hiding in the broom cupboard. Jody's behaviour transgresses the "appropriate femininity" of the era which focused on women being passive and immobile.

In Palmer's Granada television documentary about Wigan Casino (referred to earlier) the interview with a female soul fan focuses on her detailing the negotiations required with her parents in order to be allowed to go to the Casino. This reveals the lack of mobility of young women compared to their male peers. Of course, young men also had tensions with parents about attending soul events. This is especially because of the drug scene that was such a central aspect of the heyday years of northern soul. Whilst both boys and girls had to deal with parental restrictions and disapproval, there was certainly an extra layer of constraint placed on girls. As soul girl Shelly explained (in Constantine and Sweeney 2013: 69), "I never told my mother where I was going. Going to a club all night had certain connotations back then, particularly for girls, if I think back". This reference to connotations highlights the unspoken but all-powerful ideologies of the era about what girls could and couldn't do. Wilson argues that there were two barriers for women in terms of participating in the 1970s northern soul scene which were "the need to travel around the country and to stay out all night" (2007: 75). Wilson goes on to note that his female interviewees talked of having to cover up their attendance at northern soul events. All four of the women I interviewed talked about concealing or downplaying their nocturnal activities to their parents.

Conclusion

Participation in the soul scene of this period offered young men and women some freedom from, and alternatives to, traditional expectations around gender. Engagement with soul clubs gave women the opportunity to reject conventional feminine behaviour and reinvent themselves anew. As Smith argues; "[n]orthern soul is embroiled in desires for and methods of identity construction. Individuals acquire an aspect of self via scene participation" (2009: 432). The preparations for going out involved practices that were both creative and individualistic. Soul fandom provided a creative avenue to the active construction of social identity for women that was not available to them in the mainstream of the working-class communities they grew up in. Interviewee Jody expresses this very clearly:

> Music was a big thing for me. I'm artistic. I've always had that side to me. I love the theatrical ... I'd have loved to have been a writer or to act. This was my way of inventing. To be a completely different person Friday to Monday. I like Saturday Night Fever ... that's why I like it. He turned into a different creature at the weekend. I could relate to that. I thought I understand where he's coming from.

This in itself is political. The fact that these early soul girls wore items such as jeans and flat shoes signifies a gender rebellion against the female fashions of the day and a rejection of conforming to looking "feminine". They are not dressing "to be looked at" and are prioritizing functionality in order to dance as well as possible. The soul dancefloor became a space of freedom for women where they could dress and move in a way that circumvented conventional gender power relations. The platonic friendships with both men and women that were forged on the soul circuit moved beyond the "girl as appendage/girlfriend" model that dominates the discussion of youth culture in the 1960s and 1970s (see McRobbie and Garber 1978). The social interactions between men and women on the scene were mainly free from being connected to love (although romantic relationships were of course possible between people on the scene or outside of it).

Participation in soul music scenes allowed women new possibilities to be inventive, confident and independent about travel and meeting new people. It broadened their horizons and took them physically and metaphorically far away from the expectations of their gender and working-class lives. It may just be a coincidence, but all of the women I interviewed either planned to travel abroad or actually left the UK for a time.[8] It could be argued that the experiences gained on the soul scene – travelling to new places, striking up friendships with people from outside of their home communities, being creative entrepreneurs – gave both male and female soul fans confidence and resourcefulness that enhanced their future careers and life prospects.

In terms of gender, the northern soul scene is full of contradiction, and gender-based inequalities that particularly inhibit women are present within this club-based music scene. The DJs, the promoters, the record collectors, the record traders, journalists, and fanzine producers are undeniably mainly men. There is the odd female exception to the rule here and there. Yet, at the same time, women are ever-present on the scene. The average northern soul night attracts sizeable numbers of female punters. Women are far from absent on the dancefloor. The rare sixties soul music that is the focus of the scene reveres female soul singers as much as male ones. It is not a club culture where sex and courtship are centre stage (apart from in song lyrics). The focus is on friendships more than romance and courtship. In many ways, northern soul offered freedoms for women not present in other life spaces, such as escaping the "ideology of romance" and the male gaze by rejecting the mainstream fashions of the day. For young men too, the soul scene allowed them a space to express a more emotional side (Browne 2005). Gender is a spectrum and is socially constructed. The fact that men and women behaved in ways that contravened the gender expectations of the day reminds us that there is nothing natural about gender. The longevity of the scene means gender relations have shifted over time against a backdrop of changing gender structures that have taken place in wider society. Two feature films about the scene have been released in the last decade and in both instances the film producers have both been women. *Soul Boy* (2010, produced by Christine Alderson) and *Northern Soul* (2014, written and produced by Elaine Constantine) both have men as their central focus. This perhaps is in order to reflect the "authenticity" of the gender structures of the time (both films are set in the 1970s). Although these are both "fictional" films, that they prioritize male experience over that of the female one implies that the patriarchal aspects of the soul scene remain powerful and pervasive. Whether someone ever makes a film about a soul girl remains to be seen.

About the author

Katie Milestone is Senior Lecturer in Cultural Studies and Sociology at the Manchester Metropolitan University. Her research interests focus on gender and popular culture, creative industries, place and identity and popular music. Her doctoral studies at the Manchester Institute for Popular Culture on music and place, and her long-standing personal and academic interest in northern soul, led to published work and research events about the scene. The second edition of her jointly authored book *Gender and Popular Culture* will be published by Polity Press, and she is writing a Major Works Collection on the same subject for Routledge. She is currently working on research into dance music culture and gender, place and identity in the creative industries.

Notes

1. Four British women who were teenagers or in their early twenties from the mid-1960s through to the late 1970s were interviewed. Three of these women are from Manchester and the fourth is from Telford. Each of these women were regular attenders of soul events at nightclubs in Manchester and the northwest and Midlands of England. These women were contacted using personal networks and purposive sampling. None of the women are known to one another. Their names have been changed in order to preserve their anonymity.
2. The first female DJ on Radio 1 was Annie Nightingale who began working for the station in 1970.
3. Such as the images in Constantine and Sweeney's *Northern Soul: An Illustrated History* which features a range of archive photographs from the Wigan Casino period.
4. https://www.soul-source.co.uk/forums/topic/329840-the-female-connoisseurs-of-the-soul-scene/
5. The male interviewee was called Dave Withers.
6. Miners was a makeup brand. Pan stick was a foundation for the face.

7. The two-tone suit Jody refers to was a fashion staple for soul but also skinhead girls in this era. It was a skirt suit rather than a trouser suit.

8. Jane went to work in Spain as a holiday rep for five years. Deborah lived and worked in Jersey in the mid-1970s. Jody planned to work on a kibbutz but never actually went. Lisa backpacked around Europe in her early twenties.

References

Bourdieu, P. 1984. *Distinction: A Social Critique of the Judgement of Taste.* Cambridge, MA: Harvard University Press.
Browne, K. 2005. *"Soul or Nothing": The Formation of Cultural Identity on the British Northern Soul Scene.* Ann Arbor, MI: University of Michigan Press.
Constantine, E., and G. Sweeney. 2013. *Northern Soul: An Illustrated History.* London: Virgin Books.
Cosgrove, S. 2016. *Young Soul Rebels: A Personal History of Northern Soul.* Edinburgh: Polygon.
Farrugia, R. 2014. *Beyond the Dance Floor: Female DJs, Technology and Electronic Dance Music Culture.* Chicago: University of Chicago Press.
Garrett, S. 1990. "Teenage Dreams". In *On Record: Rock, Pop and the Written Word*, edited by S. Frith and A. Goodwin, 399–409. London: Routledge.
Holdsworth, N. 2013. "Boys Don't Do Dance, Do They?" *Research in Drama Education: The Journal of Applied Theatre and Performance* 28/2: 168–78.
Hollows, J., and K. Milestone. 1998. "Welcome to Dreamsville: A History and Geography of Northern Soul". In *The Place of Music*, edited by Andrew Leyshon, David Matless and George Revil, 83–103. New York: Guilford Press.
Malbon, B. 1999. *Clubbing: Dancing, Ecstasy and Vitality.* London: Routledge.
McRobbie, A. 1977. "Jackie: An Ideology of Adolescent Femininity". BCCCS Stencilled Paper, University of Birmingham.
—1994. *Postmodernism and Popular Culture.* London: Routledge.
—2002. "Clubs to Companies Notes on the Decline of Political Culture in Speeded Up Creative Worlds". *Cultural Studies* 16/4: 516–31.
McRobbie, A., and J. Garber. 1978. "Girls and Subcultures". In *Resistance Through Rituals: Youth Subcultures in Post-War Britain*, edited by S. Hall and T. Jefferson, 182–93. London: Hutchinson.
Mulvey, L. 1975. "Visual Pleasure and Narrative Cinema". *Screen* 16/3: 6–18.
Mungham, G. 1976. "Youth in Pursuit of Itself". In *Working Class Youth Culture*, edited by G. Mungham and G. Pearson, 82–104. Abingdon: Routledge and Keegan Paul.
Smith, N. 2009. "Beyond the Master Narrative of Youth: Researching Ageing Popular Music Scenes". In *The Ashgate Research Companion to Popular Musicology*, edited by D. Scott, 427–45. Farnham: Ashgate.
Straw, W. 1997. "Sizing up Record Collections: Gender and Connoisseurship in Rock Music Culture". In *Sexing the Groove: Popular Music and Gender*, edited by S. Whiteley, 3–16. Abingdon: Routledge.
Wall, T. 2006. "Out on the Floor: The Politics of Dancing on the Northern Soul Scene". *Popular Music* 25/3: 431–45.

—2008. "Rocking Around the Clock: Dance Crazes of the 1950s and 1960s". In *Ballroom, Boogie, Shimmy Sham, Shake: A Social and Popular Dance Reader*, edited by Julie Malnig, 182–98. Urbana and Chicago: University of Illinois Press.

Wilson, A. 2007. *Northern Soul: Music, Drugs and Subcultural Identity*. Cullompton: Willan Publishers.

Musical Bookmark 5

Sammy Dee photographed at The Night Owl, Birmingham, February 2017
Beverly Ann, 'He's Coming Home'. US RCA Victor 47-9269

"I managed to get that particular track off Beverly Ann in Los Angeles about twenty years ago when we went over there for a soul trip. She had the last six copies, which she was selling! So, me and my friend bought all six of them off her. I decided to keep one for myself signed by Beverly Ann herself and I sold the other two. So that particular record will always be with me and I'll never get rid of it. Absolutely cracking record as well."

Sammy Dee is a record collector, DJ, and well-known dancer on the scene. Sammy was also the first World Northern Soul Dance Champion at the Blackpool Tower Soul Weekender in 2006.

12 Northern Soul:
Life with Soul is Better, Much Better*

Dani Herranz

> Pirouettes on the parquet, unusual records, secretism, militarism without an expiry date, extreme passion, compulsive collecting, amphetamine-like speed, dance until sunrise ... the feeling is real!

The above cited are only some of the concepts that are associated with the term northern soul. But ... What is true and what is legend? Is northern soul a music? Is it still alive? And, above all, why?

Sixties: the in crowd

It all started in the only place possible – England, like all the cults that are worth it: mods, scooterists, skinheads, and of course soulies.

In the second half of the sixties the youth of northern England lived in a very different dimension to those in London. Whilst in the capital the fashions were eaten up, and "Swinging London" and pre-psychedelia annihilated everything that came before, in the north thousands of lads stayed loyal to the mod cult, listening to dark soul and R&B singers from the United States.

They continued wearing mohair suits, Levis, Harrington jackets, squared shirts with large necks buttoned up, sheepskin coats, Crombies, and Brogue shoes and went to the local youth clubs (set up for teenagers) where the local DJs made them vibrate with Motown and Stax records. They also started to play some singles produced in America, namely, "imports".

Within this mixture, two venues gave birth to the never-ending soul scene: the Catacombs in Wolverhampton, and especially the Twisted Wheel in Manchester, which in 1967 was the point of pilgrimage for teenagers from the whole of England. Its sessions usually consisted of a live performance, followed by a DJ session that went on all night, which gave them the name "allnighters".

---

*   Originally published in Spanish by *Ruta 66* (2014).

Through these performances, the soul fans could see their black North American idols in action. Legend has it that it was during a concert of Junior Walker at the Twisted Wheel, in which the members of the band performed acrobatics on stage, that the soulboys found new movements like the "backdrop" (jump and fall to the ground and bounce back up) to include in their dancing, or the "spin" (spinning oneself around at high speed and then stopping suddenly).

In 1968, Dave Godin (journalist, editor, and proprietor of the record shop *Soul City*) realized the following:

> The football fans of the Northern football clubs that came to see their teams in London and passed through my record shop had no interest in the novelties nor the great successes [hits] and so I concluded: if I want to sell soul records to my Northern clients, it is best to set aside a drawer with the type of music that they look for, and call it northern soul.[1]

What records did Dave put in that drawer? Obviously, they were soul singles recorded in the USA, but somewhat old in 1968; most were recorded between 1964 and 1966, and replicated the sound of Motown. They were also always with a high tempo, like 'Girls Are Out To Get You' (The Fascinations), 'The Right Track' (Billy Butler), 'You Gonna Make Me Love You' (Sandy Sheldon) or 'A Touch Of Velvet' (Mood Mosaics).

In the clubs – the Catacomb, Samantha's, King Mojo or, indeed, the Wheel – no alcohol was served and, as was already the norm amongst the mods, the excessive consumption of amphetamines and speed became part of the routine of the soulies, who were a constant target for the police. Drug squads carried out continuous raids of the clubs, and that was precisely the reason for the closure of the Twisted Wheel in 1971.

Seventies: Torch, Casino, and Mecca

But the closure of a cathedral was not going to stop the believers. Soon soulies found venues like Up The Junction (Crew), Clouds (Derby), or Va Va's (Bolton), until in March 1972 when the Torch in Stoke, the next big allnighter, started. And in 1973, two of the biggest clubs of the 1970s opened: the Mecca in Blackpool and the Casino in Wigan.

The Casino was without doubt the one that had the most repercussions. Led by the DJs Russ Winstanley and Richard Searling, it attracted more than 100,000 people between 1973 and 1981, and it focused primarily on the sounds of the sixties, whilst the Mecca in Blackpool, with Ian Levine and Collin Curtis on the mixing desks, explored records recorded in the seventies.

Some classics of the Casino were: 'Love Slipped Through My Fingers' (Sam Williams), 'If That's What You Wanted!' (Frank Beverly & The Butlers), 'I'm Comin' Home in the Morning' (Lou Pride); whilst in the Mecca records like 'Seven Day Lover' (James Fountain), 'Don't You Worry Baby, the Best Is Yet to Come' (Bessie Banks), or 'It Really Hurts me Girl' (The Carstairs), were played.

During these years the collector passion shot up to the extreme. A large number of dealers started to travel to the United States to look for records that had not been produced nor distributed in England, and returned with thousands of vinyl that were quickly sold in the allnighters. The great demand resulted in the creation of re-releases and some bootleggers started to create unofficial copies of the records that were most in demand.

Competition amongst the DJs to play the records that nobody else had, led to a particular custom – to cover the label with white paper and to re-label the record with the name of another singer, and even change the title when the record was introduced over the microphone. This was a very northern soul custom and called a "cover-up". In the majority of cases, the record was quickly "discovered" by other collectors and was no longer "covered-up", but some were known for years under their false name.

Eighties: Stafford, 100 Club, and the sixties mafia

With the arrival of the eighties, the young soulies were getting less youthful. The Casino, Mecca, and Cleethorpes had closed, and the scene was noticeably reduced. The new focus for the scene became the Top of the World allnighter in Stafford, with Guy Hennigan, Keb Darge, and Dave Thorley in the DJ booth.

It was a new generation with a very different vision: it was no longer necessary to play only rapid themes, nor with 4x4 rhythm. The mid-tempo records came onto the scene and even the beat ballads incorporated R&B and Latin soul. The division between music produced in the sixties and the seventies was slowly reducing. They could share the same hall, the dancers well-oiled with cross-over material – the sound of transition between one decade and another.

Meanwhile in London, Randy Cozens and Ady Croasdell started their allnighters at the 100 Club on Oxford Street. Firstly dedicated to "Rhythm 'n' Soul" and more classic tunes, from 1985 onwards this even became increasingly focused on rare soul, introducing a whole new generation of mods from London, and indeed the whole world, to the soul scene.

Ady Croasdell was, and continues to be, the person responsible for the record label Kent, which from the mid-eighties onward has published invaluable compilations, rescuing many unreleased records from studio archives. Through these compilations, Ady and Kent Records have been largely responsible for the popularization of northern soul in countries such as Germany, Italy, Sweden, France, Japan, and also Spain.

Nineties: northern soul goes global

From the nineties onwards, the northern soul scene has continued growing in numbers of followers and countries, and nowadays consists of different families: from the "Oldies Brigade", engaged in listening to the same classics again and again; to the fans of the "Up-Front" (tunes that were not played until now, which often look for influences of soul in styles like funk, beach music, disco or gospel); the "Across the Board" (orientated mainly on the tunes of the seventies and eighties); and those interested in crossover, R&B, and rhythm'n'soul. And in the middle of these sub-genres, an enormous variety of halfway options exist, and all these different groups of soulies are united always through a common feeling: an extreme passion for the music and dancing.

Some of the most prestigious DJs are Soul Sam, Mick H, Andy Dyson, and the uniquely acclaimed as No. 1: Mark Dobson (alias "Butch"). There are great events for each of these families, especially the Bamberg and Hamburg weekenders (Germany), and in Rimini (Italy). In the UK, the scene calendar offers weekenders in Cleethorpe, Prestatyn, Blackpool, and Whitby, and allnighters such as Lifeline, Togetherness, the 100 Club, Crossfire, Keele or Burnley, to mention just a few.

But it is not necessary to travel so far to live it: next May the 3rd, in the Galileo Hall of Madrid, "Someday" is taking place – a northern soul allnighter with all the magical components: impossible and super-danceable soul records; great DJs (Sean Chapman, Nigel Brown, David de Santiago, and other resident DJs); and an enormous dancefloor. The anticipated tickets are already on sale online, via *Ticketea* (limited capacity of 500 people). And on YouTube you can find a promotional video and the website for the event.

Nevertheless, no video can compete with the emotion of listening at high volume, in a hall, to these records – forgotten by the whole world, minus a handful of fanatics, aimed at your feet and your heart, forcing you to dance as if there were no tomorrow – and when the song finishes, you stand exhausted, understanding that life with soul is better, much better.

Ten northern soul blockbusters

    Precisions – 'If This Is Love'
    Rita & The Tiaras – 'Gone With The Wind'
    Tomangoes – 'I Really Love You'

Melio Souls – 'We Can Make It'
Esther Grant – 'Let's Make The Most Out Of Love'
Jesse James – 'Love Is Alright'
Sandy Golden – 'Your Love Is Everything'
George Pepp – 'The Feeling Is Real'
Wee – 'Try Me'
Lester Tipton – 'This Won't Change'.

About the author

Dani Herranz is a promoter and DJ, his most well-known events being the Autumn Mod Rally (1990s), Big Thing Allnighters (2007–12), and Someday Allnighter (2014–present), all in Valencia, Spain. In London, he was a regular at the 100 Club and Capitol Soul Club. He has been influential in creating the Spanish soul scene, which emerged in the mid-80s, with a young generation of Mods discovering the Kent compilations, and deciding that rare soul was the best music ever.

Note

1. B. Brewster and F. Broughton, *Last Night a DJ Saved my Life* (London: Headline, 1999).

NORTHERN SOUL
La vida con soul ES MEJOR, mucho mejor

PIRUETAS SOBRE EL PARQUET, DISCOS RAROS, SECRETISMO, MILITANCIA SIN FECHA DE CADUCIDAD, PASIÓN EXTREMA, COLECCIONISMO COMPULSIVO, VELOCIDAD ANFETAMÍNICA, BAILE HASTA EL AMANECER... THE FEELING IS REAL!

TEXTO: DANI HERRANZ

SOCIOS: THE IN CROWD

Todo comenzó en el único sitio posible, Inglaterra, cuna de todos los cultos que vuelven la mirada, excitados, admirados, por sus raíces musicales, sociales.

En la segunda mitad de los sesenta la juventud del norte de Inglaterra vivía en una dimensión muy diferente a la de Londres. Mientras en la capital se fraguaban las modas, y el Swinging London y la psicodelia arrasaban con todo lo anterior, en el norte, miles de chavales se mantenían fieles al ritmo rudo, enérgico, de oscuros cantantes de soul y R&B procedentes de Estados Unidos.

Seguían vistiendo trajes de mohair, Levi's, chaquetas Harrington, camisas a cuadros con grandes cuellos abotonados, abrepolais coats, crombies y zapatos brogues, y acudiendo a los Youth Clubs, donde bandas locales, de los 113 Clubs, les hacían vibrar con discos de Motown y Stax, e incluso comenzaban a sonar algunos singles en edición americana de ésos.

Con este caldo de cultivo, dos locales marcaron a fuego el nacimiento de la escena soul: The Catacombs en Wolverhampton y el Twisted Wheel en Manchester, que en 1963 y 64 era un punto de peregrinación para adolescentes de toda Inglaterra. Sus noches se extendían, un festín de DJs en un concierto, seguido de sesión de DJs toda la noche, de que vino a bautizarse como "allnighter".

En las sesiones, los chicos podían ver en acción a sus ídolos negros norteamericanos. Cuenta la leyenda que fue en una de Junior Walker, en que los fornidos negros del norte hacían acrobacias sobre la pista, al estilo de lo que los soul boys para incorporar a sus bailes movimientos como el "backdrop" (salto y caída al suelo para volver a alzarse como un muelle) o el "spin" (vueltas sobre uno mismo, a toda velocidad) y pasando en los setenta.

¿Qué discos pinchaba Dave en aquel cajón? Obviamente singles de soul grabados en los EE.UU., pero en cierto modo ya habían grabado entre 1964 y 1966, y repitiendo cañera! Fue como "Girls Are Out to Get You" (The Fascinations), "The Right Track" (Billy Butler), "You Gotta Make Me Love You" (Barry Shelley), "A Touch of Velvet" (Mood Mosaic).

En los clubs Catacombs, Samantha's, King Mojo o el propio Wheel, se servía café, Coca-Cola, Pepsi... Nada de alcohol. Como los chicos desorbitados de los Mods, el consumo desmesurado de anfetaminas y speed, se convirtió en parte...

> LA COMPETICIÓN ENTRE LOS DJS POR PINCHAR
> DISCOS QUE NADIE MÁS TUVIERA LLEVÓ A
> EXTENDER LA COSTUMBRE DE TAPAR EL LABEL
> CON UN PAPEL BLANCO, Y REBAUTIZAR EL DISCO
> CON EL NOMBRE DE OTRO CANTANTE

SEVENTIES TORCH, CASINO & MECCA

Pero el cierre de una catedral no iba a frenar a los coyotes, pronto reaccionaron, buscando nuevos lugares. La noche después que Dave y Vic Mc J (Robb), Chaude, Ken, Howie, Ian (Bobcat), Dowd, Blackpool, con Ian Levine y Colin Curtis a los mandos, explotaba en discos grabados en los sesenta.

Algunos clásicos del Casino fueron "I Love Slipped through my Fingers" (Sam Williams), "If That's What You Wanted" (Frank Beverly & The Butlers), "I'm Gonna Home in the Morning" (Lou Pride), máxime que en el Mecca se sonaban discos como "Seven Day Lovers" (James Fountain), "Don't You Worry Baby, the Best Is Yet to Come" (Bessie Banks) o "Bobby Harris We Can Do It" (The Carstairs).

En estos años la pasión coleccionista se disparó hasta el extremo; un buen número de re-editores comenzaron a viajar a Estados Unidos para rebuscar en almacenes y se edicaban ni siquiera a distribuirse en Inglaterra, sino a venderse por miles de vinilos que no se editaban ni siquiera a distribuirse en Inglaterra, sino a venderse por miles de vinilos que te marcara en las propias etiquetas se vendían en las propias etiquetas. La lucha empezó a resultar complicadísima, y que algunas plantas llegaran a crear falsificaciones.

La competición entre los DJs por pinchar discos que nadie más tuviera llevó a extender la costumbre de tapar el label con un papel blanco, y rebautizar el disco con el nombre de otro cantante. La competición entre los DJs por pinchar discos que nadie más tuviera llevó a extender la costumbre de tapar el label con un papel blanco, y rebautizar el disco con el nombre de otro cantante, a partir de los 85 más centrados en el raro soul, adentrándose a fondo en una nueva etapa en la que los soul-boys y el resto del mundo en la escena soul.

Precisamente Ady Croasdell era y es el responsable de la discográfica Kent, que desde mediados de los ochenta lleva publicando los estupendos archivos de los estudios muchos discos que no se publicaron en su día, y que fueron un impagable, rescatando de los archivos de Kent Lifeline, Together Press, Loco Club, Crossfit, H., Kosdot Rembley, por citar solo algunas.

EIGHTIES: STAFFORD, 100 CLUB Y LA NORTHERN MAFIA

Con la llegada de los años ochenta los jóvenes soulies iban siendo menos jóvenes, cerrados Casino, Mecca y Cleethorpes, y la escena se redujo sustancialmente. El Stafford fue tomando por los allnighters del Moon y el West End de Sheffield, con Guy Hennigan, Keb Darge y Dave Thorley en cabina.

Era una nueva generación con una visión muy definidas del estilo; gustaba pinchar solo temas rápidos, sin ese ritmo 4x4, mínimo es entorno a los mid-tempos, incluso las beat-ballads, también se reconocen. El R&B y el latín soul, no tenía por haber una bucha entre estos años y los setenta, podían compartir la misma sala, bien engarzados con material anterior y siempre posterior, una enorme variedad de opciones intermedias, siempre con un sentimiento común; una pasión extrema por la música.

Mientras tanto, en Londres, Randy Cozens y Ady Croasdell iniciaban sus allnighters en el 100 Club, con Londres, el público primeros decantaba dentarían habitualmente "Bruce" orientadas al rhythm'n'soul y sonidos más clásicos, y a partir de 85 más centrados en el raro soul, adentrándose a fondo en una nueva etapa en la que los soul-boys y el resto del mundo en la escena soul.

NINETIES: NORTHERN SOUL GOES GLOBAL

Desde los noventa la enorme Northern Soul ha seguido creciendo en número de seguidores, y países, y hoy en día está compartiendo por diferentes familias: desde los más clásicos hasta los fans del up-front (sonidos no pinchados hasta ahora, que a menudo bucean tesoros inéditos con material de la escena soul) hasta otras mezclas raras de funk, beach music, disco o gospel, al otro side de la board (orientando principalmente a sonidos de los 60).

Algunos de los DJs de mayor prestigio son Soul Sam, Mick H, Ady Dyson, y el indiscutible acumulado como nº 1: Ady Croasdell. Muchas de las noches de cada una de las grandes, destacando los weekends de Bamberg y Hamburgo (Alemania), Rimini (Italia), y en Reino Unido los Lifeline, Together-press, 100 Club, Crossfit, Kosdot Rembley, por citar solo algunas.

Pero no hace falta irse tan lejos para vivirlo, el próximo 3 de mayo, en la Sala Galileo de Madrid se celebra SoomeDay, una allnighter Northern Soul con todos los ingredientes indispensables: discos soul imposibles, y súper bailables, grandes DJs (Sean Chapman, Nigel Brown) y David de Santiago, más revolucionarios), y una enorme pista. Las entradas anticipadas ya están a la venta online por tickets anticipados (abrir limitada a 300 personas), y en YouTube podéis encontrar un vídeo promocional y la web del evento.

Sin embargo, dándole vídeo puedes acercarte a todo, ese disco olvidado por todo el mundo menos por un puñado de fanáticos, dirigido a tus pies y a tu corazón, bailado como si no hubiera un mañana, y el trampolín hacia el amanecer, mejor, mucho mejor. ◆

Dave Godin, creador del término Northern Soul, en su etiqueta de Londres, 1968. / Wigan Casino sus pintores de David Burrow, encuentro de underclass, en el pleno backdrop; la sala del clan coronan de baile; cabina, chica y un el disco conocido y el inoflerno 100 Club

10 bombazos Northern Soul

Presidents: «If This Is Love»
Nite & The Dunes: «Gone With The Wind»
Rita James: «I Am Family»
Mello Souls: «We Can Make It»
Ernie Gantt: «Let's Make The Most Out Of Love»
Sandy Golden: «Love Is Alright»
Jesse Jame: «Love Is Alright»
George Pepp: «The Feeling Is Real»
Javier Tipson: «This Won't Change»

Photographic Dossier

Bethany Kane

Ethan at Beatin' Rhythm, Manchester, September 2015

Emily Jane in Stoke on Trent, July 2015

Josh at The Night Owl, Birmingham, September 2016

Stephen at the Blackpool Tower Weekender, November 2016

Currently the northern soul scene is receiving great exposure through film, media, and clothing brands, giving this once very secretive scene wider recognition. Subsequently, dedicated soulies are escaping to more underground clubs and are becoming more selective in the events they choose to attend. This body of work concentrates on the younger generation and the spaces within which they construct and perform a northern soul identity. I explore the passion and dedication these individuals have for their scene and the certain elements that continuously encourage their participation.

Photographing scene participants in their personal spaces gives an insight to the life led between allnighters, highlighting elements within their environment that provoke a further understanding of the individual's personal identity and how this relates to northern soul. Taken in bedrooms, record shops, and fashion student workrooms, these photographs provide a rare insight into the permeation of scene identity into everyday life activities of young northern soulies.

About the author

Bethany Kane is a photographer who reveals lifestyles and personal narratives through by highlighting details of the environments which lie at the heart of the processes of identity construction. Her practice builds upon the knowledge and understanding she gains through her own personal experience, using retrospective photographic processes to produce insights into these rarely documented subjects. Past exhibitions include her work on the northern soul scene, punk, skinhead and Oi! subcultures.

13 Interviews with Tony Palmer, Elaine Constantine, and Liam Quinn

Interviews conducted and edited by Tim Wall*

The three interviews collected in this chapter bring in contributions on the northern soul scene from three individuals involved in the representation of the scene in very different ways. Tony Palmer was the director of the 1977 *Wigan Casino* documentary film, aired on ITV in the UK as part of the *This England* series, Elaine Constantine directed the 2014 *Northern Soul* feature film, and Liam Quinn danced and contributed to the choreography on Duffy's 'Mercy' video and coached the lead actor in *Soul Boy*, the 2010 feature film set in the early scene.

Each interview offers a different perspective from different degrees of participation in the scene, and each reveals insights not usually shared amongst members of the scene. Their comments certainly ask us to reassess many of the standard stories about some widely discussed screen representations of northern soul. Many of the other contributions to this book reference at least one of these filmic representations, and a comparison between how, for instance, Tony Palmer considers his documentary and its reception, and the ways scene insiders have discussed it, is illuminating. The material presented here was edited down from longer interviews (each passed to the interviewees for further comments and additional edits) and encapsulates the essence of their accounts of capturing aspects of the scene. Elaine Constantine used the opportunity to develop and nuance the points she made in the original interview.

Given their diversity of background, there is a remarkable consistency to the themes that emerge. Palmer was a film-maker from outside the scene, Constantine a renowned photographer keen to capture something of the

---

* Particular thanks go to Sarah Raine for her support in organizing the interviews and the transcriptions.

spirit she had herself experienced, and Quinn a young participant on the contemporary scene who offered those outside advice on capturing something of the northern dancing style. They each deal with the challenge of capturing the essence of the qualities they admire to share with those audiences who have not experienced the culture themselves, the challenge of doing so on screen, and the response of those on the scene to these very different representations.

Their interviews reveal aspects of the production of the 1977 *Wigan Casino* documentary, the film *Northern Soul*, Duffy 'Mercy' video and the *Soul Boy* film that they haven't previously shared in print. Palmer's explanations of the choices he made and his regard for those he came into contact with may well make contemporary viewers rethink many of their assumptions about how and why the film came to be made, and how it fits with Palmer's wider body of work with which they may be less familiar. Constantine shares her own views and family connection to the early days of the film which, as she herself attests, have not been brought out in earlier interviews on *Northern Soul*. Quinn reveals details of the psychological results of the negative response to his involvement in mainstream representations of scene culture. Together, they allow us an insight into the many ways that the scene has been captured in the nearly fifty years of its existence and to the production processes that deliver screen images of the northern soul music culture.

Tony Palmer

Tony Palmer is an internationally-known documentarian and film maker, who has made more than 100 films, the majority on music or music culture. He was director of the 1977 *Wigan Casino* documentary film which was aired on ITV in the UK as part of the *This England* series. This was the limit to his involvement with the scene.

How the This England Wigan Casino programme came to be made
When I did the series called *All You Need Is Love* in 1975, '76, I thought, that's it, I'm going to draw the line under all this rock and roll stuff, it's taken me away from what I really want to do. I left the BBC in '71, and Norman Swallow, the head of Omnibus at the BBC (wonderful man) went to Granada in Manchester two or three years later. Norman didn't know that I'd said I'll never make another rock film ever, but he said, we're doing a series of half an hour documentaries called *This England*, and we'd like you to do two at least. Really for Norman, I agreed. The first one, called The Mighty Wurlitzer, was bizarre. Our researcher found a man who lived in a terraced house every millimeter of which was his Wurlitzer organ; a second-hand car dealer in Norfolk had a Wurlitzer organ, cars, cars, Wurlitzer organ; and another man who lived on an island on the Norfolk Broads and this entire island was the Wurlitzer organ.

I hadn't agreed to do the second one and I said to Norman, "I've had such a good time, throw me a wobbly". So he said, "Wigan Casino". I said, "I'm not going to do a film about gambling" [laughter], and he said, "I think you should go". Norman had just heard about it and he thought it was an interesting subject and he knew that I knew a tiny bit about rock. For all he knew, I was just going to explain what northern soul was, but he also I think instinctively knew, thinking back to all my work that that isn't what I would do, that's why they wanted me to do it. Somebody on Granada management might have thought, let's do a film. Sidney Bernstein's (Chairman of the Granada Group) attitude was, we live in the north, we owe a responsibility to the north to try and understand what's going on in the north: which is in Coronation Street and of course, in the northern soul film. Wigan Casino is absolutely in that tradition, and Norman Swallow would have understood that.

I met the people who ran the club and they clearly said, I think you'd better come back and we'll have a proper meeting. So on my second visit, the following weekend, I was clearly being auditioned and I explained what I wanted. There was a sort of committee, or a representative group, it wasn't the management, it was the kids themselves. There were no DJs there. The guy that you see in the film saying, "get by and don't push at the back", he was there; he just wanted to know, from a purely practical point of view what I was supposing to do. But it was the kids who represented themselves, and I liked that. They weren't the kind of people who were remotely impressed by me saying I represent the BBC or Granada. They quizzed me what I knew about northern soul and I said, nothing [laughter], I mean musically speaking, nothing at all, but what I do know is that what I saw in the first week was something special and that's what I kept on and on and on about, I said, something special is going on.

Of the group of people I met, I think about five or six of them were clearly split; there was one half who didn't want any kind of publicity at all, and there was the other half, who really did want publicity and I later learned why and they were both the same reason. They were under very considerable pressure from the police and the local authorities, who thought that it was a den of iniquity for drugs and so the lot that didn't want me there were frightened that that's what I was interested in, 'cause I came from Granada Television. And the lot who were in favour thought that we had nothing to hide, do it and then they'll see there's something else. I think I twigged that and I was intrigued.

On both occasions I visited I was aware of two things: one, it was very dark and how the hell can you film this, because in '77, there was only very slow 16mm celluloid, which needed tons of light otherwise you couldn't film, it's not the wonders of digital camera technology in these days, sadly; and the second thing is this astonishing dancing that was going on, absolutely astonishing. They were worried about the lights because it took place in the dark, more or less, and I explained, "well, you can't film it if it's in the dark", not then you couldn't. And there was also certainly, not resentment that I came from the south, but I think it was more resentment against Granada, that represented kind of television and publicity and the fact that I didn't speak like them, as it were, that didn't endear me to them, that group of people.

I said to the committee, "I'll be back next week and I'll bring a camera and I'll bring the lights, so you can see how bad it is". I brought a cameraman and I did the lights, it was one handheld light which I was kind of waving about and much to my relief and slightly to the contrariness of their expectations, people didn't mind being filmed. Where we were with the camera and my battery light, they tended to come towards me, those who wanted to be filmed; those who didn't want to be filmed were elsewhere, but we didn't do anything else, we just filmed the dancing that first week; footage now lost by Granada.

It was agreed that I would come back and do the filming properly and I think there was a gap of two or three weeks before I did come back finally with a film crew and battery light. I wasn't aware of people walking out, absolutely not. If they did, I didn't see them. Even the first time that we filmed, I mean, I was quite amazed by how clearly people presented themselves, you know, "I'm a great dancer, film me" line, which was fine. Part of the commitment I made to the committee was that I would never interfere, I would never tell people, you know, can you do that again over here.

It was entirely a Granada film crew of three people. I said, "we're not going to be let in if we turn up with a full union crew, they'll just tell us to fuck off". I don't know how they internally agreed to it in Granada. Most of the filming took place on Thursday, Friday, Saturday day and Saturday night and Sunday morning in the swimming pool and I remember it very well. It was freezing cold, as I drove back to London after the swimming pool, and was listening to Red Rum winning the Grand National for the third time on the radio. I am the editor on all my own films, so we edited it in what was then my studio in London and the original sound was mixed in Granada. That was the schedule and I think it took about a week really, didn't take long. Took it back up, mixed the sound, showed it to the mighty trio [Sir Denis Forman (then Chairman of Granada), Sidney Bernstein (founder of Granada Television) and Norman Swallow].

Researching Wigan
On the Saturday of the second weekend, I wandered around Wigan before it got going and I was immediately aware that this town was derelict, it had been a great industrial hub and it wasn't anymore. The guy shouting "*Social-*

ist Worker, buy it here", in the film, was there in the covered market and I took him out for a cup of coffee and quizzed him about Wigan and he said that unemployment was terrible, something like 60 per cent, all the mills were closed, that was the Socialist Worker speak, but nonetheless you could see it, it was appalling.

I had done a fair amount of digging around, because it occurred to me that the structure of it had to include previous generations whose lives had been destroyed, hence the miner, hence the old lady talking about it cost a penny, it cost tuppence. I went looking for old pictures I assumed did exist. The notion that you would send a child of seven or eight to work was something so appalling to me. It's easy to say that, a jumped-up middle-class yob, my personal circumstances were nowhere near as rough as that, but they were pretty low working class. The photographs were all in the Wigan public library, which no longer exists, of course, shut down.

I do far too much rooting about. It's important. I'd never want to start filming unless I do. I'm hated – I think that's not too strong a word actually – by commissioning editors, because inevitably they want a script, and I say, when I've finished the film I'll tell you what it's about, I'll write a script then. It's a journey of exploration, I'm trying to find out something, so I go to this nightclub, I see this amazing dancing, this event and atmosphere and ambience clearly meant something to these kids, so I want to know why. It wasn't particularly exotic, it was a bit rough and ready, in an old dance hall.

It reminded me of something I'd seen an awful lot of, in '67 and '68, when I used to go to the Roundhouse quite a lot. Not the frightfully poncy Roundhouse we have now, it really was just in an empty railway shed. At two o'clockish, you'd see these twinset and pearl girls arriving, wandered up from the Kings Road carrying big shopping bags, and you'd see them about half an hour later in wonderful punkish clothes.

It was a transformation for them, because that was their world, that was what they wanted to be a part of, but they couldn't tell Mum and Dad, who lived in Chelsea. At 10 o'clock, back into the ladies' loo, back into the twinset and pearls and back to Chelsea. I just remembered all of that and what was interesting about the kids turning up at Wigan Casino, that they came as they were, fairly impoverished with no prospects, I think that was the thing, what am I going to do with my life?

Also, in my third week, the one I was there actually doing some filming, it was very clear that there were four or five wonderful dancers, but I talked to all of them and realized I needed one guy, one girl, which are the people who appeared in the film, so they were primed, they knew what I was going to do. I watched them dance and thought they were both wonderful dancers and thought, these are the two that I'm going to get to talk, as well as to dance. I did become transfixed by those two people, the girl who worked in the hospital laundry and the guy who was a metal worker and just the complete and utter uselessness of, they felt, their lives and this gave them purpose and point. As he says in the course of the film, you know, if Wigan Casino suddenly shut down, he wasn't sure what he'd do with this life, would life be worth living? He was being a bit melodramatic, but I knew exactly what he meant. They invested all of their emotional hopes and expectations into the fraternity that went to those clubs on Saturday night, that one in particular, and as somebody says in the film, you saw these busloads arrive from Scotland, from Cornwall, everywhere; it was extraordinary. That's one weakness in the film; I didn't really show that. You can't get everything into 25 minutes; that was the restriction it had to be. Three or four years later, I'd have said I can't do it in less than three hours [laughter], but I tried to be well behaved as far as Granada was concerned.

I asked both the boy and the girl, give me your five favourite records and they overlapped a bit, that's what I used. I thought, you know, they know it, they know the music, I don't. Knowing me the dancers filmed are not actually dancing to those records. The slo-mo dancing: I wanted to see it, I wanted to tell other people that what they're doing is quite extraordinary.

Then I brought in Leon Rosselson, who I had worked with before and I mean, absolutely adored what he did and I think we used two songs of his. That's his pitch, as it were, good Socialist Worker chap. I explained to him about the attitude of the main guy that we talked to and the girl in the laundry and also that I'd found this extraordinary miner, and also the dereliction of the landscape, and the pointlessness of it all. I remember saying to Leon, "what would you do if you were in those circumstances". I don't know whether he had the songs on his back burner or not, but he certainly produced four and I chose those two.

I knew very well how important Elgar was in the firmament and I also knew very well what essentially he represented, which was a world that was being swept away and he could see it and felt it and knew it and of course, that was perfect for Wigan. That moment from the Enigma Variations seems to me just right, emotionally, it just says there's something wrong here, and then the mayhem starts and it comes back several times.

Reception of the This England Wigan Casino programme
The next time I saw Norman was with the finished film and Denis was there and Sid was there actually for the first ever screening, 'cause he didn't know what Wigan Casino was either. They said, it's wonderful, thank you, next. Denis Forman did note, you made a film about Wigan Casino and northern soul and it begins with Elgar, very clever.

The people of Wigan Casino were absolutely amazed and relieved, I didn't mention drugs, didn't film drugs ... there was none in the film. I'm sure once or twice there was some pills popping here and there, but that was not the point of it. They absolutely loved it and they kept in touch. There were problems, but that had to do with jealousy at Wigan Casino; various DJs who didn't operate when I was there wanted to know why they hadn't been included and they did their best to rubbish the film a bit, but not with any serious or malicious intent. You know, this is rather a good film, I should have been in it, I think that was their attitude. The kids, I kept in touch with a few of them quite a long time and I actually went back about two years later for another film. By then, the Wigan Casino building had burnt down, but a lot of the kids were still around. We advertised for 500 people as paid extras, and an amazing number of these kids who'd been there came up and said, "I was in your film, *Wigan Casino*", "wonderful film", they all said. So, I think the kids themselves, as far as I know, liked it.

The really important point is that if I'd gone with a script and a scenario, I wouldn't have reacted in the way that I did or felt about the kids in the way that I did, both about the ambience and the music, in a way that was irrelevant, that was the thing that brought them together, but it wasn't why they came together. I did become aware of the music when I was there, but the music wasn't what I was interested in, it was the social background, both of their generation and the previous generations that was what gripped me and I thought that what they are doing is trying to find a way to make life tolerable. It's not that the music didn't interest me, but the music wasn't the thing that got me going and I think there's a story here and the story is, what shall we do with the ugly ones, those who have nothing to sell, which was then when the bloke was down the mine, when the children were working in the mills.

I went there to observe, I'll do my best to capture and understand what it is that I'm seeing and they're doing, I'm certainly not going to interfere with people in any way whatsoever. I am a participant when I take the guy into his parents' home and up into his bedroom, where he tells me, you know, what it means to him, to that extent I'm a participant, but you don't hear me. I'm just the blotting paper and he's talking, he's trusting me, as did the girl. In fact, I mean, talking to the girl was quite funny, she said at some point, obviously during the interview but she might have kept on repeating it, "you won't tell my parents I've been interviewed, will you?" I mean, the number of times people have said that, "don't tell anybody..."

Following the broadcast, Granada was telephoned by an American, who said he'd seen a bit of the film and now he's got to have a copy, and then Norman rang me and said, "this man has rung up, wants a copy, do you have any objection?" Anyway, three, four years later, out came *Flashdance*, produced by this man who'd rung up for a copy of the film. I went to see the film, it's a really good film, Jennifer Beals is wonderful, but not her dancing. But that was a connection.

In the early 2000s, we decided that we ought to rescue the film for DVD, and I must have had upwards of fifty quite virulent emails saying, you know, can't you do something about this dreadful copy that's on YouTube, dreadful pictures, dreadful sound, you must have got the film. I was unaware that it was on YouTube and it was a complete film, so I rang up Granada and said, "I want to buy a bag of film you know nothing about, and you weren't born when this film was made". She said, "Oh, I've never heard of it, I'll look it up". She said, "I've found it, what do you want to do with it?" "Can I sign a document saying you've passed that ownership to me?" Yes; that's how we got it back. We got it back principally because of that YouTube, not only got it back but we then remastered it as best we could and we did all the sound. We redid the sound digitally and I tracked down all the original recordings, we had a lot of help then from the northern soul fraternity.

Elaine Constantine

Elaine is a photographer and BAFTA nominated director of the film *Northern Soul* (2014). She has worked as a music and fashion photographer since the 1990s, and has been involved in the scene since the 1980s.

Conceiving the film
The characters in the film are partly influenced by the antics of my older brothers and partly influenced by lads generally in my area while growing up. I was born in '65, so I missed that seventies era of the allnighter scene, although in the late '70s I was actively seeking youth clubs where they played northern soul.

I didn't realize it at the time, as it was the norm, but we came from a fairly low level of society. I was an Irish Catholic in Bury, Lancashire, from a big family, the youngest of five. I had two brothers, one five years older and one seven, and two elder sisters, who were already getting married at that point, so they left the house when I was quite young.

So, I spent most of my childhood hanging around with these two brothers, who were pretty vile back then. They would always be fighting and swearing, and groups of their friends would come around and they'd all be vile together, so I had no illusions about boys being fairy-tale gentlemen. At times I really hated them, especially the younger one (we're great friends now by the way). Things were far more violent in my life back then. I felt my childhood con-

13 Interviews with Tony Palmer, Elaine Constantine, and Liam Quinn

sisted of a lot of fighting and rowing with boys, so the two fictional characters I created in the early drafts were very much that. They, for me, sum up that generation of boys, they were uncomplicated, were out for themselves and pretty rough, so that's where I got those characters from.

When it came to conceiving the film, it was more a question of wanting to do a film about northern soul than wanting to be a director and then finding a subject. With the story, it's pretty obvious stuff, but I really wanted to make people understand what northern soul was as a scene. Because the scene is pretty complicated to explain, I had to find a character who didn't get what the scene was all about and was then seduced by it, and then a second character that was already submerged in it, but was a bit of a hell-raiser. So I wanted to have one character that was very clear-headed on what he wanted to be, who took himself a bit more seriously; and someone who had that kind of personality that was too into it for his own good. When I started getting into northern soul, I noticed a good number of lads like that. They were full of drive and self-importance. Nearly everyone I met on that scene that I was attracted to was a bit like the character Matt, a bit dangerous and totally passionate about it all. You know, those characters that would be constantly questioning what was real as opposed to everything deemed to be plastic, and then declaring, "don't wear that" or "don't dance to that it's all for idiots". So it was kind of this sussed kid who wouldn't be sold on the latest trend. I loved these boys, they were the kind of boys that we all wanted to go out with.

I wanted to portray the quintessential experience of being dragged into that culture with all the passions and the highs and lows that you'd experience as a teenager. That idea that you would be seduced by this explosive passion because it would make you feel so alive after living a fairly repressed childhood existence.

Butch (Mark Dobson) provided me with a lot of inspiration for the lead character. It was his attitude and his calculated way of operating through the scene. When I sat down to write I would think of him and the effect he had on people, and it was easy to step into that world having such a focused and enigmatic character to glean from. He has more cover-ups and one-offs than any other DJ, has more quality rare records than anybody else. No-one could even begin to compete with the collection that he's got.

I got that story about dreaming of visiting America from Butch; that was his thing back then and he went on to become lauded as the best rare soul DJ of all time by his peers, so he had a very unique kind of drive at a young age. Initially he was only a collector and dealer of records up until Stafford time and then was almost pushed onto the decks by frustrated lads who wanted to hear certain records that only he owned. His whole life was and still is wholly immersed in rare soul. He came from a big family, six boys, and they all went to the Torch, the Twisted Wheel, Samantha's in Sheffield; they were organizing coaches and he was the younger brother. Butch would run to the phone box the moment the Soul Bowl record list hit the letterbox. The phone would be engaged constantly and he'd just stay in there and repeat dial until he got through to place his order, with a line of old ladies waiting outside to use the phone.

The history of the northern soul scene for me seems to play out through whichever nighters were having their heyday. I wanted to make the Shaun character have a backstory, that he'd been a regular at the Golden Torch in Stoke on Trent. This club came before Wigan. A lot of the older kids on the scene by the time the Casino came along were either veterans of the Torch or before that the Twisted Wheel in Manchester. You could look at the way someone danced and figure out what clubs they had grown up in. The Torch had a different dance style and the Sean character came with this massive kudos when he walked into John and Matt's lives.

The secondary school that I went to was full of very rough young lads, always fighting and acting up for attention. Many of them would tattoo themselves with a compass and Indian ink – scene slogans, favourite records, that sort of thing. Our teachers were jaded and wrote most kids off and treated us with scorn. When it came out, *Kes* was very real for us ... I remember it felt like watching a documentary.

That line that Steve Coogan's character comes out with: "curriculum vitae, that's Latin, you don't need to know that", and "come on meathead" or "mallet head" – these were the sorts of things you'd hear all the time.

When I was at school we didn't even do French, we didn't have a second language, can you imagine that? No one I talk to now I live in London believes me when I say that, because they think everyone in the UK did French at secondary school. We weren't deemed worth wasting the teaching time on.

Against this background for me came northern soul and it was liberating. I think the people involved that were kind of driven and dynamic, despite their background, ended up doing interesting and unusual things with their lives.

Representing northern soul
The Tony Palmer documentary, made in the mid-1970s, looking at it now, I'm not sure really hit the mark because at least my understanding of the scene is something different. It's not a geographical thing really so that part of it really irritated me. It wasn't as if the whole youth of Wigan was in attendance. Most kids in that dance hall had travelled miles to get there. From my experience of going to soul nights in the early '80s in Wigan, the area was full of kids who hated northern soul and were pretty territorial and aggressive when they caught you entering their town.

I remember seeing that documentary and the slo-mo scenes of those kids leaping about to the MVPs,[1] and it looked so spellbinding. But as I've got older and watched it again I've thought "why is he trying to link this up to the cotton mills and George Orwell", because those kids were the first generation that were rejecting that system and the idea of being stuck with the family and going to the working men's club. They weren't victims of the mills and their community, they were the first generation who were "fuck that, we're not swallowing all this shit, we're not having that, we're going to do our own thing, we'll be our own promoters, we're not going to the working men's club ... this is us, you lot, fuck off". I just think he got it so wrong there. It is a great documentary if you want to look at it in those terms, because those kids are the offspring of that horrendous industrialization of the north and the Midlands, but in a way it was the rejection of all that that created northern soul.

I thought Dave Withers (the young guy they interview), his testimony, if you like, was great though. Basically, they were mods, weren't they, they were the next generation of mods, they wanted to be modern, you know, they wanted to be transported elsewhere and do a different thing to other working-class kids.

My film didn't get to the screen until seventeen years after I'd decided to make it and it irritated me that other films about northern soul came out first and, from what I could see, were being made by people who'd had no experience of the scene and didn't have a clue.

A lot of what I think now about northern soul has come from the experience of making the film and the book. It has given me a wider understanding because before I made the film I only had my personal understanding and my friends' understanding of it. After making the film I got the opportunity to make the book and I asked a friend off the soul scene, Gareth Sweeney, to help me put the interviews together and to write that great intro, as I'm not much of a writer. Together we interviewed lots of people who we didn't previously know. I'd finished the film at this point but it would be another eighteen months before it would be released.

We did a sort of tour of northern soul's notorious history through individuals and the venues they attended. A lot of the interviews that I did for the film are in the book too, but then there's a few other DJs who I didn't know, various collectors and punters who were around before we were, in the sixties. Because it's a way of life, it's not just an obsession with music; it's an obsession with a lot of things, not least with drugs and we wanted this to come through in the interviews.

For the film, I wanted to start the story in '74 and finish in '76, because that was the eye of the storm, and that's when most of the trouble started with the drugs; all the things kicking off at that time would make for a better story because the stakes were getting higher.

During my work as a stills photographer I'd been able to represent things in the way I wanted to but this time I was representing thousands of young people's lives and I really felt the responsibility of getting things right. With the advent of social media everything's under heavy scrutiny.

When we were planning the wardrobe creation I was trying to hire the right people. We had thirty thousand followers on our Facebook page before we were even green lit, and I was posting a lot of stuff up there like wardrobe choices etc. What I used to do when we were collecting wardrobe was just throw up a picture and say, "did anyone have a jacket like this" and we would get comments back saying "yeah, but mine had a deeper collar", it was very helpful as I really did want to get the detail as accurate as possible. We wanted to try and represent the individual ethos, you know, it wasn't about the masses wearing the three-star V-neck sweater for the whole of the 1970s. It was about one guy who would wear a blazer with cuff buttons in '75, and then a few others would spring up and exaggerate on that theme for a while and it would die out within a few weeks.

I think on the scene generally the film's been received incredibly well. A lot of people who lived that life to the full and went the whole hog love it. They say "that's it, you nailed it". A percentage of people say "we enjoyed the film, the music, the dancing, but it was never like that with the drugs". I feel those people probably attended northern soul clubs but were either a bit naïve or just didn't get involved with any of the more dodgy elements. That's fair enough – not everyone who went to these venues came into such "bad company" but petty criminality focused around the supply of amphetamines was an integral part of the scene and I really think if you lived it to the absolute max, which is what my characters did, then you couldn't have avoided those types. I think also, there are quite a lot of people who want to rewrite their own history on Facebook because their sons and daughters are watching their pages and they are now saying, "I've never taken drugs in my life, how dare you even mention drugs in the same phrase as northern soul". It's also now quite cool to say you were into northern soul and so when people start coming out with stuff like that, you know they weren't really doing northern soul week-in week-out, you know they were just kind of flirting with it or whatever.

Certain individuals at Universal got behind the film, but others dismissed it and sent it down to the home entertainments department where it would only really have a DVD release. I was so devastated that the theatrical release wasn't really going to be more than a token gesture, with no London premiere, a handful of one-off screenings and DVDs being dropped through letterboxes two days later because I really wanted to spread the word that this thing was amazing beyond the people who initially knew about it.

The incredible thing that happened on the opening weekend was a result of fans petitioning local independent cinemas through an off-shoot of the Facebook page. We'd made such an effort to get it out there and we wanted it to go beyond its core audience but I think the distributors didn't want to spend money marketing it beyond the scene.

After the surprise of the successful release, various people in the film industry took it seriously and a handful of esteemed directors, writers and producers who saw it took it seriously and that's why it got its BAFTA nomination. Previously we didn't even get into the London Film Festival, or any film festivals for that matter until much later, but when the box office Top Ten hit and the DVD went to the top of the Amazon charts, with virtually no ads anywhere, suddenly things had changed. The stats were there in black and white for all to see and so suddenly people were asking questions in the film industry and our social media-led campaign became a talking piece itself.

From my perspective

I didn't get to an allnighter 'til I was seventeen and even at the age of nineteen I had only just started to get my confidence and figure out where I was going. These young men were already very dynamic at the age of fifteen and sixteen. I didn't feel an autobiographical film about a woman would work, because I seriously don't remember coming across a woman who wanted to be a DJ back then. That wasn't to say women on the scene were pushovers, the opposite in fact, but I was already telling a very unusual story to a lot of people who aren't on the northern soul scene, so I didn't want to make it about a woman being a DJ when there weren't many women who were driving that scene forward. The promoters, drug dealers, DJs, collectors, sellers, they were all men, so you're already kind of struggling to tell the story of northern soul, never mind putting a female protagonist in there for the sake of equality.

I was approached to do a Shredded Wheat ad and I didn't want to do it, so I recommended another director, 'cause I didn't make this film to then start making adverts that involve northern soul, it just cheapened it in a way. If a designer comes to me and says "I've done a collection based on northern soul" or you see catwalk pictures of some baggies and a vest with patches, I just think, you don't get it, you don't understand. This was about being modern and replacing things quickly and dictating your own fashion. Obviously, there was a time when everyone was wearing baggies and short tight t-shirts but that was soon replaced by another look as trends do. It wasn't something that stuck in 1974, it's just that the best original footage of the scene, when everyone was still young and athletic, happens to be that moment in fashion and it helped a lot that the big trousers and skirts enabled you to leap around on the dancefloor without restriction.

I think those who have been constantly doing northern soul and dress normally are appalled when they cross paths with people who still dress in baggies and are recently back out, trying to revive their youth, or re-enacting. Though I can see how, if they haven't been to allnighters since their youth, they feel that somehow that gives them back their northern soul identity.

What I wanted to do with the dancing was have an eclectic thing, where you got all these different generations of dancers coming through different clubs and all merge into one at Wigan. When I started going to allnighters there were so many different styles: from people literally just walking up and down, like a bear in a cage, to tight shuffling on the spot, to people who'd been to Stafford's Top Of The World and would barely move because they were consciously doing the opposite to Wigan. People who'd done it in these clubs in Soho in the '60s got into this thing where they'd have a lot of gesticulation, because they could only express with their hands as they were packed in like sardines. So, we invited different dancers from different eras down to these dance clubs that we were putting on for the young people who had volunteered to be in the film – people from the Torch, Twisted Wheel, Wigan, the Blackpool Mecca – and we encouraged the kids to follow different people and to express themselves within that.

When you're experiencing it en masse with people all around you, you catch a stranger's eye and it's that knowing look. I think that idea of the clap, you know, is just the moment that brings all of that culture together. When I saw *Soul Boy*, with the clapping thing ... they had them clapping above their head and you just know that some choreographer had looked at everyone dancing on a larger scale and gone, "oh it would be good if you did it this way so the camera will really pick it up visually" when in fact it wasn't this huge gesture, it was all about timing and making the right sound and almost throwing it away without giving it a dramatic movement.

When we were teaching the kids to dance we used to introduce them to all these driving tempo male vocal tracks, things like 'If This Is Love', The Precisions. I wanted them to feel the lyrics and listen to those voices, I encouraged the kids to lock themselves into the story, the romance of it so they'd get the depth of it.

For me the main thing that continues to draw me to that music is that I believe the singer and I believe their story. When you dance in a room full of people who are into it you can get into the escape of it but when you are trying to dance around people who don't know about northern soul it's difficult to get into that zone. You feel like everyone's sort of looking at you and trying to work out what it is that's happening, because it's such an odd culture to try and fathom if you are not part of it.

It's funny, I've only really talked in interviews about the process of how the film was made and how it was reacted to and I haven't actually talked much about my own experience with northern soul ... it sort of gets lost.

Liam Quinn

Liam is a DJ and dancer, he danced on the Duffy 'Mercy' video and helped prepare Martin Compston, the lead in *Soul Boy*, for the dance numbers in the film.

Duffy's 'Mercy'
I got involved in the Duffy video through an email from a good friend saying he's running an audition for a video, but he can't find any young dancers who can dance northern soul. I thought this might be a laugh, it's something I've done every weekend for the last ten years, so I took myself down on the bus to London. I walked into the studio [laughs], everything was alien; a proper dance studio with cameras set up, there must have been a couple of hundred professional dancers, in a queue signing in. I stood out like a sore thumb, 'cause I just walked in with my Adidas holdall and [laughs] I remember feeling I need to get out 'cause I'm going to embarrass myself. The producer was into northern soul: he just liked the music, and been to a few nighters, so he knew kind of what he was looking for. Anyway, everybody was limbering up. I wasn't, 'cause I wasn't used to that. I really panicked, but I thought: I went the whole way down here, let's just do it.

I was paired off with an unbelievably acrobat, athletic guy. They put on the 'Mercy' backing track so I had a bit of a beat and I thought just go with this and get back on the train to Manchester [laughs], 'cause there was an allnighter that night. So, I had a little dance just to myself; there's a wooden floor, just try and do it, get my balance and just have a little shuffle and as soon as I started warming up, the guy was like, that's it, that's what we're looking for, you just keep dancing. This amazing B-boy beside me was like, what are you doing, 'cause I was just a random guy. I instantly got the part, it was just like, look, have you got friends who can do this and I said "there's an allnighter on tonight, I'll phone all my mates, make sure they're all going and you can just do the auditions at an allnighter". All these people at the audition are professionals, but then none of them were dancing in the soul style, they were an adaption of what they thought it should be. The guy paid for me and another guy who's doing the audition to come up to the New Century Soul Club in Manchester, run by Chris Waterman, and I phoned and said, "I'm bringing these guys up, they're just going to have a camcorder and do an audition".

My friends thought it was a joke, but we were asked to come down a week later to video it, but we had never heard of Duffy and nothing's ever going to come from this. We danced for about sixteen hours, had to go and get tiger balm and rub it on our legs, 'cause everyone was cramping up so much [laughs]. I helped choreograph the whole thing; he should be there and they should be there; the break bit, if it was a northern soul track, this is what happens. I brought CDs with me and we danced all day to rare soul tunes, but then he played the backing track when he videoed us dancing. He was like, would that part work well? I was like, no, when there's a little break, there'll be people doing acrobatics, and make sure when he comes out of a spin where the break ends, that's the part where we would be coming up from a drop or landing from a flip or stopping from a spin. I was trying to direct him in that way, so it looked proper. So, what people are seeing us dancing to is probably not 'Mercy', it was Rita and the Tiaras or some rare soul track.

When Duffy became number one, I got a phone call off one of the other guys and he was, just like, you will not believe what I've just seen on TV. My initial reaction was we're all moving away! [laughter] We'll never show our faces again! 'Cause we knew that the backlash was just creeping and it wasn't acceptable for us to be doing something like that. Soul Source, personal, nighters, everything, oh man, it was crazy. It was the first time in a long time – since probably that Wigan documentary – that it had hit the sort of mainstream. It was me and a couple of other pals, mainly myself, 'cause I was probably just more well-known because I was DJing. You can't imagine now, a few years later, but I didn't go to any nighters for about three years, it was that bad, it put me off the scene, really bad, I just bought records and listened to music. Someone was physical one night, there was somebody else just trying to be very passive aggressive and other ones were just very, very demeaning online. I'm just more annoyed that, I would let that slide, that scene was something that meant everything to me, had done for so many years, it was everything. People said, oh yeah, you'll do anything, and I was like, what, I've been doing the nighters for years, I've been travelling the country, buying records, I never asked for it, I got a couple of hundred quid to do something, I had no idea it was going to be massive, so I never went looking for that sort of attention, but then it came.

Dancing
I never really thought about how I danced. I just made it up by myself. I always liked to dance in my bedroom when I was younger, just to funk music, but during the nights at Mecca, you just sort of do it anyway. It might come up when I see people dance in movies and different things like that, it just looks all a bit staged, people flicking their arms up and I can tell, I can actually tell

when I look at it and go, "no!". That's why the Duffy thing, I think, was done so well because we were actually dancing to rare soul there, so there was a sort of realism there. It was just a bit of fun, we never imagined ever that that was ever going to go to number one, it was just a case of doing it for a couple of hundred quid.

In the moment, when I'm dancing to the record, or when we were dancing to the tracks that were being played, maybe subconsciously, but when I'm dancing, say when that break comes up, I'm going to kick, but I don't really plan it. It's always been a feeling for me, 'cause there's some things, mid-tempo and whatever, I've always just done whatever feels right. It just came out of me when you hear that big massive break, I was so built up inside 'cause I loved the tune and you want to scream the lyrics to the high heavens, probably it always relates to something back in what's going on with you at the time, I think that as well, 'cause there's that release. I don't think there's much thought about the actual actions, like the actual moves as such, if you want to call them that.

I started dancing specifically northern, it must have been 1999, 2000, when I went over to Liverpool to a club called the Sink Soul Club, from my home in Ireland. None of my friends were into it, it was just my thing and I just had to go and try and find somebody else [laughs], and then I went to this sort of club called the Magnet and there was a nightclub, the Sink Soul Club, I found it online. I just happened to come across it and my Mum was a bit, like, what are you doing [laughs], I was like, no, I've got to do this, I've got to go over, and there was about six people on there that night and it was mainly sort of mod types, but there was a woman actually who was dancing, who I still know, and she's still very much on the scene and dances, but it was a lady that was dancing that just totally took me, I just stood at the side and I watched her all night in this tiny little underground club. I remember her coming up and saying come on, have a go, 'cause there was only around six people in this club, but the music was amazing. I can even remember tunes, like one of the best moments that night was hearing David Ruffin's 'He Who Picks The Rose', 'cause it was the only track that I knew all night [laughs], so it was like, yes, I know this song. It wasn't a northern night, but it was more sort of soul, bit of northern, bit of R&B, I just watched this lady's feet and just the way she flowed, you find your own way.

You used to get the old guys going, oh, you can tell he went to Wigan, the way he danced, but I loved it, I just love all the different styles, I love modern soul as well, and some of them people are just amazing. There was one guy at the big weekender at Blackpool, it's years and years ago and he danced and everyone was watching all the people jumping up and flipping, but there was one guy at the side, he hardly moved, but he just done this tiny wee shuffling, I've never seen anybody, he just was so unique and it wasn't anything extravagant, but flippin' hell, I could have watched him all night. Every track he danced, it was like, oh, you just knew he loved it more than anyone else at that moment on the planet and just his movement, whatever way he has, that's, for me, he did the best [laughs], not the guys doing all the acrobatics.

There's no proper way, the only proper way is somebody going and dancing the way they want to dance. I absolutely can't stand seeing the dancers in some of the clubs sometimes and they're just like, you can tell by their face they're not enjoying it or that they're not really, it's just like, you know, I'm dancing in a square, I'm doing this, flick my hands, I'm going to do a little drop, I'm waiting for it, you know what I mean, it's like, oh come on. Don't get me wrong, each to their own, as long as they're enjoying themselves. I would never judge anybody, but one thing I suppose I'm totally conscious of is, you can tell if someone has either been taught how to dance or they have watched a video of another person and copied it, so it is interesting; that's going to happen if you get dance classes. I think people thought I used to take dance classes or something, I've never taken a dance class in my life, I got asked to teach that guy in the *Soul Boy* film, but if you do get people taking dance classes, well, then it could technically be creating a lot of carbon classes of people just dancing alike, but that's alright.

Soul Boy
With the film it's a different kettle of fish, totally different kettle of fish, 'cause I just had to, 'cause I went, obviously, on that Duffy tour. The *Soul Boy* film came and unfortunately, that was just a monetary thing. I was, again, in between two jobs and it seemed pretty harmless and all the good people on the scene, 'cause there is a lot of good people on the scene with a bit more foresight and they were like, this is what it needs, it needs new blood, it needs to be out there, so you know, it carries on legacies and everything. So I just went for that, but that was a different kettle of fish, it had its good points, you know, bad points as well. It was low budget and, you understand, it's a film; it's not a documentary, so I had to take that on board and I was just asked to train the main actor, Martin Compston, how to dance and I'd never trained anybody in my life.

I travelled to Glasgow two, three times a week and with him just sat in the studio and I brought the CDs and I had to think about what I did (when I danced) and it was really difficult. I just kind of said: do this. So, I had to try and break everything down into a real simplified version and I almost went back to sort of going, here's the oldies guys and we can do the same. That was the easiest way of doing it, 'cause I knew that what they did was very simple steps, and it wasn't really how I danced myself, so yeah, it was really tough.

Again, on a personal basis, I don't know, it was for a film, fair enough; it's not real and people I think lose sight of that. It is a film, it's not real, the person isn't really dancing northern soul, they don't really love it as much as maybe you do; may it would be better to sit back, relax and enjoy the film for what it is. It's very hard to portray reality, it's on the screen, so I had a difficult time trying to talk to the producers or other people and saying, look, this is wrong, you're showing this wrong, the dance hall scene, it was like, no, take it out, doesn't happen, not reality [laughs]...

I felt for Shimmy Marcus, because I actually met him again, on Soul Source, as it happens. If you're not on the scene, you're not in a clique, your film is not going to be supported, you know, so a lot of people didn't know Shimmy Marcus but I actually met him at Sleepless Nights soul club in Dublin. He was a guy who did go to soul nights but just wasn't on the scene, unfortunately. It was a sticky situation, it was so low budget, they had literally no money left, they had to cut things quick, so they just went with it. I did sit around and try and help them as much as possible, but I could only try and do what they asked. I did say, "this is too difficult, do you know what I mean, it's not real". I think once I'd seen past that, I was like, it is a film, it's not reality, and they're trying to do something good. They give it a go, it's the first one, and it only enhanced young people's awareness of the music, which is still the main thing, the soundtrack is absolutely brilliant, that's one thing that is good and the film is not actually that bad.

In its testament, I met someone, we've just opened a bar here, we obviously play a lot of like northern and soul, funk in the bar here and a couple came up from Belfast for the day and they don't know me from Adam and they randomly were like, a northern soul track came on, oh, we've got this in the car, we've got that *Soul Boy* soundtrack. I genuinely had never seen these people in my life and I didn't let on, never even told them and they were like, oh yeah, it's one of our favourite films and they were a really cool couple. That was the reason they know about northern soul.

Years later, I thought, ah, do you know what, it's played a part in a lot of positive ways. The film itself got a backlash, wasn't supported by the soul scene as a whole, because obviously there was two going on, such as the soul scene in life, people want to make allegiances and they don't want to support everything, so it's just the way it goes, unfortunately.

I know Paul Sadot really well, and me and him used to dance years ago and go to the good clubs. I have a lot of good memories of Paul and he had a lot of friends. He did ask me at one stage to come along (and be part of *Northern Soul*), but I was on the floor with the backlash, I was really appreciative, but, "oh no, seriously, I can't". Loads of my friends were involved in London, dancing on it and getting trained. I think it was great, it was good, a bit darker; they went for edgier kind of feel, and Paul's amazing, he was a dance teacher himself. I'm just one guy who never taught and I only had to teach one person in a month and that was like working with him a couple of days a week. So, I kind of felt a wee bit like, ooh, this is tough, but you know, it was fun. Again though, I feel when I watch it, it's still watching a lot of carbon copied dancers flicking their hands in the air; it's not personally what's right for me, and I don't feel the realism, like I didn't feel it with *Soul Boy*. You can say all the cliché things in the world, you can say, oh, I love this, but I don't think it does a lot to enhance the scene and again, it was great but – I think just a personal opinion – just go to nights, just go to the scene, just go and dance.

About the author

Tim Wall is Professor of Radio and Popular Music Studies, and Associate Dean for Research in the Faculty of Arts, Design and Media at Birmingham City University. He undertook his doctorate on black music and radio at the Centre for Contemporary Cultural Studies at the University of Birmingham. He researches into the production and consumption cultures around music and the media, mixing historical analysis with contemporary investigations. His publications include the second edition of *Studying Popular Music Culture*, and recent research as varied as the politics of dancing on the northern soul scene, US dance fads from 1955 to 1965, music radio online, the transistor radio, personal music listening, music on television, jazz collectives, and *The X-Factor*. He has been a devotee of northern soul since his teens in the 1970s, and can still be found on the dancefloor on some weekends.

Note

1. MVPs, 'Turning My Heartbeat Up'. 1971. Buddah Records – BDS 469.

Musical Bookmark 6

Harriet Dakin photographed at Brighton Pier, March 2017
David Bowie, 'Knock on Wood'. UK RCA – 2466 1972

> "It's David Bowie and I choose it because Bowie was the first person that got me into music. He was the first person that I listened to and I thought 'wow!' It's his cover of Eddie Floyd's *Knock on Wood*. It was also the first time I'd ever heard a soul song, I suppose, so that really got me into soul as well. Covers of older songs are often more accessible than the [original] songs themselves and then you go on that journey of finding the originals."

Harriet Dakin is a music enthusiast and dancer. She danced on the Brit Awards during Pharrell William's performance of 'Happy' and has appeared in other northern soul related music videos.

14 Nostalgia, Symbolic Knowledge and Generational Conflict

Lucy Gibson

Much journalistic literature on northern soul treats it as an historical subject and phenomenon of the past. It is only in the past decade that academic research has begun to explore the longevity of northern soul culture. This chapter explores how fans have retained a long-term commitment by continuing active involvement within the northern soul scene.[1] It also considers some of the ways the past and present interrelate and manifest in fans' lives. Exploring commitment illustrates the meaning and socio-cultural experiences of sustained fandom. I argue that nostalgia, memory and familiarity play a role in northern soul as fans acquire symbolic knowledge through their ongoing allegiance and demonstrate an understanding of scene etiquette and associated practices. Symbolic knowledge and familiarity ultimately cements a fan's position as a genuine "soulie".[2] This is not to suggest that older fans are "clinging onto" their youth; rather, they look back on their past and, in turn, this informs their present involvement. The chapter also highlights the male-dominated nature of northern soul and explores generational tension amongst original scene members and younger newcomers as issues of ownership and status can lead to contention between traditionalists and those that feel the scene should progress.

The chapter draws on key findings from data collected between 2006 and 2008 in a study of how ageing shapes participation in music scenes (Gibson 2010); one facet of this research involved a study of northern soul. In 2010, Professor David Sanjek organized a symposium at the University of Salford: *Rare Records and Raucous Nights: Investigating Northern Soul*. This chapter is based on a paper I presented at the symposium; thus the discussion is based on data collected in the mid-2000s and is not making claims about the northern soul scene today. Indeed, more recent data collection would be welcomed for comparative analyses a decade on. Within my research, three primary sources were used to collect data: participant observation at northern soul events, and both face-to-face and email interviews with fans. Several secondary sources were also used, namely journalistic accounts, websites, internet message boards/forums and promotional material. Participant observation took place at seven northern soul events in a number of areas throughout the north-west of England, including Bury, Blackburn, Prestwich, Manchester, Wigan, and Warrington. To gain a broad view of the northern soul scene and fans' experiences, both small and large-scale events were attended. They varied in capacity and venue form: some were traditional dance-hall/ballroom styles with large wooden dancefloors, whilst others resembled a more contemporary nightclub or public house setting, or were typical of civic/municipal centres. Most events entailed at least two rooms to cater for sub-genres such as "oldies"/classics and modern/"crossover", and a separate area where fans are able to purchase, sell and trade records and memorabilia.

I was an "outsider" with very little prior knowledge of northern soul culture, music and general scene activities. My first experience of attending an event was plagued with not knowing what to expect. I entered venues excitedly and anxiously but with a very open mind. Two demographic aspects affirmed my outsider status – my young age in comparison to the majority of people in attendance, and my gender. The majority were aged forty and above and male; I was around twenty-four years old at the time, and female; this led me to feel rather conspicuous during my initial experiences of northern soul culture. Nonetheless, friendly "regulars" soon made me feel at ease and once I had attended a couple of different nights and certain faces became relatively familiar, conversations with fans helped me to gain an understanding of the customary behaviour of fans and DJs, music sub-genres, dancing styles, drug consumption, record bar areas and dancefloor etiquette. Nicola Smith's (2009a) positioning as a young female initial outsider was similar. Her work provides a useful discussion of the merits of being a young outsider rather than a "fan-researcher" (Smith 2009a: 444) and some of the issues that can arise in studying longstanding music scenes. In respect of my position as a researcher, fans were viewed as experts within the field and encouraged to share their experiences and stories of long-term involvement in northern soul. The following discussion is based on key findings from participant observation at events, five face-to-face interviews and fifteen email interviews with fans aged between thirty-five and sixty-one, and secondary data analysis of various sources. The age of participants is significant: whilst there was a small minority of younger people evident at events my research aimed to move beyond the preoccupation with youth in popular music studies and was interested in the notion of cultural commitment, the formation of music taste, and how ageing shapes involvement in music scenes. Thus, a sample of fans aged over thirty was used.

Nostalgia and familiarity

Northern soul has been in existence for over fifty years. Many events take place across the UK at nightclubs, traditional dance halls, bars, social clubs, working men's clubs and town halls and there is a strong following from original fans and a smaller number of younger newcomers. Many DJs who began playing records in the 1960s, 1970s and 1980s continue to do so to hundreds and even thousands of soulies at events across the UK. During fieldwork, fans suggested there were more events than during the 1970s' so-called halcyon days of the scene. An array of allnighters, fortnightly and monthly events and annual weekenders were available for fans to attend in the UK and globally. Northern soul records are still found in the vaults of American record companies and "new" releases of sixties material and "modern" soul continue at the time of writing. "Oldies" and newer favourites are played at events across the country. This combination of past and present offers an avenue for long-term fans to reminisce whilst also providing an element of freshness through new sounds played during events. The scene, as Smith (2009a) alludes, entails a fascinating interplay between old and new, tradition and progression, which is symptomatic of its longevity and fragmentation as it has evolved over time. Whilst Smith (2006: 176) suggests: "This is the same scene as evident in the 1970s with one obvious difference – the age of the participants", I would argue that the scene has in fact altered in part due to the increasing age of participants and subsequent changes in behaviour and practices (e.g. dancing, recreational drug taking) but also due to some fans' desire for the scene to progress and incorporate newer records. Indeed, Smith (2009a) does in fact hint at change later in her writing despite this earlier contention.

Fans often made reference to nostalgia as a reason for the longevity of northern soul. A fifty-year-old male fan talking on the BBC programme, *Inside Out*, reflects this view:

> You hear a tune you love and in the first few beats you're eighteen again (BBC TV, *Inside Out West Midlands*, 4 October 2004).

For some fans, participation in the scene evokes youthful memories and can contribute to a reprise of one's youth and a sense of attachment and belonging. This echoes Katie Milestone and Joanne Hollow's (1998) claim that the northern soul scene increasingly revolves around memory and familiarity rather than rarity. In Andy Bennett's study of the continuing significance of punk rock music for older fans, he claims that punk's longevity was celebrated as a "living culture" rather than viewing it in a nostalgic sense (2006: 229–30). I argue that for northern soul fans, it is not as clear-cut as Bennett suggests for older punks; nostalgia and familiarity are significant in some fans' continued involvement, particularly when they want to hear the same "oldies" played during events (explored in further depth later in this chapter). Thus, northern soul fans' experiences show the tension between perceiving their involvement as nostalgia or as a "living culture" to be enjoyed in adulthood. A 48-year-old male describes going to the Cleethorpes weekender in 1993 after a long break from the scene:

> I saw so many faces I knew, the records hadn't changed, the dancing was the same, it was just as though I had walked into a recurring dream, except the faces were a bit older, stomachs not so firm. I thought that I shouldn't be there, I thought it was "wrong", I thought they were very sad people hanging on to a past youthfulness which had danced into their dreams and aspirations fuelled by the music I love. Then in 1999 I went to a weekender in Skegness, the same feelings, it was out of joint, but as I attended the next two events I had stopped thinking they (and I) were trying to live in the past and realized that the passion for northern soul which I had as a teenager and early twenties was still real, the music was still true to my soul and when I danced it was not recapturing my youth but more like putting on a comfy pair of slippers, sort of coming home, although it felt like I had never been away.

This fan stresses the familiarity and sense of belonging derived from returning to active participation in northern soul. He claims he is not hankering after the past and his youthful lifestyle, but rather, he is regaining his enthusiasm for northern soul – a familiar aspect of his identity to maintain and evolve during adulthood. This is not a case of "arrested development" (Calcutt 1998) or a refusal to "let go" of youth. It can be conceived more as "evidence that youth styles and lifestyles are migrating up the age scale and that as the 1960s generation ages they are taking some of their youth-orientated dispositions with them" (Featherstone 1991: 100–101). Contemporary lifestyles have arguably become increasingly independent of specific age groups.

Through participation in northern soul, it is evident that fans are able to recapture youthful memories and recall past events and times of pleasure within their lives. Arguably, for some engaging in familiar leisure pursuits from one's adolescence is a reprise of youthful attachment and identification. Smith (2009a – also included within this edited collection as Chapter 4) focuses primarily on identity and a fan's changing sense of self in her discussion of nostalgia. She suggests that northern soul fans "are not nostalgic about the scene but about the loss of the youth experience of the scene. Nostalgia is thus an internal sense of separation" (2009a: 442). Whilst I agree with this to an extent, I would add that some fans *are* nostalgic about elements of the scene such as the music, vinyl records, and scene-specific cultural goods and knowledge and aim to preserve it. In support of Smith (2009a), we can consider Andrew Blaikie's (1999) analysis of ageing and popular culture, which discusses the notion of a mind/body dichotomy where the true – perpetually youthful – self is disguised behind old skin. He asserts, "cohorts tend to retain the values of their youth throughout life" (p. 214). Moreover, Stephen Hunt (2005: 182) argues that in contemporary society it appears to be more acceptable that middle-aged people will try to put the "biological clock" back if they have the time and money to make the effort. Such an attempt to retain youth is increasingly accepted as legitimate. Currently, he postulates, a whole age cohort is refusing to adopt the middle-age role. This is the so-called generation of baby-boomers – those born between 1946 and 1964 – who have reached mid-life in postmodernity and a culture of endless choice and lifestyle preferences. A number of northern soul fans belong to this cohort and their involvement in the scene could be interpreted as an attempt to resist and redefine traditional definitions of middle age, and manage their changing sense of self. Participating in music scenes during adulthood shows how there is a blurring of traditional lifestyle preferences in respect to age as the consumption of music has traditionally been viewed as a youthful sphere of social life.

A contentious issue within northern soul, and one that relates to the tensions associated with nostalgia and evolution, concerns the music played during events. Opinions differ in terms of whether DJs should play what are commonly known as "oldies": songs that were popular during the late 1960s and 1970s and are now regarded as northern soul "classics". Or whether DJs should incorporate more "modern" and recently discovered soul music into their playlists. Smith's (2009a) analysis is highly relevant here. She identifies two "ideal-types" in respect to the extremes of northern soul fans' experience: nostalgics and progressives. For Smith, nostalgics are those fans that want to hear the "oldies" of the 1960s, 1970s and are committed to protecting "the specifics of northern soul" (p. 440). Progressives, in contrast, are "committed to exploration, discovery and development within the scene" (ibid.). I would agree with Smith's categorization of fans and add that some fans feel progressives are in the minority. The following quotation from a 42-year-old male DJ and promoter makes reference to this:

> 85 percent of people in the scene are there for nostalgia, recapturing youth, familiar music and friends. For the other ten or fifteen percent, music is everything and they want new rare stuff played all the time.

This DJ describes the tendency for the majority of fans to want to hear the same records that they experienced when they originally developed a passion for northern soul. For other fans, hearing the same songs and "oldies" at events is tiresome and newer, rarer songs are coveted as they want the scene, and their musical knowledge, to evolve. A male 42-year-old fan describes his experience:

> There are still so many records that we've not heard and discovered, not as many now but I can still go to a club and hear seventy percent of music that I've never heard before.

For this progressive fan, northern soul is viewed as a "living culture" (Bennett 2006) and one that provides new musical experiences despite its longevity and often nostalgic tone.

Whilst fans tend to want to hear familiar music during northern soul events, the majority refrain from wearing clothes associated with the scene to symbolize their attachment. Like the punks in Bennett's (2006) study, northern soul fans have modified their image, and their reflexive conception of themselves as soulies has become more subtly expressed. Fans have altered their commitment and made their identification to northern soul more implicit as they have grown older, as this 49-year-old male suggests:

> I love the clothes in the scene, although this isn't as important these days, the music and bonding with people is more important.

And similarly, a male 48-year-old describes his views on displaying his attachment to northern soul through style:

> I'm proud of my northern soul journey and heritage but I don't wear any of the "uniform" or badges or carry those allnighter bags around anymore, one wouldn't know my passion for northern soul unless one actually knew me, that's ok, it's a feeling, some might say religion (I wouldn't say that) but if it was my religion it would be between me and my conscience, a personal thing, nobody else's business, until I get to a venue or converse on the "net".

Again, akin to the punks in Bennett's (2006) research, commitment to northern soul is not communicated explicitly through clothing; there is a mutual understanding among many soulies of the "internalization of commitment" (Bennett 2006) existing in a fan's ongoing, yet matured, identity as a "soulie". Commitment to northern soul is commonly embodied by fans through their knowledge and understanding of the music and culture rather than being objectified through clothing and stylistic cultural goods associated with the scene. Older fans' clothing is more a reflection of their age than their attachment to the northern soul scene. This demonstrates that fan behaviour and scene aesthetics have changed over time and somewhat contradicts the earlier point regarding a blurring of traditional lifestyle preferences and age via music scene involvement. Arguably, fans do work within established age expectations despite their adult involvement in what has been commonly perceived to be a youth pursuit. Few fans at events continue to nostalgically objectify their commitment to the scene through their choice of attire. The northern soul style typically entails carrying holdall bags adorned with patches to signify affiliation to certain venues, wearing high-waisted flared trousers, polo shirts, full circle skirts, vests, white ankle socks, and brogues. These items were very rarely witnessed at events. Those fans who do choose to continue to symbolize attachment through external style did tend to talk about and view the scene in a nostalgic way. Conversely, some fans wearing typical northern clothing and accessories were younger novices, rather than original fans, and embraced the fashion as a "retro" nod to northern soul's stylistic history and tradition. This trend was also noted by Smith (2009a) in her analysis of the ageing northern soul scene. She argues that this may be a tactic employed by young newcomers to exhibit knowledge of the scene's history and counter any conflict derived from their status as a young fan.

There is an interesting paradox within northern soul culture in terms of the role of nostalgia and familiarity. Although musically the majority of fans regard their identification with the scene sentimentally, their ongoing attachment to northern soul, and the internalization of commitment as they age, means that fans do perceive northern soul as a "living culture" (Bennett 2006) or, as Smith (2009a: 441) puts it, "an active (as opposed to a retro) scene". This is even more apparent with those fans wanting to hear "new" songs still being uncovered rather than the same "oldies" event after event. Although Bennett (2006) condemns the pathological discourse existing in studies of older music fans who, it is claimed, refuse to "let go" of their youth, it appears that in the case of northern soul culture, nostalgia and familiarity do play a significant role. This is not a desperate clinging on to youth; it is more a tendency to fondly acknowledge the past, their sense of self, tastes and admiration for certain songs, artists and DJs whilst actively participating within the present-day scene: a sense of the past within the context of the present.

Symbolic knowledge, credibility, and rarity

In her seminal study of electronic dance music, Sarah Thornton (1995) argues that club cultures are "taste cultures" in opposition to the mainstream. She draws on the work of Pierre Bourdieu and coins the term "subcultural capital" to conceive of "hipness" within club cultures and electronic dance music scenes. Thornton (1995: 11–12) argues that: "subcultural capital confers status on its owner in the eyes of the relevant beholder". Within club culture it is about fashionable haircuts, record collections, being "in the know" through the use of current slang, and performance of the latest dance styles. Subcultural capital refers to awareness and familiarity of songs, artists, record labels, venues, DJs, promoters, vernacular, and in some cases ownership of key artefacts and cultural goods. For Thornton (1995: 11), however, subcultural capital is a youth phenomenon: "it affects the standing of the young just like its adult equivalent" cultural capital; northern soul culture provides evidence against this as adults possess so-called subcultural capital in the form of symbolic knowledge and cultural goods within the scene.

The term "scene" is used here to describe northern soul since I do not view it as a distinct subculture in the theoretical sense of the word. I would suggest that subcultural theory does not apply to ageing fans or groups of music fans and, similarly to Peter J. Martin (2004), the notion of symbolic representations, resources and knowledge is more fitting as it allows for any fluidity that may occur as fans and music scenes age. Symbolic forms of knowledge and subcultural capital are in some ways similar; both bestow status on the individual, contribute to a sense of belonging and can play a significant role in the construction of one's identity as a northern soul fan. Whilst symbolic knowledge can arguably be obtained via various means (e.g. Smith's (2012) exploration of subcultural capital exchange for the children of soulies), being a long-term fan and ageing within the scene, undoubtedly affords the acquisition of symbolic knowledge. The longevity and sustained nature of commitment to the scene can help to cement one's identity as an original northern soul fan.

For Thornton (1995), club cultures entail "hierarchies of taste" in opposition to the mainstream; these hierarchies and forms of subcultural capital are anchored in knowledge of the latest records, "white labels", niche media, fashion styles, promoters, DJs, events, festivals, and so on. Forms of symbolic knowledge can authenticate a person's identification as an enthusiast for a particular music scene; it can act as proof of fervour by providing evidence of a person's expertise and experience. Northern soul can also be described as a culture revolving around taste which diverges from the mainstream. Yet it does not neatly fit into subcultural theory definitions due to the ageing nature of the scene and its participants. Fans of northern soul do, however, openly distinguish themselves from other mainstream and underground taste cultures in a similar vein to subcultures. A crucial aspect of this distinction is the auto-denomination used by some fans to describe and differentiate between themselves and others. Many respondents used the term "soulie" in defining themselves and their identification to the northern soul scene. In contrast, some fans referred to outsiders as "handbaggers". Soulies are positioned by some as "true" northern soul fans who possess symbolic knowledge of conventions within the scene. Conversely, handbaggers – who have been given their name due to dancing around handbags, a cultural faux pas in northern soul – are unaware of the cultural codes and behave somewhat inaptly during events. A female 45-year-old fan's comments highlight this distinction:

> There is never any trouble from people who are genuinely on the soul scene. I have found out over the many years of being on the soul scene that true northern soul people dancing if they bump into you will automatically put up their hand and apologise instantly for catching you on the dancefloor even if it's not their fault. There is also a level of etiquette on the dancefloor which personally I believe only true northern soul people appreciate – for example if someone is already dancing on the dancefloor you don't encroach their space – a bad venue is having people on the dancefloor with cigarettes, drink and the dreaded handbags – it's a no go area for soulies!

The fan refers to specific cultural practices in the scene which only "true" northern soul fans understand and conform to. Thus, this supports Tim Wall's (2006) analysis which argues that an understanding of the dancefloor etiquette alongside the ability to display the particular dance movements within the scene helps to create a sense of belonging to a community and cultural solidarity amongst scene members. Moreover, this sense of belonging and cultural solidarity is enhanced over time as fans develop and build upon their possession of symbolic forms of knowledge. Handbaggers do not possess sufficient understanding of accepted practices in the scenes. Handbaggers were easily identified during fieldwork and a number of fans expressed contempt towards this group; interestingly, this was an issue discussed more by female research participants than males. The term handbagger has clear gender implications as it is women who carry handbags and stereotypically place them on the dancefloor to dance around in mainstream pub and club cultures. Despite this connotation, the term is applied to all outsiders, regardless of gender, that demonstrate a lack of symbolic knowledge concerning accepted behaviour and etiquette within northern soul.

Smith (2009a: 438) provides a valuable typology of participants in a scene with longevity such as northern soul. This typology acknowledges varying types of scene membership and the interpretation of "non-established participants" is particularly salient for this chapter. There are "non-members", which includes the "passer-by" and "day-tripper"; and "members", which refers to both "mature" and "young" "newcomers". The handbagger discussed herein is arguably an addition to Smith's typology of participants. The handbagger is similar to the non-members but attends more regularly than the "passer-by" or "day-tripper". The age of the newcomer is highly relevant: for Smith (2009a), there is an age-related conflict as young newcomers experience difficulties in relation to scene acceptance due to their age. It is suggested that mature newcomers are less conspicuous due to their older appearance; they "'fit in' in terms of age and thus experience fewer problems of access" (Smith 2009a: 439). Indeed, in earlier work by Smith (2006), a similar argument is put forward regarding age-related conflict in the scene that is not experienced by older or adult newcomers. This rejection of young newcomers, Smith (2006: 188) claims, is a means of older soulies preserving self-esteem.

This chapter reveals how handbaggers are viewed more negatively than the proposed categories in Smith's (2009a) typology and as such constitute an additional area of contention. Whilst I acknowledge age is an important source of conflict, I would add symbolic knowledge works in a similar vein by creating tension between scene participants. Handbaggers tend to be mature newcomers who do not wish to become established scene participants but, arguably, are attending events often fairly regularly due to feeling comfortable surrounded by people of a similar age. Handbaggers problematize Smith's (2009a) view that tension associated with newcomers is age-related and focused primarily on the young. They can be categorized as mature newcomers that are positioned negatively by soulies as outsiders, as they lack appropriate symbolic knowledge of northern soul culture. In agreement with Smith (2006) such conflict relates to a fan's sense of self, social identity, and nostalgia. Smith suggests "nostalgia is relevant to the conflict of age in northern soul as it creates a unique subjectivity for the older soulie that the newcomer *cannot*[3] possess" (2006: 186). Whilst age is stressed here, I suggest that this is also the case for the mature novice or handbagger.

It was clear that some people attending northern soul events were not "genuine" enthusiasts, and their involvement may have been due to feeling at ease being surrounded by people of a comparable age and the sociable nature of the scenes. A male 50-year-old reiterates this view:

> Some [events] are more commercial than others. Commercially I mean the sounds played will be more popular records that may have crossed over into the mainstream, so you get more non-soul fans attending because it's a good local night out, where they can dance to records they know and quite often they are the only events on that cater for the over 40s. If this crowd attend a rare soul night they often vote with their feet and remove themselves elsewhere, as they don't really appreciate the music being played.

This fan mentions a lack of events, leisure activities and club nights catering for middle-aged audiences which leads to an increasing number of outsiders participating in the scene. Despite many fans' critical perceptions of this, some did express positive attitudes by welcoming newcomers into the scene (a theme explored later in the chapter).

Long-term participation in northern soul cements a fan's commitment to the scene due to the acquisition of symbolic knowledge, and crucially, involvement in social networks with key individuals within the scene. These vital demonstrations that one is a genuine "soulie" are maintained and amplified over a number of years through ongoing allegiance to the scene. As this male 42-year-old explains:

> Getting into the scene is like serving an apprenticeship, you have to work your way in and up. With DJing, it's very hard for someone to just come into the scene and DJ straight away, even if they owned all the records. It's about association and who a person knows.

Possessing a wealth of experience and knowledge of records, clubs, DJs, and labels can lead to development of social capital and prestige within the northern soul scene. For the fans that are passionate about dancing rather than DJing or record collecting, symbolic knowledge in the form of cultural goods can have a similar effect. A 59-year-old male, who was a frequent attendee of Manchester's Twisted Wheel club, which is commonly referred to as the "original" northern soul club, highlights this:

> I once went to a northern soul dance in Warrington and as I wasn't a regular there the people on the door ... asked me if I knew what sort of dance it was, I said "I think so" and produced my original Twisted Wheel membership card. I can only describe the change in their attitude as dramatic. They at once became in awe of the card and immediately called all sorts of other people to see it and insisted that without question I went in without paying.

This example reveals the importance of credibility and authenticity in northern soul culture. This quest for authenticity is further epitomized by the scene's emphasis on rare vinyl. Many fans believe that DJs should only play original records at events, and reissues, bootlegs, pressings, and more recent technologically-advanced musical formats such as CDs, MP3s or other digital formats should be disregarded.[4] In discussions on a northern soul website forum the "OVO" (Original Vinyl Only) policy at numerous venues is frequently debated. Venues are generally criticized if they do not adhere to the OVO policy and allow DJs to play pressings, reissues/bootlegs, and CDs. Such venues are often labelled CRAP – CDs, Reissues and Pressings. A 60-year-old male stated at one northern soul event, "any venue worth its salt will only play vinyl! CDs are ok for cheap copying and listening to at home but any venue that plays them just isn't right". Although a relatively small number of CDs are sold in the record trading areas at events, the popularity of vinyl illustrates the fans' desire for original, authentic, and rare soul records. Equally, this means that the cost of rare records is often very high and only a small number of DJs and collectors can afford the rarest vinyl; arguably, this could lead to elitism within the scene. Some fans expressed a sense of frustration as they felt rarity is sometimes more important than quality; a male 53-year-old believes that "if nobody is dancing then the monetary value and how rare the record is doesn't matter".

Elements of northern soul culture are dominated by white males. For example, in respect to gender, there were a high number of male DJs, promoters, and record traders compared to females. And, in terms of ethnicity, there were a small number of people from black and minority ethnic origins. Just one research participant was of a mixed racial background and all other interviewees were white. This was an unintended consequence of convenience and snowball sampling. At events, rooms playing modern soul had people in attendance of black and Asian origin but rooms or clubs playing traditional 1960s/1970s soul attracted a predominantly white audience. Wall's (2006) analysis of dancing touches upon gender relations within the northern soul scene; a theme which in her previous work (1997) and her paper with Joanne Hollows (1998), Katie Milestone overlooks. Issues of gender are however discussed in Smith's wider thesis (unpublished PhD, 2009b) and by Katie Milestone in Chapter 11 of this edited collection. Wall's (2006) focus on dancing highlights a move towards gender parity as women occupy a central space on the dancefloor. However, I argue that other aspects of the scene, such as DJing and record collecting, illustrate the male dominance within northern soul.

Andrew Wilson (2007) also briefly comments on gender relations in the northern soul scene. In his analysis of the 1970s scene he argues that "there were fewer female participants in the Scene than male" (2007: 75). For Wilson, there were two deterrents to female participation: the need to travel around the country and the all-night nature of events. Wilson also notes that females were "invisible" in central activities of the scene such as collecting rare records. He draws on the observations of one of his respondents who states, "there were hardly any girls collecting records, and often the girls you did see with records were holding them for their boyfriends" (Wilson 2007: 76). Wilson's arguments are still relevant. While his observation refers to 1970s northern soul culture when it was perhaps more apparent, arguably, female fans continue to experience some issues in the realm of record collecting, trading, and DJing within the scene.

The number of female DJs, promoters and collectors has risen in the past few years; nonetheless, some female respondents commented upon the difficulty of establishing credibility as a DJ. As a 40-year-old female fan explains:

> It takes years to be accepted and taken seriously on the soul scene. If you happen to be a woman it is that much harder. The soul scene is definitely a male orientated scene – without doubt and to be taken seriously on your own merit is hard, very hard. On your own merit, I mean for your knowledge, for your record collection, for your passion and for your commitment, regardless of whether you have a boyfriend/husband who is someone on the scene.

This DJ has experienced difficulty in gaining status in the scene due to her gender; however, she is now successful. Following twelve years of participation, at the time of data collection, she holds three DJ residencies at northern soul events around the UK. When questioned about her experiences as a female DJ, despite holding three residencies, she is reluctant to identify herself as a DJ, stating: "It's funny really because I don't actually think about myself being a 'female' DJ. In fact, to be honest I don't really think of myself as being a DJ at all, although I guess I probably am". Whilst this "pro-am" self-image could be interpreted as a potential lack of dedication to the scene and underlying reason for taking twelve years to secure residencies, I would suggest her modesty is perhaps a reflection of the fact that she has experienced hostility from men in the scene and because she is engaging in an activity that is traditionally understood as a male domain. When she first began to buy records during the 1980s she explains that she used to send a male friend to buy them on her behalf because she didn't feel confident enough to go and buy them herself. She explained that female collectors were virtually unheard of in the 1980s and women who did buy records were perceived as buying them for their boyfriend or husband. She described a few incidences where men have expressed negative attitudes towards her:

> I remember once, must be at least eighteen years ago, I was looking through a DJ's sales box. I won't mention him by name. Anyway, I was looking through his box when he suddenly slammed down the box shut on me and said with a sneer on his face, "A man's got to do what a man's got to do". Another instance was when another well-known DJ turned round and said, "Why don't you run along and get yourself a part-time job in a patisserie." Needless to say, I ignored that 24-carat gold nugget of wisdom. Then just two weeks ago I had

a guy I had never met before but knew vaguely through a northern soul forum came up to me and said, "This might sound sexist", and before he said anything else I said, "But are all the record's mine...?" I just knew what he was going to say and then left him standing there with my husband and went off to dance. He then turned to my husband and said, "They're your records really, aren't they mate?"[5]

The experiences of this female DJ exemplify the tendency for knowledge and expertise, particularly in relation to DJing and collecting vinyl, to be masculinized in the world of northern soul. Women are accepted in the scene as dancers, although men demonstrate the more elaborate moves, but their ability to DJ or possess a large record collection is often questioned. The female DJ alludes to the masculinization of knowledge as she believes that "there are very few females that I can sit down with and have a conversation about records. Don't get me wrong, there are loads of girls I know who know names/titles of songs they like. However, if I wanted to talk about a certain record label or about a particular producer or discuss what musicians played on what tracks it would have to be a bloke." Thus, women who participate in the scene tend to adopt the accepted roles of dancer and enthusiast rather than DJ, promoter, or record trader. Women are involved in the scene but often on a more marginal level than men because DJing, promoting venues and events, and collecting records are traditionally viewed as a male preserve.

Generational conflict

There are differing opinions concerning "young" novices participating within the northern soul scene. Although the vast majority of fans were aged between forty and sixty, a small number of teenagers and people aged under thirty were present at events. As a researcher aged around twenty-four at the time, I experienced no signs of hostility from fans. However, my presence at events did cause some individuals to make comments such as "Aren't you a little young to be in here?" and "Are you really into this? It's way before your time, isn't it?" Fans often approached me to engage in conversation because they felt it was interesting to gain a younger person's perspective on the scene and were interested in the research.[6] Despite this, there is some evidence of generational conflict in the northern soul scene.

These statements reveal the differing approaches to young newcomers in northern soul. All research participants welcomed the involvement of young enthusiasts in the scene; however, this may reflect the fact they were being interviewed by a "young" researcher and did not want to appear unfriendly. Positive attitudes towards young newcomers were summed up by one fan as evidence of older fans feeling more youthful if they are surrounded by younger people; this differs from Smith's (2009a) suggestion that young fans problematize the subjective sense of self for the ageing fan and serve as a reminder of an older fan's past youth. In contrast however, and in support of Smith's (2009a) other arguments, there was evidence that some fans feel threatened by the arrival of young people "taking over" the scene and transforming it from the familiar musical culture they have been a part of for many years. On a website forum dedicated to northern soul, one fan shares his experience of negative attitudes towards young people in the scene:

> [I] can remember getting into a "discussion" several years ago at Warrington Parr Hall with some old timer, told him it was great to see a younger element there and he looked at me and said, "Nope, don't like youngsters at venues – they make me feel old".

In contrast, another fan highlights, via an online forum, a more positive view:

> Youngsters should be encouraged whether they DJ or are just part of the crowd. At the last 100 Club there were some (teenage?) girls dancing their little hearts out and they hadn't just stumbled into the venue by accident. Also two mods who looked about sixteen but stood there soaking up the atmosphere!

A few fans take their children to events and younger people in the scene often have parents who introduced them to northern soul music and culture during their childhood. Indeed, Smith's (2012) work on parenthood and the transfer of capital in the northern soul scene explores this phenomenon in some depth. Within my research, a male 42-year-old DJ explained how he often takes his 15-year-old son to events because he feels the scene cannot last forever and the current crowd needs to be perpetuated by younger fans. He stated: "older people can show resentment towards younger people for not knowing certain things and the established practices in the scene. I get annoyed because we need younger people to get involved or else the scene will die out." In a similar vein, some fans discussed their anxiety over the future of northern soul, and in particular, records losing value because of a lack of interest from younger generations.

The website forum dedicated to northern soul provides further evidence of ongoing debates concerning young newcomers in the scene. A fan discusses a new young DJ:

> This kid was great! He's not only a serious DJ with several well-stacked boxes of his own originals and his own sound system but he clearly loves the music and dances with all the passion and energy a

14 Nostalgia, Symbolic Knowledge and Generational Conflict

16 year-old can muster. Yep. 16 years old! Credit where credit's due. He clearly has the same passion about what he does as many of us did when we started out at the same age and it was refreshing to see someone less than 40 yrs old behind the decks who could play with a level of professionalism which would put many to shame.

Check him out if you get the chance. This is exactly what the scene needs IMO.[7]

This DJ's father is known in the scene as a fan who began his participation during the 1970s. In response to the initial post above, other fans ask what the DJ's specific music tastes are, for example, whether he plays "oldies", or "7ts", or newer records, how he can afford to buy records, and (rather pessimistically) if they belong to his father. In another forum post, a fan discusses her experience of other young DJs attempting to establish themselves on the scene and states:

We took [DJ's name] on as a resident when he was 14 years old – playing his own OVO – not his dad's. I noticed when he was DJing out and about, if he played "current biggies or floor fillers" he got slated by those who thought he was playing "same old same old" and told him that he was shite and should be doing something new, and when he mixed it up a bit and had less of a dancefloor reaction, he'd still get slated for it by those who want something they know. What used to really piss me off was if [DJ's name] would play something and get a mild reaction, but should older DJs play the same record, then the reaction was different and they were a DJ god!

Another thing to look out for is jealousy. There are some guys out there who feel the younger DJs shouldn't be DJing and don't deserve their spots because they haven't put the 30+ years in.

Something else young DJs have to put up with is that many many people feel the need to give them advice or express their opinion of the young 'uns in a patronising and condescending way.

This extract reveals how older fans situate themselves as "critical overseers" (Bennett 2006) of northern soul scenes (a role that is also discussed in Chapter 8 by Raine and Wall). Like the older punks in Bennett's study, older northern soul fans "articulate a discursive practice ... designed both to celebrate the survival and development" of northern soul scenes and to self-impose the older fans' "collective authority, won through age and longevity of commitment" to northern soul, "to supply critical judgement on the scene and those involved in it" (Bennett 2006: 228). There appears to be a dichotomy in terms of both positive and negative generational relations within the northern soul scene, as Smith (2006; 2009a, 2009b; 2012) has explored. Older fans feel it is their duty and entitlement as long-serving participants to pass on their knowledge, expertise, and guidance to younger enthusiasts. The above extract shows how some fans feel that this direction is sometimes expressed in a disdainful manner due to resentment towards younger fans. In addition, the evidence suggests younger fans have to work hard to gain status and recognition as a DJ, and older DJs are given more credit due to the longevity of their commitment. Smith's (2012) research highlights a rather positive relationship between "soul parents" and their "soul child(ren)" consuming northern soul music and actively participating within the scene together; the evidence here is more aligned with Smith's (2006; 2009a) previous work as it demonstrates some of the tensions associated with intergenerational involvement in the scene. Moreover, for younger newcomers that are not introduced to the scene via their parents and have not accrued familial subcultural capital (Smith 2012) or symbolic knowledge, credibility is evidently difficult to obtain within the scene. As Smith's (2012) research suggests, the "soul child" (Smith 2012) arguably gains more acceptance on the scene through their status as the child of an original and established scene member. They are perhaps viewed less suspiciously due to their inherited symbolic knowledge and subcultural capital. There is a need for future research to add to debates on generational conflict and draw on the experiences of younger newcomers by investigating their perceptions of any tensions existing within the scene.

Conclusion

This chapter has contributed to existing analyses concerned with the dynamics and nuances of northern soul as a long-standing music scene. Focusing on key themes such as nostalgia, symbolic knowledge, and generational conflict reveals a number of contradictions within the scene. Northern soul culture entails an interplay between the past and present – the past self is imbued in the context of the present. Nostalgia clearly plays a role, and leads to tensions, within the scene. This is evident in debates regarding playing "oldies" that provide fans with a sense of familiarity and belonging, or embracing more modern records and formats allowing the scene to evolve. A further contradiction is evident via fans' ongoing attachment to northern soul. This could be interpreted as a form of negotiating traditional expectations of adulthood; yet fans' internalization of commitment, exemplified through changing clothing and accessories, indicates how fans do work within perceived age-appropriate demands. Such tensions surrounding change and continuity reveal how fans may want to protect the scene and its characteristics, yet ageing and scene longevity inevitably impact on fans' experiences and the nature of the scene.

Whilst previous work (e.g. Smith 2009a) has focused primarily on age as a source of conflict within the scene, this chapter demonstrates that mature so-called handbaggers are a further contentious issue. Symbolic knowledge and apparent dedication to the scene are highly significant for soulies. Whilst I recognize the importance of age in creating tension within the scene as young newcomers can and do experience hostility, here we have seen how lacking crucial symbolic knowledge in relation to the codes and conventions of the scene can also cause conflict for *adult* novices. Indeed, the term "handbagger" is also significant in highlighting the masculinization of knowledge and expertise within the scene. This is particularly the case when considering the relative lack of female promoters, DJs and record traders/collectors, and difficulties gaining credibility for female DJs and fans. Whilst women are accepted in the realm of dancing as Wall (2006) suggests, this chapter illustrates that gender equality is not as evident within other areas of northern soul culture. The paradoxical nature of generational relations in northern soul has supported Smith's (2006; 2009a; 2012) work and revealed further contention surrounding intergenerational involvement in the scene. Differing attitudes towards young newcomers have revealed the tensions and contradictions regarding change, familiarity, and the future of northern soul. While much journalistic writing on northern soul suggests the scene is historical and ceases to exist in any meaningful sense, the academic research discussed in this chapter highlights how the scene entails contradictory dynamics in recent years. Indeed, the northern soul scene is still very much alive with highly committed fans, and the longevity of the scene has impacted on the aesthetics, practices and identities of fans in several interesting ways.

About the author

Lucy Gibson is Senior Lecturer in Applied Health and Social Care at Edge Hill University, UK. Her doctoral research explored popular music and the life course and investigated themes of cultural commitment, lifestyles and identities amongst fans of northern and rare soul, rock, and electronic dance music (EDM). She has published and presented academic work on popular music and ageing, the extension of youth cultural practices in adulthood, and the ageing body. Her research interests broadly focus on ageing, youth culture, community engagement, well-being, and online research methods.

Notes

1. Some fans made reference to scenes in the plural sense or used the term "northern and rare soul". I acknowledge diversity within the scene and am not attempting to homogenize it; I recognize there are numerous local, translocal and virtual scenes (Bennett and

Peterson 2004) that coexist within northern soul culture. However, for this chapter, I use the term "northern soul scene" as an umbrella term for fans' varying interpretations and terminology.

2. A common auto-denomination used by northern soul fans.
3. Author's own emphasis.
4. This refers to 2006–2008 – the fieldwork period.
5. Email interview data; punctuation errors are respondents' own.
6. Research was conducted overtly and I openly made notes during events; this often prompted conversation and on occasion led to a later interview as scene members would be interested in the research and fieldwork process. If research had been conducted covertly, my experience as a young person in the scene could have been more negative as I was not attempting to establish myself as a soulie.
7. IMO refers to "in my opinion" and is commonly used as an abbreviation in online interactions.

References

Bennett, A. 2006. "Punk's Not Dead: The Continuing Significance of Punk Rock for an Older Generation of Fans". *Sociology* 40/2: 219–35.
Bennett, A., and R. A. Peterson. 2004. *Music Scenes: Local, Translocal and Virtual*. Nashville: Vanderbilt University Press.
Blaikie, A. 1999. *Ageing and Popular Culture*. Cambridge: Cambridge University Press.
Calcutt, A. 1998. *Arrested Development: Pop Culture and the Erosion of Adulthood*. London: Cassell.
Featherstone, M. 1991. *Consumer Culture and Postmodernism*. London: Sage.
Gibson, L. 2010. "Popular Music and the Life Course: Cultural Commitment, Lifestyles and Identities". Unpublished PhD thesis, University of Manchester.
Hollows, J., and K. Milestone. 1998. "Welcome to Dreamsville: A History and Geography of Northern Soul". In *The Place of Music*, edited by A. Leyshon et al., 83–103. New York: Guildford Press.
Hunt, S. 2005. *The Life Course: A Sociological Introduction*. New York: Palgrave Macmillan.
Martin, P. J. 2004. "Culture, Subculture and Social Organization". In *After Subcultures*, edited by A. Bennett and K. Kahn-Harris, 21–35. London: Palgrave Macmillan.
Milestone, K. 1997. "The Love Factory: The Sites, Practices and Media Relationships of Northern Soul". In *The Club Cultures Reader: Readings in Popular Cultural Studies*, edited by S. Redhead, 152–67. Oxford: Blackwell.
Smith, N. 2006. "'Time Will Pass You By': A Conflict of Age: Identity in the Northern Soul Scene". In *Perspectives on Conflict*, edited by C. Baker et al., 176–95. Salford: University of Salford.
—2009a. "Beyond the Master Narrative of Youth: Researching Ageing Popular Music Scenes". In *The Ashgate Research Companion to Popular Musicology*, edited by D. Scott, 427–45. Farnham: Ashgate.
—2009b. "Performing Fandom on the British Soul Scene: Competition, Identity and the Post-Subcultural Self". Unpublished PhD thesis, University of Salford.
—2012. "Parenthood and the Transfer of Capital in the Northern Soul Scene". In *Ageing and Youth Cultures*, edited by A. Bennett and P. Hodkinson, 159–72. Oxford: Berg.

Thornton, S. 1995. *Club Cultures: Music, Media and Subcultural Capital*. Oxford: Polity Press.
Wall, T. 2006. "Out on the Floor: The Politics of Dancing on the Northern Soul Scene". *Popular Music* 25/3: 431–45.
Wilson, A. 2007. *Northern Soul Music, Drugs and Subcultural Identity*. Oregon: Willan Publishing.

15 The Voice of Participants on the Scene

With commentary from Mark Duffett, Sarah Raine and Tim Wall, and the voices of "Dean", "Esther", "Rob" and "Nancy"

This chapter presents the perspectives of four participants on the northern soul scene followed by academic analyses from three academic approaches. Following the editorial position of the whole book, as academic authors of this chapter we seek to let participants on the scene speak "for themselves", while at the same time offering up distinct academic analyses of what they say and do. This is not because as academics we think the voices cannot be understood in their own terms, but because we want to place the talk of scene participants side-by-side with the sorts of analyses usually undertaken by academics. In doing so, we want to show how the experience of "being there" can be framed to draw out what such experience offers to those outside the scene who study popular music cultures more generally.

What academics write about music cultures can often be seen as removed from the lived experiences of a participant, unnecessarily weighed-down with an unfamiliar technical language, and sometimes a disrespectful intrusion into other people's lives. There is a danger in the academic study of popular music culture that all we do is highlight two different cultures (a northern soul scene culture and an academic culture) misunderstanding each other. For this reason, we wish to lay bare the process of analysis which is often hidden in the books and articles published by academics, and we have self-consciously sought to give equal weight to the words of scene participants.

Like the whole book, this chapter speaks to two audiences with different purposes. Firstly, we want to reveal to scene participants how music culture academics work with the material we generate through interviews and our observations as participants ourselves. And secondly, we want to address other music culture academics, to use approaches with which they will be familiar to help those outside the scene understand what northern soul participants say and do. In doing both, we hope to present various ways that academics might study and engage with the people who constitute the scene they research.

This chapter, therefore, begins with short extracts from longer ethnographic interviews conducted and recorded by Sarah Raine with four current participants on the scene. In each case we have anonymized the accounts to "cover-up" the identity of the original speaker. This is a common practice in academic work, which seeks to protect the speaker from the unforeseen implications of what they say, and to focus on what is said, rather than which individual said it.

What "Dean", "Esther", "Rob" and "Nancy" have to say comes, in each case, from early sections of hour-long open conversations which explore the perspectives of a variety of participants on the scene. The four "voices" were chosen from a larger group of twenty scene participants whose broader contributions forms the basis of another publication by Sarah Raine (2018) on the experiences of the younger generation of the scene. The particular extracts were chosen from the rest of her interviews to demonstrate the range and variation of engagement that is evident in the totality of interviews she conducted, and our experience of the contemporary northern soul scene as a whole. They offer up an insight into the voices of men and women, older and younger fans of soul who express their love for the music and the scene through a range of practices: from collecting vintage clothes to DJing. Ultimately, they represent some interesting themes that have emerged from a larger research project and yet are distinctive to the individuals to whom she spoke.

These recorded conversations took place at a range of places: a conservatory in rural Staffordshire; a dance studio in Birmingham; Sarah's sitting room; and university fashion workrooms in the Midlands. Each place offered a quiet and familiar space of their choosing for the speakers, and gave each soul fan a chance to recover from the excesses and booming speakers of weekend events. The four participant voices below explain how each individual found their way into northern soul and, for Dean, how he started DJing at events.[1] Sarah used the question "how did you get into northern soul" as a means to open up the conversation and to identify potential strands of scene-related engagement to explore as the conversation progressed and, for this chapter, created four distinct voices from one initial prompt. The voices have been edited by the authors for clarity only, offering northern soul participants the space to share their own considerations of the scene.[2]

As such, different voices make up this piece. The participant voices were contributed by men and women of a range of ages; but all currently very active on the scene. They demonstrate that there is no one experience of participation, and what they offer us is far from a singular, consistent or considered narrative. These stories illuminate the personal processes used by the speaker to make sense of experience on an individual level, and to define the boundaries of the scene and their relation to and within it. Furthermore, these articulations of self and scene were all told in the midst of a complex process of both establishing and demonstrating personal knowledge of scene boundaries in conversation with another self-identified northern soul scene member, who is also the researcher.

The short extracts from the four participants are followed by approaches taken by three academics from three different fields of study. We each approached the analysis of these voices differently. In speaking to this book's wide readership, we have made these differences, and what they reveal, explicit; to add our voices as an open consideration of academic practice. Therefore, within the remaining parts of this chapter we set out our different "frames" of analysis and approaches to understanding what is being said by the interviewees. In totality, this provides both overlapping and distinctive insights into what it means to be a northern soul participant.

Firstly, Mark Duffett, a widely-respected music fandom researcher, considers the statements of Dean, Esther, Rob, and Nancy as fan voices through a thoughtful rethinking of the conventions and preoccupations of fan studies, and in doing so raises important questions about class and ethnicity. Mark is not himself a participant on the scene, and his response mainly comes from looking in detail at what our four participant voices have to say and the way that they say it. His frames of reference for analysis come from studies of the cultural geography of northern Englishness, and thinking this through broadly sociological frames of class and ethnicity and his knowledge of popular music culture history. He does so in a form and through words familiar to other academics, making his particular approach understandable to others in overlapping but disparate fields. Fan studies has developed sophisticated ways to think about music or media consumers as active participants in defining the meanings of contemporary culture. In many ways, it offers a distinctive approach that rejects both earlier versions of the fanaticism of fandom as a psychological weakness or mass hysteria, or the collectivized semiotics of music participants as subcultures.

Following this, Tim Wall considers the participant voices from the perspective of the field of cultural studies, focusing in particular on the themes that emerge across all the interviews. He also draws upon his experience of the scene from the 1970s through to the present day, and a wide range of studies of different aspects of popular music culture. Tim analyses the discursive construction of what the participants said and how they position themselves in the scene. His analysis takes the form of a critical discourse analysis, which explores what is said as a construction of major sets of ideas about cultural identity, knowledge and power. In this case what it is to be a participant of the northern soul scene (and what is not an authentic claim to membership); what common senses of knowledge about the scene are in circulation and how do individual accounts relate to these shared stories; and finally, who gets to define what the scene is and what authentic participation means.

Finally, Sarah Raine draws upon her background in anthropology, as a scene participant in the 2010s, and her current multidisciplinary research on the experience of young scene members. Tim and Sarah have worked together on developing a critical multigenerational understanding of the scene by engaging in a joint analysis which is apparent in Chapter 8 and in Raine and Wall (2017). They also share an interest in the way each speaker positions her or himself as a scene insider, adapting key scene stories and knowledge to fit with individual experiences. In this earlier work, Sarah and Tim have reflected on their own research and their own participation to understand the scene as a multigenerational and international community which is characterized by different levels and periods of experience, and that are in turn valued comparatively within the scene.

Given the diversity of age across the participant voices we capture, the role of generation on a multigenerational scene is a major part of their discourse, with Sarah's analysis linking this discussion to Chapter 8 and considering the ways in which participants, from different generations, use common stories about the history of northern soul to position themselves within the scene. Sarah's discussion goes beyond the particular participant voices included within this chapter, to place them within and link them to the wider cultural processes of northern soul that she explores through her ethnographic research. She considers these discourses specifically in relation to how different generations position themselves in relationship to the history and histories of the scene itself.

As academics, we seek to make visible the ways in which individual and shared meaning is created and communicated within a music culture, and to consider how these contribute to the patterns of behaviour which come to typify the cultural memberships of the speakers. This chapter, therefore, becomes not only an opportunity for soulies to speak, but for us to consider and demonstrate the ways in which academics listen, analyse, and respond to these voices.

Four participant voices

Dean, 57
I started DJing about '82 in Trowbridge. I'd met a friend called Alan Smith, I met him in a club in Chippenham, watching Junior Walker. And we got together and started, and he was a mod, got started talking and he said, "Oh,

I like all this northern soul". I said, "Well, you know, I've been doing this since I was sixteen". So we got into it through that. We started this club and I can remember this first night we had, all these young kids came in with Specials on their back, and I went, "You lot, you can fuck off" … "Why, won't you just play The Specials and stuff like that?" I went, "No, I'm not, it's just northern soul". And I think about it now and I think, why did I say that? I should have embraced them but I didn't, because up until a certain time, northern soul, to me, I love punk, but when the punk scene was going on I was into northern soul, and I couldn't see anything past northern soul, I was totally, utterly tunnel vision into that music and nothing else. I got into punk actually about '79, '80, when it had all sort of gone and died … And that's when I started to appreciate other music …

I think the whole, the whole genre of the reggae, the skinhead scene, the rocksteady, and, and the mod and the, and the soul and the northern, it all … It all sort of interlinks in some way. I'm seeing northern soul more as a, not as a genre anymore. I don't even know what northern soul is anymore … If you say, what is northern soul, I could not answer that question, 'cause whatever I tell you today, I can tell you 100 times over the next 100 days and I could tell you something different … It's a scene, you know what it is, I'll tell you what it is, to me, it's just a dance scene. It's a dance scene and people play records and people dance and people go to socialize … And you know what, to me, it's that simple. There's a record and it's got a beat and a rhythm, and if you like it, you'll dance to it.

When I was a young kid, I didn't think, oh, that's this. I just danced, I didn't think, I'm not dancing to this 'cause it's this. I went to a northern soul do and they played this music and I, and I danced to all of it, I didn't think this is that … I didn't put a, a name on it. And that's what's, what's happened, we've all put names on things now. And the Mecca sound, that's when people said, I'm not dancing to that …

But with Mod comes clothing, it's always been very much about clothing, the music and, you know, how you look. The soul thing has never been like that, 'cause it's always been music first and the dancing. It's always the music. I actually think with mod, probably, the clothing is probably more important than music because that comes with it, and scooters. But with northern, you know, music is number one, by a mile, and the dancing, yeah!

Esther, 31
I'd been brought up on Motown, my Dad loved Motown, he loved like James Brown and Diana Ross and all that and so he got me into that. And then my Mum was a huge Michael Jackson fan, so she got me into Michael Jackson, Jackson Five, so I've always had this passion for the Motown sound, and I

always loved going to Motown nights and all soul nights and stuff. When I lived in Leeds for that two years working up there, there was lots of clubs there where they did Motown and northern soul nights and I was just like, "What's this northern soul? I don't understand".

I went to the HiFi Club in Leeds and it was, on their Friday nights they have northern soul and Motown night and I was just like, okay, this is, it's interesting, 'cause it does sound kind of the same. So I started to YouTube songs and I was like, actually, you can tell the difference. Like there is a more raw, gritty element and, and me being there, preferring contemporary dance, raw, gritty, grounded, like more real and more, I don't know, personal, then I felt like, oh, actually, I prefer this northern soul, soul sound to the Motown sound and then when I started watching all these videos of people dancing and all these allnighters and I was like, I just love that people are just dancing by themselves, just going for it, there's none of this dancing around the handbag, or being with your friends or have to, like, look in a certain way or look pretty.

As a dancer, I've always liked dancing by myself anyway; I'm not one of these [dancers] who likes salsa and rock and roll, 'cause that's all partner stuff. I always prefer having like my own freedom and like the freedom to do what I want and I feel with northern soul you get that you can just be in this bubble and close off everybody in the room and stuff and just, kind of just dance and express yourself in a way and with the raw, gritty sound. I think that suits me and my personal way, that I want to express myself. I feel like Motown's very high, happy up here, where northern's real, and I feel that's where I am as a dancer.

The northern soul scene is about people watching, 'cause they love the music and they love the style, so they love to watch, not because they're stood going, "Oh, look at her, ooh" … It is part of the culture that you do that on the side of the dancefloor. I've found myself doing it as well, like I do watch, it's to steal people's moves mainly … But I do want to watch, you know? And everybody on that dancefloor must be conscious that people are watching, it's not like people go, I don't care, like … Everyone must have that at the back of their mind, we're all human … Like we all want to be loved. Especially 'cause I, I'm a new person, I think being a younger person into it, you have the pressure of, like, the older ones kind of going, "Well, that's not what we used to do, that's not northern soul".

Rob, 22
My Dad used to go to Cleethorpes, St Ives, he never used to like Wigan, and then I was growing up, I just always had Motown in the background, northern soul. I got into like mod stuff and like skinhead stuff in school, err, so I'm

like, into like scooters and stuff and then I went to, I'd just see an allnighter on Facebook ... And Rachel said that she was going, so I sent a message, "Oh, do you want to, do you want to go?" So, so we ended up going, and I met some fucking brilliant people on the first night ... Who I'm still mates with now ... And then that was it then, I just carried on going.

My Dad's not into it anymore. He left his records round his mates and the kids got in, smashed them all up, every one. And, now he's like, now when he's seeing records going on eBay he's, oh, I used to have that ... And they're going for like thousands and it's like, bloody hell ... 'Cause he was dead into them, yeah. He loves my record collection, he treats them like they're his, you know, yeah. It does my head in, 'cause he, he's always like, he knows which ones I like and he's looking on eBay all the time ... Oh, found this one and he's put them on my watch list and like filling it up with shit. It treats it like his own and that's, that's what he loves now, he just, he just likes listening to the music ...

[Northern soul], [i]t's about hardship, isn't it? I was in the car earlier, me and Patrick went to the market earlier and JJ Barnes' 'Lucille' come on, and Patrick is like "This is northern soul!" He says all northern soul is made up of upbeat love songs ... And it made me think all the way home, that's all it is ... It's just love songs, so it just takes you away from the shit, that's all.

I can, I can relate to the funk stuff as well ... You relate in different ways, but it's all, but yeah, will admit, I got, I got really into the funky stuff and I've kind of pulled back ... I'm finding loads of like traditional northern songs and that's making me want to hear them ... It's nice, well, that's, we can go to SoulFunktion and we can hear the funky stuff, but I wouldn't want to go every weekend to the funk do. I want to go to, and then I go to like Rugby to hear anything across the board, um, I go to Nuneaton to hear my oldies ... I just like to experience it, it all ...

I think you move the scene on by just going out and doing it every weekend and finding new records. Records are drying up, in a way, that's, that's why we can't get any of the funky stuff ... That's just your northern records are drying up, but you do still find them ... You do, you, they are still coming out. I don't think, I don't think you have to be all new records to move it on, I think you can go back to the past, and some of the stuff that was played maybe once or twice at Wigan and then dropped, and then everyone think it's an old, yeah, it's an oldie ... But, but it's yet to have its time, so it can have its time now. There's still records like that.

Nancy, 18
I think I've always been interested in like sixties and seventies clothing and then when I turned eighteen, I was really excited to go clubbing and I thought, oh,

15 The Voice of Participants on the Scene

this is going to be great and then after a while, it had worn off and I thought, there must be something else out there that involves what I'm wearing and what I feel and, like, where I want to be with, a, like eras. And then it just happened through Instagram, because I had followed people who wore the same sort of outfits and then looked at what they're interested in, like the music and I met a girl called Sam and she'd gone to this allnighter and then I realized it was in Hinckley, and then she ended up being from Nuneaton, so she invited me to the Coop allnighter and I went for the first time and I just felt differently than I did about any other music and it made me feel alive, and I thought this is where I'm meant to be.

I hadn't really looked any further than that and then I kind of just discovered it from there. I mean, some people say, "You found it online?" But I, I accept where we are today and that it is about social media and that's what the world is ... And I accept that. I used to be a bit embarrassed about things like that, but it is the 21st century. It's what we do, and I can still be a part of something that I love, even if it is included in things like that. I mean, most people that I've, I've met either like online or in person, they, I mean, their parents would be into it and they've been brought up ... And then there is a few people that are just randomly, like, "I don't really know how I got here, it's just I feel more like myself now than I ever have". And I do think that social media does play a big part in [it], because I wouldn't, I wouldn't have found out unless, unless of that; I didn't really know anyone that even liked to dress the same.

I think when I first started, I just enjoyed going to vintage fairs, going to car boot sales, and picking up stuff to wear and then since, actually finding a sub-culture that I enjoy, I think I, I dress more ... [pauses]... well, you like to say it, authentic ... But whereas before, I was, it was always a bit mismatched, I always kind of wanted to be different. And then, like, if I do look through, back through my [Instagram] posts, have changed quite a lot, especially like, like cutting my hair short, and things like that, because I've, I've seen more and I understand more about it, where before, I just, it was an interest but it wasn't who I am as a person, whereas now, you know, what I wear and how I look is, is who I am.

When I first sort of got into this, I was a Pop Boutique girl and that was like your sixties mod starter kit. But it's just, I don't think it's like the same, I like to wear things that when I buy them smell a bit dusty because there's a history there, and that's what I love, is that it's, it's had a, like a past to it and that's actually been there and been in that generation ... See, I would absolutely love a record player, but obviously, being a student, it's something that I have not saved up for yet, you know, I'd love to go record collecting and have a record player ... But at the minute, I use YouTube ... And I, I hate that I use YouTube, but I don't put myself down about anything anymore because I'm still listening to it for the same reason, just because it's not accessible to me on a record player ... Doesn't mean that I don't believe in it or love it or it doesn't make me feel anything.

Thinking about northern soul scene participants as music fans
Mark Duffett

Thinking about the participants in the northern soul scene as music fans raises some interesting questions. To analyse the specificity of any particular fandom, we consider what participants *know* and what they *do* as intersecting dimensions. The distinction between these two aspects, of course, is artificial, but it may help to improve understanding. So, what do northern soul fans know?

Firstly, we can say that northern soul fandom locates itself in relation to working-class identity. I am not suggesting that all northern soul fans are working class, but rather that the phenomenon perhaps still posits a kind of "ideal type" of participant. To speak of music fandom *purely* in relation to class might lead us towards such frameworks; locating northern soul fandom as escapism, compensation, or alternative community. Though these are discursive resources through which fans sometimes speak, they do not fully explain fandom. For instance, when Rob talked about songs lifting fans from their own daily drudgery ("It's just love songs, so it just takes you away from the shit") he also implied escapism – perhaps even fantasy – associated with the pleasures of the weekend as a departure from the daily grind.

The two male interviewees, Dean and Rob, mark out a cultural distinction through their use of swearing in their interviews. Sociologically, swearing in public, in the UK, has always been freighted with class connotations. To understand this, it might be worth considering the long history to this distinction by drawing upon the historian Jeffrey Richards' discussion of national identity. After quoting E. M. Forster's claim from 1920, that English values were essentially those of the middle classes (self-improvement, education, restraint, good manners), Richards then referenced the Victorian distinction between the "rough" and "respectable" working class: "The 'roughs' lived a life of immediate gratification, particularly in sex, drink and violence. This always provided a potential alternative image for Englishness but it was largely kept underground until the 1960s when a social and cultural revolution occurred" (Richards 1997: 18). Embodied by changes in youth culture, in Britain the 1960s "revolution" overturned traditional social and cultural hierarchies. It established the cachet of northern and working-class culture, and – in association with this – promoted greater incidence and acceptance of swearing in the public sphere.

In relation to African-American music, the idea of "escaping the daily grind" connects to structural notions of racial exploitation. Historically, northern soul emerged in the long wake of rock 'n' roll, a genre that raised questions of cross-racial empathy through youth culture. In the early 1960s, white, *middle-class* British music fans consequently became fascinated with the earlier culture and music of the Mississippi Delta. Their blues fandom inspired the musical productivity that eventually bore fruit in the R&B music of the British Invasion. This white R&B boom was based on a kind of trans-Atlantic, cross-racial fascination, one that registered empathy at the same time that it implied geographic and social distance.

In its premise, northern soul seemed to modify rather than abolish the "Thames Delta" equation. Northern, white, working-class, British fans were, in socio-economic terms, much better off than the poorest African-American citizens. Their consumption patterns offered a unique form of patronage: celebrating black musicians who missed out on the benefits of stardom. This challenges the sociological explanations that those most susceptible to racist ideologies come from working-class culture.

Beyond racial allegiance, British northern soul fans also distanced themselves, in Bourdieuan terms, from more ordinary Motown fandom. They originally displayed subcultural capital by seeking out, discussing and playing various rare, "gritty", non-Motown, soul recordings. What this means, ironically, is that the distinct tastes of northern soul fans also separate them from other factions of the same class. Interest in one faction of the African-American music that missed the charts allowed fans to build *literate* identities around a music genre that implied an *ethical* approach. It was a culture *primarily* based on a specific music taste (rare soul), as opposed to personal style (in mod), or "attitude" (with punk). As one respondent makes clear, however, all these different subcultures, with their various racial politics and alliances, are interlinked rather than opposed.

These areas of cross-racial communitarianism and cultural refinement suggest that northern soul fans actually eschew "roughness". Their music concerns, instead, appear based on empathy for black folk elsewhere; people who, like those in northern British working-class society, have been historically oppressed by socioeconomic disparities. The limit point to this kind of discussion, however, is that it reflects a prehistory of northern soul itself. What may once have been licensed by ethical imperative has now arguably become musical pleasure, the pretext for a great night out or record-collecting interest.

In terms of what northern soul fans do, it is evident that, just like other fan cultures, they pursue a wide variety of practices. Research in fan studies stresses that individuals are never passive consumers. Instead, they use their interests socially, engage in activities that transform the materials given to them, and organize collectively (see Jenkins 1992 and 2006). Fan fiction is commonly referenced as an example of such "transformative" practice. That type of thinking, however, comes out of research on television fan cultures. At least before the age of social media, the "transformative" aspect of popular music fandom was less obvious, precisely because so many practices were routine, industrially sponsored or based on personal self-fashioning (style). It is, for example, hard to understand buying records, listening, dressing appropriately, socializing, going out, dancing and getting intoxicated as examples of engagement in "transformative labour" – at least in the fan fiction sense – though such things are associated with the social and personal transformation of each individual. More generally, music culture practices like DJing and music making are very much "transformative" in that they rework cultural forms, but pop studies does not use that language to consider them, and fan studies implies that this reworking matters only when it is an amateur or "folk" activity.

The practices pursued by northern soul fans might variously be seen as stereotypically subcultural (drug taking, marathon dancing), clubbing-orientated (dressing up, going out, DJing), or fannish (collecting records, discussing music). Such typologies of practice are, however, limited, because the distinctions are not tenable in real life. It is not simply that "music fan" and "clubber" are mutually enforcing roles. Rather, they are constructs unsuited to capturing the complexity of scene participation. Fandom itself can mean pursuing a range of activities as an enthusiast. The precise combination and relative importance of different elements will depend on the individual. As an analogy here, we might think about religion – not because northern fans "worship" the music, but because participation in religious activity itself can also mean all sorts of different things to different people: separation from society; a role in relation to society; a way to express class or gender; acceptance by a community; participation in an institution or hierarchy; pursuit of a social life; adherence to theology; doctrinal differences; spiritual feelings; mysticism … To draw a parallel, people participate in the northern soul scene in many different ways, each emphasizing some practices and relegating or avoiding others. This can reveal the wider licensing of different social identities too. For instance, in relation to gender: Dean's claim that northern soul was never about "how you look" is contradicted by Nancy's interest in visiting vintage fairs.

There are three final aspects of northern soul fan practice that are worthy of further note. First, some practices appear, in a sense, universal, or at least very pervasive. They are much more widely shared popular music pursuits through which each individual's specific form of identification with northern soul is marked out. Other practices are more circumscribed. We might also speak of fan practices that mark participation in northern soul as distinct. For example, by noting that participants watch others perform the spectacular dance moves that characterize the phenomenon, Esther's discussion implies community support rather than voyeurism. Interest in the dancers almost seems vicarious, as if they have an ambassadorial function for others in the community. Thus, there is also an *enacted ethics* of the northern soul scene, expressed here as it has developed as a community of practice. Second, new practices become prominent as time goes by. Nostalgia grows and technologies change. Fans, old and new, now speak of going on eBay rather than visiting independent record shops; using Instagram; vintage clothes shopping. Third, there are gaps in the picture. While northern soul fandom contains record collecting and other such practices that are typical of most music fandoms, the scene also marginalizes or avoids certain kinds of fan activity. In particular, here, in comparison to some other music fan cultures, an interest in stardom and celebrity is relegated and configured around specific subcultural heroes. Northern soul fandom thus combines residues of the ethics that influenced the genre's formation (spreading the "soul love", as it were) with new forms of enactment as a living culture.

Positioning oneself in the northern soul scene

Tim Wall

In their accounts, all four participants explain their way into the scene through very different routes and set out what they feel is their position. In doing so, they also seek to explain what northern soul is in essence, most often setting out what it means to them. Dancing, buying records, and DJing are all characterized as scene practices, but social media is also cited, including feelings of a degree of incongruity about the role of a twenty-first-century technology in a scene that has its roots in the twentieth century.

Dean, now in his late fifties, explicitly answers a question about how he got into DJing in the 1980s, but also makes some effort to show that he engaged with the scene from the 1970s. These "I was there" personal narratives have an important role for participants who are old enough to have engaged as one of northern soul's first generation, and when Dean narrates the early 1980s encounter with an acquaintance which started his DJing career, he positioned himself in relation to his younger friend with the assertion that: "well, you know, I've been doing this since I was sixteen".

It is also notable how strong this theme is within Esther's and Rob's account, with both referencing a familiar relationship with an earlier generation, and in Nancy's when she expresses a semiotic sense of identification. For Esther, in her early thirties, it is the claim that "I'd been brought up on Motown" and for Rob, 22, "my Dad used to go to Cleethorpes, St Ives". Nancy's sense of connection is less personal, but no less intense, based upon her supposition that "I think I've always been interested in, like, sixties and seventies clothing". All three locate their entry into the scene as occurring through attendance at specific venues, but they also present this as evidence of an increasing understanding of the scene. Each initially attended local events – Esther attending a northern night at a Leeds basement club, Rob an allnighter, and Nancy at a Hinkley sports club – and they all narrate that they made an immediate commitment; in Rob's words, "and then that was it". For Nancy, the engagement was profound – "I just felt differently than I did about any other music and it made me feel alive, and I thought this is where I'm meant to be". For two participants, social media played an important role with Esther using YouTube to listen to northern sounds, Rob seeing an advert for his first allnighter on Facebook and then making contact with a friend who was going. Nancy used Instagram to explore clothes and image, along with YouTube to access northern records she wanted to hear.

None of the respondents use any of the widely-circulated simplistic definitions of northern soul, exploring more complex senses. Unsurprisingly, they all seek to explore music as an essential way to understand the scene, usually by drawing definitional lines, making clear distinctions with other musics or practices. There is a variability in their accounts as they verbalize northern soul as an abstract idea beyond their own biographical engagement. Dean explicitly rejects any notion that it is a music genre, arguing that it is a culture demarcated by scene-defined music and dancing, and he contrasts northern soul with what is for him a separate mod scene, where he sees clothes as being more important. Nevertheless, he also explicitly links the music and British scenes associated with reggae/skinhead/rocksteady and mod/soul/northern and emphasizes the changing nature of the northern scene as new music is played. Rob picks up the issue of the developing soundtrack, although he connects this even more firmly to the question of finding new records to play.

Esther's sense of northern is in part a musical one – which in her construction is "raw", "gritty", "grounded" and, most of all, "real" when compared with the Motown music she had grown up with – and in part defined by forms of solo dancing. These definitions are strongly linked in Esther's account to the personal meanings of the scene, which she describes through a certain form of freedom to "kind of just dance and express yourself in a way and with the raw, gritty sound. I think that suits me and my personal way that I want to express myself". More generally, and perhaps unsurprisingly, each participant defines the scene through their primary role upon it. As we've seen, for Esther it is a music to be danced to, for Rob it is defined by the supply of music and the venues in which it is played, and for Nancy by stylistic considerations. They all, though, in their own way seek to get at an essential (often essentialist) sense of the scene, and they all make distinctions between what, for them, northern soul is and what it is not. Dean's account reveals a more complex version in which he tells the story of an emerging appreciation of a wider range of music, and a sense that northern soul is connected in sophisticated ways to other musics and to other British music scenes. More broadly, he places this within an ever-changing music and scene, but one which at its roots has dancing, something that he sees as beyond the scene's obsession with categorizing its own field of music played, and the differences between these diverse musics and those which are not "northern".

It is, though, in the generational differences that each interviewee makes their most distinctive observations. Certainly, all three younger participants make explicit reference to their position as a younger entrant to the scene, and the way their participation is shaped by this position. For Esther, this is articulated by her sense of being watched and judged when on the dancefloor, for Nancy her uncertainty of the authenticity of engaging with the scene online and through visual images and digitized music, and for Rob his attempt to go back to records played earlier in the scene's history that are today neglected. Unsurprisingly, as a longer time participant, Dean's sense of self is the most secure, and he offers a growing acceptance of the entrance of younger participants as his own more pluralistic views develop.

Scene identity, generation, and northern soul history

Sarah Raine

For Dean, as a regular attendee and later DJ at many of the original 1970s venues, personal experience of the historic scene is central to his placing of self within the mythologized scene past, and in critiquing the insider knowledge of others. By contrast, as younger participants, Esther, Rob, and Nancy are unable to demonstrate an experiential understanding of the scene throughout its existence. However, they all adopt existing roles as dancer, DJ, or collector, and position themselves as knowledgeable members by reference to common insider stories as part of their personal narratives.

Such activities are also evident in the creation and reposting of online texts through which scene participants discuss the nature and history of the scene.

In Chapter 8, we noted the importance of such self-documenting processes as ways in which scene participants dealt with the insider/outsider positioning of both people and the media texts they produced, by deriding and ridiculing "outsider" documents as inauthentic accounts of the scene and its history. In a pattern repeated in many music cultures, the dominant discourses of the northern soul scene place their music and related practices in strict opposition to a constructed mainstream. An "authentic" or "real" experience is felt to be only possible through a rejection of mainstream technology, mediations, behaviour, and places. By extension, histories written from within the scene make a claim to greater authenticity and receive greater scene support.

Perhaps more importantly, within this discussion of the options open to different generations in securing an authentic position as an insider, telling stories about the scene (either though personal narrative or online self-documentation) provides the storyteller with a means to publically validate their insider status. We can see these issues emerging within the points made by my interviewees, but they become even more prominent in the ways online contributors to northern soul forums, reference, and produce, histories of the scene as a form of personal legitimization.

As I began to explore in Chapter 8, most of the online discussion concerning written northern soul histories involve older members of the scene in their forties, fifties, and sixties. Front covers of books are reposted in northern soul related groups, claimed to be the "best" written history of the scene, or acting as a prompt for a discussion about the value of the book. Authors of books also use the online network of Facebook alongside public events to promote and sell their publications, many of which are self-published or printed by smaller, independent presses. Similar to the common photographs of recently acquired records waiting to be catalogued, boxes of newly minted books are posted online as photographs or short videos that pan across the room, commonly accompanied by a northern soul record playing close by. These books are eagerly anticipated by this older, inside audience, and once received, publically critiqued in terms of its contribution to scene knowledge.

During my wider ethnographic research, older, male DJs and record collectors also spoke to me about being interviewed for books, considering or actually writing their own account of the scene. In addition to being an object worthy of discussion within themselves, books were often used by these individuals as a means of legitimizing their own knowledge, with a point verified through referencing a publication. These published scene histories remain a key part of this ongoing engagement with northern soul practices and music, providing not only access to scene knowledge, but also a means to verify or legitimize their own understanding when talking to others:

> I mean, if you look at Soul Sam ... He's been doing it, and have you read his story in, in, in my book? You should read his story, it's great ... [Y]ou know, he used to play when the bands were on in the sixties, he used to put records onto a single Dansette record player behind a curtain at his local club ... (Michael, 62).

For the younger participants, the northern soul past is explored through television and film mediations, rather than the expensive self-documented written histories,[3] the online activities of soul fans producing hour-upon-hour of free documentaries, films, and online fan videos on YouTube, in addition to scene-related websites and Wikipedia offering scene "facts".[4] Feature-length films and the use of older footage in online fan mediations (generally posted on YouTube and/or shared through Facebook) are common sources of initial introduction to the scene for some of its youngest participants in the UK:

> I sat with my Dad on the couch and we watched [the] *This England* footage of Wigan Casino. It just kind of hit me and I just thought, this is really cool and it's different from what people at school were into, like, I was never able to get into, like, the dance music and things ... A lad called Harry, he got into northern soul through the Northern Soul film, you know, Elaine Constantine's film, and he watched that and was blown away by it. He messaged me on Facebook, and he said, "I want to come to a soul night, like, but there's like no one at school who's into it, do you mind if I come with you?" (Bobby, 19).

Bobby tracks his entrance into the scene through Palmer's documentary, and he situates his friend as having been inspired by a film mediation of the scene. As Bobby notes, such entrances may be supported through an initially online insider network of younger members, and developed into offline friendships at northern soul events. In addition to recruiting new participants, online videos of the historic scene are used by the younger generation to access knowledge and to develop skills, particularly dancing (as argued by Raine 2018). The use of these videos has led to the persistence of particular acrobatic dance movements, replicated from Palmer's documentary footage, and a related valuing amongst the younger generation of what they term "tricks":

> Oh, [the Wigan documentary] is amazing. I've watched it so many times, it's that guy who does the high kick ... [My dance style is] kind of a mishmash of people's different styles with kind of my weird kind of way, but literally just watching people and watching YouTube and practising in the kitchen (John, 25).

The mediated nature of these videos is understood by the younger participants, but they continue to be viewed as an accessible means to develop the knowledge and skills required of a scene insider within a scene that values its past. Rather than turning to insider publications, the younger members of the scene map out the key mythologized history through their online activities, creating and reposting texts that perpetuate insider origin myths, and using these to position themselves as knowledgeable members through on- and offline storytelling.

Conclusions

Through his analysis of the four participant voices, Mark considered the unique nature of northern soul fandom in terms of other fan practices. Through this approach, he also identified a central "ethic" of the scene as a "fan community" in an empathetic relationship between producers and listeners, and how this is becoming less central as the scene moves into a new time of technology and culture.

Tim's analysis focuses on the individual processes of positioning of self and scene indicated within the four narratives of Dean, Esther, Rob, and Nancy. Generational differences become apparent through this discussion, and the increased flexibility and pluralistic nature of Dean's engagement as an "original member" of the scene is particularly highlighted, communicating the comparative valuing of his participation over those who found their way to northern soul at a later date, through family or friends.

Picking up on these generational differences, Sarah's section elucidates the role that these stories of self play in establishing and maintaining the boundaries and particular forms of the northern soul scene. By placing these individual narratives in a wider understanding of scene engagement, Sarah explores what these acts of storytelling *do* as a wider practice of claiming membership within an insider music scene.

This chapter provides a diversity of voice, both of the fan and the academic. The four participant voices do not always agree, but these shared experiences and meanings are communicated alongside individual attempts to make a shared engagement personally meaningful, and in this the diverse but identifiable nature of the northern soul scene is evident. The academic voices, too, differ, bringing together three different but overlapping ways of considering engagement within the northern soul scene, demonstrating that each approach reveals a different insight. Using a range of approaches means that we can identify the unique nature of northern soul participation, that we can understand these narratives as individual claims to membership, and that these individual claims both establish and maintain shared understandings of what northern soul is or should be. This engagement with a range of different, and at times contrasting, participant voices is particularly important for northern soul studies which has been primarily focused on the past or a typical and voice-less engagement, and a valuing of "authentic" or "expert" insider accounts. The repetition of particular music scene histories and the dominance of certain types of voices (predominantly older and male) in popular music studies more widely suggests that this is not an issue to be found in northern soul research alone. Through this collaborative and many-voiced approach, we can provide a layered understanding of meaning, questioning not only *what* people say about their engagement in music scenes, but *why* they say it and what these stories *do*.

About the authors

Mark Duffett is Reader in Media and Cultural Studies at the University of Chester, where his research interests focus on music fandom. He has edited and co-edited special editions of *Popular Music and Society*, *Rock Music Studies*, and *IASPM@journal* and presents his work internationally. His well-known critical survey of fans studies, *Understanding Fandom*, was published by Bloomsbury in 2013, and his studies of Elvis Presley, *Elvis* for Equinox and *Counting Down Elvis: His 100 Finest Songs* for Rowman & Littlefield, were published in 2017.

Sarah Raine is a Research Fellow at Birmingham City University. Her research into the ways in which the younger members of the northern soul scene negotiate their place in a multigenerational community that values "original" participation has been published in a range of journals and books. She is co-managing editor of *Riffs: Experimental Writing On Popular Music*, review editor and special issue guest editor (2018) for *IASPM@Journal*, and the network coordinator for *Jazz & Everyday Aesthetics*. She has been attending northern soul events in the UK and Spain since 2012.

Tim Wall is Professor of Radio and Popular Music Studies, and Associate Dean for Research in the Faculty of Arts, Design and Media at Birmingham City University. He undertook his doctorate on black music and radio at the Centre for Contemporary Cultural Studies at the University of Birmingham. He researches into the production and consumption cultures around music and the media, mixing historical analysis with contemporary investigations. His publications include the second edition of *Studying Popular Music Culture*, and recent research as varied as the politics of dancing on the northern soul scene, US dance fads from 1955 to 1965, music radio online, the transistor radio, personal music listening, music on television, jazz collectives, and *The*

X Factor. He has been a devotee of northern soul since his teens in the 1970s, and can still be found on the dancefloor on some weekends.

Notes

1. Dean was chosen as a well-known and respected DJ, but one who played records that existed on the musical edge of the northern soul canon. As Sarah was interested in the ways in which the musical canon of the scene was constructed through what older and established DJs said and did, Dean's initial engagement with DJing (rather than the scene more generally) was the focus of the interview.

2. Dean, Esther, Rob, and Nancy were each given access to their edited contributions to this chapter, alongside the three academic analyses through which their words were considered, before publication.

3. Such publications tend to be printed as a limited edition and through independent presses; older publications are therefore particularly expensive. More recent autobiographical accounts can be bought cheaply online, but books that claim to set out a history of the scene or the "northern soul sound" start at around £40.

4. This online engagement mirrors contemporary record-collecting practices, with the young record collectors in my wider research sourcing the vast majority of their records through online global marketplaces such as Discogs and eBay (see Raine 2018).

References

Jenkins, H. 1992. *Textual Poachers: Television Fandom and Participatory Culture*. New York: Routledge.

—2006. *Fans, Bloggers, Gamers: Exploring Participatory Culture*. New York: New York University Press.

Raine, S. 2018. "A Little Togetherness: Making Claims, Negotiating Boundaries, and Forging Meaning as a Younger Member of the British Northern Soul Scene". PhD thesis, Birmingham City University.

Raine, S., and T. Wall. 2017. "Participation and Role in the Northern Soul Scene". In *Keep It Simple, Make it Fast! An Approach to Underground Music Scenes (vol. 3)*, edited by P. Guerra and T. Moreira, 75–86. Porto: University of Porto, Faculty of Arts and Humanities.

Richards, J. 1997. *Films and British National Identity: From Dickens to Dad's Army*. Manchester: University of Manchester Press.

Photographic Dossier

Richard Oughton

Felix Barreira Alvares (DJ and promoter) at Soul Suor and Sacanagem Allnighter, Sao Paulo Santa Cecilia, November 2015

Dancer at Soul Suor and Sacanagem Allnighter, Sao Paulo Santa Cecilia, November 2015

Dancer at Prague Allnighter, Praha 7, June 2015

Aaron, The Empire Soul Allnighter, Wigan, September 2016

The photographs chosen for this dossier focus on current participation within the northern soul scene and bring together images from a range of British, European and worldwide events, focusing on the multigenerational nature of contemporary northern soul participation. Through my work, I seek to harness the unsurpassed power and immediacy of the photographic image to record the intense physicality and emotional connection between dancer and music – as both a deeply personal and collective experience.

About the author

Richard Oughton's photography focuses on underground British subcultures including northern soul, mod, ska and skinhead with their pathognomonic aesthetic and rituals. His work captures the importance of both individual identity and collective sense of camaraderie that underpins these cultural movements. He has rapidly established himself as a popular and integral purveyor of images which reflects the scene as it continues to evolve.

16 I'm Still Looking for Unknowns All the Time:

The Forward (E)motion of Northern Soul Dancing

Paul Sadot

"Drifting offshore": stepping into the unknown

Around 2005, while DJing in the main room at Middleton Northern Soul All-nighter near Manchester, I opened my set with a then unknown rarity by Jonathan Capree, titled 'Gonna Build Me a Mountain'. This was followed with the little-known 'I Never Thought' by Sammy Campbell; the same Sammy Campbell who wrote the classic 'Job Opening' also on the Queen City label in 1967. Halfway through Campbell's track, a woman dressed in the iconic 70s northern soul regalia, including circle skirt and ankle socks, approached the front of the stage holding an A4 piece of paper. Anticipating a request, I moved to the front of the decks to investigate. On the paper in large letters were the words "can you play something faster!" Taken aback – neither of the two tracks were, to my ears, slow – but not wanting to disappoint, I reached for Freddie Scott's 'I'll Be Gone', a furiously fast-paced 45. As the previous track faded, I announced the request for a faster track, jumping from the stage onto the dancefloor to get "in it".[1] To my further surprise, the person who had requested something "faster" remained seated, looking furious, whilst consulting with a group of similarly dressed companions. This same group then made a complaint to the organizer because they did not know any of the music that I was playing. On reflection, I speculated that the issue was not one of pace, but rather one that was bound to notions of familiarity and tradition on the northern soul scene that might be understood by examining the way in which people position themselves, in relation to musical preferences, on the scene.

I open with this anecdote because the constant search for new discoveries has always been a powerful ethos and one of the driving forces of the underground northern soul movement; in record collector Jock O'Connor's words the "enemy being apathy and repetition" (quoted in Constantine and Sweeney 2013: 197). Unknown records have always been played and it is the process by which now established classics were first introduced to the dancers. The Oxbow 45 by Jonathan Capree, for instance, is now highly regarded and noted as a classic of the past fifteen years. In this chapter, then, I build upon this personal experience to explore the close relationship between music and the way in which people dance. I am myself implicated and positioned in all this, and conscious that I represent a group of self-identifying long-term members of the scene. While I bring the views of a particular group of participants to this discussion, I also bring the insider's knowledge of the scene and its development.

Informed by this, I construct a historically-located soundscape of the scene which moves away from the Wigan Casino sounds that tend to dominate the discourse of northern soul, to illustrate how music has diversified as the scene moved on, and how this ethos continues today. The music played on the northern soul scene is incorporated from a wide range of music genres, and northern soul dancing is closely linked to the nature of music played on the dancefloors. To this end, I discuss this evolving musical diversity on the scene, set against notions of fixity, historical re-enactment and pastiche, and their relationship to a version of northern soul dancing that has gripped the imagination of outsider media and academic accounts for some time. In doing so, I explore how these versions of the scene are often acted out by insiders on the oldies scene and examine the possible impact on the dancing styles of younger participants. Throughout the chapter I include references to records which demonstrate the breadth of genres, sounds and tempos that fall under the expansive banner of northern soul, and inform the dancing styles of participants. This creates the discography listed at the end of the chapter, and reveals the nuanced difference and individuality produced by evolving musical tastes within the scene. I argue that it is this process of change that defines the scene, rather than that of a dominant, homogenized and formulaic sound, step or style.

I take a strategy that combines elements from each of the earlier approaches taken to explore the scene. These include the autobiographical (see, for example, Cosgrove 2016; McKenna 1996; Nowell 2001 and others), the academic-ethnographic (see, for example, Smith 2009a, 2009b; Robinson 2013; Hollows and Milestone 1998), as well as academic-autoethnographic (see, for example, Wall 2007, 2006; Wilson 2007). As a scene insider and academic researcher of popular dance, I interrogate existing literature on northern soul dancing exploring notions of identity, corporeality, movement, and spatial politics. This chapter, therefore, draws on personal recollections, extensive embodied experience, corporeal expertise, pedagogical "know how", interviews with intergenerational participants, and academic analysis of insider and outsider narratives. I aim to articulate ideas surrounding the evolution of musical tastes, the relationship of these tastes to the development of the individual over time, and their impact on dancing style(s). I trace the diversity of dance style at points in time and how northern soul dance has changed over time, bringing out something of the tension between changing musical taste/dance style on the scene and an "oldies" culture that has a tendency to essentialize northern soul as a music, stylistic and dance culture. My focus, then, is on what can be seen as the underground, or rare soul, northern soul scene which mostly takes place in small venues, rather than the large "oldies" allnighters that are run by Gold Soul, Butlin's and other commercially-focused promoters.

"My proposal": a 360° consideration

Acknowledging the depth and complexity of northern soul, viewing it as a sub-cultural dance scene that has survived autonomously for five decades, we must exercise caution when considering the scene through notions of musical and corporeal fixity. I therefore argue for a 360° perspective that embraces corporeal and conceptual considerations in the discourse of northern soul, moving beyond homogenizing dominant narratives. I urge scholars and commentators to move beyond the linear pattern of thought derived from dominant Casino-centric myths and legends, to a broader way of thinking that acknowledges nuanced diversity in the spaces, the music and the dancing. To achieve this, one must recognize that many venues encircle(d) the history of northern soul, and that a wide range of sounds have emerged from the maverick DJs that fuel the demand for new discoveries.

A claim to insight through a personal insider narrative is not sufficient, and we need a richer, more pluralistic and historically dynamic sense of the scene. Even when academic researchers can claim insider status, the extent, duration, and intensity of that experience, along with the reliability of personal recollections, calls for consideration. Individuals attending allnighters across a multitude of venues and locations over several decades will have a different insider experience to those who have taken a prolonged break from the scene, or someone who attends mostly soul nights, or indeed someone who only participated in the Wigan Casino years. Furthermore, the insider experiences of dancing on amphetamines (or not) informs individual participation, experiences and recollections in contrasting ways.

Corporeal authenticity in northern soul dancing is a slippery notion to define and, as Tim Wall (2006) has argued, "a full analysis requires an exploration of the relationship of physical movement to space, music and senses of identity" (p. 431). However, several academic studies, including Milestone (1997), neglect these considerations and my analysis builds on Wall's observation that they attempt to articulate the present by reifying certain historical myths attached to the scene. Through the assertion of musical exemplars and homogenous footwork these studies discuss northern soul dancing as if there were a ubiquitous style that spanned the decades of its development. For example, Milestone (1997: 163) describes it as "a distinctive acrobatic style of dancing [involving] spins, handsprings and backdrops". However, in accord with Wall, I argue that an expected style, or en masse acrobatic movement, has never dominated the underground northern soul scene, and that eclectic influences have always existed.

The breadth of musical taste that emerged at many large venues beyond Wigan Casino indicates that dancing styles developed reciprocally. Like many scene participants I have embraced a very wide spectrum of music and dance over the years, exploring, amongst other things, jazz funk, Capoeira, and UK jazz dance, and these multiple components influence(d) how I dance(d). During the period that Wigan was running (and beyond), many participants, including myself, attended nationwide alldayers, such as Nottingham Palais, Cleethorpes Winter Gardens and Manchester Ritz, where DJs played an eclectic mix of music including, in Constantine and Sweeney's words "the latest Jazz Fusion and New York disco sounds [played] alongside newly discovered sixties records" (2013: 174).

I observe that the dancing has been *circular* as much as it has been "side-to-side". By this I mean that participants dance in a manner that rotates their body in circular, rather than linear patterns. The reasons for the circular travel are multiple, resonating from the desire to orientate oneself with the other dancers, and embracing notions of flow, peer observation, energy and unity, flirtation, performance, competition, connectivity, and the marking of space. I put it this way in Constantine and Sweeney (2013: 152):

> There'd be moments of euphoria together ... You'd look over and see someone's face and there'd be that shared recognition of the same euphoria ... There was unity and exchange and togetherness with that.

This style of dancing, as if contained in one's own, corporeally demarcated, small circular space, within the larger space of the dancefloor, also allows for the possibility of 360° kinesthetic connection and empathy[2] with one's peers, a perception through movement that re-adjusts continually throughout the record, as dancers connect in various ways with those around them. This 360° framework embraces Wall's (2006) discussion of northern soul dancing wherein he describes a side-to-side step linked to the dancer's urge towards orientating themselves on the dancefloor.

I do not, though, want to suggest that dancers move in an unbroken circular trajectory but that, driven by multiple and competing incentives, such as kinesthetic exchange with fellow dancers, scoping-out of competition, and unspoken call and response dance-offs, they continually change direction and re-orientate themselves throughout the record. Dancers travel both left and right using moments of linear side-to-side footwork, but also footwork that turns the dancer effortlessly on the spot. This might be combined with short elegant spins or half turns that blend into a holistic notion of a 360º domain of participation on the dancefloor. In this way, within the space of a single record, dancers can orientate themselves in relation to their surroundings, relating to the holistic energy and entity of the dancefloor as a corporeal feedback mechanism. Personally, I gravitate towards dancers with whom I feel a kinesthetic connection, with whom I share a drive, intensity, and honesty when dancing, orientating myself within the wider space of the dancefloor by seeking out such individuals, clusters or collectives to dance amongst. It is here that I am able to experience a tacit and nuanced call and response exchange that, for me, exemplifies my "growing up" on the northern soul dancefloor. No longer do I perform physical excess bound to the myth of the spectacular (youthful) acrobatic northern soul dancer. It would be out of place within the melodies, beats, and dancefloors that I have travelled through in the new millennium. When I first heard records such as the Turbines' 'We Got to Start Over', Kae Williams' 'Our Love is Dying' or, more recently, Ron and Joe's 'Go Away and Stay', I was driven towards the dancefloor with the same excitement and wonder as when, as a 15-year-old, I first felt the Tomangoes' 'I Really Love You' pounding (literally) through my body at a St Ives allnighter. But, whereas my competitive youthful drive, amphetamines and the Tomangoes converged in a spectacular acrobatic display, Ron and Joe, Kae Williams or the Turbines draw out an entirely different response: spectacular acrobatics cannot find space in these records. They elicit something that matches the intensity of my youthful acrobatics, or perhaps even supersedes it, but it is nuanced and digs deep into a kinesthetic mechanism that has grown within me over the years: we might dare to call it soul.

"Point of View"

Point of View 'I'm Superman', a recent and rare discovery on the northern soul scene, is far from the pounding classic 60s soul sound. Such is the richness of the soundscape of the northern soul dancefloor that I might, alternatively, have used '(It Depends on the) Point of View' by the Blue Jays, to demonstrate how changes were afoot at Stafford and Warrington Parr Hall shortly after the Casino's closure. Other illustrations are plentiful throughout the scene's history. Two current 45s are Sag War Fare's 'Don't Be So Jive' and John Harris', 'Hangin' In', although these have, in many ways, already become classics on the underground northern soul scene which shows that collectors and DJs have never stopped searching for new "records with history", and that this is the continuum that defines northern soul and its dancing.

Since the millennium the scene has grown again, attracting new, younger participants and a steady influx of ageing returnees. When thinking about this latter group, I have offered the opinion elsewhere that they "missed twenty or thirty years of brilliant music" in the intervening years (Sadot, quoted in Constantine and Sweeney 2013: 207). This new mixture of differently positioned groups on the northern soul dancefloor raises interesting questions about participation on the scene. For many of the returnees, exemplified anecdotally in my introduction, there is a sense of displacement when confronted by unfamiliar music in a northern soul venue, having fallen out of the habit of dancing to unknowns.

The engagement with the scene by younger participants and returnees is also reflected in the adoption of what I earlier called iconic 70s regalia of northern soul. This was only a fleeting fashion for a couple of years in the latter half of the seventies, and not adopted by all scene participants, its iconic status achieved through media representations of northern soul focused on the Wigan Casino footage in Tony Palmer's (1977) *This England* documentary. This fleeting moment, captured in one of the few moving image representations of the scene, has become for many the defining representation of northern soul past and present, enforcing the idea that a northern soul uniform defines the scene participants, which led *Guardian* journalist, Tim Jonze, to describe donning "some suitably baggy trousers [for] the Sheffield City Hall soul night", in his 2014 article on northern soul dancing.

Where an individual's agency – in Ahearn's (2001) terms their "socioculturally mediated capacity to act" (28), and in this case their capacity to dance – is challenged, they experience displacement; eviction from the security of home which impacts on the participants' mobility. On the northern soul scene, this dialectical relationship is dictated by the music, which itself is tied to pervasive expectations of tradition and continuity evident within the discourses of the scene. Displacement calls into question the participants' ability to orientate themselves, the loss of hierarchical privileges associated with familiar spaces and occupancy of a section of the dancefloor, and demands a reconfiguration of the personal and collective space of dancing. Likewise, unfamiliarity with the rhythmic space in the music means a loss of a sense of security. The interplay between these elements affords participants the potential to control a piece of space via dancing, to become highly skilled in a piece of geography of their own making. Mobility in this sense, defined by the geography of the dance space, becomes a powerful idea, permeated with ideas of moving on, and moving within, the "hierarchies" defined by musical tastes within the scene. As cultural geographer Peter Adey notes, "mobility cannot be conceived of without its opposite, that means immobility" (Adey 2009: 5).

New York Times critic, John Lahr, suggests that, "[if] history is a fable agreed upon ..., so too is identity, which is a story not only arrived at by the individual but conferred by the group" (1990: 10). Myths and fables lurk in the recollections of participants on the northern soul scene, including those who were once on the scene but left for various reasons, those who joined more recently, and those who never left the scene. For those who visited the scene only briefly during the commercial heyday of Wigan Casino – in Stuart Cosgrove's words, a "venue to be remembered in legends and stories, some real and some imaginary" (1982: 38) – the dominant narrative is particularly strong. However, writing in 1982, shortly after the closure of the Casino, Cosgrove noted even then that "the oldies and newies schism has remained a problem until the present day" (41). "Oldies" and "newies" in Cosgrove's comment refers to the records played in a venue, with oldies the tracks that have been played on the scene for many years and newies the relatively unknown records that are emerging on the scene. New records emerge on the scene via the sets of records played by DJs who constantly search for undiscovered sixties and seventies soul records that they might introduce to the dancers, in a part of the scene referred to as an "upfront" scene.

Little has changed over the decades and this schism has remained a permanent fixture of the northern soul scene, with the ongoing binary division between overground oldies and underground newies going back to the Friday oldies allnighter at Wigan Casino in the late seventies. During this period, for Cosgrove and many others, the Casino "increased its output of old Northern standards and at times was guilty of playing records that had no real place on a soul scene" (1982: 41). The oldies strand of this binary has, during the past decade or so, started to dominate general outsider, and many returnee insider, perceptions of northern soul. This "Casino-centric" lens within representations of the scene perpetuates many of the myths associated with that period, such as en masse acrobatic dancing, spinning, and clapping, uniformed clothing styles, and a fixed chart of music that has come to define an unchanging northern soul ideal. For Karl White (2016), chronicler of early 80s Top of the World venue in Stafford, "much has been written about the Northern Soul scene up to the demise of The Wigan Casino, but very little has actually been written about what followed". This, perhaps, contributes to the limited perspective of many narratives and studies. The "Casino-centric" lens covers merely eight years of northern soul's history, but often lays claim to its past, present, and possible future, perpetuating emblems, be they fashion, records, or dancing styles, that are anachronistic in the pre-and post-Casino context.

Contrary to this dominant discourse, the scene did not die with Wigan Casino. It returned to an underground status, away from the media spotlight, where a "new order" of venues, DJs, collectors and dancers evolved and music tastes, people and dancing all changed. As a prime example, Stafford's Top of the World ran from 1982 to 1986, and in Constantine and Sweeney (2013) words, "set the tone for what was to happen to the scene ever since [, and] led the way in pioneering new types of records which could be classified as Northern Soul" (183). Embracing multiple genres including R&B, modern, crossover, mid-tempo, big ballads, fast paced 60s, Latin soul and more (all in the same room), Top of the World made a lasting impact on what was to come. For Constantine and Sweeney:

> at its heart the Northern Soul scene has never really been retrograde in character. While it primarily focuses on music with history, the ideal was to always move forward ... There was a framework, an ethos, and that ethos was largely a Mod one, but it wasn't about merely looking back in a reverential, re-enactment society manner (Constantine and Sweeney 2013: 211).

"I can almost believe": problematic paradigms

Although the scene I know has always encouraged this "creative space", this should not be considered the universal space and experience that is open to all scene participants. As one of my younger interviewees put it:

> You are often told how you should dance, what you should wear and not wear, why are young people there. There is a lot of deference to how it should be done and young people get a lot of hate at some events already, so if we do something different it causes comments. We get a lot of advice like "why did you do that, you should have done it like this", you do get told what to do sometimes so if you are a young insecure kid from say Manchester or Wigan, and you're quite shy to go to those events, because they are quite intimidating, and then you try something new on the dance floor and someone says that to you. You think I'm never going to do that again.[3]

This testimony, as well as those of other younger participants I interviewed, illustrates the presence of perceived dominant hierarchies, which is further enforced by the behaviour of older scene members telling younger dancers how they should, and should not, dance. Observations at musically contrasting events leads me to conclude that these behaviours are primarily associated with the oldies scene, where restrictive perceptions of authenticity appear to be dominant, held in place through notions of tradition and historical stability that are played out through musical and corporeal fixity: how one should dance and what one should properly dance to. By contrast, dancing on the upfront rare soul scene is not so bound to such intensely perceived ideas of how a participant should or should not dance.

At oldies events, notions of temporality and tradition are bound to a fixed catalogue of oldies records which allow participants to display highly rehearsed performances on the dancefloor, which in turn, as Wall (2006) notes, support the dancers' claim to insider status: a corporeal incarnation of perceived authenticity. This style of dancing can be conceived of as "spectacularized", and can be traced to a specific period in the scene's history which roughly spans 1975–1981, employing the "demonstrative" use of arms, acrobatic movements, and clapping on the beat at key points in the record (that was very much a part of the style at that time for many, though not all, dancers). This style, where participants act out the lyrics of the record, is often used by media onlookers as the exemplar of northern soul dancing when, in fact, it existed for only a short time. Like many pieces of the bricolage of northern soul dancing, it mostly disappeared post-Casino as the music and venues changed.

If we take Tim Wall's (2006) idea of the close link between music and the practised performance and demonstration of insider knowledge via dancing, and apply it to the oldies scene, we can see that the ethos of preserving fixed musical tastes allows status to be asserted and maintained. The reliability of a fixed musical chart – where the songs, and often the detailed lyrics, are embodied in the participants – assures a safe space in which to perform northern soul identity via dancing. Oldies scene participants perceive a temporal and corporeal link with authenticity, and consequently a perceived idea of what northern soul dancing is and should properly be, and some younger participants become subject to domination by older members claiming authenticity at oldies events: played out through an explicit policing of dance performances.

However, as Constantine and Sweeney (2013: 143) again point out, dancing "evolved like any other facet on the scene. It wasn't stuck in one particular mode and it was a constantly changing, dynamic means of expression, which was for many the essence of the scene". Assertions of homogenous corporeal conformity in northern soul dancing is problematic. One such example is the use of Stuart Cosgrove's (1982) portrayal of northern soul dancing. Cosgrove notes that it is not only about the acrobatics "that catch the eye of the onlooker, [but] it is more importantly the ritual elegance of a dance style that glides from side to side but refuses to adopt a name" (38). Whilst descriptions of northern soul dancing as "*side to side*" and "*sideways*" may be true in some cases, they are far from universal. Used anecdotally by a current wave of northern soul dance teachers, they perpetuate and validate the side-to-side footwork motif, and by standing in front of the students and assimilating the format of a standard exercise class, these teachers call for participants to move in lines, and so creating a linear, flattened and dimensionally subverted style that resembles the "line dancing" format. In this commercial context, we might ask what is lost when a popular dance form is taken from its vernacular setting, to become formularized, codified, and homogenized, *and* what is lost when the music becomes cursory, and the movement stultified.

Equally problematic is the misunderstanding that northern soul music customarily follows(ed) a pounding 4/4 upbeat track. Venues such as the Highland Room at the Blackpool Mecca, which left an indelible imprint on the music and dancing styles during the same period as the Casino, introduced many records now regarded as classics, such as the Carstairs' 'It Really Hurts Me Girl' and The Voices of East Harlem, 'Cashin In'—both released in 1973 and, at the time, the cause of controversy for many participants, who regarded them as too modern or too funky. Northern soul histories often note that, in response, Wigan Casino promoter Russ Winstanley banned these types of "new sounds" being played at his allnighters, widening the divide between the musical constellation of the Mecca and the Casino. However, for those who were thrilled and excited by the new sounds, who accessed the tunes corporeally, whose souls were moved by them, who wanted to get "in it", the dancing style changed. It would be difficult to describe these tracks as upbeat, and the spectacle of acrobatics could not express the nuanced instrumentation, the complex percussion, or the deep lyrical narrative.

The breadth of beats and sounds embraced by the northern soul soundscape continued to evolve and, in response, so did the dancing. Styles in northern soul dancing were venue-centric in terms of the music played and the physical space available, and a reflection of the musical evolution within the scene. The modern funkier sounds emerging from places such as the Highland Room[4] were met with tighter and more nuanced footwork with the dancers' torsos and legs shedding the dynamic angularity and demonstrative gestural nature of the driving beat style of dancing, encouraging the participants to dance in the music, rather than at it, or on it, giving an overall impression of relaxed coolness, as opposed to the dynamic athleticism associated with the brasher style that gripped Wigan Casino and other venues.

DJ, Ian Levine, recalls that Blackpool Mecca had "many great female dancers [and] even though Northern Soul came to be quite a macho scene the girls at the Mecca could really dance" (Levine, in Constantine and Sweeney 2013: 146). Yet representations of northern soul dance fail to explore these particular female corporeal narratives in their discourse of northern soul (see, for instance, Robinson 2013; Smith 2009a, 2009b) and this is an area that needs to be researched and articulated in depth in the future. What is clear is that the complex dialogue between music, dancing, venues, and the positioning of scene participants cannot be underestimated, and that there is a need to challenge generalized expectations of what northern soul dancing is, by demonstrating the limitations of the Casino-centric lens when it is used as a "macro", rather than "micro", viewpoint.

"It's Just an Illusion": a case of misdiagnosis

My previous involvement in portraying northern soul dancing has led to approaches from commercial producers who want me to choreograph "authentic" northern soul dancing for their projects. They inevitably use the reference-point footage of the spectacularized image of northern soul dancing from Tony Palmer's Wigan Casino documentary, an image that through its reuse in almost all subsequent documentaries on northern soul, has laid claim to the northern soul's past, present and future. Palmer's glimpse into Wigan Casino is one of the few filmic documentations of the northern soul scene in the 1970s and many outside commentators often, erroneously, interpret this highly edited footage as a true portrayal of today's northern soul scene.[5] Wigan Casino has also been constitutive in the perpetuation of northern soul dancing stereotypes by some insiders[6] failing to acknowledge that these images were caricatured by the production values of the film's director, and are not universally indicative of a musically, and corporeally, nuanced and diversified scene. This has been fuelled by other media excursions such as Duffy's 'Mercy' music video (2008) and the more recent feature film *Northern Soul* (Constantine, 2013).

Using such sources is at its most problematic in Laura Robinson's (2013) work, which draws on Duffy's 'Mercy' and Palmer's documentary as an evidential base. She refers to *This England*, by discussing "a sea of dancers all gliding in perfect unison" (183), and goes on to further reify northern soul dancing as being embodied "through the uniformity and simplicity of the side-to-side gliding step" (185). However, the film is a montage of bridging shots, cross-cutting, jump cuts, long shots, slow motion, and other methods pulled together in an editing suite. Dancers can be seen bouncing, skipping, and in places stepping, stomping, and shuffling. I personally shift(ed) my footwork between stomping, shuffling, and floating depending upon my connection with a particular record. "Stomping" and "shuffling" are terms that have been in use on the northern soul scene for at least four decades, though some dancers interpret the meaning differently.

In my case "stomping" means quick footwork where the feet momentarily touch the floor in transition, but remain in flight most of the time and where the legs are slightly bent at the knees whilst maintaining almost straight alignment. By "shuffling" I refer to a style where the feet remain on the floor, dancing into the ground, knees relaxed and bent, whilst simultaneously driving across it: the torso position varies amongst dancers. "Floating" is a style I refer to that developed in response to slower big ballad and mid-tempo records that emerged from Stafford and beyond, such as Jack Montgomery, 'Don't Turn Your Back on Me' (Barracuda) or Sir Caesar, 'Show Me the Time' (Ride). Here, the dancers move across the beat, in different directions, creating an elegant, floating motion that often uses turns and tight, flowing spins.

These explorations, calling upon "expansive corporeal texts"[7] within the dance style, often result(ed) in individual nuanced hybridizations of footwork, which in turn add(ed) to the lexicon of movement, a continuum that still subtly evolves today: as new corporeal shifts emerge in response to sub-categories of genres within the scene, including "funk-edged soul", "soulful gospel" and "ghetto soul" (or soul with a message).[8] Furthermore, some of these terms have long been used on the scene to denote footwork styles that change in response to the music. So, for instance, historically, footwork would change if dancing to certain late sixties or seventies records.[9]

Palmer's footage has since been taken out of context and co-opted by inside and outside commentators as spectacle reminiscent of Anna Beatrice Scott's assertion that commodified dance demands that the "performing body, and hence the performance, must be reduced to its most tantalising parts for the maximum effect in a minimum amount of time and space" (Scott 2001: 113).

Dave Wards, a dancer who was filmed for *This England*, and who appears in the out-takes wearing a P-Funk shirt, recalls that:

> 1977 was a time of change, the Casino promoters started to "ban" certain new records because they were too funky ... I didn't rate circus acrobatics or side-to-side stomping, although these are the dancers who feature on *This England*. I hate the clips on YouTube, they are out of sync and backed by the wrong music ... [I was dancing to] Ton of Dynamite![10]

Wards's testimony captures some of the misconceptions that might arise from analysis that is estranged from a deeper understanding of the scene.

Wigan Casino footage was filmed over two hours when many records were played and danced to, and the postproduction dubbing uses tracks that may not have been played, and edited mostly out of synch with the dancers' movements. There are also claims that many dancers boycotted the event altogether (see Ritson and Russell 1999: 230), or hid in the shadows in protest at the cameras being allowed access to "their" venue, and that Tony Palmer was "under orders to film only those who sought him out" (Jelbert 2010). Some even argued that between them, in their drive towards commercialization, the Casino owner Gerry Marshall, and the promoter and primary DJ Russ Winstanley, had "taken Northern Soul to the brink of caricature" (Constantine and Sweeney 2013: 110). Dave Conway, another dancer who was present at the filming of *This England*, suggests:

> ... far from a normal Saturday/Sunday niter. Many regulars stayed away. The smaller-than-usual crowd numbered unfamiliar faces. The dancefloor was brightly lit and clusters of on-lookers were standing around. The cameras homed in on anyone spinning around then falling down. Such were the theatrics, the music at the time, and later when dubbed, was irrelevant as the acrobats threw themselves to the floor when the camera approached rather than at a significant break in the track. The programme might have titillated some nostalgic Northerners but it was a travesty for the Casino and a slur on the Northern Soul scene that the media keep trying to match even today.[11]

The myth of the spectacular northern soul dancer owes much to a co-optation of Palmer's documentary footage that can be analysed through the combined lens of historical re-enactment and pastiche,[12] that in Jameson's words "tend[s] to obliterate difference and to project an idea of the historical period as massive homogeneity" (Jameson 1991: 3). In other words, it presents an imagined history that draws on common northern soul iconography: baggy trousers, demonstrative acrobatic dancing, and 4/4 beats. This historico-pastiche is apparent in the carefully constructed images of the Shredded Wheat, 'Live from the Heart' (2015) commercial, supported by not-so subtly anachronistic and clichéd clothing, music and imagery. Here, stereotypical expectations of "northern-ness" and northern soul were seen dancing across UK television screens, employing a process of homogenization, and the obliteration of difference, described by Jameson in his treatise on capitalism as "the insensible colonisation of the present by the nostalgia mode" (1991: 12).[13] The trend towards historico-pastiche and the fetishization of the Casino years, now appears to dominate many northern soul events across the UK.

Conclusion: "Look at your Soul"

I have discussed an ethos based upon the discovery of new records, upon which the scene was founded, and still evolves. In doing so, I have challenged the assumption that "everyone dances the same" at northern soul events, whether in the seventies, or today. Furthermore, I have demonstrated how this motif is enforced by various forces, both internal and external to the scene, for a range of motives and outcomes.

People of different tastes, styles and experiences have always danced northern soul, simultaneously, and at different periods in time. Temporality and location *are* key factors in any assessment of northern soul dancing, as is, in the contemporary setting, the relationship between a mass of ageing fans and an influx of younger participants. Whilst many young dancers might parry explicit attempts at soul policing, coercion is certainly a factor in the reification of the dancing style at oldies events. There appears to be a space of self-conscious reverence to northern soul's perceived elders. It is a mythologized space that is enforced through already mediated versions of what "proper" northern soul dancing is and should be. Corporeal departures from traditional versions of northern soul movements and styles, nuanced or otherwise, amongst younger dancers are rare. For many younger participants nowadays, the weight of history can be more coercive, re-imagined and played out via tactics of soul policing on the oldies dancefloor.

There is no homogenized, authentic step in northern soul dancing. There is, however, an original reference point, an ethos of progressive movement that embraces rare soul music, dancing, community, life, and a distrust of mainstream culture and the media. This is the locus of the original form that informs the poise and dignity of a scene musically and culturally in flux. On the northern soul scene, people dance in different ways; it is not unique to be unique within it. Some people are "in" the music, as when they jump up to a tune they don't know and "feel" a way through it, whilst others might be seen as "out" of the music, going through motions they have gone through many times to the same tune, almost re-enacting and performing the emotion they once felt when they were "in" it. And then there are those who mix the two together. Observation is the true method of northern soul dancing, that and experimentation.

Like Butch quoted in Constantine and Sweeney (2013), "I'm still looking for unknowns all the time" (p. 213),[14] for me, and many others on the scene, the search for "new discoveries" is aligned with the articulation of what the "soul" encounters in life: the unknowns. The need to hear and dance to a "new" lost voice, to find a cathartic release that reflects the "very moment" of being "in" life, has always been the unswerving continuum of the scene. Space, place and time inform this negotiation. Many of the records that I have danced to over time have, of course, remained with me. They are treasured encounters: I dance to them "when" I need to, and "how" I need to, but my corporeal repository of soul is not a fixed proposition; it is rather a lifelong evolution.

Freddie Scott's "sermon-inspired" lyrics for 'I'll Be Gone'[15] capture this evolution of an individual over time: from adolescence to adulthood, to older adulthood, and so on. We might even think of this in terms of the holistic development of the individual, encompassing mental, physical, social, emotional and spiritual growth or decay; moving towards a destination unknown. Whilst I acknowledge that not all dancers may have the desire, space, or competence to develop throughout their participation, it would also be naïve to assume that these intrinsically human characteristics do not relate to many individual participants on the northern soul scene, reflected in their musical tastes and in their dancing.

About the author

Paul Sadot is completing his practice-based doctoral research in dance at the University of Chichester. He commissioned, produced and directed the acclaimed stage play *Once Upon a Time in Wigan* (2003–2005) and was the choreographer and acting coach for Elaine Constantine's 2014 BAFTA-nominated feature film *Northern Soul*. He has appeared in numerous documentaries on northern soul, and in 2017 he choreographed the Gucci *Soul Scene* campaign. He has danced to northern soul for over four decades. His chapter in the *Oxford Handbook of Hip Hop Dance Studies* is awaiting publication.

Notes

1. I use this phrase to denote a reflexive doing, a being "in" the music, a non-reliance on formulaic patterns that often come from dancing four beats to the bar, on the beat. But, instead, dancing across, or on the off-beat, exploring what the music holds. The scene includes many participants who dance in this individual way.

2. "Kinesthesia" refers to "sensations of movement and position", whilst "empathy" can be seen as "projecting oneself into the object of contemplation" (Reynolds and Reason 2012: 18–19).

3. Lauren Fitzpatrick is a 22-year-old dancer who has been attending allnighters and soul nights since 2012. She placed second in the World Northern Soul Dance Championships in 2012 and 2013 (Interview with the author, 22 June 2016). My other interviewees, Charlotte Hindley, 22, Jordan Wilson, 20 and James Whitehead, 32, have all experienced similar attempts at policing their dancing by older members at oldies events.

4. Examples of this can be heard in the following: 'Music Maker' by King Sporty on Tashamba (1970s); 'Charade' by The Four Tracks on Note (1974); 'Wrong Crowd' by Prince George on D.P.G. (1970s).

5. Many extant documentaries about northern soul use Palmer's footage to reveal the perspective of their coverage and the, often, limited extent of their research. Examples are numerous and can be found online such as: *Way of the Crowd* directed by J.D. Moore (2002) and *Northern Soul: Keeping the Faith* directed by Maurice O'Brien for BBC2, *The Culture Show* (2013).

6. Insiders can also be seen to perpetuate this demonstrative, spectacularized version of northern soul dancing through the emergence of studio classes, dance lessons and DVD tutorials; see: http://www.nightowl-media.co.uk/index.asp?pageid=288676 and http://www.dancenorthern.com/

7. I use this term to indicate that northern soul dancing is expansive rather than restrictive, made up of "many different movements" and "ways of moving" that are intricately bound to musical development, holistic development, venues, tastes and other factors.

8. Whilst the northern soul scene has always absorbed other musical genres, UK events such as *Soul or Nothing* and *DDA* began focusing on these particular genres in more depth as far back as 2004. Soul with a message is the subject of Norwegian rare soul collector, DJ and historian Tommy Søvik's thesis, "Speak Ghetto Speak: Political Soul in USA 1960–1980" (2014), where he coins the acronym SWAM. See: https://www.duo.uio.no/handle/10852/46077. DJs in Norway, Sweden, Spain, France, Australia, USA and elsewhere also contribute greatly to these developments. Records such as Wally Coco, 'Message to Society' (Florentine), Bongi and Nelson, 'Do You Remember Malcolm?' (Editions Syliphone Conakry), Boco, 'Running the Mardi Gras' (Laughing Eye) and Sacred Four, 'Somebody Watching You' (Champ) illustrate these emergences. Though the true nature of underground northern soul music's evolutionary ethos ensures that these references will be somewhat dated by the time of publication.

9. Examples of these would be World Column's 'So is the Sun', Frankie Crocker, 'Ton of Dynamite', or the frenetic Seventh Wonder, 'Captain of My Ship'.

10 Dave Wards's testimony can be found on the P-Funk thread of the fan base *Soul Source* (2013). Available at: http://www.soul-source.co.uk/soulforum/topic/142684-p-_-funk/ (accessed 5 December 2016).

11. In interview with author, 6 December 2016.

12. I use pastiche to denote the use of a combination of different, often idiosyncratic, fragments that are employed to present an imagined version (imitation) of northern soul.

13. However, I do not want to suggest a simple binary wherein commodification is the enemy of the northern soul, because these dimensions have always been there. The scene has always had a political economy. Dance hall owners, event promoters, record dealers, drug dealers and bootleggers are amongst a cast of characters that participate(d) in an exploitative economy (to different degrees) that exists within the scene.

14. Butch (Mark Dobson) is regarded by many as the world's number one northern soul DJ in terms of the original ethos of moving forward musically. He has been the resident DJ at London's 100 Club since 1996 and introduced countless new discoveries to the scene that are now regarded as classics.

15. "When I was child, I walked like a child, I talked like a child, I acted like a child. Now I'm a man I'm through with my childish ways. You see I leave my child like a butterfly, I spread my wings and take to the sky, I'll be leavin."

16. Where no date of release/location information is available an approximation based on evidence research has been made by the author. I would like to thank Karl White for his generous help and support in compiling the detailed information regarding release dates and recording locations.

References

Adey, P. 2009. *Mobility*. London: Routledge.
Ahearn, L. 2001. "Agency and Language". *Annual Review of Anthropology* 30: 28–48.
Constantine, E., and G. Sweeney. 2013. *Northern Soul*. London: Virgin Books.
Cosgrove, S. 1982. "Long After Tonight is All Over". *Collusion* 2: 38–41.
—2016. *Young Soul Rebels*. Edinburgh: Polygon.
Fitzpatrick, L. 2016. Interview with the author, 22 June.
Hindley, C. 2016. Interviewed by Paul Sadot, 30 November.
Hollows, J., and K. Milestone. 1998. "Welcome to Dreamsville: A History and Geography of Northern Soul". In *The Place of Music*, edited by A. Leyshon, D. Matless, and G. Revill, 83–103. New York: Guildford Press.
Jameson, F. 1991. *Postmodernism, Or the Cultural Logic of Late Capitalism*. New York: Duke University Press.
Jelbert, S. 2010. "Tony Palmer's Wigan Casino film comes to DVD". *The Guardian*. Available at: https://www.theguardian.com/music/2010/apr/15/the-wigan-casino-tony-palmer (accessed 26 December 2016).
Jonze, T. 2014. "How to Dance to Northern Soul". *The Guardian*. Available at: https://www.theguardian.com/lifeandstyle/2014/sep/18/how-to-dance-to-northern-soul-1970s-dance (accessed 11 April 2017).
Lahr, J. 1990. "The World's Most Sensational Absence". *New York Times Book Review*, 84: 10.
McKenna, P. 1996. *Nightshift*. Argyll: S.T Publishing.
Milestone, K. 1997. "The Love Factory: The Sites, Practices and Media Relationships of Northern Soul". In *The Club Cultures Reader: Readings in Popular Cultural Studies*, edited by S. Redhead, 152–67. Oxford: Blackwell.
Nowell, D. 2001. *Too Darn Soulful: The Story of Northern Soul*. London: Robson Books.
Reynolds, D., and M. Reason. 2012. *Kinesthetic Empathy in Creative and Cultural Practices*. Bristol/Chicago: Intellect.
Ritson, M., and S. Russell. 1999. *The In Crowd: The Story of the Northern and Rare Soul Scene*. London: Bee Cool Publishing.
Robinson, L. 2013. "Keeping the Faith: Issues of Identity, Spectacle and Embodiment in Northern Soul". In *Bodies of Sound: Studies across Popular Music and Dance*, edited by S. Cook and D. Sherril, 179–92. London and New York: Routledge.
Scott, A. B. 2001. "Dance". In *Culture Works: The Political Economy of Culture*, edited by R. Maxwell, 107–130. Minneapolis: University of Minnesota Press.
Smith, N. 2009a. *Performing Fandom on the British Northern Soul Scene: Competition, Identity and the Post-Subcultural Self*. Manchester: University of Salford.
—2009b. "Beyond the Master Narrative of Youth: Researching Ageing Popular Music Scenes". In *Ashgate Research Companion to Popular Musicology*, edited by E. Scott, 427–47. Oxon/New York: Routledge.

Wall, T. 2006. "Out on the Floor: The Politics of Dancing on the Northern Soul Scene". *Popular Music* 25/3: 431–45.
—2007. "Dancing, Northern Soul Style". *Wall of Sound*. Available at: https://wallofsound.wordpress.com/2007/12/20/dancing-northern-soul-style/.
Wards, D. 2013. "P-Funk". *Soul Source*. Available at: http://www.soul-source.co.uk/soulforum/topic/142684-p-_-funk/ (accessed 5 December 2016).
White, K. 2016. "The Stafford Story". *Soul Underground*. Available at: http://www.soulunderground.co.uk/page21/page13/ (accessed 6 December 2016).
Whitehead, J. 2016. Interview with the author, 22 June.
Wilson, A. 2007. *Northern Soul: Music, Drugs and Subcultural Identity*. Cullompton, UK: Willan Publishing.
Wilson, J. 2016. Interviewed by Paul Sadot, 30 November.
Winstanley, R., and D. Nowell. 1996. *Soul Survivors: The Wigan Casino Story*. London: Robson Books.

Discography[16]

The Blue Jays. 1965. '(It Depends on the) Point of View'. Jay, Wilmington, Delaware.
Boco. 1974. 'Running the Mardi Gras'. Laughing Eye, New Orleans, Louisiana.
Bongi & Nelson. 1971. 'Do You Remember Malcolm?' Editions Syliphone Conakry, Paris, France.
Sammy Campbell. 1966. 'I Never Thought'. Queen City, Plainfield, New Jersey.
Jonathan Capree. 1968. 'Gonna Build Me A Mountain'. Ox Bow, Maryland, Washington, DC.
Carstairs. 1973. 'It Really Hurts Me Girl'. Red Coach, N.Y.C.
Wally Coco. 1978. 'Message to Society'. Florentine label, Florence, South Carolina.
Frankie Crocker. 1969. 'Ton of Dynamite'. Turbo label, Englewood, New Jersey.
De-Larks. 1965. 'Job Opening'. Queen City, Plainfield, New Jersey.
The Four Tracks. 1974. 'Charade'. Note, Birmingham, Alabama.
John Harris and the Soul Sayers. 1967. 'Hangin' In'. Kerston, Germany.
The Illusions. 1971. 'Just an Illusion'. Freedom, Alexandria, Louisiana.
Jerri Jackson. 1971. 'I Can Almost Believe'. Parallax, N.Y.C.
King Sporty. 1970. 'Music Maker'. Tashamba, Miami, Florida.
Lovations. 1969. 'Drifting Offshore'. Cap City, Washington, DC.
Jack Montgomery. 1967. 'Don't Turn Your Back on Me'. Barracuda, Detroit, Michigan.
Point of View. 1974. 'I'm Superman'. Instant, New Orleans, Louisiana.
Prince George. 1970. 'Wrong Crowd'. D.P.G. Norfolk, Virginia.
Ron & Joe. 1968/69. 'Go Away and Stay'. Megatone label, Lynchburg, Virginia.
Sacred Four. 1975. 'Somebody Watching You'. Champ, Johnson, Tennessee.
Sag War Fare. 1971. 'Don't Be So Jive'. Libra label, Orlando, Florida.
Scott, Freddie. 1967. 'I'll Be Gone'. Shout label, N.Y.C.
Seventh Wonder. 1976. 'Captain of My Ship'. W.G., Alabama, Tuskegee.
Sheila Wilmer. 1971. 'Look at Your Soul'. Whole Soul, Philadelphia, Pennsylvania.
Sir Caesar. 1964. 'Show Me the Time'. Ride, Los Angeles, California.
Soul Incorporated. 1967. 'My Proposal'. Coconut Groove, Mount Morris, Michigan.
The Tomangoes. 1968. 'I Really Love You'. Washpan, Detroit, Michigan.

The Turbines. 1968. 'We Got to Start Over'. Cenco, Los Angeles, California.
The Voices of East Harlem. 1973. 'Cashin In'. Just Sunshine, N.Y.C.
Williams, Kae. 1967–69. 'Our Love is Dying'. Unissued, Philadelphia, Pennsylvania.
World Column. 1969. 'So is the Sun'. Tower, Los Angeles, California.

Musical Bookmark 7

Kev Roberts photographed at Thorpe Salvin, Nottinghamshire, February 2017
The Esquires, 'How Could It Be'. US Bunky Records 7756

> "This is a song that I had forgotten all about it 'til one of my DJs played it at the King's Hall Stoke and it reminded me about how I love soul music, northern soul. It's one of the greatest group sounds of all time in my opinion: so much going on, it's a very busy record. They're out of Milwaukie, Wisconsin, just a tremendous group, and anyone who wants to feel good about northern soul take a listen; it's the real business."

Kev Roberts DJed at Wigan Casino in its heyday, ran Goldmine records in Manchester, and authored *The Northern Soul Top 500* with David Carne. He now runs Goldsoul promotions.

17 "Groove Me":

Dancing to the Discs of Northern Soul[*]

David Sanjek[1]

> I think we have to be very cautious about interpreting those moments of connection. We know what that language articulates because we know about the intensity of pleasure that we discover. But I think sometimes that language of an essential particularity, which we use to explain those moments of affiliation and linkage, represents a kind of shortcut to the more obviously political work involved in explaining how solidarity happens and how culture, technology, and language mediate that solidarity. I think if we could be just a little harder on ourselves before we start celebrating, we might have something more worthwhile – a more politically coherent understanding of what those fragile solidarities add up to (Paul Gilroy).[2]

Common sense would seem to dictate that infatuation constitutes a relatively uncomplicated phenomenon. In the most rudimentary terms, a person temporarily succumbs, in one manner or another, to an overwhelming interruption of their ordinary equilibrium. However long they remain in the presence of the agent of this disorientation, their center of gravity, so to speak, collapses. One might draw upon a romantic vocabulary in order to provide the most appropriate characterization of this sensation: a swoon – or, perhaps just as accurately, employ that vivid English colloquialism: "gobsmacked". Whatever the precipitating phenomenon, whether it be the most elevated or altogether down to earth, the end result remains the same. The architecture of our interior topography undergoes a tectonic shift. We consequently feel compelled to inspect each and every step we take, as though the inclination to trip over ourselves was almost unavoidable.

If the experience of infatuation can be recounted in a more or less universal manner, the various trajectories that the emotions are able to traverse

---

[*] Originally published in Jill Terry and Neil A. Wynn (eds), *Transatlantic Roots Music: Folk, Blues and National Identities* (Jackson: University Press of Mississippi, 2012).

remain uncountable. The human heart may well contain a finite set of chambers, but the affections are able to attach themselves to an infinite number of targets. Perhaps the most persuasive argument against the purported monogamous nature of human beings might well be the fickle behavior of our consciousness. We flit from perception to perception, leapfrog from one position to another as though we rarely exceed, whatever our age, the conceptual overload experienced by infants that William James famously characterized in *The Principles of Psychology* as "one great blooming, buzzing confusion".[3] We exist in a continuous state of potential intrigue, promiscuously attracted to any number of divergent avenues of infatuation.

Making sense of that oversaturated set of circumstances can be somewhat less oppressive if we harness our attention to one of those occasions when a set of individuals become mutually absorbed by an identical target, engage in a kind of collective embrace, and thereby become classified as fans. Fascination with what have been determined to be specifically demarcated communities of fans has consumed many an academic and average person alike. This takes place not simply due to a kind of analytic shorthand but also because these conglomerations might be thought of as the institutionalization of infatuation. It is possible to think of fan communities as what occurs when what would otherwise appear to be random acts of solitary rapture achieve a kind of critical mass. Lawrence Grossberg has frequently and eloquently written of the "affective alliances" that arise when two or more individuals recognize and act upon their mutual investment of time, consciousness, and cash in a common object. He recognizes as well that the act of being consumed by popular music in particular cannot be separated from whatever other activities might potentially take up a portion of our lives. Consequently, "The meaning and effect of specific music always depends on its place within both the broad context of everyday life and the potentially multiple, often specific contexts and alliances of other texts, cultural practices (including fashion, dance, film), social relationships, emotional investments, and so forth".[4]

Understanding any specific act of infatuation requires that we distinguish and dissect those "contexts and alliances"; make sense of how we attach ourselves to a particular form of music; why we do so; and what the consequences, intended and potentially inadvertent, might be. As Paul Gilroy points out in the epigraph with which we began, "moments of connection" that result in a demonstrable "intensity of pleasure" will remain perennially fragile constructions until or unless we unpack and interrogate the impulses that give rise to those routinely overpowering sensations. And when we find ourselves seized by song, dominated by rhythms on the dancefloor, or flummoxed by the fabulous vocal arabesques of an inspired singer, a good deal of unpacking will have to be done. Invariably, the baggage that accompanies the experience of popular music challenges our capacity for juggling disparate discourses, intersecting ideologies, colliding forms of consciousness. In the process, we might well find that intertwined with pleasure is some form of polemic, even if that construction of consciousness does not emerge overtly or even coherently in the rapturous experience from which it originates.

To that end, let us take a specific fan community and a time-honored attachment by several generations of aficionados to a particular form of music – African American rhythm & blues – and the resulting alliance that has come to be known now for some forty years as northern soul. Its parameters as a mass audience phenomenon can be described quite simply. Starting in the early 1970s, a group of working-class English men and women developed a mutual embrace of a specific repertoire. They came together to listen and dance to that playlist at clubs by and large located in the North of England, hence the topographic determination of the group's name. At the same time, if the culture that bred the music these individuals favored was urban, their place of residence tended not to be overtly cosmopolitan. As Katie Milestone observes, most northern soul communities occur in small towns in the northwest of England, like Wigan, Blackburn, Morecambe, Cleethorpes, and Tunstall, places on the margin that remain "peripheral to the concentration of economic and cultural power in city centres".[5] Nothing terribly complicated brings them together, simply a common passion for a specific form of popular culture and the desire to join a community of fellow fanatics.

However, the more one investigates the phenomenon of northern soul, the less simple it appears. Several questions about geography, race, and ideology arise. First, there is the matter of the transatlantic migration of the material, the fact that one national culture embraced the performances of a portion of another. In this case, something led these individuals to seek out meaning and identity in the recordings not of their country, but that of America. Why were they drawn across the Atlantic and how did they characterize their fascination with a foreign culture? Second, there is the issue of the cross-racial element of the process: for the most part fans of northern soul were and are white while the recordings they sought out were created and marketed by African Americans. What led them to cross racial barriers that often exclude rather than include outsiders? Finally, what conscious and unconscious ideological claims can be said to attach themselves to what might otherwise seem nothing more than a spirited engagement with recorded commercial music? The fans of northern soul do not appear to have promoted any explicitly polemical positions regarding either the material they admire or the individuals who create it; yet simply by seeking it out, and drawing the public's attention often to recordings that were obscure if not completely unknown, this group appears to have engaged in work that possesses ideological dimensions.

In the remainder of this essay, I will examine four issues that arise from these vexing questions. First, what is the composition of the discography they constituted, and how does it demarcate a particular portion of the rhythm & blues repertoire as innately superior to better-known and publicly popular recordings? It needs to be stressed that at the present time, when cultural canons routinely are overturned, the advocates of northern soul constructed just such a hierarchy of validated sounds. They identified and advocated for a very specific body of recordings that in their minds stand out by virtue of being, by and large, drawn from the least commercially successful and in some cases altogether unreleased portion of the rhythm and blues repertoire. What cultural capital is amassed by such a set of choices, and what positions are thereby issued about commercialism? Second, what relationship is projected between the two nations of the United States and England, and how is the geography from which the music originated imagined? Is there any implicit desire on the part of the northern soul community to engage with the tangible topography and the citizenry of another society, or has the actual territory given way to a landscape of the emotions and the imagination? Third, how has the northern soul community integrated issues of race, and what determination might be made about the kinds of bonds that elude and perhaps eradicate lines of potential hostility that can originate through the acquisition and acclimation of commercial products? Finally, what specific ideological statements might be intertwined within particular acts of pleasure, and might something be emancipated on the dancefloor other than the inhibitions of the audience? The hope is that asking such questions will allow us to be a bit harder on ourselves in the manner that Paul Gilroy invites, and allow northern soul to be understood as the complex and consequential phenomenon that it has been and continues to be for a number of people.

Before continuing, some further details about the phenomenon itself are required. Northern soul has been said to have originated in Manchester at the Twisted Wheel venue (1963–71), where the DJ Roger Eagle began to spin his private stash of U.S. rhythm & blues singles and attract an audience of like-minded individuals.[6] Initially, the northern soul scene depended on self-directed cultural entrepreneurs such as Eagle to provide the sounds, as American soul imports did not start to enter the UK in any systematic fashion until 1968.[7] Previously, collectors had to rely on individual initiative, private contacts, and trips across the ocean to acquire material. The success of the Twisted Wheel also benefited from the emerging scene in Manchester as the city had come to compete alongside Hamburg as the "Fun City of Europe".[8] The freewheeling atmosphere temporarily abetted that reputation, until an overweening moral panic ensued that focused on drug sales and consumption in public venues as well as an absence of administrative oversight by the owners of those venues. Attention was drawn to these activities by J. A. McKay, Manchester's chief constable, in reports filed in 1964 and 1965.[9] He conjured up an image of unsupervised, adolescent vagrants, wandering from club to club, strung out on hashish or amphetamines.[10] The ensuing melange of "quasi-facts, clichés, innuendoes and indignant moral outrage" that appeared in the local press stirred up politicians to take action and led to the 1965 Manchester Corporation Act.[11] Its statutes responded to the desire on the part of the city council and other forces for regulation and control of errant youths as well as helping promote efforts at modernization of Manchester's city center. Subsequent statutes threatened prosecution of club owners should consumption of illegal drugs take place on their premises, even if the proprietors remained unaware of the purported crime. This and other regulations enabled the powers that be in Manchester to eliminate the kind of behavior that collided with the promotion of civic stability and transformation of the city center into a shopping arena.

Despite these interventions, the Twisted Wheel retained its pre-eminence past the end of the decade as the scene's reputation spread. The visit by music journalist and record promoter Dave Godin to the venue in 1970 led to his promotion of the emerging northern soul phenomenon in his column featured in the publication *Blues & Soul* – as well as the initial printed coinage of the appellation northern soul. Godin (1936–2004) was the outstanding proponent – one might even say propagandist – for American rhythm & blues in England at the time and a revered figure among aficionados of the genre. Initially a devotee of the Detroit-based Tamla-Motown affiliated record labels, he founded the Tamla-Motown Appreciation Society, established a professional relationship with the company, acted as its representative, and opened a London-based shop and label, Soul City, as an outlet for the products. In that 1970 column he drew attention to a series of characteristics that typify the northern soul scene to this day: how ingratiating and collegial the attendees were –"none of the stand-off-ishness in the North that plagues human relationships in the South"; the expertise of the dancers – "I never thought I'd live to see the day where people could so relate the rhythmic content of Soul music to bodily movement to such a skilled degree in these rigid and armoured isles!"; and the top-notch caliber of the selections chosen by the DJs – "a focal point for that aware and elite minority who are not content with the lifeless pulp that constitutes the bulk of the manipulated "hit" parade".[12]

Godin's description could apply equally well to the subsequent venues that followed in the wake of the Twisted Wheel and retain to this day their reputation as the locus *mundi* of the northern soul universe, principal among them the Golden Torch in Tunstall, Stoke on Trent (1971–72), and the Wigan Casino (1973–81).[13] The latter eventually acquired international plaudits when it received the designation of #1 discotheque from the U.S. music industry publication *Billboard* in 1978. It also served as the focus for the 1977 Granada documentary, directed by Tony Palmer, presented on the series *This England*. The opening sequences achieve through parallel editing a painful juxtaposition between the industrial bleakness of the area and the experiential expansiveness of the venue. In particular, the entrancing shots of astonishingly acrobatic male dancers reinforces the virtually utopian dimension of the space as a vehicle that could unclog all manner of bottled-up energy and otherwise assaulted individuality. Some attendees disliked if not loathed the program. They objected to how Palmer had used "unusual camera angles [to] distort and objectify the dancers and (the lights being on) [how] the camera focuses on 'working-class signifiers' such as muscles, sweat and tattoos. Rather than the allnighter looking fast and exciting, it seems strange, dreamlike and suspended in time".[14] By literally casting light on their countercultural enclave, they felt that Palmer extinguished some of the aura they had attached to its atmosphere. (Tim Wall's 2006 essay "Out on the Floor: The Politics of Dancing on the Northern Soul Scene" provides the most detailed and theoretically sophisticated commentary about the dancefloor. Among other things, it does not dwell on the masculine acrobatics and consequently illustrates that there was more than one way to announce one's identity than simply to spin elastically about the floor.)

Palmer's film did illustrate how much northern soul remained a nocturnal phenomenon, and that the absence of daylight and banishment of anything affiliated to the diurnal reinforced the specialness of the activity. Oddly enough, the venues were by and large alcohol-free, as local ordinances did not permit the sale of anything other than soft drinks at such a late hour. It should therefore come as little surprise that the scene was routinely drug-enhanced, as the ingestion of amphetamines in particular brought about not only the pleasure of the high but also served as a means of keeping bodies upright long past the crack of midnight. Andrew Wilson, a participant analyst, provides the most detailed and evenhanded study of this dimension of the scene in *Northern Soul: Music, Drugs and Subcultural Identity*. He reinforces how the crowd thought of their drug of choice not as an escape from reality but a means of "being in control, on the ball and smart"; that the absence of moral shibboleths affiliated to their use reinforced the sense of group identity and moral code.[15] As much as anything, amphetamines encouraged if not reinforced "Those experiences – the physiological sensations, confidence, fast thought and talk – together with the upbeat music and sense of camaraderie, all combined in a very real and exciting way".[16]

The incitement of that camaraderie might have been a factor in the absence of sexual predation on the dancefloor as well as off. It certainly allowed both men and women the opportunity to express what might otherwise have been submerged portions of their personality. People assuredly sought out partners and physical gratification away from the venue itself, as though to keep the site unsullied and undefined by gender competition. The absence of testosterone-driven feistiness in the northern soul scene has been frequently observed. Dave Godin wrote of it in his 1970 article: "There was no undercurrent of tension or aggression that one sometimes finds in London clubs, but rather a benevolent atmosphere of benign friendship and camaraderie". Katie Milestone speaks of the "lack of pressure to conform to heterosexual definitions of masculinity" that made gay men feel welcome and straight men encouraged to drop their guard.[17] The degree to which dance remained the *raison d'être* of northern soul allnighters reinforces not only the commanding presence of the DJ but also the crucial dimension of the tracks he chose to play. The phono-centric nature of the northern soul community cannot be underestimated. The participants remain irretrievably entranced by what lies within the grooves of vinyl, the sounds that could be perfected in the recording studio.

That is not to exclude that occasions arose when live performers took to the stage of venues. Kimasi Browne enumerates, in his rewarding and richly detailed 2005 U.C.L.A. PhD thesis "'Soul or Nothing': The Formation of Cultural Identity on the British Northern Soul Scene", some of the individuals and groups that appeared on the scene. The list incorporates many estimable names, yet remains far from exhaustive.[18] Furthermore, even when filled to capacity, a venue like the Golden Torch, where Chicago-based Major Lance wowed the crowd in 1972 and recorded a widely selling live album, did not exceed much more than fifteen hundred. These occasions, memorable as they certainly were, nonetheless pale in comparison to the impact of one perfect recording after another, the customary fare of allnighters. One gets the feeling that if the crowd needed to choose between the raw sounds of the stage or the cooked compositions of the studio, they would opt for the latter every time. Their understanding of authenticity encourages the embrace of technology and the perfected manipulation of sound achievable only through the tools available with recording technology.

To some degree, this perspective flies in the face of certain long-standing and emphatically asserted propositions amongst certain popular music audiences. It particularly critiques the antipathy held by many consumers toward corporatism, often expressed in romantically uncritical denunciations of the industry, their stranglehold upon creativity, and promotion of the second-rate at best. It is most persistently addressed in the rhetoric of the "sell-out", an equation of commercial success with creative emptiness, predicated on the assumption that the only bargain that can be struck between an artist and an executive need be Faustian. Northern soul communities do not typically denounce the marketplace or the players who hope to succeed within it on the basis of its demanding definitions of success. They instead often become obsessed with individual record labels and aim to acquire everything released by them, whereas others who focus on rock music, in particular, as their principal enthusiasm would assume that approach feeds the proposition that too many companies adopt a rubber-stamp mentality and force-feed the public the same kind of product over and over. What one community might denounce as formulae, the other defends as house style.

If advocates of northern soul do not renounce the marketplace, they undeniably romanticize and rejoice in the entrepreneurial behavior of small-scale musical enterprises. Therefore, almost as a kind of reflex, they tend to elevate the obscure over the obvious, the unappreciated over the applauded. Should you examine the lists of favorite tracks included throughout the volumes by Winstanley and Nowell,[19] even the more than averagely well-versed fans of rhythm & blues find themselves confronted with a virtually alternate or parallel universe. Many if not most of the names referred to in their books challenge any assumption of the power of commercial charts or the promotional opportunities enhanced by radio airplay. To illustrate, here are some of the artists incorporated by these authors in their respective canons: the Tomangoes, Little Bryant, the World Column, Eddie Foster, Don Thomas, Mel Britt, Sam and Kitty. And a number of the labels remain equally recondite: JJ, Criminal, General American, In, Wise World, Sharae, Sassy. Less than a footnote even in the most in-depth histories of the genre, they would remain not simply unknown but obliterated altogether were it not for their resurrection by northern soul. Admittedly, this perspective would seem to conflict with the aforementioned attitude toward corporatism. How can you assume that only the best rise to the top if so many who deserve that designation remain prostrate on the floor? Yet the impression given by fans of northern soul is that this situation arises out of oversight, not some kind of institutional obliviousness. Were the public only to be made aware of the power of these tracks, their superiority would be undeniable; just look at the dancers that they inspire!

For the fans of northern soul, the perfection of these recordings remains a self-fulfilling proposition that requires only an audience's open eardrums. That even extends to recordings that never in fact entered the commercial arena. A number of northern soul DJs and collectors valorize test pressings: printed but not merchandised material that, for one reason or another, remained withheld from the public. One of the most treasured and highly appraised items in the northern soul canon is Frank Wilson's 1965 'Do I Love You (Indeed I Do)'. Written and recorded by the artist for the Soul subsidiary of the Motown label, only two copies are believed to exist and have been appraised for as much as £15,000. Purportedly, having laid down the track, Wilson was challenged by label owner Berry Gordy to choose between performance or production, and he elected (quite successfully, at that) for the latter. Again, even if such items seem to exist outside the commercial process altogether, their eventual success and financial valuation within the northern soul community reinforces the assumption that they would have achieved their deserved recognition if only the appropriate circumstances arose.

Acquiring or simply appreciating such discs allows individuals to accrue that non-monetary but undeniably estimable currency that Sarah Thornton famously dubbed *subcultural capital*.[20] The virtually universal anonymity of these recordings outside the northern soul community tends to guarantee the membership of that fraternity a kind of desired differentiation from the general audience of mass culture consumers. Not only do their eardrums pick up and respond to rhythms that others fail to apprehend, but they would also appear to operate on another wavelength altogether, a privileged sphere of comprehension that allows them to assimilate compositions that elude their contemporaries. Yet how else did this community benefit, in their eyes, from this perceptual bankroll? One can hypothesize that it permitted them, among other things, to set themselves apart from their neighbors to the south, particularly those from the national center in London, who are assumed (then and now) to act as the nation's cultural barometer. There has been a long-standing cult of northern-ness as a region apart and a state of being separate from the rest of the country. George Orwell drew attention to this geographical divide more than seventy years ago in *The Road to Wigan Pier* (1937). He observed that working-class inhabitants of the region have typically characterized themselves as more rooted in the everyday as against the frivolous attraction to fashion and novelty in the South. Orwell writes, "it is only in the North that life is 'real' life, that the industrial work done in the North is the only 'real' work, that the North is inhabited by 'real' people, the South merely by rentiers and their parasites".[21] Commentators on northern soul have linked this sense of regional exclusivity with their fascination with such comparatively unknown music. Katie Milestone points to how the region seemed to reject the urban fascination with the counterculture during the 1960s; the North and Midlands of England evidenced "a working-class rejection of the growing middle-class culture of hippies, acid and progressive rock".[22] In addition, the fact that many of the recordings they admired came from a city, Detroit, similarly associated with manual labor and industrial technology added to the attraction.

In other words, here was something the elite failed to notice or appreciate, until those off the beaten track laid down the gauntlet. Engagement with northern soul also allowed its fans not to be completely defined by their day jobs or the position in the class system to which they were thereby assigned. Neither their salaries nor the substance of their labor could singularly validate their lives or act as means of appraising their worth. Furthermore, as many of the initial denizens of the community either themselves spurned or were turned aside by the community of higher education, their considerable knowledge about the artists they admired and the music they worshipped could be considered a sort of self-conferred higher degree, a means of registering and rewarding their autodidactic proclivities. As the information about this music was, like the discs themselves, not readily available, they had to make the effort as self-motivated researchers to recover the information from oblivion. They could not depend on the music press or other elements of the mass media to sort out that data, but had to dig in the trenches by themselves, and this long before the facilitation of such activities by the internet.

However, as wide-ranging and self-initiating as these enterprises might be, they nonetheless do not comprehensively address the sphere of rhythm & blues. Not only does the northern soul community approach the genre in a phono-centric fashion, they also fail to transpose their engagement with the cultural universe conjured up in these grooves to the physical geography from which they originated. While such a gesture could not be considered a requirement, it nonetheless tends to be an activity taken up energetically by many other popular music communities. In the process, various locations acquire virtually totemic resonance as embodying something inalienable from that particular genre. One can observe this phenomenon carried out in various visual representations of music making. To stick to the North American continent, let us consider, for example, the final edition of the *Observer Music Monthly*, which contains a two-page spread of "mythic locations" entitled "Home Is Where the Art Is".[23] It depicts the façades of Sun Studios in Memphis, Chess Records in Chicago, the Capitol Records tower in Los Angeles, and the purported crossroads in Mississippi whereupon Robert Johnson is said to have stood before the devil and delivered over his soul in return for his extraordinary musical proficiency. Or regard the opening sequence of Rachel Liebling's 1994 documentary *High Lonesome: The Story of Bluegrass Music*, which shows the genre's paterfamilias Bill Monroe rummaging through the ruins of his birthplace, as though somehow from among its battered remnants he might extract the very genesis of his genius.

Various communities in the United States have recognized this phenomenon and utilized it successfully to solicit attention to and tourist attendance of their municipalities, among them Chicago, Memphis, New Orleans, and the state of Mississippi, as well as Nashville, Tennessee, which, along with other gestures, advances the Ryman Auditorium as the certified home of country music. Local economics have not suffered in the slightest from the insinuation that to stand upon these sites is to occupy not simply physical space but the end points of communally embraced pilgrimages.

The resonance is hard to resist, as Marybeth Hamilton observes in the introduction to *In Search of the Blues: Black Voices, White Visions*. She, like many others, gravitated to the Southern delta from which the genre is said to have originated. Hamilton endeavored to leave behind all the mythology attached to the region in order "to get a handle on the pilgrim experience, to reconstruct the breathless hunt for the blues' authentic origins".[24] Once there, however, she found herself almost unwittingly succumbing to the enticement of the atmosphere, sucker-punched by what some would dismiss as nothing more than oversold scenery. As she writes, "I found myself wholly caught up in that story. Everywhere seemed to demand to be photographed ... At some level I knew that these photos were hackneyed, that they had been taken by every blues pilgrim before me. But the power of the tale was too strong to resist, that sense of stepping out of history, and entering a mythic, primordial world".[25]

The northern soul community seems not to buy into this investment in geographically driven nostalgia. The sounds they revere could well float in an unattached arena, grounded only by the duration of the very grooves from which they emerge. One certainly gets this sense from what collectors anecdotally recount in the volumes by Winstanley and Nowell about their exploits in the United States. They rarely stepped outside the precincts of record stores, where they could rummage through endless boxes of unsold product in search of rare gems. More to the point, even the information compiled about the songs they admired and the artists they incorporated in their canon stayed routinely attached to the fruits of their professional labors, not the communities from which they came or the culture they represented. You do not get the sense of the presence of something that resembles what Warren Zanes speaks of as the "imagined South" in his examination of *Dusty in Memphis*, Dusty Springfield's 1969 recording.[26] Zanes draws attention to how a physical location can become enhanced and embroidered for outsiders through its acoustic presence in the cultural landscape. Recordings created in that place—even, as with Springfield, by outsiders, in her case an English woman—are able to assist in the activation of "a particularly *phonographic* kind of seeing, involving a mental framing based on leaving some things in and some things out".[27] Certain sounds, he infers, evoke a sense of place, a kind of geographical aura, which is both rooted in tangible topography and wrenched altogether from it by the imagination. The act of listening to that recording can serve as a virtual passport for the mind to return to the location.

In her 2009 PhD thesis "Performing Fandom on the British Northern Soul Scene: Competition, Identity and the Post-Subcultural Self", Nicola Smith cogently explains that quite another relationship to cultural geography appears to overtake most participants in the northern soul community. She argues that when they listen to these recordings, the individual tracks exist as pretty much little more than sites for the exercise of fandom, not the repository of a whole way of life or the reflection of their geographical origin. These songs might possibly conjure up or allude to a community somewhere on the other side of the Atlantic, but they do not reverberate with the complexities of their point of origin. Consequently, one might argue, to hear the releases of the Motown label does not lead to their decoding into information about Detroit. By listening to them in a new locality and not affixing them to their original home, the northern soul community engaged in an act Smith dubs "[re]marking", whereby "a record is able to possess a new identity, and subsequently a new significance, via alterations in the modes of cultural consumption".[28] The artist(s) become thereby more or less absented from their own endeavors, as they achieve consequence only by virtue of what they have left affixed to the vinyl itself. This leads to the paradox that, when artists elevated in this sphere appear live in person, the audience virtually disconnects them from their present circumstances and validates them only as the vehicle for the record they revere. Even if they sing, with all the impact upon their skills of the passage of time, they are then, in effect, virtually lip-synching, for what resonates for the audience remains nothing more or less than the material technologically committed to memory many years before.

If participants in the northern soul community were able to accumulate certain kinds of cultural capital through their engagement with the repertoire, to what degree were they simultaneously permitted to test and possibly transform fixed notions of race and ethnicity? As earlier stated, by and large the vast majority of the community was white, and their opportunities for face-to-face interaction with members of other races remained limited, not only by the inherent restrictions of British society but also by the physical separation of those individuals into self-defined enclaves. Therefore, absent an interpersonal avenue for social integration, they opted instead for a phonographically driven metamorphosis. The dancefloor itself and the attendant activities of allnighters became the catalyst through which some kind of osmosis might transatlantically be brought about that would achieve a cultural and potentially an ideological transformation. The anecdotal evidence contained in Winstanley and Nowell, as well as the ethnographic data integrated into Browne's and Smith's theses, validate such a proposition. The respondents' attitudes toward one another, issues of gender, their own bodies, and public manifestations of pleasure underwent a sea change. They consequently found their personalities rendered more elastic and accommodating, as flexible in their identities as the limbs of the most adept dancer. You get some sense of this alteration in the interview with an unidentified young man contained in Tony Palmer's documentary. He speaks eloquently and longingly about his hunger for some alternative to the humdrum routine of his industrial occupation and the undeniable satisfaction of that emptiness at Wigan Casino. The consequences of either an interruption or complete cessation of that way of life baffle him, for he cannot imagine what could replace the means by which his personality is integrated through the community of northern soul. He has widened his horizons, and the prospect of collapsing them back into the narrow confines of his residential community horrifies him.

At the same time, how did those horizons incorporate some elaborated understanding of the very individuals who created and performed the repertoire that instigated this fascination with African American music? If the 45s played by DJs triggered some momentous effects, was one of them a realigned sense of race? This question nags at anyone who investigates the sphere of northern soul. It seems difficult to believe that the members of this community did not transfer something of their affection for African American music to their comprehension of the complications of race and racism. However, by and large, in most writing about the subject, the issue of the racial position of the community rarely arises. The investigation of the recordings themselves or their creators rarely exceeds the hagiographic. They do not elicit or seem to entertain how these recordings might be part of a larger social context, ideological construction, or racial dynamic. Unlike, for example, the English fans of American blues, they did not translate their appreciation into acts of performance, initially mimicking the material they loved and eventually allowing it to become the fuel for their own compositions. The comments made by participants in the community about the repertoire consequently remain, for the most part, effusive rather than interpretive. For them, the incontrovertible superiority of the recordings they treasured required no theoretical or intellectual justification. That should come as no surprise, as even being asked to convey how the scene influenced their personalities appears to have left any number of respondents dumbstruck. They seemed to exclaim without actually stating, "how can one parse out the principles of pleasure?"

By contrast, Kimasi Browne's dissertation provides the most elaborate dissection of the material itself into subcategories and unpacks the manner with which it achieves its effects. He conveys the fact that while the consumers of this repertoire felt overwhelmed by its elements, one can sympathetically dissect the musicological means with which that astonishment was achieved. However skillfully Browne assesses the techniques employed, one simultaneously acquires a sense of the problematic dimension of race that remains encoded within the northern soul canon. Some element of the phenomenon one might call a racial imaginary comes across: the conscious and unconscious means by which members of one race imagine the members of another. In the case of the northern soul community, some of the means by which this process occurs partake of long-standing conventions that verge on if not exceed the questionable. One of the many means through which audiences construct a sense of another race is through cultural products that are embedded in those communities and carry over into their daily lives the communal patterns and personal characteristics that emerge from the process.

In the case of the rhythm & blues genre, the material most admired by the northern soul scene can be broken into two spheres: what Browne calls the "stompers" or "floaters" that enabled many of the dancers, particularly the men, to enact their graceful arabesques; and the slower and often achingly emotional ballads that Browne, Dave Godin, and others have dubbed deep soul. One can extrapolate from these categories a kind of racial imaginary that conceives of African Americans as being alternately rhythmically adept or emotionally assertive. They can command a dancefloor and appear to possess abundant reservoirs of soul.

It does not take a great deal of thought to discern how questionable these propositions can be, which implicitly value African Americans not for the wholeness of their identities but, instead, for their capacities for unrestricted physicality and unmediated emotionalism. That is not to imply that the denizens of the northern soul sphere overtly caricature the community they so admired, but it does raise the question of just what racial propositions arise from an aesthetic agenda; what polemics reside, implicit or explicit, in pleasure? Can one inadvertently reduce the very identity of a body of individuals while simultaneously becoming personally enlarged by the effusively lauded cultural expressions of that set of people? It could be possible that the white English working class share with their African American cultural compatriots something of the problematic relationship about which Paul Gilroy inquires between the black people of privilege and the poorer members of that larger community. He wonders: "Maybe privileged people remain dependent on poor people for their soul, or their access to soul comes via the cultures those people erect against their sufferings, which the elite do not share ... maybe there's a kind of estrangement from the vernacular which the elite experience as form of ambivalence".[29] The ethnographic studies of the northern soul community have yet to dig deep and dissect these confounding questions. For the moment, we can only propose that the sphere of northern soul undeniably supports and salutes African Americans, but it remains possible that in doing so it also simultaneously incorporates some longstanding and unquestioned assumptions, even generalizations, about those individuals. While it would be excessive in the extreme to imagine that the northern soul community could solve the dilemma of race all on their own, it does bear asking: What might be the ideological dimensions of this phenomenon? Can one unleash some manner of claim about the constitution of society on the dancefloor when your principal objective is to engage in acts of pleasure initiated by the commercial products released by the recording industry? The answer to these propositions may not be simple, but it does bear mentioning that ideological claims appear in many guises; even when one does not adopt a form of discourse that overtly engages with polemical gestures, a political proposition may nonetheless emerge. The work of Robin D. G. Kelley, one of the preeminent African American scholars and a cogent chronicler of liberation movements, acknowledges the intractability of political systems, and his work has eloquently given witness to the often, even routinely frustrated efforts of those who batter against oppression. At the same time, however, he advises that we do not allow that struggle to limit the kind of thinking that circumvents the boundaries of immediate circumstances. He inquires, "How do we produce a vision that enables us to see beyond our immediate ordeals?"[30] Kelley elaborates upon this position when he asserts:

> the desires, hopes, and intentions of the people who fought for change cannot be easily categorized, contained, or explained. Unfortunately, too often our standards for evaluating social movements pivot around whether or not they "succeeded" in realizing their visions rather than on the merits or power of the visions themselves. By such a measure, virtually every radical movement failed because the basic power relations they sought to change remain pretty much intact. And yet it is precisely these alternative visions and dreams that inspire new generations to continue to struggle for change.[31]

Kelley draws inspiration from the proclamation of African American poet Jayne Cortez that we try to envision ourselves "somewhere in advance of nowhere".[32]

Perhaps that is the only place where those "fragile solidarities" that Gilroy speaks of in our epigraph could occur? In *Discographies: Dance Music, Culture and the Politics of Sound*, Jeremy Gilbert and Ewan Pearson take up the issue of how and when these "fragile solidarities" could arise in a dance-centered arena. For them, the answer does not come down to a matter of whether or not some form of dance culture, such as northern soul, could topple the destructive consequences of capitalism or race or gender. Instead, they advocate an investigation of at what point that form of culture succeeds in "negotiating new spaces", opening up admittedly limited but nonetheless consequential alternatives to the repressive dynamics of contemporary society.[33] Gilbert and Pearson write, "it is not a simple question of dance culture being 'for' or 'against' the dominant culture, but of how far its articulations with other discourses and cultures (dominant and otherwise) result in *democratizations* of the cultural field, how far they successfully break down existing concentrations of power, and how far they fail to do so".[34] As stated earlier, members of the northern soul community did feel that the environment and the recordings it emphasized widened their sense of themselves and the world about them. Whether or not it has also led to the kind of "democratizations" of which Gilbert and Pearson write would require further study and ethnographic engagement with members of the community.

In conclusion, what took place on the turntables of the Wigan Casino and elsewhere on the northern soul circuit whenever these recordings were played had an effect on those "concentrations of power", even if it did not issue in explicitly polemical gestures on the part of the participants. While neither the audience nor the DJs involved might have been able to achieve the objective liberation of the creators of the works of music they so admire, what they have incontrovertibly done, time after time after time, is to set free the voices of African American performers and producers who would otherwise remain silenced, erased altogether from history. Some might ask, would not attention have been drawn to the recordings admired by the northern soul communities by other individuals if this scene had never come into existence? The chances are narrow, it would seem, for many if not most of the individuals they idolized had fallen off the radar of pretty much the entire North American record-buying public. Conceivably, the activities of later DJs who were engaging in digging in the crates in order to sample unknown sounds could have come across them, but there is no guarantee.

It does not seem altogether an exaggeration to assert that the northern soul community transposes the act of emancipation that has yet to occur fully on a social plane for African Americans, and people of color everywhere, into a social context through the vehicle of dance and the communal adoration of commercial recordings. They freed up for consumption and commendation the voices and experiences of the performers who created and marketed the recordings they loved. Pleasure can, it would seem, co-exist with polemics, as I imagine Kelley, and others, advocate. On the dancefloors of Britain for some four decades or more, the denizens of the northern soul community have launched themselves into this uncontained and endlessly animating sphere wherein we feel in our feet those "moments of affiliation and linkage" Gilroy encourages. At a moment in time when some commentators have announced the dawn of a post-racial age, the continuing friction and outright combat between racial communities reminds us that the fractiousness has not yet been quelled. Therefore, if we can, through affiliation with the northern soul community, achieve some acquaintance with the mythic Land of 1,000 Dances, then we might as well more fully imagine, and perhaps then bring into existence, that "somewhere in advance of nowhere" that lures us to believe harmony genuinely can reside in the civic sphere.

About the author

David Sanjek (3 September 1952–29 November 2011) was formerly Professor of Popular Music and Director of the University of Salford Music Research Centre, and a widely respected researcher of music, film, media and popular culture and a leading member of the International Association for the Study of Popular Music (IASPM). He is particularly well known for the update of Russell Sanjek's (his late father) long history, *American Popular Music and Its Business* (Oxford University Press, 1988). He had been Director of the Archives at BMI Broadcast Music, Inc. and acted as an advisor to the Library of Congress, the Rock and Roll Hall of Fame and the Rhythm & Blues Foundation.

Notes

1. This book is dedicated to the memory of David Sanjek.
2. Paul Gilroy, quoted in Richard C. Green and Monique Guillory, "Question of a 'Soulful Style'", in *Soul: Black Power, Politics and Pleasure*, edited by Richard C. Green and Monique Guillory (New York: New York University Press, 1998), p. 255.
3. William James, *The Principles of Psychology* (Cambridge, MA: Harvard University Press, 1981), p. 462.
4. Lawrence Grossberg, "Reflections of a Disappointed Music Scholar", in *Rock Over the Edge: Transformations in Popular Music Culture*, edited by Roger Beebe, Denise Fulbrook and Ben Saunders (Durham, NC: Duke University Press, 2002), p. 34.
5. Katie Milestone, "The Love Factory: The Sites, Practices and Media Relationships of Northern Soul", in *The Clubcultures Reader: Readings in Popular Cultural Studies*, edited by Steve Redhead with Derek Wynne and Justin O'Connor (London: Blackwell, 1997), p. 157.
6. Dave Haslam, *Adventures on the Wheels of Steel: The Rise of the Superstar DJs* (London: Fourth Estate, 2002), pp. 155–56.
7. Milestone, "The Love Factory", p. 154.
8. C. P. Lee, *Shake, Rattle and Rain: Popular Music Making in Manchester 1951–1995* (Devon, UK: Hardinge Simpole, 2002), pp. 68–70.
9. Ibid., pp. 69–70.
10. Ibid., pp. 70–77.
11. Ibid., p. 79.

12. David Nowell, *Too Darn Soulful: The Story of Northern Soul* (London: Robson, 2001), pp. 44, 46, 48.

13. Milestone, "The Love Factory", p. 153.

14. Ibid., p. 161.

15. Andrew Wilson, *Northern Soul: Music, Drugs and Subcultural Identity* (Cullompton, UK: Willan, 2007), p. 85.

16. Wilson, *Northern Soul*, p. 86.

17. Nowell, *Too Darn Soulful*, p. 47; Milestone, "The Love Factory", p. 157.

18. Kimisi Lionel John Browne, "'Soul or Nothing': The Formation of Cultural Identity on the British Northern Soul Scene" (Dissertation, University of California, Los Angeles, 2005), pp. 410–11.

19. Russ Winstanley and David Nowell, *Soul Survivors: The Wigan Casino Story* (London: Robson Books, 2003); Nowell, *Too Darn Soulful*.

20. Sarah Thornton, *Club Cultures: Music, Media and Subcultural Capital* (Hanover, NH: Wesleyan University Press/University Press of New England, 1996), pp. 10–11.

21. George Orwell, *The Road to Wigan Pier* (New York: Berkeley Medallion, 1961), p. 99.

22. Milestone, "The Love Factory", p. 154.

23. "Home Is Where the Art Is", *Observer Music Monthly* 76 (January 2010): 33.

24. Marybeth Hamilton, *In Search of the Blues: Black Voices, White Visions* (London: Jonathan Cape, 2007), p. 1.

25. Ibid., pp. 2–3.

26. Warren Zanes, *Dusty in Memphis* (New York: Continuum, 2003), p. 84.

27. Ibid., p. 86.

28. Nicola Smith, "Performing Fandom on the British Northern Soul Scene: Competition, Identity and the Post-Subcultural Self" (Dissertation, University of Salford, 2009), p. 136.

29. Green and Guillory, *Soul*, p. 62.

30. Robin D. G. Kelley, *Freedom Dreams: The Black Radical Imagination* (Boston: Beacon, 2002), p. x.

31. Ibid., p. ix.

32. Ibid., pp. x, xii.

33. Jeremy Gilbert and Ewan Pearson, *Discographies: Dance Music, Culture and the Politics of Sound* (London: Routledge, 1999), p. 160.

34. Ibid., p. 161, original emphasis.

Musical Bookmark 8

Jenny Wilkes photographed at BBC West Midlands, The Mailbox, Birmingham, January 2017
Wigan's Ovation, 'Skiing in the Snow'. UK Spark SRL 1122

"When I was about fourteen, my friend Patrick was a little older than me so he was allowed to go to Wigan and I wasn't. He would play me the latest records he'd bought to see if I liked them and this is the one that I really remember as being the first one that made me think, 'Oh yeah like this'. I know it's not the critics' favourite, but 'Skiing in the Snow' is important to me because it's the record I remember that got me into northern soul. If you play it now it'll always get me on the dance floor and that's what my radio show is all about: taking people back to where they were when they heard those records first."

Jenny Wilkes DJs on *The Soul and Motown Show* for BBC Radio West Midlands.

Critical Reflection

Tim Wall

In the introduction, as editors of this book, we set out our commitment to develop insights into northern soul as a music culture through activities of co-production. The final volume brings together contributions from twenty-one individuals in a variety of forms. We have republished six key articles and book chapters, which together constitute a foundational body of work on northern soul, commissioned a further ten essays, several based upon the papers presented at the Salford northern soul symposium, and brought together three photographic dossiers, three interviews, and eight specially commissioned portraits. The final book certainly lives up to the ambition to combine traditional academic work with contributions from scene participants, to capture a diverse range of viewpoints and positions on the scene and draw upon different academic traditions, and to have the ideas tested through further conversations within the music culture we are exploring. There is certainly no single explanatory narrative or linear history of the scene to be found here, and in this we have realized our goal of capturing the pluralism of views about what the scene means to its participants and have placed very different perspectives side-by-side.

Such an approach demands that we were explicit as editors about our role, and the discussions amongst the three editors were just a prelude to the debates that unfolded at both the Salford and Birmingham symposia. That should not be taken to mean that as editors we have not been involved in actively challenging our contributors about both their ideas and the way they are expressed. We hope in the end that they found this a positive engagement. It certainly resulted in some enlivened debates, multiple redrafting, and increased insights on all sides. Likewise, as editors we have been eager to be open about our sense of purpose and willingness to listen to those we engage with. In doing so, we have explicitly developed an approach to academic research into music cultures that builds upon a wider philosophy shared by others, but more often stated than executed. We have been particularly attentive to questions of insider and outsider roles, grappling with matters of subjectivity and objectivity, and of address and re-address. In the end, though, the book must also stand as a contribution to the field itself, and as an engagement between academia and the cultural world we study.

We closed the edited contributions to this book with a reprint of Dave Sanjek's essay on the northern soul scene, itself a development of a paper presented to the original Salford northern soul symposium. In it he sought to explain northern soul to a readership of university academics interested in folk music forms and national identities. As an outsider academic, Dave saw the infatuation amongst British music fans with forms of American rhythm and blues and pop that are at the heart of northern soul as part of a wider set of affective alliances that form the scene. As Dave, and other contributors point out, the music at the heart of northern soul isn't made within the fan community and, while the scene has its own political economy, its central commodity is reused from elsewhere; centrally, the meanings of the music are remade for purposes never imagined by the originators. In many ways, the themes of Sanjek's essay became the agenda for the book, and the design of the symposium became the model for the co-produced project available to you here.

Dave's questions about the music that is collected and played in the scene, about the way our own (predominantly) British experience relates to that of the people who originally produced the music, and about the way the commercial production of this music has been turned into subcultural activities of the scene are explored throughout the other chapters. His short account of the origins of the scene calls upon a list of clubs cited in most histories, but he also usefully looks at the way that scene has been mediated to a wider audience, and introduces some of the academic work which had been written to explain the scene to other popular music and cultural studies researchers. That has been the agenda of many of the other contributors, too. Most of the writing about the scene has come from within the scene, in the form that in Chapter 8 Sarah Raine has termed "self-documenting" histories: books that construct a common narrative on the scene's origins and development.

By contrast, the contributions to this book collectively rethink most of the certainties of those stories, make the contemporary scene as important a focus as its past, set out previous academic work for scrutiny and critique, and extend the way the scene is explored to the work of photographers and film makers. Sanjek's chapter, therefore, is a pivotal one in writing about northern soul. Like this book, it builds upon the work that has come before, and it frames northern soul in ways in which other academics can understand, placing the scene within debates about music authenticity, identity, and the global age that academic readers would know and understand. Many will want to dispute things in Dave's essay, but this in itself demonstrates the value of

Critical Reflection 333

taking a different view of something that seems already to make sense, especially to those who have immersed themselves in the culture.

Likewise, the aim of the book to explore diverse aspects of the scene from distinct perspectives through different forms of investigation is predicated on the belief that this will challenge many of the certainties which underlie the way northern soul is presented. In reflecting on this experiment in popular music scholarship, we must ask some searching questions. What has been revealed, how do the contributions sit with each other, and as a whole what does it mean? More fundamentally, what does an exercise in popular music studies from the outside and the inside say about northern soul scholarship and popular music studies as an academic field? Do we end with a more sophisticated understanding of northern soul? Given now that all this has been said and shown, where does it leave us? And, indeed, where does it leave popular music research?

Where we've come from

The first chapters of the book reprint four of the earliest attempts to understand important aspects of northern soul produced between 1982 and 2009, and they each self-consciously respond to each other by offering very different takes on what is meaningful in popular music cultures and this scene in particular. Stuart Cosgrove's celebration of one of the scene's defining clubs, Wigan Casino, along with Tony Palmer's television documentary *Wigan Casino* are the first attempts to explain northern soul to a wider readership. They coincided with a burst of new academic writing which sought to develop popular music cultural studies, the most notable of which were Simon Frith's (1978) *The Sociology of Rock*, Dick Hebdige's (1979) *Subculture: The Meaning of Style*, and Angela McRobbie's articles, "Settling Accounts with Subculture: A Feminist Critique" and "Dance and Social Fantasy" (1980 and 1984, respectively).

Although it took sixteen years from the publication of Cosgrove's article for academics to apply such frameworks to northern soul culture, Joanne Hollows' and Katie Milestone's chapter builds upon Cosgrove in dealing with the exclusiveness of the scene, and the production/consumption divide that characterizes northern soul, to reconsider those ideas of community and subcultural theory which had been established at the time that the scene first emerged. In this way, northern soul became a case study through which the effectiveness of academic analytical frames could be tested. My own (2006) contribution took a very different line, focusing less on the macro-theorization of the scene and the idea of space as continental geography, and starting instead with what people actually did on the enclosed spaces of the dancefloor. This was part of a return to the ethnographic in popular music culture, linked to a post-Foucauldian notion of identity rooted in everyday practices. Nicola Watchman Smith's contribution fits nicely between the Hollows and Milestone approach and my own, taking a more sociological line and placing the scene even more explicitly within earlier attempts to understand youth music subcultures, both critiquing those approaches and exploring the perspective of "soulies" on an aging scene that was embraced by new generations of participants.

This twenty-five year span of writing and research also reveals a diversity of published sources and the rising journalistic and academic interest in the continuing scene and its origins. The articles also demonstrate something of the different ways popular music cultures were being studied. Cosgrove's article appeared in *Collusion* magazine, itself somewhat obscure in its day, representing a then newer and more eclectic, more academically informed, music journalism that treated the margins and obscure history and present of a global popular music with equal reverence, but it only managed five issues before it disappeared. The Hollows and Milestone chapter appears in a study of the relationship of music and place with an international scope, while my own study slotted into a special journal issue of *Popular Music* on dancing, and Watchman Smith's graced the pages of a major work on popular musicology. They do share much in common, though all see northern soul as distinctive, possibly unique within popular music culture, and maybe even strange and impenetrable to outsiders; and they all use northern soul to explore wider issues (music, culture, place, dance, age), mainly to critique wider approaches in music journalism and academic orthodoxy.

Cosgrove is impressively prescient about the role the Casino venue would have in the later scene in his "obituary and critique" of the Wigan 1970s all-nighter, and the Casino is referenced in all but one of the chapters that follow. Drawing on Jimmy Radcliffe's 'Long After Tonight Is All Over' as the title for his article, Cosgrove turns this subsequent staple of northern soul compilations and Casino histories into a metaphor for the venue's continuing significance. The venue is cited in all the contributions to this book and receives the most attention of any subject. For the chapters collected here, though, the venue is seen variously as a mythologized pinnacle to a dark shadow over the vitality of the contemporary scene. This tension between the scene's past and present is one of the major recurring themes of the book, and several authors address this directly. For Andrew Wilson, it represents a commercialized nadir which destroys the close community of the early scene, and for Paul Sadot it plays an unhelpful symbolic role in the contemporary scene, determining a fixed ideology which Sadot argues is an anathema to what he sees as a true spirit of Britain's rare soul scene.

More generally, it is notable how many of the chapters take a sizable part of their length to recount a history of the scene, and this would have been even more prominent without some editing intervention. However, while Hollows and Milestone tell a clear story of a diversity of clubs in the late sixties/early seventies, leading to rarer and faster records at The Torch and Casino, and a conflict of ideology with the DJs at the Mecca, to a post-Casino small club underground, Wilson, Sadot, Barrett, and Milestone's new chapters deliver more nuanced histories. Although Wilson and Sadot are both academics (a criminologist and a dance researcher), their accounts are strongly influenced by their insider status. This allows them to draw upon a personal understanding of the scene and its history, in which both of them have been intimately involved, but also makes their articles into a passionate case for a distinctive and committed version of the scene and its history. This claim for ownership is undoubtedly a characteristic of northern soul for all participants, and of all popular music (sub)cultures. My own chapter with Sarah Raine on myths on/of the scene focuses on an analysis of how such stories about the scene's past are constructed and what they mean for different groups on the contemporary scene. Working with Sarah has certainly made me shift perspective quite significantly in the way I understand history. I had already established an idea of northern soul histories as mythologies while writing my 2006 article, but working with Sarah, who is from a younger generation of scene participants, I came to understand how history works differently for different members. We both shared an anthropological/cultural studies imperative to make the taken-for-granted strange, and like Lucy Gibson, we see a command of the scene's history as symbolic knowledge which cements a participant's position as a genuine "soulie". Gibson's work is all the more valuable because it is rooted in an ethnographic study of northern soul nights between 2006 and 2008, and her outsider position is used to interpret what her respondents said about their sense of belonging and cultural memory. Katie Milestone's account of women's memories of their participation in pioneering clubs in England offers a very different narrative from the usual male account of the scene's early history, and Dani Herranz's journalistic outline of the northern soul scene in Spain demonstrates not just how broad the northern soul community has become, but also how it folds back into similar narratives about the scene's past.

As editors, we were particularly keen to deal with the two important screen media representations of the Casino, the 1977 documentary *Wigan Casino*, and 2014 fiction feature film *Northern Soul*. Rather than contrasting the representations of each film in a textual analysis, we interviewed their directors and presented the interview as an edited, but long-form statement. Although these two media representations are widely cited, and critiqued within the scene, the interviews with their directors offer something not produced before: a highly personal and insightful exploration of the motivations and production processes which realized the films in the form they took. At one level, the films represent binary opposites: documentary vs fiction; contemporary vs retrospective; television vs theatrical/digital distribution; outsider vs insider understanding; and quick turnaround vs long-burn production cycles. Palmer's distant, but very committed position, and his interest in historicizing 1970s northern soul culture produced a mainstream documentary many are critical of, but Palmer's account makes sense of how and why the documentary took the form that it did. Constantine has been interviewed many times about the film, but this account is much more personal, rooted in her own family history and personal familiarity with the scene from the 1980s. What emerges, though, are two very different takes on what northern culture is about, even if they both agree that involvement was a transformative experience for those involved.

The photographic contributions to the book offer something dramatically different. From John Barrett's strikingly up-close-and-personal images of scene participants in the 1990s and early 2000s, to Bethany Kane's and Richard Oughton's more coolly-observed capture of a younger generation on the contemporary scene, all three provide an insider's view of different ages of northern soul. Barrett's images are matched by his equally personal account of why he got involved in photographing soulies at northern nights. These three portfolios, and the written chapters, are interspersed by William Ellis's "musical bookmarks", with the stylized form he developed in his *One LP* series of portraits of musical commitment. The very different way in which this scene can be represented in the still image is plain here, even before one compares it to the committed documenting of the past and present of the scene which is apparent in northern soul online forums.

Matters of mediation pervade the contributions as much as issues of position and perspective. John Barrett makes a compelling argument about his role as photographer as storyteller and narrator within his own work, and apparent in both Kane's and Oughton's photographs. The form and address of the media record of the scene's history, along with the positioning of authors in relation to scene participation are explicit in my chapter with Sarah Raine in another way, and we explore the way that such activity mythologizes the scene. We hope that the book shows that it really is possible to feel warm affiliations with such myths and study their origin and significance. The same point is implicit in the diversity of contributions on offer here. It is no coincidence that Palmer's *Wigan Casino* programme and Cosgrove's article captured something of a moment in the documentary and journalistic movements. Palmer's characteristic techniques of musical and cultural juxtaposition were part of an experimental mode that offered an alternative to the news realism approach that dominated television documentary at the time. Cosgrove's writing is someway between new journalism in the way it used subjective account and literary style, sociological analysis in the way it explored drug use, obsessive record collecting and dancing, and historic account in the way it records the engagement of Britons with black America and the soundtrack of the Casino's dancefloor. The work which follows took a noticeably more traditional academic mode, although I attempt to place myself solidly in the account. Wilson's autobiographical account is moving and at the same time very revealing, persuasively imploring us to rethink the role of drugs, and what is often seen as the dark side of the scene. Paul Sadot's use of anecdote offers us new ways to bring ourselves effectively and critically into important discussions about the scene and ways to write popular music cultural histories.

By contrast the new contributions are far more diverse, and it is interesting to read how researchers who first analysed the scene return to create new takes on the scene many years later.

What's the northern-ness of northern soul, what constitutes a northern soul identity, and how does it link to African-American culture?

Palmer and Cosgrove make much of the politico-cultural geography of northern soul, by highlighting its northern-ness. For Hollows and Milestone, this sense of "northern-ness" is seen to be constructed in relation to a southern English cultural hegemony, just as much as rare record collecting reversed the usual economic dynamic of the mainstream music industry. They then take this further, to an argument about "interregional affiliations" between the northern Englishness of northern soul and the northern US states' black culture which hosted the production of the records subsequently played on the scene. They do seek a nuanced understanding of this relationship, and shy away from a suggestion that there is an equality of position between African Americans and white British working-class youth, but their contention that there is a shared interpretative community embracing Detroit and Manchester is challenged elsewhere. This is a view shared by the (then former) *Blues & Soul* journalist and political activist, who makes a similar point in the introduction to John Barrett's 2003 book, a quote John reproduces in his article collected here. My 2006 article explicitly challenges the thesis, pointing out that the northern-ness of northern soul is originally constructed by a London-centric sense of the English provincial cities, and the term only gained widespread usage during the mid-seventies branding of British record companies' back catalogue for the dancefloor, and the companies' attempts to create new recordings that used the scene to make pop hits. I explicitly discussed these issues with Tony Palmer in the interview, and his points about his own cultural background in the English south, his place in a London-based media, and crafting a documentary about a North of England nightclub for a Manchester-based broadcaster make interesting reading.

It is in this discussion of northern soul's link to North America that this book makes a more significant contribution. While Cosgrove contends that British soulies try to "relive and imitate the imagery" of African-American culture, and Hollows and Milestone propose their idea of an interpretive community, I argue that it is simplistic to even consider 1960s and 70s African-American culture as a single interpretative community, let alone embrace the issue of British identification with and through black music forms. This is not to deny that many European and white American soul fans construct a relationship with African-American culture, but that the relationship of northern soul to black America is much more conditional, and is far more about the cultural possibilities it offers for creating an alternative English identity, than an unequivocal support for the liberation struggle taking place in the US at the time. I also make the point that the northern "soul" records played on the 1970s scene were mainly early 1960s bi-racial pop dance music, rather than the later 1960s black identity music, termed soul, and that funkier and overtly soulful records struggled to find a place on a scene dominated by stompers.

In this context, Joe Street's examination of the life of Dave Godin, as much a political agitator as a soul fan, and consistently critical of many of the activities central to the scene, is important in moving away from many simplicities of the notion of the scene as a unified community. This will undoubtedly be controversial because, as Sarah and I show in our myths chapter, Godin is widely cited in histories of the northern soul scene as the man who named the scene. As Street accounts, Godin's commitment to soul and black music in general was a highly politicized one, linked to his own left-liberationist views, and played out in the British black music media to which he regularly contributed. Godin's strong political commitment was not shared by the *Blues & Soul* editor and by many of its readership. Street contends that while for many soul fans the music could be divorced from the socio-political contexts in which it was produced, for Godin music and dancing had meaning beyond hedonism and collective local identity, and the economic impact of many core practices within northern soul hurt the black artists who made the music. When Godin wrote "keep the faith – right on now!" he wasn't just addressing a solidarity amongst British soul fans, but trying to mobilize it for a greater political purpose. As his many columns on the subject show, Godin was a staunch critic of both the cover-up and the bootleg culture that emerged in the 1970s, and always linked records back to the political and economic place they were created. The analysis Sarah and I make of Dave Godin's role in the origin myths of the scene suggest he ultimately had greater success as a mythologizer than raiser of political consciousness, although his regular columns were at least highly influential on my own political perspectives as a young white British man.

The voices of scene participants are included in Chapter 15, and in the extracts from interviews with Sarah Raine they obviously stand and speak for themselves. Senses of identity and finding a place in the scene pervade what they say. Just as interesting, are the academic interpretations. Mark Duffett's focuses on working-class identity, and what he calls cross-racial communitarianism and cultural refinement, in processes of escapism, compensation, or alternative community. However, Duffett notes that while many of the cultural practices of the northern soul scene may be seen as similar to those in other fan communities, he also theorizes that the scene has a strong emphasis on community, rather than individual notions of identity. John Barrett also makes a point of explicitly seeing northern soul as rooted in working-class communities, and reflecting values of "camaraderie, solidarity, unity, thrift, loyalty, respect, and pride in community (and nation), inclusiveness, cordiality, integration and support". His prose is as eloquent as his photographs in this respect, but a number of the authors challenge such narratives, less for what they celebrate and more for what they miss out. Class is a particularly difficult issue to explore, and it is easy to see it as an overly determining factor, with crude notions of class solidarity and escape from the factory system predominating. They are certainly there in the narrative of Palmer's Wigan Casino, and this seems to reflect the left-liberal political position that comes out in the interview with him presented here. By contrast Elaine Constantine offers a much richer discussion, which often touches on the way the scene attracted individuals to express their talents and explore alternative life opportunities. These ideas are a clear and consistent theme in her film. Few studies of northern soul have picked up on Watchman Smith's suggestion that identity on the scene is performative and linked ideas of postmodern playfulness. She argues that long-term participants, and those who have returned to the field, do so to "possess an identity and a form of cultural involvement that results in the achievement of scene-specific status, personhood and subsequent selfhood".

Katie Milestone's new essay for this book explores and challenges the assumption made by most histories of northern soul, and implicit in its main cultural practices, that music culture expertise is a male domain. Gibson rather dolefully notes that while women are increasingly accepted as dancers, men usually undertake more elaborate moves, and women's ability to DJ or commit to record collecting is often questioned. Milestone, along with Gibson, sees these as examples of persistent notions of "appropriate" gender roles, but her primary research suggests a far more complex set of gender relationships, and that the scene's empowering and alternative gender role opportunities are limited in mainstream culture.

It is, though, in the area of generational identity on the scene that this book raises some of the most interesting questions. To some extent this reflects a wider interest in aging in popular music (see, for instance, Bennett and Hodkinson 2012), although as a multi-generational scene, northern soul is especially ripe for these considerations. Gibson's research, conducted between 2006 and 2008, sees the scene as a space in which older members reprise their youthful memories to achieve a sense of attachment and belonging, and so suggests that this strong identity creates generational conflict, with examples drawn from online discussions. A decade later, Sarah Raine's research highlights generational differences which she headlines in both her contributions to this book. Firstly, by noting that standardized histories of the scene are learned as an oral history at events and reinforced by extensive online material. She suggests that the ability of members of the younger generation to master and reproduce these standard stories is central to the way they can secure a place on the scene. Second, she notes the challenges of securing space on the dancefloor or existing roles as DJ or collector.

Political economy and social practice

Northern soul culture is built around some core activities: dancing, DJing and events promotion, and record collecting. While they are often noted in relation to other analytical considerations, such as gender and generation discussed above, they are strangely under-represented in studies of the scene. In fact, as I have noted elsewhere, this failure to deal with the detail of music culture practices is commonplace in popular music studies, which tend to pick up on broader social issues (Wall 2013). Cosgrove does deal with each, but only in passing, and we see glimpses of these in documentaries like Palmers', in the fiction of *Northern Soul* and *Soul Boy*, and in the stylized representations of pop videos and adverts which call on what we could call "northern soul cool" in twenty-first century British popular culture in which retro-referencing is routine. Liam Quinn's discussions about trying to recreate a dance style to meet the needs of mainstream directors is revealing, though his account of the response from the northern soul community is disheartening in a culture that values and celebrates the friendliness and solidarity of participation.

My own account of dancing on the scene was the first to explore the physicality of northern soul dancing in any detail, and the way competence in interpreting records and executing skilled moves is an important sign of scene membership. Given that so much of popular music culture revolves around dancing, its neglect within popular music studies is limiting, but such a neglect in studies of a dance music culture is strange to say the least. In part, this is because we lack a developed accessible vocabulary to talk about dancing to music, and partly it is because to the outsider dance is at best seen through a very limited lens of the spectacular. This is especially so in northern soul. Paul Sadot's discussion, then, is particularly important, and he rightly seeks to push beyond the basic analysis I set out when discussing ways in which we move on the dancefloor. He challenges overly rigid expectations of what constitutes northern soul dancing, arguing that dancing has always adapted to changing music on the scene, and he champions an open approach to dance, especially as a means to better include a new generation of soulies.

Both John Barrett's and Richard Oughton's photographs capture important aspects of dance, even if they tend to isolate the individual, rather than emphasize northern soul's collective dance form brought out by both me and Paul Sadot. The way Palmer's documentary and *Soul Boy* emphasize the spectacular, gymnastic side of northern soul dance reproduces this outsider positioning. Interestingly, the northern soul cool pop videos of the like of Duffy's 'Mercy' are strangely closer to the communal dance characteristic of the all-nighter, even more than Constantine's *Northern Soul*. The interview with Constantine is particularly revealing, as the director explains the enormous amount of work that went into developing the dancing skills of the extras and lead players, and the importance dancing has within the narrative. Likewise, Hollows and Milestone explore mobility as a core value within the scene, although they link it to notions of working-class day tripping and sacred pilgrimage, and Andrew Wilson's autobiographic story has an impressively positive end result. For Watchman Smith, the cultural practices of northern soul are primarily competitive, focused on acquiring identity, status and prestige through dance competency, DJ skills and record collecting connoisseurship. Although other authors note similar characteristics, such propositions are not well developed. This is particularly noteworthy because even a superficial familiarity with northern soul DJing practice, and its particularly limited performative skillset, reveals that it is very different from other dancefloor cultures.

Similarly, record collecting on the scene, and the veneration of original release pressings of obscure releases by local US labels that at best achieved regional hit status is an exaggerated case of the sort of male activities discussed by Will Straw (1997). In this respect Ady Croasdell's essay, which takes in UK-based bootlegging, its internationalization, and the reissue CD companies of the 1980s and 1990s, is particularly important. His insights into this dark side of the scene reveal how much the economy of northern soul depended upon an exaggerated version of the exploitation that sits at the heart of the recording and releasing of African-American music. Croasdell's personal commitment, and that of the Ace record label for which he works, is especially gratifying. There is a need, though, for similar investigations of other aspects of the political economy of northern soul, including promotion and DJing. The results are unlikely to be as morally concerning, although they would reveal something of the ego-driven entrepreneurialism that has built the scene, as well as something of its location in a new music industry business model which emphasized the dancefloor and dance music as new areas for exploitation. Sometimes the mythological histories and commitments to collectivism obscure some basics of the operation of music cultures.

What next?

The commissioned essays, interviews and photographs that constitute this book offer exactly the sort of greater diversity of perspective, approach and style we imagined, but they also raise many fruitful avenues for further examination, especially in terms of identity and political economy. If the book stimulates continued respectful, but critical, engagement with this important, but idiosyncratic, scene we will all have made a significant contribution to popular music cultural studies.

Although the overwhelming majority of contributors are from academia, the majority of the academics offering new work to this book participate in the scene, and over 40 per cent of the new contributors draw their expertise from outside academia, but from within the scene. This is reflected in the form of contribution they make, either through photographic dossiers or through interview as well as written accounts, and personal accounts and perspectives are strong elements of their work. Collectively, they reveal indispensable insights into the study of northern soul, and useful templates to understand popular music culture more generally.

Projects like this one also raise important questions about the relationship between the academic and the culture they study. As well as asking questions about who the people on a scene are, we need to ask who we are, and how our positions as participant and researcher relate to our academic engagement with the scene. In particular, we have to ask how we negotiate the line between insider and outsider, between advocate and analyst. Our insider knowledge enables us to detail what happens and how it is important on the scene, but we need the distance generated by our academic training to see the absences and relationships of scene practices, as well as the mythologies the stories we tell generate. So, I end by proposing a question to other popular music academics: do we as insider academics tend to reproduce scene myths as ways to validate our own involvement and celebrate the importance of the scene to which we belong? At their best, these chapters display how a reflexive engagement between insider academics and participants can produce a richer set of insights. There is a challenge in this for us all.

References

Bennett, A., and D. Hodkinson. 2012. *Ageing and Youth Cultures: Music, Style and Identity*. London: Berg.
Frith, S. 1978. *The Sociology of Rock*. London: Constable.
Hebdige, D. 1979. *Subculture: The Meaning of Style*. London: Routledge.
McRobbie, A. 1980. "Settling Accounts with Subcultures: A Feminist Critique". *Screen Education* 34 (Spring): 37–49.
—1984. "Dance and Social Fantasy". In *Gender and Generation*, edited by A. McRobbie and M. Nava, 130–61. Atlantic Highlands, NJ: Houndmills/Basingstoke, UK: Macmillan.
Straw, W. 1997. "Sizing Up Record Collections". In *Sexing the Groove: Popular Music and Gender*, ed. S. Whiteley, 3–16. London: Routledge.
Wall, T. 2006. "Out on the Floor: The Politics of Dancing on the Northern Soul Scene". *Popular Music* 25/3: 431–45.
—2013. *Studying Popular Music Culture*. London: Sage.

Index

Page numbers in *italics* denote illustrations. **Bold** page numbers denote tables. Song titles are shown in single inverted commas.

100 Club, London 218

Abbey, John 85, 126
Abercrombie, Nicholas 110
Ace Records 91–5, 97
acetate records 87, 93
Adey, Peter 298
adults and music cultures *see* ageing popular music scenes
African-American culture
 appreciation of music 102
 cross-racial communitarianism 227, 339
 identification with 53–4
 imitation of 13
 relationships with 315, 325–6, 337–8
age of participants 24, 41, 50, 73, 252
ageing and popular culture 252, 340
ageing popular music scenes 60–77
 continuing music scenes 61
 northern soul, ageing of 69–75
 participation, ageing of 67–9
 researching ageing participation 75–6
 scenes, ageing of 61–7
Ahearn, L. 297
allnighters 174–7, 181, 186–8, 204
America
 distance from 103–4
 empathy with 104–6, 109, 168, 277
 identification with 27–30, 53–4, 337
 see also African-American culture
amphetamines 13, 180, 181, 182, 186, 188, 189–93
 see also drugs
Andes, Linda 67–8
anthropological approaches 152, 335
Appadurai, A. 26–7
artists
 absence of 109–11, 323
 anonymity of *see* cover-up; white labels
 promotion of 123–4
Audio Arts 87
Audio Arts Strings, The 87
authenticity
 alien authenticity of music 99
 of history 143–4
 inauthenticity and northern soul 22
 of northern soul 22, 26, 110, 160, 258–9, 282, 300
 and (re)marking 111–14
autobiographies 145, 146, 156
 see also interviews; subcultural heart of northern soul

baby-boomer generation 252
'Baby Reconsider' (Leon Haywood) 83
'Baby You're The Fire' (The Del Satins) 88
Baker, Madelon 87
Banks, Bessie, 'Go Now' 129
Banks, Darrell 16
Banks, Tony 89, 165
Barrett, John
 Keeping the Faith 165–73
 photographic dossier 174–7, 178, 336
Barthes, R. 152
Bauman, Zygmunt 63
'Beautiful Night, The' (Jimmy Thomas) 89
bedroom culture, female 208
'Before It's Too Late' (Jackie Day) 87
Benjamin, Walter 130
Bennett, Andy 250, 254
Bernstein, Sidney 229
Bihari brothers 87, 91
Binnick, Bernie 84
BJD 84
Black Magic 88–9
Blackburn, Tony 17
Blaikie, Andrew 252
'Blowing My Mind To Pieces' (Bob Relf) 88
Blue Cat 13
Blues & Soul 85, 126–7, 145, 147–8
Bob Wilson Sounds, The, 'Strings A Go Go' 87
Bobby (interviewee) 283
Bolton, Chris 187
bootlegging 15, 27, 83–90, 96–7, 130
Bourdieu, Pierre 24, 201–2
Brackett, D. 55
Braggs, Johnny 16
Brake, Michael 67

Bratton, John 84
Brewster, Bill 136, 191
British Broadcasting Corporation (BBC) 122–3
British Phonographic Industry (BPI) 83, 92, 96
Brophy, Brigid 128
Brown, James 54–5
Brown, Ruth, '(Mama) He Treats Your Daughter Mean' 121
Brown, Tim 103
Browne, Kimasi 104, 203, 318, 324–5
Brunswick 94
Bund, of Schmalenbach, social relations of 22, 32–3
burglaries of chemist shops 182, 186, 190–3
Burton, Chris 187
Buster, Bill 84

Cameo-Parkway 84, 93
Casino, Wigan
   allnighters at 23
   commercialization of 188
   fame of 317
   female clothing at 205–6
   layout of 203
   music policy of 16–17, 217–18, 298–9, 303
   obituary of 11
   replacement for 18
   seediness of 12
   significance of 334
   symbolic role of 298–9, 302, 304
   see also Wigan Casino (documentary)
CD market 94–6
Central, Leeds 187–8, 191–2
Chambers, Iain 27, 101–2
Chandler, Lorraine, 'Love You Baby' 88
Chapman, Mary 200
Chapman, Sean 81
Charades, The, 'Dreaming Up A World Of Fantasy' 88
Charly Records 91
Charmaines, The, 'Eternally' 86
Checker Board Squares, The, 'Double Cookin'' 87–8
chemist burglaries 182, 186, 190–3
children of scene members 72–3, 262, 264, 273–4
Churchill, Trevor 92
civil rights movement 124–5
Clark, Ian 89
Clarke, Gary 21
Clarke, Jeff 185–6

Clarke, Tony, 'Landslide' 84
class, issues of 339
   see also working-class culture
clothes and accessories 31, 45, 168–9, 185, 205–8, 238, 253–4, 297
clubs
   atmosphere of 132–3, 148, 318
   attributes of 49
   capacity of 318
   coding of music for place 106–9
   consumption spaces 31–2, 34
   importance of particular 31, 34
   layout of 203, 206
   seediness of 12
Cohen, Phil 183
collections of material 145–6, 150–1
Collins, Jez 158
Columbia Records 86
Columbia Special Products 93
'Come On Train' (Don Thomas) 16–18
commercialization of the scene 192–3
commitment to northern soul
   generational conflict 261–4, 340
   infatuation 312–13
   interest in the scene, measurement of 146–7
   nostalgia and familiarity 250–4
   research methods 248–9
   symbolic knowledge, credibility, and rarity 254–61
community, soul 31–3, 132–6, 313
compilation albums 91, 94
Compston, Martin 244
Congress of Racial Equality (CORE) 124–5
Connell, J. 106, 113
Constantine, Elaine
   on clothes (from *Northern Soul: An Illustrated History*) 205
   on dance 300
   on music 295
   Northern Soul (film) 234–41, 336, 341
   perspectives of 155–7
   on Top of the World, Stafford 299
Contours, The, 'Just A Little Misunderstanding' 85
Conway, Dave 304
Cooke, Sam 55
copyright laws, relaxation of 97
Cosgrove, Stuart
   on the appeal of soul 29
   on Casino, Wigan 298
   on dancing 42, 46, 300–1
   insider status of 155–6

interpretation of lyrics 109
on legends and memories 24
on origins of northern soul 22
on respect for the music of Black America 28
on schism between oldies and newies 298
on tattoos 207–8
on travel safety 209
on women 157
on women in northern soul 198, 200, 203
writing of 337
courtship and sex 204
cover-up 15, 105, 110, 130–1, 218
see also white labels
CRAP (CDs, Reissues and Pressings) venues 258–9
Croasdell, Ady 82–3, 89, 91, 93, 98, 218–19, 342
Crocker, Frankie, 'Love Man' 16
cultural studies approaches 152, 335
Cummings, Tony 131
Curtis, Johnny 186

Dakar 94
Dakin, Harriet 247
dance competitions 170
dancefloor
    cultural space of 44, 201–3
    etiquette of 49, 256
    mobility on 297–8
    moving in space on 48–51
'Dancing In The Street' (Martha and the Vandellas) 123
dancing, politics of 41–56, 341
    dance styles 12, 45–51
    ecstasy of dance 43
    media and academic focus on 41–2
    politics of dancing 51–5
    theorizing dance 42–5
dancing, style of 292–305, 341
    acrobatic dance moves 45, 47, 217, 283, 296
    choreographing dance 302–4
    circular dance moves 295–6
    dance steps 46, 217, 240
    dance styles 200–4, 241–2, 244–6, 295–6, 300–3, 305
    dance teaching 301
    dance technique and competence 45–7, 202–3, 341
    evolution of dance 299–302
    footwork 48, 296, 301–3
    glide style of dance 46, 296

growth of the scene 296–9
a perspective on 294–6
recreating dance styles 241–2, 244–6, 340
side-to-side dance moves 42, 46, 295–6, 301
solo dance styles 200–2
Twist, The, dance craze 201
to unknown records 292–4
Date Records 86
Day, Jackie, 'Before It's Too Late' 87
Dean (interviewee) 271–2
Deborah (interviewee) 208
Dee, Sammy 215
Deep Soul 85
Dees, Sam 94
definitions of northern soul
    attributes of northern soul 20, 61, 100, 186, 314–23
    characteristics of the scene 12
    coining of the term 134
    by participants 272–4, 280–1
    scene myths 153
    as a subculture 188
    Wikipedia entry 2, 147
Del Satins, The, 'Baby You're The Fire' 88
Detroit labels 14
Dewhirst, Ian 191
digital bootlegging 96–7
Disco Demand 89
DJs
    gender of 198–9, 260–1
    music selection 54, 131
    role of 26–7, 110–11, 131–2
    younger people 262–3
'Do I Love You ('Deed I Do)' (Frank Wilson) 86, 319–20
'Double Cookin' (The Checker Board Squares) 87–8
Doyle, Barry 130
'Dreaming Up A World Of Fantasy' (The Charades) 88
dress code 168–9
Driscoll, Julie 207
drug-related crime 182, 186, 189–95
drugs 12–13, 217, 315–17
    see also amphetamines
Duckett, Yvonne 206
Duffett, Mark 270, 276–9, 284, 339
Duffy, 'Mercy' 241–2, 341
Dyer, Richard 42–3

Eagle, Roger 315
East Moor approved school, Leeds 183–4

economics of soul 25, 128–32, 136
eighties, music of 90
Elgins, The, 'Heaven Must Have Sent You' 85
Ellis, William *see* musical bookmarks
Elson, Frank 127, 188
EMI 89
Emily Jane 119, *119*, 223
Englishness 276
Esther (interviewee) 272–3
'Eternally' (The Charmaines) 86
ethnicity and cultural identity 53–5
ethnicity of northern soul 259
ethnographic methods 75–6
Evison, Dave *175*
exchange of records 25–6, 199–200
external exploitation 192

Facebook groups 158–9
fandom, conflicting 73–5
fans 75–6, 252–3, 255–6, 278–9, 313
    see also members, scene; participants
Farrugia, Rebekah 198–9
Fiske, John 112
Flashdance (film) 234
folk discourse 22, 25
Foster, Eddie 86–7
Fountain, James, 'Seven Day Lover' 15
friendship of the scene 168, 189, 204, 211

Garrett, Vernon, 'If I Could Turn Back The Hands Of Time' 87
gender and northern soul 197–212, 259–61, 339–40
    androgyny on the dancefloor 206
    clothes and accessories 205–8
    dancing 52, 200–4
    DJs and record collectors 259–61
    gender freedoms 204–5
    travel and mobility 208–10
    vinyl culture 198–200
generations, relationships between 159–61, 261–4, 271–6, 280–1, 340
Gibson, C. 106, 113
Gilbert, Ian "Gilly" 95
Gilbert, Jeremy 43, 127, 326–7
Gill, J. 43
Gilroy, Paul 29, 44, 102, 313, 325
Glinert, E. 106
'Go Now' (Bessie Banks) 129
Godin and the British soul community 120–36, 338–9
    inconsistencies of Godin 135
    life and early activism of Godin 121–5

politics and economics of soul 126–32
soul community 132–6
Godin, Dave
    on atmosphere of clubs 318
    and bootlegging 92
    coining of "northern soul" 24, 217, 316
    and *Keeping the Faith* (Barrett) 166–7, 171–2
    and musical appreciation 102
    and record labels 85
    role of in northern soul 316
    writing about the scene 147–9, 338–9
Goffman, E. 45
Golding, Bernie 18
Goldmine Records 95–6
Gordy, Berry 106–7, 123, 153–4
Grapevine 89, 91, 97
Gray, Dobie, 'Out On The Floor' 41, 47–8, 54–5
GRC/Moonsong 94
Grossberg, Lawrence 313

Hamilton, Dave 95
Hamilton, Marybeth 322
handbaggers (outsiders) 256–7
Harem Records Inc 95
Haywood, Leon, 'Baby Reconsider' 83
'Heaven Must Have Sent You' (The Elgins) 85
Hebdige, Dick 45
Hetherington, K. 32
'Hey Girl Don't Bother Me' (The Tams) 85
Hideaway, Manchester 166
hierarchies of taste 255
hippy culture 206
historico-pastiche representations 304
history 20–34
    a brief history of northern soul 22–4
    media texts and history 145–6
    northern-ness of northern soul 24–5
    place, pilgrimage, and identity 31–4
    rarity, exclusivity, and commodity exchange 25–7
    urban north UK and USA 27–30, 337
    see also myths on/of the northern soul scene
history and insider/outsider status 144–52, 155–60, 335
hitchhiking 209
Hodkinson, Paul 63–4
Holdsworth, Nadine 202
Holland, Samantha 68
Holliday, Billie 12
Hollows, Joanne 53, 104, 109, 250, 259

Human Beinz, 'Nobody But Me' 186
100 Club, London 218
Hunt, Stephen 252

identification by fans 255–6
identity
    affinity, concept of 183–4
    formation of 32–3, 62–3, 67–9, 74, 102, 281–4
    performative nature of 64–6, 339
    place, pilgrimage, and 31–4
'If I Could Turn Back The Hands Of Time' (Vernon Garrett) 87
In Records 86–7
insider status
    and dance 46, 294–6, 300
    exclusiveness of the scene 25–7
    and history 144–52, 155–60, 335
    and identity 281–2
instrumental records 87–9
integration, racial 124–5
internal exploitation 192
Internet 96
    see also online activity about northern soul; social media, use of
interpretive community concept 29
interregional affiliations 28, 337
interstitial leisure spaces 181–2
interviews
    Bobby 283
    Dean 271–2
    Deborah 208
    Elaine Constantine *(Northern Soul)* 234–41, 341
    Esther 272–3
    Jane 203, 205
    Jody 199, 203, 205–10
    Liam Quinn *(Soul Boy)* 241–6, 340–1
    Lisa 199–200, 205–7
    Nancy 274–6
    Rob 273–4
    Shelly 210
    Tony Palmer *(Wigan Casino)* 228–34
Invitations, 'Ski-ing In The Snow' 17
issues of northern soul 315–28
    attributes of northern soul 315–23
    competence in the soul scene 45–8
    competitive nature of northern soul 52–3, 63, 68, 74, 170, 341
    cultural ownership of music 100–3
    ethicity of the scene 168, 279
    growth of the scene 296–9
    ideological statements and pleasure 327–8

    music, range of 315
    race 315, 323–6
    relationship with America 315, 325–6
    typologies of practice 278–9
'I've Got Something Good' (Sam and Kitty) 16

Jackson, Billy 93
Jade Owl 86
Jagger, Mick 128–9
James, Etta 12
James, William 313
Jameson, F. 304
Jane (interviewee) 203, 205
Jenkins, Henry 30
JFM (radio station) 24
Jody (interviewee) 199, 203, 205–10
Jones, Linda 16
Jopling, Norman 122
'Just A Little Misunderstanding' (The Contours) 85

Kane, Bethany 8, *222–5*, 226
Keeping the Faith (Barrett) 166–7, 171–2
Kelley, Robin D. G. 326
Kent (UK label) 91, 94–5, 97, 218–19
Kent (US label) 94
King, Jeff 82–3
King's Hall, Stoke on Trent *174–7*
Koslicki, Steph 184

La Discotheque, Soho 181
labels *see* record labels
Lahr, John 298
'Landslide' (Tony Clarke) 84
Langlois, Tony 110
Laws, Eloise, 'Love Factory' 30
'Lay This Burden Down' (Mary Love) 87
Legend, Tobi, 'Time Will Pass You By' 11–12, 69–70
leisure spaces 181–2
'Let The Music Play' (Didi Noel) 13
Levine, Ian 17, 23–4, 130, 132, 302
liminal spaces 31, 33–4
Lisa (interviewee) 199–200, 205–7
live performances 109–10, 114
London, England 24–5, 181
'Long After Tonight Is All Over' (Jimmy Radcliffe) 11
Long, Paul 158
Longhurst, Brian 110
'Love Factory' (Eloise Laws) 30
Love, Mary, 'Lay This Burden Down' 87
'Love You Baby' (Lorraine Chandler) 88

'Love You Eternally' (The Sweet Things) 86
Lyman, Frankie 12
Lyntone 84
lyrics, empathy with 109

Madrid, Spain 219
Maffesoli, Michel 62–3, 65–6
magazines 24, 41, 145
'Magic Touch, The' (Melba Moore) 93
Malbon, Ben 43–5, 51
'(Mama) He Treats Your Daughter Mean' (Ruth Brown) 121
Manship, John 164
Marcus, Shimmy 245
marginalization of northern soul 21
Marshall, Gerry 304
Martha and the Vandellas, 'Dancing In The Street' 123
Martin, Peter J. 255
Marvelettes, The, 'Please Mr. Postman' 122
masculinity 52, 200–4, 206
mass media 12, 17, 23–4
master tapes 93
Matthews, Sherlie, 'My Sugar Baby' 88
Matza, David 183
Maximilian, 'The Snake' 90
MCA 85, 91
McKenna, Paddy 186
McRobbie, Angela 33, 52, 200, 202, 206, 208
meaning
    artists, absence of 109–11
    authenticity and (re)marking 111–14
    coding of music for place 106–9
    creating distance in northern soul 103–4
    cultural authentication 143–4
    cultural capital, distribution of 24–5, 53
    making of new 99–115
    questionable home of northern soul 100–3
    real, making something 30
    reimagining music 111–14
    reinvention of the scene 172–3
    transatlantic empathy 104–6
Mecca Highland Room, Blackpool 17, 133, 217–18, 301–2
members, scene 70–1, **71**, 257–8
    see also fans; participants
'Mercy' (Duffy) 241–2, 341
Middleton, Richard 21
Milestone, Katie
    choice of music 130
    dancing 294–5
    gender relations 259

geography of northern soul 53, 314, 320
industrial living 104–5, 109
memory and familiarity 250
Mirwood 87–8
Modern 87, 93–4
Mods 14, 181, 216
    see also neo-Mods
Mojo 85
Moore, Melba, 'The Magic Touch' 93
Moss, Graham 124, 128
Motortown Revue 107
Motown (label) 14, 54, 85–6, 122–3, 153–4
Motown sound 106–8, 123
multigenerational scene 159–61, 261–4, 271–6, 280–1, 340
Munden, Dave 129
Mungham, Geoffrey 204
music, range of 15–16
    appeal of soul 29–30
    bi-racial pop sound 54, 153
    boundaries of 113, 186, 315
    at contemporary events 252–3, 258–9, 263, 292, 300
    dates of 54
    distinction from mainstream music 51–2
    evolution of 22–3, 217–19, 301
    new categories of 90
    new discoveries 292–3
    obscurity of 101, 108, 152–3
    schism between oldies and newies 298
    session artists 89
    tailor-made music 88, 113–14, 115n1
    tempo of music 23–4
musical bookmarks 6, 336
    Emily Jane 119
    Harriet Dakin 247
    Jenny Wilkes 330
    John Manship 164
    Kev Roberts 311
    Sammy Dee 215
    Sean Chapman 81
    Tom Page 10
Musicor Records 93
'My Sugar Baby' (Sherlie Matthews) 88
mythologizing process 152
myths on/of the northern soul scene 142–61
    documents and myths 154–9
    multigenerational scene 159–61, 340
    origin myth 144–9
    self-documenting as myth-making 143, 149–54
    see also history

Nancy (interviewee) 274–6
Nashville, Tennessee 93, 321
national identity 276
Negus, Keith 101
neo-Mods 50, 90
    see also Mods
neo-tribes 60, 63–4, 66
'Nobody But Me' (Human Beinz) 186
Noel, Didi, 'Let The Music Play' 13
northern soul
    ageing of 69–75
    books about 155–7, 282–3
    documents and myths 154–9
    studies of 41
    traditions of 31
    value of 25–6
Northern Soul (film) 212, 234–41, 283, 335–6, 341
northern-ness
    of northern soul 24–5, 320, 337–8
    urban north UK and USA 27–30, 337
nostalgia 72–5, 250–4, 321–2
Nowell, David, 'Too Darn Soulful' 153–5

O'Connor, Jock 292
Old Soul 82–3
older members of the scene 160
    see also ageing popular music scenes
online activity about northern soul 157–9, 281–4
    see also social media, use of
origin myth 144–9
Orwell, George, *The Road to Wigan Pier* 320
Oughton, Richard 9, *287–90*, 291
Out Of The Past 84
'Out On The Floor' (Dobie Gray) 41, 47–8, 54–5
outsiders
    handbaggers 256–7
    and history 147–9, 335
    outgroup status 180, 182–3
OVO (Original Vinyl Only) policy 258–9

Page, Tom 10
Palmer, Tony 145–6, 228–34, 336
'Papa Oom Mow Mow' (The Sharonettes) 89
Parker, Charlie 12
Parrish, Dean 109–10
participant voices 268–85
    four voices 271–6
    identity in the scene 281–4
    participants as music fans 276–9
    positioning oneself 279–81

research methods 269–71
participants
    ageing of 67–9, 75–6
    displacement of 297–8
    as music fans 276–9
    types of 70–3, **71**, 252, 256, 292
    see also fans; members, scene
Pearson, Ewan 43, 127, 326–7
Peel, John 127
Perry, T. 106
Phillips, Esther 12
photographic dossiers 7–8, *174–7*, 178, *222–5*, 226, *287–90*, 291, 336
photographing the soul scene 165–73
    Keeping the Faith (Barrett) 171–2
    later soul revival 172–3
    narratives 168–71
    working-class culture 167–8
pilgrimage 32, 322
playing the subcultural game 64–6, 339
'Please Mr. Postman' (The Marvelettes) 122
police raids 189, 217
politics and economics of soul 126–32
politics of dancing 51–5
Polydor 85
post-subcultural theory 60–7, 339
Probe 85
production and consumption of music 25–7, 31–2
Propp, V. 152
provinces of Britain 24–5
Pye 89

Quinn, Liam 241–6, 340

race, issues of 315, 323–6
racial exploitation 277
racial segregation 124–5
Radcliffe, Jimmy, 'Long After Tonight Is All Over' 11
radio programmes 24
Raine, Sarah 269, 271, 281–4
rarity, importance of 25–7, 152–4, 259, 277, 292–3
RCA 89, 94
Ready, Steady, Go! (television show) 123
record labels 13–14
record production 82–98, 342
    bootlegging 83–90
    CD market 94–6
    digital bootlegging 96–7
    licensing 91–2
    Mechanical-Copyright Protection Society (MCPS) 92

new record companies 90–2
unissued tracks 93–4, 97–8
records
   as commodity 26
   exchange of 25–6
   gender and 198–200
   prices of 15, 25
   rarity of 152–3
   reissued music 91
   unknown records 292–3
regional identity 24–5, 28
Relf, Bob, 'Blowing My Mind To Pieces' 88
religious associations 33
Renfro 86
Reynolds, S. 43
rhythm & blues music 321–2
Richards, Jeffrey 276
Ritson, Mike 136, 155–6
Ritz Ballroom, Brighouse 165
Road to Wigan Pier, The (Orwell) 320
Rob (interviewee) 273–4
Roberts, Kev 101, 109, 311
Robinson, Laura 302
rock aesthetic, dominance of 43
Rolling Stones 128–9
'Rosemary What Happened' (Richard "Popcorn" Wylie) 15
Rosselson, Leon 232
Roundhouse, London 231
Rowe, Tim 171
Russell, Stuart 136, 155–6

Sadot, Paul 245–6, 334, 337, 341
Sahlins, M. 152
Said, Edward 29
Sam and Kitty, 'I've Got Something Good' 16
Sanders, Bobby 86
Sanjek, Dave 332
Sardiello, Robert 67
Savage, Jon 121, 135–6
Scepter 93
Schmalenbach, Eugen 22, 32
Scott, Anna Beatrice 303
Searling, Judith 205
Searling, Richard 18, 22–4, 27
seaside resorts 31
segregation 124–5
Selby, Brian 84
Selecta Disc, Nottingham 84, 88
self-documenting 149–54
selfhood, creation of *see* identity, formation of
'Seven Day Lover' (James Fountain) 15
sexism 260–1

Shalamar 89
Sharonettes, The, 'Papa Oom Mow Mow' 89
Shelly (interviewee) 210
Shepherd, J. 29–30
Shields, Rob 31–3
Shredded Wheat commercial 179, 239, 304
Shuker, Roy 111
Sink Soul Club, Liverpool 243
'Ski-ing In The Snow' (Invitations) 17
'Ski-ing In The Snow' (Wigan's Ovation) 17
skinheads 183
Smith, Alan 271–2
Smith, Nicola Watchman
   ageing in the scene 60–77, 204–5, 251, 254, 262
   children and parents in the scene 264
   competitive nature of northern soul 63, 68, 74, 341
   identity formation 210
   longevity of the scene 250
   (re)marking of northern soul 112–13, 115, 323
   research work 249
   typology of participants 70–3, **71**, 252, 256
   women on the dancefloor 203
   young newcomers to the scene 257
'Snake, The ' (Maximilian) 90
social lives of things 26
social media, use of 274–6, 279–80
   see also online activity about northern soul
Soho, London 181
Soul Boy (film) 212, 240, 244–6, 341
Soul City (label) 85, 129
Soul City (shop) 120, 128, 134
soul clap 46, 52, 240
soul community 31–3, 132–6, 313
Soul Fox Orchestra, 'Thumb A Ride' 89
Soul Sounds 83–4
Soul Source (website) 159
Soultown 86
Soussan, Simon 17, 86–9, 95
Spain, soul in 219, *221*
Stoke Heath Borstal, Shropshire 184–6
Straw, Will 26, 28, 199
'Strings A Go Go' (The Bob Wilson Sounds) 87
style 31, 45, 205–8
   see also clothes and accessories
subcultural capital 254–5, 277, 320
subcultural heart of northern soul 179–95
   allegiance to a subculture 183–4
   Borstal experiences 184–6
   chemist burglar, making of a 190–3

deviant leisure 181–3
  rogue element of 189, 191
  soul scene to subculture 187–90
  subculture and scene 193–4
subcultural identity 32–3
subcultural theory 21–2, 62, 255
  see also post-subcultural theory
subcultures 21, 180, 182, 188–9, 194–5
Suttles, Gerald 182
'Suzy's Serenade' (Bob Wilson) 87
Swallow, Norman 228–9
swearing, use of 276–7
Sweeney, Gareth 157, 205, 237, 295, 299–300
Sweet Things, The, 'Love You Eternally' 86
Sweetman, Paul 63, 65
symbolic knowledge, credibility, and rarity 254–61

T. B. (label) 89
Tamla Motown (label) 89, 123, 153
Tamla Motown Appreciation Society (TMAS) 102, 122–5
Tams, The, 'Hey Girl Don't Bother Me' 85
Tannock, Stuart 74–5
Taylor, Andy "Tats" 95
Taylor, Ginger 165
Terra Shirma, Detroit 14
This England see *Wigan Casino* (documentary)
Thomas, Don, 'Come On Train' 16–18
Thomas, Jimmy, 'The Beautiful Night' 89
Thornton, Sarah 42, 254–5, 320
'Thumb A Ride' (Soul Fox Orchestra) 89
Till, Emmett 127–8
'Time Will Pass You By' (Tobi Legend) 11–12, 69–70
'Too Darn Soulful' (David Nowell) 153–5
Top Gear (radio show) 127
Top of the World, Stafford 90, 218, 240, 299
Torch, Tunstall, Stoke on Trent 23, 187, 236, 318
tournaments of value 27
transatlantic empathy 104–6
transformative labour 278
travel
  acts of pilgrimage 32, 322
  importance of 31–2, 208–10
  night-trips 31
Twisted Wheel, Manchester
  atmosphere of 132–3, 148
  décor of 203
  layout of 206
  reputation of 11, 185, 258, 315–16
  sessions at 216–17

USB memory sticks 97

Va-Va, Bolton 188
venues see clubs
videos, online 158
Villa 87–8
vinyl records, resurgence of 96–7

Wall, Pat 203
Wall, Tim
  on dancing 200–1, 256, 259, 295, 300
  on identity and dance 294
  on participation 270–1, 279–81, 284
  on women and dance 202
Ward, Andrew 43
Ward, Brian 153
Wards, Dave 303
Waterman, Chris 172
Welsby, Paul 166
White, Karl 298
white labels 27, 84, 131–2
  see also cover-up
Whymark/Williams, Dave 84
Wickham, Vicki 123
Wigan Casino see Casino, Wigan
Wigan Casino (documentary)
  dancing in 302–4, 317
  as documentation of the scene 145–6, 297
  gender patterns 204, 210
  making of 228–34, 236–7, 335–7
  and younger participants 283
Wigan, Greater Manchester 230–1
Wigan's Ovation, 'Ski-ing In The Snow' 17
Wikipedia entry for northern soul 2, 147
Wilkes, Jenny 330
Williams, Paul 94
Wilson, Andrew 199, 204, 259, 317, 334, 337
Wilson, Bob, 'Suzy's Serenade' 87
Wilson, Frank, 'Do I Love You ('Deed I Do)' 86, 319–20
Wilson, Jackie 55
Winstanley, Russ 17, 301, 304
Withers, Dave 232, 237
women
  ageing of 68
  and dancing 50, 52, 302
  histories of 157
  in relation to "handbaggers" (outsiders) 256
  see also gender and northern soul
working-class culture 31, 167–8, 276–7, 339
Wylie, Richard "Popcorn", 'Rosemary What Happened' 15

young people
- entering the scene **71**, 72–4, 257, 261–4, 299–300
- and music 60, 67
- younger members of the scene 160, *222–5*

youth culture 205
youth identity, search for 101
youth subculture 21
YouTube videos 158

Zanes, Warren 322

www.ingramcontent.com/pod-product-compliance
Lightning Source LLC
Chambersburg PA
CBHW071953220426
43662CB00009B/1110